Cisco Router Configuration, Second Edition

Allan Leinwand

Bruce Pinsky, CCIE #1045

CISCO SYSTEMS

CISCO PRESS®

Cisco Press
201 West 103rd Street
Indianapolis, IN 46290 USA

Cisco Router Configuration, Second Edition

Allan Leinwand and Bruce Pinsky

Copyright© 2001 Cisco Press

Cisco Press logo is a trademark of Cisco Systems, Inc.

Published by:
Cisco Press
201 West 103rd Street
Indianapolis, IN 46290 USA

Printed in the United States of America 1 2 3 4 5 6 7 8 9 0   04 03 02 01

First Printing December 2000

Library of Congress Cataloging-in-Publication Number: 00-109754

ISBN: 1-57870-241-0

Warning and Disclaimer

This book is designed to provide information about Cisco router configuration. Every effort has been made to make this book as complete and as accurate as possible, but no warranty or fitness is implied.

The information is provided on an "as is" basis. The author, Cisco Press, and Cisco Systems, Inc., shall have neither liability nor responsibility to any person or entity with respect to any loss or damages arising from the information contained in this book or from the use of the discs or programs that may accompany it.

The opinions expressed in this book belong to the author and are not necessarily those of Cisco Systems, Inc.

Trademark Acknowledgments

All terms mentioned in this book that are known to be trademarks or service marks have been appropriately capitalized. Cisco Press or Cisco Systems, Inc., cannot attest to the accuracy of this information. Use of a term in this book should not be regarded as affecting the validity of any trademark or service mark.

Feedback Information

At Cisco Press, our goal is to create in-depth technical books of the highest quality and value. Each book is crafted with care and precision, undergoing rigorous development that involves the unique expertise of members from the professional technical community.

Readers' feedback is a natural continuation of this process. If you have any comments regarding how we could improve the quality of this book or otherwise alter it to better suit your needs, you can contact us through e-mail at ciscopress@mcp.com. Please make sure to include the book title and ISBN in your message.

We greatly appreciate your assistance.

Publisher	John Wait
Editor-in-Chief	John Kane
Cisco Systems Program Manager	Bob Anstey
Managing Editor	Patrick Kanouse
Acquisitions Editor	Tracy Hughes
Senior Editor	Jennifer Chisholm
Copy Editor	Krista Hansing
Technical Editors	Henry Benjamin
	Kevin Burgess
	Andre' Paree-Huff
	Dave Sumter
	Michael Truett
Cover Designer	Louisa Klucznick
Compositor	Steve Gifford
Indexer	Tim Wright
Proofreaders	Chrissy Andry
	Gayle Johnson

CISCO SYSTEMS

Corporate Headquarters
Cisco Systems, Inc.
170 West Tasman Drive
San Jose, CA 95134-1706
USA
http://www.cisco.com
Tel: 408 526-4000
     800 553-NETS (6387)
Fax: 408 526-4100

European Headquarters
Cisco Systems Europe
11 Rue Camille Desmoulins
92782 Issy-les-Moulineaux
Cedex 9
France
http://www-europe.cisco.com
Tel: 33 1 58 04 60 00
Fax: 33 1 58 04 61 00

Americas Headquarters
Cisco Systems, Inc.
170 West Tasman Drive
San Jose, CA 95134-1706
USA
http://www.cisco.com
Tel: 408 526-7660
Fax: 408 527-0883

Asia Pacific Headquarters
Cisco Systems Australia,
Pty., Ltd
Level 17, 99 Walker Street
North Sydney
NSW 2059 Australia
http://www.cisco.com
Tel: +61 2 8448 7100
Fax: +61 2 9957 4350

Cisco Systems has more than 200 offices in the following countries. Addresses, phone numbers, and fax numbers are listed on the Cisco Web site at www.cisco.com/go/offices

Argentina • Australia • Austria • Belgium • Brazil • Bulgaria • Canada • Chile • China • Colombia • Costa Rica • Croatia • Czech Republic • Denmark • Dubai, UAE • Finland • France • Germany • Greece • Hong Kong • Hungary • India • Indonesia • Ireland Israel • Italy • Japan • Korea • Luxembourg • Malaysia • Mexico • The Netherlands • New Zealand • Norway • Peru • Philippines Poland • Portugal • Puerto Rico • Romania • Russia • Saudi Arabia • Scotland • Singapore • Slovakia • Slovenia • South Africa • Spain Sweden • Switzerland • Taiwan • Thailand • Turkey • Ukraine • United Kingdom • United States • Venezuela • Vietnam • Zimbabwe

About the Authors

Allan Leinwand is the Chief Technology Officer and Vice President of Engineering at Telegis Networks, Inc. Previously, as Chief Technology Officer and Vice President of Engineering for Digital Island, Inc., he was responsible for the technical direction of the company's global network and content distribution strategy. Before Digital Island, he was a Consulting Engineering Manager at Cisco Systems, Inc., responsible for the global network design of customer networks. Allan received his BS in Computer Science at the University of Colorado at Boulder in 1988, and has been working in internetworking technology and solutions for large corporations since that time. He teaches graduate computer networking courses for the University of California, Berkeley; has published many papers on network management and network design; and is the co-author of the Addison-Wesley text *Network Management: A Practical Perspective,* Second Edition.

Bruce Pinsky, CCIE #1045, is the Vice President of Product Engineering and Network Infrastructure at Telegis Networks, Inc. Previously, as Chief Information Officer, Vice President of Solutions Engineering, and Chief Network Strategist of Digital Island, Inc., he was responsible for the direction and deployment of corporate technology infrastructure and advanced technology research. Before Digital Island, Bruce was a Senior Internetwork Support Technologist at Cisco Systems, Inc., and was responsible for the escalation of complex customer technical issues. He received his BS in Computer Science at California State University, Hayward, in 1988, and he has been working in internetworking technology and systems integration for large corporations and consulting firms before and since that time. One of the original Cisco Certified Internetwork Engineers, Bruce has expertise in such topics as network troubleshooting and protocol analysis, network design and configuration, and workstation and server-based operating systems. He routinely teaches courses on network configuration, design, and troubleshooting, and is co-inventor of patented routing technology.

About the Technical Reviewers

Henry Benjamin, CCIE, CCNA, CCDA, B. Eng., is a Cisco Certified Internetwork Expert and an IT network engineer for Cisco Systems, Inc. He has more than 10 years of experience in Cisco networks, including planning, designing, and implementing large IP networks running IGRP, EIGRP, and OSPF. In the past year, Henry has focused on architectural design and implementation in Cisco internal networks across Australia and the Asia/Pacific region. He is the author of a book dedicated to passing the CCIE written exam and has helped with many other titles related to Cisco IOS. Henry holds a Bachelor of Engineering Degree from Sydney University. This review is dedicated to his sick mum.

Kevin Burgess has been doing network design, analysis, and maintenance for the past 10 years. As a Network Engineer with EDS for the past five years, he has worked on various projects across Canada. Kevin holds certifications from Novell and Cisco and is currently working on his CCIE.

André Paree-Huff, CCNP, MCSE+I, ASE, A+, Network+, I-Network+, has been working in the computer field for more than 8 years. He is currently working for Compaq Computer Corporation as a Network Support Engineer, Level III, for the North America Customer Support Center in Colorado Springs, Colorado. André handles troubleshooting of network hardware, specializing in Layers 2 and 3 of the OSI model. André has co-authored four network-related technical manuals and has been a technical editor on many others. He is currently working toward his CCIE.

Dave Sumter, CCIE #4942, CCDP, has been in the networking industry for close to five years and has been concentrating solely on Cisco solutions for the last three years He works for Cisco Systems, Inc., in South Africa. Dave's current duties involve the design of large-scale campus and WAN solutions for corporate and government clients in South Africa. Other duties involve the ongoing training of Cisco partners and participation in the examination of CCIE candidates at the CCIE routing and switching lab in South Africa.

Michael Truett, CCNP, is a network engineer for a large organization specializing in VoIP. He is currently working on his CCDP and CCIE. His strength lies in the area of network design, implementation, and troubleshooting for large networks on many different media types, including Frame Relay and satellite. In his spare time, Michael also teaches several classes on Cisco routers and switches.

Dedications

Allan Leinwand would like to dedicate this book to his family and friends, who have provided continual support, suggestions, encouragement, and insights throughout the writing of this book.

Bruce Pinsky would like to thank all his friends and family, who have provided their support in helping to make this book a reality. An extra special thank you goes to his wife, Paula, and sons, Eric and Kyle, for their tireless support during the many nights and weekends dedicated to the completion of this text.

Acknowledgments

We would like to say thank you to the diligent and persistent efforts of Tracy Hughes, the entire Cisco Press staff, and our technical reviewers in helping to complete this book.

Contents at a Glance

Contents

Introduction

Cisco Systems, Inc., is the leading global supplier of internetworking hardware and software, with more than 100,000 devices deployed throughout public and private internetworks each year. At the time of this writing, these devices carry more than 80 percent of the public Internet's traffic. The aim of this book is to help novice Cisco users with the basic administration of their internetworking devices.

Each of these devices has Cisco proprietary operating system software called the Cisco Internetwork Operating System (IOS). The Cisco IOS software is a complicated real-time operating system consisting of multiple subsystems and tens of thousands of possible configuration parameters. Using straightforward, chronological descriptions and practical examples, this book focuses on the Cisco IOS software with respect to configuring, operating, and maintaining internetworking devices. In addition to covering general aspects of the IOS, we consider it in the context of the three most popular networking protocols used today: the Transmission Control Protocol/Internet Protocol (TCP/IP), Novell Inc.'s Internetwork Packet Exchange (IPX), and Apple Computer Inc.'s AppleTalk.

Objectives

The central objective of this book is to make the Cisco IOS software easy to configure, operate, and maintain for novice users. The IOS documentation that comes with each Cisco product covers multiple CD-ROMs and offers a comprehensive look at each command, with all the relevant options. The documentation often intimidates and confuses people when they are trying to configure a Cisco product for a basic internetwork.

This book is intended to serve as a supportive, more focused partner to the available documentation by covering the commonly used IOS commands and the most popular options. Through the use of copious examples, illustrations, and Cisco IOS software configuration output, we explain the use of the IOS for a variety of users and internetworking configurations. An example internetwork for a fictitious company, Zoom Integrated Products (ZIP), is a context throughout the book to help illustrate concepts. As we introduce configuration commands and strategies, we also implement them for the specific devices and topology of the ZIP network.

Audience

This book is intended for any beginning user of the Cisco IOS software. Advanced users will also find this reference valuable because of the many examples and tips for using common IOS features.

We assume that the reader has some general background in the various types of internetworking equipment, such as hubs, bridges, switches, and routers. Coverage of the intricate details of these types of equipment is outside the scope of this book, but we review them briefly with respect to the Cisco IOS software. Likewise, comprehensive introductions to TCP/IP, AppleTalk, and IPX are left to the several fine texts already available, some of which are referenced at the end of each chapter. Instead of duplicating existing references on specific internetworking equipment and protocols, this book concentrates on the use of these technologies by products that run the Cisco IOS software.

Organization

Chapter 1, "Getting Started in Internetworking," reviews the OSI reference model and gives an overview of the general types of internetworking devices that are at issue in this book: bridges, switches, and routers. The chapter concludes by describing a complete example internetwork for the fictional Zoom Integrated Products (ZIP) company.

Chapter 2, "The Basics of Device Configuration," describes the basic information that you need to know about a Cisco device, starting with its configuration out of the box. Topics covered include how to access the console port, basic terminal configuration, Cisco IOS software setup mode, context-sensitive help, privileged mode, and the IOS configuration command structure. This chapter also explains some of the physical characteristics of a Cisco device, such as accessing random access memory (RAM), saving configuration information to nonvolatile RAM (NVRAM), and transferring Cisco IOS software images to Flash memory.

Chapter 3, "The Basics of Device Interfaces," explains what you need to know about the various network interface types found on a Cisco device. The chapter introduces each of the following interface types and gives examples of how to configure the Cisco IOS software for each: Ethernet, Fast Ethernet, Gigabit Ethernet, Token Ring, Fiber Distributed Data Interface (FDDI), High-Level Data Link Control (HDLC), Point-to-Point Protocol (PPP), X.25, Frame Relay, Asynchronous Transfer Mode (ATM), Digital Subscriber Loop (DSL), and Integrated Services Digital Network (ISDN). The chapter includes explanations of how to use Cisco IOS software commands to examine interface status and health.

Chapter 4, "TCP/IP Basics," explains the basics of the Internet Protocol (IP): subnetting and routing. The chapter also shows you how to use the Cisco IOS software to configure IP addresses, IP routes, IP routing protocols (RIP, IGRP, OSPF, EIGRP, and BGP4), IP network security, and dialup IP. Other IP nuances in the Cisco IOS software, such as Domain Name Service (DNS) configuration, IP broadcast forwarding, DHCP services, and redundancy, are also explained.

Chapter 5, "AppleTalk Basics," covers a variety of topics, starting with an overview of the AppleTalk protocol suite. The chapter then covers the IOS configuration of AppleTalk cable-ranges, zones, routing protocols (RTMP and EIGRP), AppleTalk network security, and dialup AppleTalk.

Chapter 6, "IPX Basics," first overviews the components of the Novell Internetwork Packet Exchange (IPX) protocol: network numbers, the Service Advertising Protocol (SAP), and routing. Next is coverage of using the IOS to configure IPX addresses, multiple LAN encapsulation methods, routes, routing protocols (RIP, NLSP, and EIGRP), IPX network security, and dialup IPX.

Chapter 7, "Basic Administrative and Management Issues," explains other basic configuration items in the IOS that you need to understand. These items include access control, using Secure Shell (SSH) to access an IOS device, logging messages, network management protocols, and clock/calendar control. The chapter shows how to configure the Simple Network Management Protocol, the Terminal Access Controller Access Control System (TACACS and TACACS+), the Remote Authentication Dial-In User Service (RADIUS), and the Network Time Protocol (NTP).

Chapter 8, "Comprehensive IOS Configuration for the ZIP Network," gives complete IOS configurations for the entire example ZIP network. This chapter summarizes the configuration examples seen throughout the text.

Book Features and Elements

This book utilizes a number of elements and conventions to help present information as clearly as possible and to reiterate key concepts. One convention already noted is the practice of using a single example network throughout the book as a context for configuration samples. You can find an illustration of the ZIP network on the inside front cover for convenient reference.

Naturally, configuration code forms a central element of this book. Code fragments are presented in a distinctive typeface (monotype) for easy identification. Input that must be typed by the user is distinguished by bold in code fragments. Individual code terms that appear in paragraphs are presented in bold.

Other elements used in this text are as follows:

- **Notes**—Sidebar comments that are related to the discussion at hand but that can be skipped without loss of understanding or continuity.

- **Tips**—Sidebar comments that describe an efficiency, shortcut, or optimal way of using the technology.

- **Further Reference**—Sidebar passages that identify sources of further information on text topics.

- **Summary tables of commands**—Reference and reiteration of the most important new commands and syntax introduced; these appear at the ends of relevant chapters.

A Brief History of Cisco Systems

Cisco Systems originated with Len and Sandy Bosack, a husband and wife working in different departments at Stanford University. They needed to enable their computer systems to communicate with one another. In developing a solution for this problem, they built a device called a gateway server. The gateway server helped the machines in the two departments at Stanford University communicate through the use of the Internet Protocol (IP). That was in the mid-1980s.

Not long after this achievement, Len and Sandy decided to take a chance and attempt to produce a commercial gateway server product. The first development and production facility for Cisco was the Bosacks' living room. In 1984, cisco Systems, Inc., was founded, and a new era in internetworking was formed.

Note the lowercase *c* in the company's original name; there are many rumors and explanation regarding it. It has been interpreted as an attempt to confuse editors when they are beginning a sentence with the company name; a mistake made by lawyers drafting the company name; a ripped piece of paper that originally said San Francisco Systems, Inc.; and just a name intended to be unique. We do not share the truth here because we prefer to keep the mystery alive—choose the answer that you prefer. In 1992, the company name was changed officially to Cisco Systems, Inc. The move to the capital *C* was met with some hesitancy by the cisco faithful, but today the name Cisco Systems, Inc., is used by most, except perhaps the die-hard engineers from the days of cisco Systems.

The first gateway product from Cisco was the Advanced Gateway Server (AGS), followed soon by the Mid-Range Gateway Server (MGS), the Compact Gateway Server (CGS), the Integrated Gateway Server (IGS), and the Advanced Gateway Server Plus (AGS+). These products are now known as the old alphabet soup products from the company. The next generation of products began to emerge in 1993 with the Cisco 4000 series routers, which was soon followed by the Cisco 7000, 2000, and 3000 router series. The family of Cisco products continues to evolve today, following this convention of using product numbers rather than names, with products such as the Cisco 12000 routers and Catalyst 6500 switches.

In the mid-1990s, Cisco began to diversify its product line from routers to other internetworking products, such as LAN switches, ATM switches, WAN networking products, IBM connectivity, and more.

With all the diversification of Cisco products, the inherent complexity of the Cisco IOS software, and the widespread growth of internetwork implementation, network designers and managers can feel overwhelmed by the amount of information that they need to sift through to even begin configuring a network with Cisco devices. At its core, this book has the objective of distilling the essentials needed to configure the Cisco IOS software from the vast amount of available information and documentation. Our goal in writing this book was to make the impressive products of Cisco, which from their beginning have been solving internetworking problems, as accessible to novices as they are to the veteran users of the IOS.

The OSI Reference Model—Review of the seven layers of tasks that make communications systems operate.

Types of Internetworking Devices—The main devices on an internetwork: bridges, switches, routers, and access servers.

An Internetwork Example—A specific internetwork topology that is used as an example throughout the book.

CHAPTER 1

Getting Started in Internetworking

This chapter helps you start learning about internetworking. Understanding this complex topic is the first step toward understanding the Cisco Internetwork Operating System (IOS). The IOS provides the intelligence that Cisco products require to perform their various internetworking tasks. The IOS is an operating system with a proprietary user interface, command set, configuration syntax, and so on. The IOS is to Cisco devices as Windows 2000 is to IBM-compatible personal computers. The IOS runs on all the Cisco products discussed in this text.

We encourage you to have a firm grasp of the internetworking principles surveyed in this chapter before you attempt to understand the complexities of the Cisco IOS. *Internetworking* is a term used to describe the collection of protocols and devices that interoperate on data networks. This chapter gives you the basic understanding of the subject; it is not meant to give you comprehensive coverage of the subject (which could take multiple books to cover completely). If you need a more extensive introduction to internetworking, a few good texts are cited in the "References" section at the end of this chapter.

When you finish this chapter, you should be comfortable with the OSI networking model and have a basic understanding of how bridges, switches, routers, and access servers work. Chapter 2, "The Basics of Device Configuration," introduces you to the basics of configuring a Cisco device.

The OSI Reference Model

The Open System Interconnection (OSI) reference model is a principle of internetworking that you must understand to appreciate the way Cisco devices operate. The OSI reference model is a seven-layer architectural model developed by the International Organization for Standardization (ISO) and the International Telecommunications Union-Telecommunications (ITU-T). It is used universally to help individuals understand network functionality. The OSI reference model adds structure to the many complexities involved in the development of communications software. The development of communications software involves many tasks, including dealing with multiple types of applications, transmission strategies, and physical network properties. Without structure, communications software might be difficult to write, change, and support.

NOTE   ISO is an international organization founded to promote cooperation in technological developments, particularly in the field of communications. ITU-T, on the other hand, is a global organization that drafts standards for all areas of international analog and digital communications. ITU-T deals with telecommunications standards.

The OSI reference model is divided into seven distinct layers. Each layer performs a specific, distinct task that helps communications systems operate. The layer operates according to a set of rules, which is called a *protocol*. In addition to following the rules of the protocol, each layer provides a set of services to the other layers in the model. The seven layers of the OSI reference model are the application, presentation, session, transport, network, data link, and physical layers, as shown in Figure 1-1. In the following sections, we briefly review each layer, starting with the application layer.

Figure 1-1   *The OSI Reference Model Contains Seven Layers*

Application	Layer 7
Presentation	Layer 6
Session	Layer 5
Transport	Layer 4
Network	Layer 3
Data link	Layer 2
Physical	Layer 1

The Application Layer

The application layer provides the interface to the communications system, which the user sees. Many common applications are used today in an internetwork environment, such as web browsers, File Transfer Protocol (FTP) clients, and electronic mail. An example of application layer communication is a web browser downloading a document from a web server. The web browser and server are peer applications on the application layer that communicate directly with each other for the retrieval of the document. They are unaware of the six lower layers of the OSI reference model, which are working to produce the necessary communications.

The Presentation Layer

The presentation layer deals with the syntax of data as it is being transferred between two communicating applications. The presentation layer provides a mechanism to convey the desired presentation of data between applications. Many people infer that the look and feel of the environment of a computer desktop, such as the way all the applications look and interact uniformly on a computer by Apple Computer, Inc., is an example of a presentation layer. In fact, this is not a presentation layer, but a series of applications using a common programmer's interface. One common presentation layer in use today is Abstract Syntax Notation One (ASN.1), which is used by protocols such as the Simple Network Management Protocol (SNMP) to represent the structure of objects in network management databases.

The Session Layer

The session layer allows two applications to synchronize their communications and exchange data. This layer breaks the communication between two systems into dialogue units and provides major and minor synchronization points during that communication. For example, a large distributed database transaction between multiple systems might use session layer protocols to ensure that the transaction is progressing at the same rate on each system.

The Transport Layer

The transport layer, Layer 4, is responsible for the transfer of data between two session layer entities. Multiple classes of transport layer protocols exist, from those that provide basic transfer mechanisms (such as unreliable services) to those that ensure that the sequence of data arriving at the destination is in the proper order, that multiplex multiple streams of data, that provide a flow control mechanism, and that ensure reliability.

As you will see in the next section, some network layer protocols, called connectionless protocols, do not guarantee that the data arrives at the destination in the order in which it was sent by the source. Some transport layers handle this by sequencing the data properly before handing it to the session layer. *Multiplexing* of data means that the transport layer can simultaneously handle multiple streams of data (which could be from different applications) between two systems. *Flow control* is a mechanism that the transport layer can use to regulate the amount of data sent from the source to the destination. Transport layer protocols often add reliability to a session by having the destination system send acknowledgments back to the source system as it receives data.

In this text, we discuss the three commonly used transport protocols: the Transmission Control Protocol (TCP) that is used on the Internet, Novell's Streams Packet Exchange (SPX), and Apple's AppleTalk Transport Protocol (ATP).

The Network Layer

The network layer, which routes data from one system to another, provides addressing for use on the internetwork. The Internet Protocol (IP) defines the global addressing for the Internet; Novell defines proprietary addressing for the Internetwork Packet Exchange

(IPX), its client/server architecture; and Apple's AppleTalk uses the Datagram Delivery Protocol (DDP) and proprietary addressing for communicating between its machines on the network layer. In later chapters, we explore the specifics of each of these types of network layer addresses.

Network layer protocols route data from the source to the destination and fall into one of two classes, connection-oriented or connectionless. Connection-oriented network layers route data in a manner similar to using a telephone. They begin communicating by placing a call or establishing a route from the source to the destination. They send data down the given route sequentially and then end the call or close the communication. Connectionless network protocols, which send data that has complete addressing information in each packet, operate like the postal system. Each letter, or packet, has a source and a destination address. Each intermediate post office, or network device, reads this addressing and makes a separate decision on how to route the data. The letter, or data, continues from one intermediate device to another until it reaches the destination. Connectionless network protocols do not guarantee that packets arrive at the destination in the same order in which they were sent. Transport protocols are responsible for the sequencing of the data into the proper order for connectionless network protocols.

The Data Link Layer

Layer 2, the data link layer, provides the connection from the physical network to the network layer, thereby enabling the reliable flow of data across the network. Ethernet, Fast Ethernet, Token Ring, Frame Relay, and Asynchronous Transfer Mode (ATM) are all Layer 2 protocols that are commonly used today. As you will see throughout this text, data link layer addressing is different from network layer addressing. Data link layer addresses are unique to each data link logical segment, while network layer addressing is used throughout the internetwork.

The Physical Layer

The first layer of the OSI reference model is the physical layer. The physical layer is concerned with the physical, electrical, and mechanical interfaces between two systems. The physical layer defines the properties of the network medium, such as fiber, twisted-pair copper, coaxial copper, satellite, and so on. Standard network interface types found on the physical layer include V.35, RS-232C, RJ-11, RJ-45, AUI, and BNC connectors.

NOTE   Many people add an eighth layer to the top of the OSI reference model, the political layer. Although used in jest, the term *political layer* is often accurate because all lower layers of the OSI reference model are encapsulated within the politics involved in the organizations that design a data network.

The Data Exchange Process

These seven layers all work together to provide a communications system. The communication occurs when a protocol on one system, which is located at a given layer of the model, communicates directly with its corresponding layer on another system. The application layer of a source system logically communicates with the application layer of the destination system. The presentation layer of the source system passes data to the presentation layer of the destination system. This communication occurs at each of the seven layers of the model.

This logical communication between corresponding layers of the protocol stack does not involve many different physical connections between the two communications systems. The information each protocol wants to send is encapsulated in the layer of protocol information beneath it. The encapsulation process produces a set of data called a *packet*.

NOTE   Data encapsulation is the process in which the information in one protocol is wrapped, or contained, in the data section of another protocol. In the OSI reference model, each layer encapsulates the layer immediately above it as the data flows down the protocol stack.

Starting at the source, as shown in Figure 1-2, the application-specific data is encapsulated in the presentation layer information. To the presentation layer, the application data is generic data being presented. The presentation layer hands its data to the session layer, which attempts to keep the session synchronized. The session layer passes data to the transport layer, which transports the data from the source system to the destination system. The network layer adds routing and addressing information to the packet and passes it to the data link layer. The data link layer provides framing for the packet and the connection to the physical layer.

At Layer 1, as shown in the figure, the physical layer sends the data as bits across a medium, such as copper or fiber. The packet then traverses the destination network from Layer 1 to Layer 7. Each device along the way reads only the information necessary to get the data from the source to the destination. Each protocol de-encapsulates the packet data and reads the information sent by the corresponding layer on the source system.

As an example, consider what occurs when you open a Web page using a Web browser. Given a URL, such as www.telegis.net, your browser asks the TCP to open a reliable connection to the Web server that is located at www.telegis.net. (Many applications that use TCP skip the presentation and session layers, as we do in this example.) TCP then requests the network layer (IP) to route a packet from the source IP address to the destination IP address. The data link layer takes this IP packet and encapsulates it again for the particular type of data link leaving the source system, such as Ethernet. The physical layer carries the signal from the source system to the next system en route to the destination, such as a router.

The router de-encapsulates the data link layer; reads the network layer information; re-encapsulates the packet, if necessary, to place it on the next data link en route to the destination; and routes the packet appropriately.

Figure 1-2 *Data Flow from a Source Application to a Destination Application Through the Seven Layers of the OSI Reference Model*

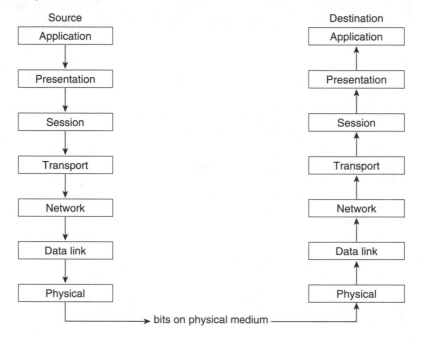

This process continues until the packet reaches the destination IP address. At the destination IP address, the data link layer de-encapsulates the packet, sees that the destination IP address is the local system, and passes the data in the IP packet to the transport layer. The transport layer ensures the reliability of the connection and passes the data from your Web browser to the www.telegis.net Web server. The Web server then responds to your Web browser request and sends a Web page of data back to your browser (using the same process, but with the source and destination IP addresses reversed).

Cisco devices covered in this book operate at the physical, data link, and network layers of the OSI reference model and read information in these layers to carry data from one location to another. Throughout this book, we reference these layers and explain how the Cisco IOS uses the protocol information at each layer. Some Cisco devices, such as bridges and switches, operate at the data link layer. Other Cisco devices, such as routers, operate at the network layer, as shown in Figure 1-3. We describe the various types of internetworking devices in the next section.

Figure 1-3   *An OSI Reference Model Depiction of Data That Travels from a Source Host, Through a Cisco Switch, Through a Cisco Router, and Then to a Destination Host*

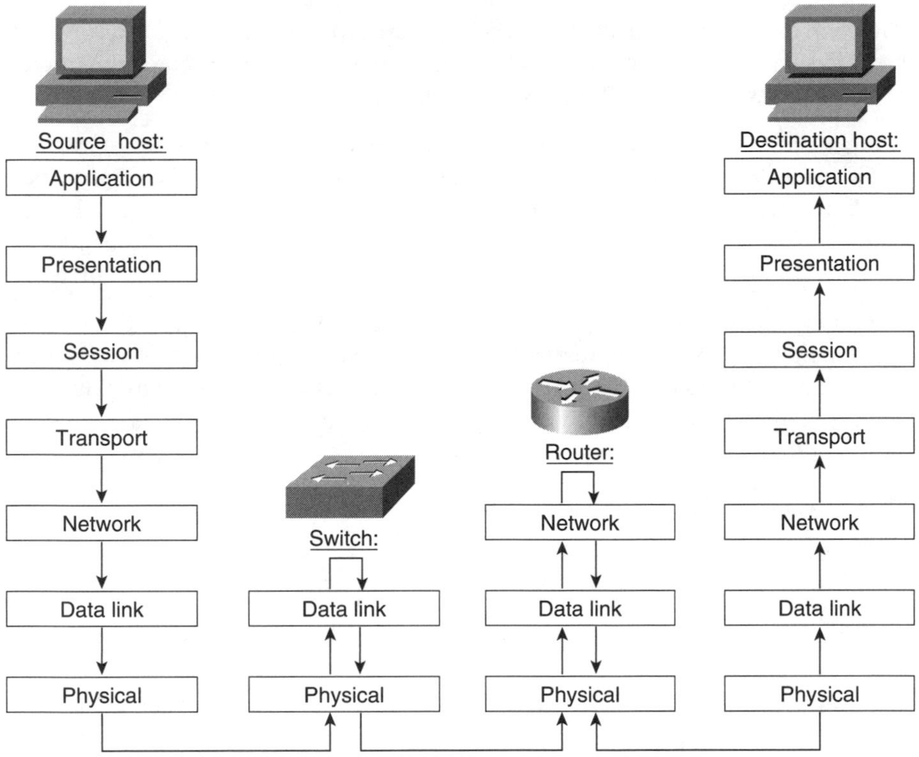

Types of Internetworking Devices

Cisco devices fall into three main categories: bridges and switches, routers, and access servers. We discuss bridges and switches first.

Bridges and Switches

A *bridge* is a network device that operates at the data link layer. A bridge connects multiple data link layer network segments into a single logical network segment. There are many different types of bridges:

* Transparent or learning
* Encapsulation
* Translational

- Source-route
- Source-route translational

Although the Cisco IOS implements each of these types of bridging, we discuss only the first three types of bridging in this book. Source-route and source-route translational bridging are used in Token Ring environments.

Bridging allows for physical and logical separation of traffic when necessary to reduce traffic loads on a network segment. The main advantage of bridging is to ensure network reliability, availability, scalability, and manageability by segmenting a logical network into multiple physical pieces. We examine bridging as it relates to routing throughout this text.

A bridge performs its function by examining the data link layer information in each packet and forwarding the packet to other physical segments only if necessary. The information concerning which packets to forward to which network segments is learned by the bridge and kept in a forwarding table. The forwarding table includes a list of known data link layer addresses and the associated network segment where these devices are believed to exist, as shown in Figure 1-4.

Figure 1-4   *The Forwarding Table Maps Data Link Addresses to Physical Network Segments*

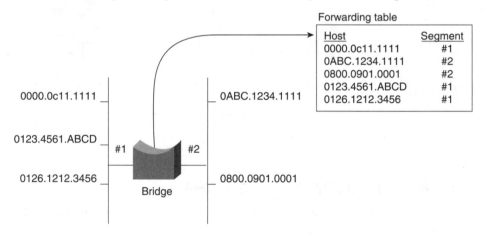

Bridges communicate with one another to determine the best method of forwarding packets to a given data link layer destination using a Spanning Tree Protocol. This protocol allows bridges to build a loop-free topology over which to forward packets. A *loop-free topology*, a topology that guarantees that a packet reaches every segment of a network exactly once, is needed in a bridging environment to avoid broadcast storms and to avoid multiple parallel bridges forwarding a packet multiple times to a given segment. A *broadcast storm* is a network segment event in which a *broadcast packet*—that is, a packet meant for every station on the segment—is sent in a continual loop until the segment is overloaded with traffic.

The simplest form of a bridge, a *transparent bridge*, can handle the connection of only like data link layer protocols. *Encapsulation* and *translational bridges* can be considered transparent bridges, with the additional functionality of enabling different data link layer protocols to interoperate.

An encapsulation bridge encapsulates an entire data link layer frame in another data link layer, which allows transparent bridging between like data link layers to occur when they are physically separated by a second, different data link layer. For example, two encapsulation bridges, each with one Ethernet port and one serial port, can bridge Ethernet network segments when they are connected by a serial link. The serial link is a different Layer 2 medium than is Ethernet. Encapsulation bridging allows the entire Ethernet frame to be bridged from one segment to another when separated by the serial link because the bridge encapsulates the Ethernet frame in the serial link data link protocol. The result is that the devices on the two Ethernet segments that are joined by the encapsulation bridges believe that all the devices are attached to a single, logical Ethernet segment.

Another type of bridge is a translational bridge. A translational bridge performs the function of a transparent bridge between different types of data link layer protocols. For example, a translational bridge may translate Ethernet frames into Token Ring frames on the data link layer. If two devices are on different mediums connected by a translational bridge, they appear to be on one logical network segment. The transparent interconnection of two different mediums can provide the necessary connectivity for two devices that need to communicate solely at the data link layer.

A Cisco *switch* is essentially a multiport bridge that runs the IOS. A switch, which functions at the data link layer, performs the same basic functions as a bridge. The essential difference between a bridge and a switch is not technical, but packaging.

A switch may have more ports than a bridge, cost less per port than a bridge, and possess embedded management functions that a bridge does not have. Yet, when you examine the functionality of bridges and switches within the context of the OSI reference model, they do not differ. Many switches have multiple ports supporting a single data link layer protocol, such as Ethernet, and a smaller number of high-speed data link layer ports used to connect to faster mediums, such as ATM or Fast Ethernet. If a switch has two or more different interfaces to two or more data link layer protocols, it can be considered a translational bridge. Many switches today have interfaces that operate at multiple speeds, such as Ethernet, Fast Ethernet, and Gigabit Ethernet.

Figure 1-5 shows a small switched internetwork.

Figure 1-5 *A Small Switched Internetwork*

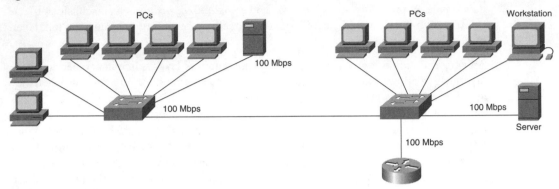

Routers

A *router* is a device that directs packets through the network based on network layer information. We focus on three network layer protocols in this book: IP, IPX, and AppleTalk. A router understands the network layer addressing in a packet and it has algorithms, called routing protocols, that build tables to determine the route that a packet should take to reach its final destination. For a multiprotocol router—one that understands multiple network layer addressing formats and routing protocols, such as a Cisco router— the router keeps a separate routing table for each network layer protocol that is being routed, as shown in Figure 1-6.

Figure 1-6 *A Multiprotocol Router Keeps a Routing Table for Each of Its Network Layer Protocols*

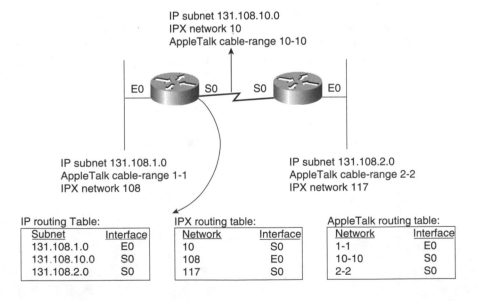

A bridge or switch connects two or more physical networks into a single logical network, while a router connects two or more logical networks and routes between them using information that is built by routing protocols and kept in routing tables. The advantages of a router (as compared to using any type of bridge) are that it physically and logically breaks a network into multiple manageable pieces, allows for control of routed packets, and routes many different network layer protocols at the same time. In this book, we discuss many router configuration options in the Cisco IOS.

Access Servers

An *access server*, also called a *communications server*, is a device that connects asynchronous devices to a network. A common application of an access server is to connect a computer communicating over a modem to the Internet. The access server combines the functions of a router with the functions of an asynchronous protocol.

If a machine connects to an access server via an asynchronous interface, the access server provides the software that allows the machine to appear to be on the network. For example, an access server may have 16 asynchronous ports and a single Ethernet port. Any device that connects to an asynchronous port appears to be on the Ethernet where the access server resides, which allows people running IP, IPX, or AppleTalk to work from a remote machine, just as they would if they were on the local network. We discuss the configuration and functions of access servers throughout this book.

An Internetwork Example

Figure 1-7 shows the network that we use as an example throughout this book.

This network is used to examine the use of the Cisco IOS in the following environments:

- Various local-area network (LAN) technologies, such as Ethernet, Fast Ethernet, Gigabit Ethernet, Token Ring, and the Fiber Distributed Data Interface (FDDI). (See Chapter 3, "The Basics of Device Interfaces.")

- Various synchronous and asynchronous wide-area network (WAN) technologies, such as HDLC, PPP, Frame Relay, ATM, and ISDN. (See Chapter 3.)

- IP routing. (See Chapter 4, "TCP/IP Basics.")

- IPX routing. (See Chapter 6, "IPX Basics.")

- AppleTalk routing. (See Chapter 5, "AppleTalk Basics.")

Figure 1-7   *The Zoom Integrated Products Internetwork*

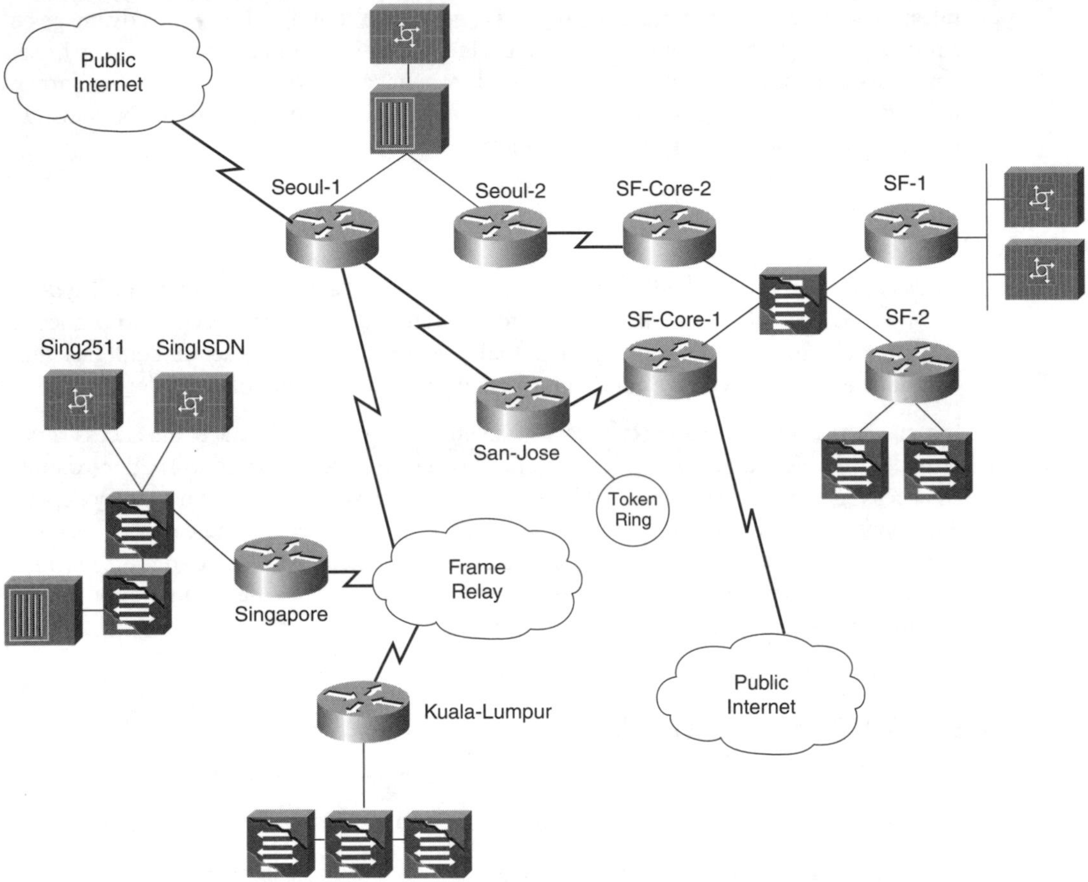

This network belongs to a fictitious company named Zoom Integrated Products (ZIP). ZIP, which has its corporate offices in San Francisco, California, makes components for the semiconductor industry. Its Asian sales headquarters are located in Seoul, Korea. Both the corporate offices and the Asian sales headquarters have connections to the public Internet. ZIP also has manufacturing facilities in Singapore and Kuala Lumpur, Malaysia.

The ZIP network uses Frame Relay to connect Singapore and Kuala Lumpur to Seoul. Seoul has ISDN BRI dialup facilities. At its corporate offices, the ZIP network has a

Gigabit Ethernet backbone and three Fast Ethernet network segments—two for high-speed connections to office suites and one for a LAN, where access servers reside for corporate dialup users. There are additional access servers for local dialup users in Seoul and Singapore. The corporate offices are connected to its sales headquarters via redundant HDLC links. A manufacturing assembly facility, which is located in San Jose, California, has dual HDLC links—one to the corporate offices and one to the sales headquarters in Seoul. The San Jose facility uses a Token Ring network on the assembly floor.

ZIP uses a variety of internetwork protocols on its network, including AppleTalk, IP, and IPX. Cisco switches are used for desktop connectivity, and routers interconnect each site and each location. (Each router is identified by name in Figure 1-7.) Most locations have at least one access server for remote dialup users.

The ZIP internetwork is representative of many internetworks throughout the world in that it uses multiple network layer protocols and wide-area network protocols, uses a combination of routing and switching, and has access servers to handle connections from asynchronous devices. Although it is only an example, this network and its complexities are typical of internetwork deployment today. As we progress through this book, we will use the ZIP network as an example and show you how to configure all the Cisco IOS devices necessary to make this fictitious network a reality.

Summary

Having completed this chapter, you should be comfortable with the OSI networking model and should have a basic understanding of how bridges and switches, routers, and access servers work. Next, Chapter 2 introduces you to the basics of configuring a Cisco device. Keep in mind the following central concepts from this chapter:

- The Cisco IOS is the operating system that runs Cisco devices.
- Cisco devices covered in this book operate at three layers of the OSI reference model: physical, data link, and network.
- The Cisco IOS uses protocol information at each layer of the OSI reference model.
- Bridges and switches operate at the data link layer and connect multiple data link layer network segments into a single logical network segment.
- Routers operate at the network layer and direct packets through the network based on network layer information.
- Access servers connect asynchronous devices to a network, allowing the device to appear to be on the network.

References

The following references explore the subjects in this chapter further:

Halsall, F. *Data Communications, Computer Networks, and Open Systems,* Fourth Edition. Reading, Massachusetts: Addison-Wesley Publishing Company, 1996.

Perlman, R. *Interconnections: Bridges, Routers, Switches and Internetworking Protocols,* Second Edition. Reading, Massachusetts: Addison-Wesley Publishing Company, 1999.

Peterson, L. and B.S. Davie. *Computer Networks: A Systems Approach,* Second Edition. San Francisco, California: Morgan Kaufmann Publishers, 1999.

Preliminary Configuration Steps—The basics of configuring a Cisco device running the IOS, starting with what to do when you receive the device in a shipping box.

The Help System—How to use the Help system in the IOS.

Nonprivileged and Privileged Modes—The two predefined user levels for accessing a Cisco device.

Memory Configuration Issues—Description of two of the memory types found on Cisco devices, NVRAM and Flash memory.

User Configuration Mode—The IOS method to perform dynamic configuration from a user prompt, from memory, or from a server.

Configuration Commands—Structure of configuration commands used by the IOS and examples of basic configuration commands.

CHAPTER 2

The Basics of Device Configuration

This chapter explains the basics of Cisco IOS configuration, which are used throughout the remainder of this book. We begin with the fundamental issue of setting up a device after it is "out of the box" and cover the most fundamental components of the IOS, including Help features, memory configuration, and the structure of configuration commands. The ZIP network, which was introduced in the previous chapter, serves as a context for device configuration examples.

Preliminary Configuration Steps

All IOS devices are configured with the minimal configuration possible from the factory. For example, bridges and switches are set up to forward and run a spanning tree on all ports, but they are not configured for advanced features, such as filtering. For routers and access servers, Cisco provides a minimal configuration that requires you to give input before the devices can perform their functions. When you receive your router or access server, all the interfaces on the device are turned off, or administratively downed.

To set up a Cisco device, first plug the device into an electrical outlet and find the power switch located on the back of the device. If you turn on the power switch (sometimes labeled as 1), the device powers on and shows the status LEDs on the front panel.

A notable exception to this convention is the popular Cisco 2500 series routers. This specific series of routers does not have any status LEDs on the front of its devices to show that they are powered on, but its devices each have one status LED on the back near the auxiliary (AUX) console port.

NOTE   Many of the LEDs associated with other components of the device, such as LAN or WAN interfaces, may not turn on until you have configured them. It is not possible to configure LAN or WAN interfaces without power and without entering the proper IOS configuration commands.

The Console Port

The next step in configuring an IOS device is to find the console port. Every Cisco device has a console port that is used to access the device from a directly attached terminal. The console port is often an RS-232C or RJ-45 port labeled "Console."

After locating the console port, you need to attach a dedicated terminal or PC with a terminal emulator. Cisco provides the necessary cables to connect to the console port with each device. If you have a dedicated terminal to connect to your device, you might use an RS-232C connector on the terminal, connect this to an RJ-45 cable, and then attach this assembly directly to the device.

Some devices, such as the Cisco 7500 router, require you to use an RS-232C connector on both ends of the RJ-45 cable, whereas other devices, such as the Cisco 2500 series, do not. If you plan to use a PC to connect to the device, you might have to attach a DB-9 connector to the serial port of your PC and then use the RJ-45 cable to connect to your device. If your IOS device has an RJ-45 console port (such as a Cisco 2500 series or Cisco 3600 series router), you need only the proper connector from the RJ-45 to your console (often an RS-232C connector) or personal computer (often a DB-9 connector).

After establishing the physical connection from your terminal or PC to the device, you need to configure the terminal to communicate with the device properly. You should set your terminal (or terminal emulation program on your PC) to support the following settings:

- VT100 emulation
- 9600 baud
- No parity
- 8 data bits
- 1 stop bit

After these settings are correct, you should power on your device. You should see a banner similar to this code from a Cisco 7206 router:

```
System Bootstrap, Version 12.1(1), SOFTWARE
Copyright (c) 1986-2000 by cisco Systems

Restricted Rights Legend
Use, duplication, or disclosure by the Government is
subject to restrictions as set forth in subparagraph
(c) of the Commercial Computer Software - Restricted
Rights clause at FAR sec. 52.227-19 and subparagraph
(c) (1) (ii) of the Rights in Technical Data and Computer
Software clause at DFARS sec. 252.227-7013.
           cisco Systems, Inc.
           170 West Tasman Drive
           San Jose, California 95134-1706
Cisco Internetwork Operating System Software
IOS (tm) 7200 Software (C7200-P-M), RELEASE SOFTWARE 12.0(5)
```

Bridges and switches running the IOS may or may not show a banner similar to this, depending on the model of the device and its functionality. Regardless of the banner shown, you should see some output on your terminal or terminal emulator when you power on the device. Depending on your terminal emulation and settings, you may have to press the Enter or Return key on your terminal's keyboard before you see some output.

If you do not see any output on your terminal or terminal emulator, check the connections and ensure that the terminal settings are correct. You might also want to refer to Cisco's *Getting Started Guide*, which ships with each device.

The System Configuration Dialog

During initial power on, all routers and access servers enter the System Configuration Dialog mode. This interactive mode appears on the console screen and asks you questions to help you configure the basic items in the IOS. The System Configuration Dialog prompts you first for global system parameters and then for interface-specific parameters.

When entering System Configuration Dialog mode, you should see the following code:

```
--- System Configuration Dialog ---
At any point you may enter a question mark '?' for help.
Refer to the 'Getting Started' Guide for additional help.
Use ctrl-c to abort configuration dialog at any prompt.
Default settings are in square brackets '[]'.
Would you like to enter the initial configuration dialog? [yes]:
```

NOTE   The prompts and interface options shown here may not be exactly the same as shown on your router. The IOS customizes the System Configuration Dialog automatically, depending on the platform and the interfaces installed in your router. This example was done using a Cisco 2500 series router.

You can then press Return or Enter to begin the System Configuration Dialog:

```
Would you like to enter the initial configuration dialog? [yes]:
First, would you like to see the current interface summary? [yes]:
```

The following interface summary is for a device direct from the Cisco factory; it has not been configured yet. Therefore, all interfaces are shown as not configured (indicated by NO in the OK? column). The interfaces do not have IP addresses assigned, so this column shows a value of **unassigned** for each interface. The Method column refers to how the interface was configured, such as manually or automatically from the network. At this time, the interfaces are not set. The last two columns refer to the status of the interface and the data link protocol that is running on the interface. By default, on a new device, all interfaces begin in a **down** status and with a **down** data link layer protocol.

```
Interface      IP-Address    OK?   Method    Status   Protocol
Ethernet0      unassigned    NO    not set   down     down
Serial0        unassigned    NO    not set   down     down
```

Interpreting the interface summary further, an Ethernet is a local-area network (LAN) interface, and a serial is a wide-area network (WAN) interface. The interface name Ethernet0 denotes the first Ethernet LAN in the device, and the interface name Serial0 denotes the first serial WAN in the device. Cisco labels the device with these names on the physical ports on the outside of the unit. The various types of LAN and WAN interfaces are discussed in Chapter 3, "The Basics of Device Interfaces."

The next few steps concern configuring the name of the device, a logical name to associate with this physical hardware, and passwords for the device. Let's start with the device name. Use the Singapore router from the ZIP network as a sample device to be configured:

```
Configuring global parameters:
 Enter host name [Router]: Singapore
```

TIP   The IOS accepts the answer shown in brackets ([]) as the default entry to questions. This example shows the default answers being entered for clarity.

As you see in the next section of this chapter, the two levels of commands in the IOS are privileged and nonprivileged. You must configure a password for each device. This password is the key to entering privileged mode. Privileged passwords should be kept confidential and treated the same as superuser or system administrator passwords. It is strongly recommended that you use the enable secret method and not the older enable password method of setting the password, because the **enable secret** command uses a one-way cryptographic algorithm. To facilitate all IOS options, you set both methods in this example, but all examples in the rest of this text use the enable secret method. You should set the enable secret to !zippy2u and the enable password to !zippy4me:

```
The enable secret word is a one-way cryptographic secret that is used
instead of the enable password word when it exists.
  Enter enable secret: !zippy2u
The enable password is used when there is no enable secret
and when using older software and some boot images.

  Enter enable password: !zippy4me
```

A virtual terminal is a logical terminal connection to an IOS device. By default, all IOS devices allow five simultaneous virtual terminal Telnet sessions (numbered 0 through 4). When the IOS device is active on a network, you can use the Telnet program to access all IOS functions from the virtual terminal in the same manner as accessing the device from the console port. For example, you can use a virtual terminal to connect to a router and to then enter privileged command mode with the enable secret password. At this point, we will set the virtual terminal password for all five virtual terminal sessions to Zipmein:

```
Enter virtual terminal password: Zipmein
```

We set all virtual terminal passwords to be the same because when users connect to a router, they often do not specify the virtual terminal they want to connect to and instead connect to the first one available.

The next steps in the Systems Configuration Dialog involve setting the desired protocols. You should enable the Simple Network Management Protocol (SNMP) on your device now. SNMP configuration is explained further in Chapter 7, "Basic Administrative and Management Issues." For now, enable SNMP and accept the default community string of public:

```
Configure SNMP Network Management? [yes]: yes
  Community string [public]: public
```

The System Configuration Dialog now asks if you want to configure the DECnet protocol, Digital Equipment Corporation's network layer protocol. Because you do not need this protocol on the ZIP network, type **no**:

```
Configure DECnet? [no]: no
```

You are using AppleTalk with multizone networks. (AppleTalk is discussed further in Chapter 5, "AppleTalk Basics.")

```
Configure AppleTalk? [no]: yes
    Multizone networks? [no]: yes
```

You are also using the Novell IPX protocol on the ZIP network:

```
Configure IPX? [no]: yes
```

The Internet Protocol (IP) is the main protocol on the ZIP corporate network, so you enable it here. When you enable it, the IOS asks you to pick an IP routing protocol that is used by routers to pass routing information. You do not enable the Interior Gateway Routing Protocol (IGRP) as your routing protocol. We show you how to configure IP routing protocols in Chapter 4, "TCP/IP Basics."

```
Configure IP? [yes]:
    Configure IGRP routing? [yes]: no
```

After the section on protocols, the IOS setup command queries you for information about each specific interface on the device. For each LAN and WAN interface on the device, you are asked for protocol-specific information. The various types of LAN and WAN interfaces are covered in Chapter 3, and protocol specifics, such as IP addressing, IPX network numbers, and AppleTalk cable ranges, are covered in subsequent chapters. The ZIP router in Singapore has a single Ethernet LAN interface and a single Frame Relay WAN interface. You configure IP, IPX, and AppleTalk on each as follows:

```
Configuring interface parameters:
Configuring interface Ethernet0:
```

The following question asks if the interface being configured is in use—that is, whether you want the interface to be turned on and not administratively turned off. You should turn on the interfaces Ethernet0 and Serial0 for the Singapore router:

```
Is this interface in use? [no]: yes
```

You should tell the router to run the IP protocol on this interface and to use the IP address 131.108.1.1 and the subnet mask 255.255.255.128 for Ethernet0. The details of IP addressing, subnetting, and configuration are covered in Chapter 4.

```
Configure IP on this interface? [no]: yes
    IP address for this interface: 131.108.1.1
Number of bits in subnet field [0]: 9
    Class B network is 131.108.0.0, 9 subnet bits; mask is /25
```

The ZIP network in Singapore also runs Novell IPX and AppleTalk. To enable these protocols, you need to give an IPX network number and an AppleTalk cable-range. The details of IPX are covered in Chapter 6, "IPX Basics." AppleTalk is covered in Chapter 5.

```
Configure IPX on this interface? [no]: yes
    IPX network number [1]: 4010
  Configure AppleTalk on this interface? [no]: yes
    Extended AppleTalk network? [no]: yes
    AppleTalk starting cable range [0]: 4001
```

You also need to configure interface Serial0 on the router with the same network layer protocols as follows:

```
Configuring interface Serial0:
  Is this interface in use? [no]: yes
Configure IP unnumbered on this interface? [no]: no
  IP address for this interface: 131.108.242.6
  Number of bits in subnet field [0]: 14
    Class B network is 131.108.0.0, 8 subnet bits; mask is /30
Configure IPX on this interface? [no]: yes
    IPX network number [2]: 2902
Configure AppleTalk on this interface? [no]: yes
    Extended AppleTalk network? [no]: yes
    AppleTalk network number [1]: 2902
```

The output of running the System Configuration Dialog is a configuration command script that is interpreted by the device. The System Configuration Dialog itself does not configure the device, but it makes a configuration command script, which is then interpreted by the device and used for configuration. This is the language you need to understand to configure all Cisco IOS products. The remainder of this text explores this scripting language. You probably can already draw connections between the questions asked by the System Configuration Dialog and the following configuration command script.

The following configuration command script is created:

```
hostname Singapore
enable secret 5 $2zu6m7$RMMZ8em/.8hksdkkh78p/T0
enable password !zippy4me
line vty 0 4
password Zipmein
snmp-server community public
ip routing

ipx routing
appletalk routing

no decnet routing

!
interface Ethernet0
```

```
ip address 131.108.1.1 255.255.255.128
ipx network 4010
appletalk cable-range 4001-4001
appletalk discovery
no mop enabled
!
interface Serial0
ip address 131.108.242.6 255.255.255.252
ipx network 100
appletalk cable-range 2902-2902
no mop enabled
!
end
Use this configuration? [yes/no]: yes
[OK]
Use the enabled mode 'configure' command to modify this configuration.
Press RETURN to get started!
```

When you press the Return key, the router gives you the following prompt:

```
Singapore>
```

At this point, you have entered EXEC mode, or the mode used to execute commands within the IOS. Let's first consider the Help system before going into EXEC mode.

The Help System

The Help system in the IOS is available in EXEC mode to help you issue commands to a device. The Help system is context-sensitive, meaning that the help given depends on what you are trying to do with the IOS. For example, if you enter **?** at the device prompt, the following information appears:

```
Singapore>?
Exec commands:
  <1-99>           Session number to resume
  access-enable    Create a temporary Access-List entry
  access-profile   Apply user-profile to interface
  attach           attach to system component
  clear            Reset functions
  connect          Open a terminal connection
  disable          Turn off privileged commands
  disconnect       Disconnect an existing network connection
  enable           Turn on privileged commands
  exit             Exit from the EXEC
  help             Description of the interactive help system
  lock             Lock the terminal
  login            Log in as a particular user
  logout           Exit from the EXEC
  mls              exec mls router commands
  mrinfo           Request neighbor and version information from a multicast
                   router
  mstat            Show statistics after multiple multicast traceroutes
  mtrace           Trace reverse multicast path from destination to source
  name-connection  Name an existing network connection
  pad              Open a X.29 PAD connection
  ping             Send echo messages
--More--
```

This is only the first help screen available, and the output has been limited in this example. For a complete listing of EXEC commands, you might want to consult the Cisco IOS Software Command Summary, which can be found at www.cisco.com/univercd/cc/td/doc/product/software/ios121/12lcgcr/index.htm. Note that the IOS commands are listed on the left side of the help screen, and a brief explanation of each command is listed on the right. Some commands are executed in a single word; the Help system communicates this by showing that your only option is to enter a carriage return after the command, denoted by the <cr> in the display:

```
Singapore>lock ?
<cr>

Singapore>lock
```

When you use the Help system, the IOS does not require you to repeat the command after you ask for help. In the previous example, the word **lock** is repeated by the IOS automatically after the Help screen appears.

You can also use the Help system to find the available completion options for a given EXEC command. As you will see throughout this text, the IOS has many commands available to show the current status of the device. Many of these commands begin with **show**. In the following information, you can see all of the possible options after you type the word **show**:

```
Singapore>show ?
  alps          Alps information
  backup        Backup status
  bootflash:    display information about bootflash: file system
  bootvar       Boot and related environment variable
  calendar      Display the hardware calendar
  cef           Cisco Express Forwarding
  ces           CES Show Commands
  clock         Display the system clock
  context       Show context information about recent crash(s)
  dialer        Dialer parameters and statistics
  disk0:        display information about disk0: file system
  disk1:        display information about disk1: file system
  drip          DRiP DB
  dss           DSS information
  flash:        display information about flash: file system
  fras-host     FRAS Host Information
  history       Display the session command history
  hosts         IP domain-name, lookup style, nameservers, and host table
  ipc           Interprocess communications commands
  location      Display the system location
  management    Display the management applications
  microcode     show configured microcode for downloadable hardware
  mls           multilayer switching information
  modemcap      Show Modem Capabilities database
  mpoa          MPOA show commands
  ncia          Native Client Interface Architecture
  ppp           PPP parameters and statistics
  rmon          rmon statistics
  rtr           Response Time Reporter (RTR)
  sessions      Information about Telnet connections
  sgbp          SGBP group information
  slot0:        display information about slot0: file system
  slot1:        display information about slot1: file system
  snmp          snmp statistics
```

```
syscon          System Controller information
tacacs          Shows tacacs+ server statistics
terminal        Display terminal configuration parameters
traffic-shape   traffic rate shaping configuration
users           Display information about terminal lines
version         System hardware and software status
vpdn            VPDN information
```

```
Singapore>show
```

Note that the IOS repeats the initial portion of the command you typed so that you do not have to repeat it.

The Help system in the IOS also completes partial commands when you use the Tab key. If you enter an unambiguous EXEC command and then press the Tab key, the IOS completes the command. As an example, we'll show you the **show sessions** command, which lets you see all the Telnet sessions on an IOS device:

If you enter

```
Singapore>show sess
```

and then press the Tab key, the IOS completes the command:

```
Singapore>show sessions
```

If you enter an ambiguous command, such as

```
Singapore>show s
```

the IOS cannot complete the command. This is an ambiguous string, possibly meaning **show sessions** or **show snmp**. Pressing the Tab key at this point causes the terminal bell to ring on most systems.

TIP

You do not have to use the full command in EXEC level in the IOS—an unambiguous string defaults to the proper command. This means that the commands **show sess** and **show sessions** produce the same output.

The **show sessions** command is different from the **session** command. The **session** command enables you to connect to a virtual console session of a hardware module on the IOS device. Some IOS devices have multiple hardware modules that each have their own virtual console access. Examples of this are the Route Switch Module (RSM) and the Asynchronous Transfer Mode (ATM) module in a Catalyst switch. You can specify the module that you wish to connect to using the **session** command followed by the module number. For example, if you have an ATM module as the third module (typically in the third slot of the device) in a Catalyst switch running the IOS, you can do the following to access the module:

```
Router>session 3
```

```
Trying ATM-3...
Connected to ATM-3.
Escape character is '^]'.

ATM>
```

You have now established a session to the ATM module. This is different from a Telnet session to the router itself, and all commands that you now execute are performed by the ATM module.

Nonprivileged and Privileged Modes

You can execute two basic levels of commands from the EXEC mode. The first level is nonprivileged mode. Nonprivileged mode is denoted on the device prompt with the greater-than (>) character after the device name, such as the following:

```
Singapore>
```

In this mode, you can examine the status of the IOS device but cannot change any parameters.

The second level of commands comprises the privileged commands, also known as *enable mode*. To enter privileged mode, you must know the **enable secret** password on the system. You can then enter the EXEC command **enable** to switch from nonprivileged to privileged mode:

```
Singapore>enable
Password:
Singapore#
```

In the previous example, when prompted for a password, you enter the enable secret password (in this case, **!zippy2u**), which is not echoed to the terminal. An IOS device in privileged mode changes the > character in the prompt to a hash mark (#). To move from privileged to nonprivileged mode, use the EXEC command **disable**:

```
Singapore#disable
Singapore>
```

Notice that in privileged mode, more commands are available than in nonprivileged mode, as indicated by the Help system:

```
Singapore#?
Exec commands:
  <1-99>            Session number to resume
  access-enable     Create a temporary Access-List entry
  access-profile    Apply user-profile to interface
  access-template   Create a temporary Access-List entry
  attach            attach to system component
  bfe               For manual emergency modes setting
  calendar          Manage the hardware calendar
  cd                Change current directory
  clear             Reset functions
  clock             Manage the system clock
  configure         Enter configuration mode
  connect           Open a terminal connection
  copy              Copy from one file to another
```

```
debug            Debugging functions (see also 'undebug')
delete           Delete a file
dir              List files on a filesystem
disable          Turn off privileged commands
disconnect       Disconnect an existing network connection
enable           Turn on privileged commands
erase            Erase a filesystem
exit             Exit from the EXEC
format           Format a filesystem
help             Description of the interactive help system
lock             Lock the terminal
login            Log in as a particular user
logout           Exit from the EXEC
microcode        microcode commands
mkdir            Create new directory
mls              exec mls router commands
more             Display the contents of a file
mpoa             MPOA exec commands
mrinfo           Request neighbor and version information from a multicast
                 router
mstat            Show statistics after multiple multicast traceroutes
mtrace           Trace reverse multicast path from destination to source
name-connection  Name an existing network connection
ncia             Start/Stop NCIA Server
no               Disable debugging functions
pad              Open a X.29 PAD connection
ping             Send echo messages
ppp              Start IETF Point-to-Point Protocol (PPP)
pwd              Display current working directory
reload           Halt and perform a cold restart
rename           Rename a file
--More--
```

Note that the preceding output has been truncated for brevity.

Memory Configuration Issues

Of the three portions of memory on an IOS device, two hold the device configuration. The third holds the IOS operating system. The difference between the configuration commands and the IOS operating system is that the configuration commands are used to configure the device and the IOS operating system is the software that runs on the device.

You learn about the two types of memory that hold IOS configuration commands—random-access memory (RAM) and nonvolatile random-access memory (NVRAM)—in this section. You also learn how to load the IOS operating system to a third type of memory on the device, electronically erasable programmable read-only memory (EEPROM), also known as Flash memory. To execute any memory-related commands on a device, you need to be in privileged mode (as shown in the following examples).

Device Configuration Memory

The current, or running, configuration of an IOS device can be seen by using the EXEC command **show running-config**. The output of this command lists the IOS configuration commands that the device is running, as follows:

```
Singapore#show running-config

Current configuration:
hostname Singapore
enable secret 5 $2zu6m7$RMMZ8em/.8hksdkkh78p/T0
enable password !zippy4me
line vty 0 4
password Zipmein
snmp-server community public

ip routing
ipx routing
appletalk routing
no decnet routing

!
interface Ethernet0
ip address 131.108.1.1 255.255.255.128
ipx network 4010
appletalk cable-range 4001-4001
appletalk discovery
no mop enabled
!
--More--
```

The output has been truncated for brevity.

The running configuration of a device is held in RAM, which is erased if the device loses power. You must save the current configuration to NVRAM, called the startup-config, if you want the device to resume the same running configuration after a power cycle. The EXEC command **copy**, which copies from the first memory location to the second, is used to save the running configuration to NVRAM:

```
Singapore#copy running-config startup-config
[OK]
Singapore#
```

You have now saved the current running configuration in RAM as the startup configuration in NVRAM. You can use the **copy** command in the reverse manner also, copying from the startup configuration to the running configuration as follows:

```
Singapore#copy startup-config running-config
[OK]
Singapore#
```

You might want to copy your startup-config to your running-config so that you can revert to your startup-config after making configuration changes on a device. For example, imagine that you make some configuration changes on a device. You observe the behavior of the device and decide that the changes were incorrect. If you had not copied your running-config to startup-config, you could copy your startup-config to your running-config. When you copy from the startup configuration in NVRAM to the running configuration in RAM, be aware of the merging of IOS configuration commands that could occur (see the section "Merging and Superseding of Configuration Commands," later in this chapter).

If you want to view the startup configuration, issue the EXEC command **show startup-config**:

```
Singapore#show startup-config

Using 1240 out of 7506 bytes
!
hostname Singapore
enable secret 5 $2zu6m7$RMMZ8em/.8hksdkkh78p/T0
enable password !zippy4me
line vty 0 4
password Zipmein
snmp-server community public

ip routing
ipx routing
appletalk routing
no decnet routing
!
interface Ethernet0
ip address 131.108.1.1 255.255.255.128
ipx network 4010
appletalk cable-range 4001-4001
appletalk discovery
no mop enabled
!
--More--
```

The output has been truncated for brevity. Note that the first line of the startup configuration shows the amount of NVRAM that the configuration uses and the total NVRAM on the device.

The startup configuration matches the running configuration after a **copy running-config startup-config** command is issued. However, if you configure the device (as explained in the next section) and do not save an altered running configuration to the startup configuration, the device reverts to the last configuration saved in the startup configuration the next time it gets power-cycled.

You can erase the startup configuration using the **erase startup-config** command:

```
Singapore#erase startup-config
Erasing the nvram filesystem will remove all files! Continue? [confirm]
[OK]
Singapore#
```

If you now reload your router by turning off the power or by using the privileged EXEC command **reload**, the device startup configuration is blank. This sequence of events— erasing the startup configuration and reloading the device—causes the IOS device to begin with the System Configuration Dialog, as discussed earlier in this chapter.

IOS Flash Memory

Flash memory is the location where a Cisco device holds the binary executable IOS images that constitute the operating system for the device. Do not confuse IOS images with IOS configurations. As you have seen earlier in the chapter, an IOS configuration tells the device its current configuration, while an IOS image is the actual binary program that parses and executes the configuration.

Depending on the amount of Flash memory you have installed and the IOS image size that you want to store on the Flash memory, your device can hold multiple IOS images. If you have multiple IOS images on a given device, you can configure which image the device executes after a reload. You can copy IOS images received from Cisco to your IOS devices using several different TCP/IP-based file transfer protocols, including the Trivial File Transfer Protocol (TFTP), the File Transfer Protocol (FTP), and the UNIX remote copy protocol (rcp). We will discuss using both TFTP and FTP for transferring the IOS software image to your device. Although rcp is an available protocol, it requires configuration of both your IOS-based device and your rcp server, which is beyond the scope of this text. Additionally, the use of rcp presents certain security risks that are better addressed with additional IOS and network proficiency.

Deciding whether to use TFTP or FTP to transfer the IOS image from a server to your IOS device depends on several factors:

- The availability of TFTP or FTP on your server or workstation (as provided by your server administrator). If your server administrator does not allow TFTP, for example, you will need to rely on FTP to perform the transfer.

- The type of network connection that is available from your server to your IOS device. If your server is on a LAN that is directly connected to your IOS device, TFTP will perform adequately, and the transfer time will likely not be excessive. If your server is several LAN or WAN hops away, FTP will perform better and reduce the transfer time of the IOS image from the server to the device.

- The level of security that you wish to maintain for the transfer of your IOS image from the server. TFTP does not require any kind of identification or authentication to perform the transfer. FTP requires a username and password to perform the transfer.

NOTE   We strongly recommend that you contact your local Cisco support channel to help you determine which IOS image to run on your routers.

Using TFTP for IOS Image Transfer

Before you can transfer an IOS image to your device, you need to have the IOS image file on a TFTP server. If you do, use the **copy tftp flash** command to initiate the transfer. In the following example, we copy the IOS image c2500-i-l.120-5.P.bin onto the Singapore router. Note that the Singapore router shows you the current contents of the Flash memory and then asks you for the IP address of the TFTP server and for the name of the IOS image before confirming the copy process. As a final step, the device verifies that the file has been loaded without error:

```
Singapore#copy tftp flash
System flash directory:
File  Length   Name/status
```

```
  1    2980876  c2500-is-mz.111-3.P.bin
[2980876 bytes used, 5407732 available, 8388608 total]
IP address or name of remote host [255.255.255.255]? 131.108.20.45
Name of file to copy ? c2500-i-l.120-5.P.bin
Copy c2500-i-l.120-5.P.bin from 131.108.20.45 into flash memory? [confirm]
Loading from 131.108.20.45:
!!!!!!!!!!!!!!!!!!!!!!!!!!!!!!!!!!!!!!!!!!!!!!!!!!!!!!!!!!!!!!!!!!!!!!!!!!
!!!!!!!!!!!!!!!!!!!!!!!!!!!!!!!!!!!!!!!!!!!!!!!!!!!!!!!!!!!!!!!!!!!!!!!!!!
!!!!!!!!!!!!!!!!!!!!!!!!!!!!!!!!!!!!!!!!!!!!!!!!!!!!!!!!!!!!!!!!!!!!!!!!!!
!!!!!!!!!!!!!!!!!!!!!!!!!!!!!!!!!!!!!!!!!!!!!!!!!!!!!!!!!!!!!!!!!!!!!!!!!!
!!!!!!!!!!!!!!!!!!!!!!!!!!!!!!!!!!!!!!! [OK - 1906676/4194240 bytes]
Verifying via checksum... vvvvvvvvvvvvvvvvvvvvvvvvvvvvvvvvvvvvvvvvvvv
vvvvvvvvvvvvvvvvvvvvvvvvvvvvvvvvvvvvvvvvvvvvvvvvvvvvvvvvvvvvvvvvvvvvvvvv
vvvvvvvvvvvvvvvvvvvvvvvvvvvvvvvvvvvvvvvvvvvvvvvvvvvvvvvvvvvvvvvvvvvvvvvv
vvvvvvvvvvvvvvvvvvvvvvvvvvvvvvvvvvvvvvvvvvvvvvvvvvvvvvvvvvvvvvvvvvvvvvvv
vvvvvvvvvvvvvvvvvvvvvvvvvvvvvvvvvvvvvvvv
Flash verification successful. Length = 1906676, checksum = 0x12AD
```

NOTE   All EXEC commands that use the network to perform an action return an exclamation point
(!) character when successful and a period (.) when unsuccessful.

If you want to perform the reverse of the previous process—namely, copy an IOS image
from the Flash memory on a device to a TFTP server—use the EXEC command **copy flash
tftp**. We recommend that you keep a copy of all your IOS images on a server and make
backups of these files regularly. When upgrading IOS images, it is imperative to have the
last known working IOS image for your network on a server. This precaution enables you
to revert to a working IOS image by using the **copy tftp flash** command in the event of an
unforeseen IOS caveat.

You can view the contents of Flash memory at any time using the EXEC command **show
flash**:

```
Singapore>show   flash
System flash directory:
File  Length    Name/status
  1    1906676  c2500-i-l.120-5.bin
[1906676 bytes used, 6481932 available, 8388608 total]
8192K bytes of processor board System flash
```

NOTE   Some Cisco IOS devices execute the IOS image from Flash memory and cannot overwrite
the image while it is executing. These Cisco IOS devices use the Flash load helper system
to copy IOS images from a TFTP server.

Using FTP for IOS Image Transfer

Unlike TFTP, FTP requires a username and password to both identify and authenticate the IOS device and its administrator to the FTP server prior to the transfer of the IOS software image. Two methods are used to provide the username and password for the transfer:

- Specifying the username and password as part of the **copy ftp** EXEC command

- Predefining the username and password via the global configuration commands **ip ftp username** and **ip ftp password**

The former is useful when many different individuals perform software image upgrades to the router. The latter is useful when only one individual performs the upgrades or when a specific login account and password have been set up for the express purpose of transferring the IOS software images. In either case, the corresponding username and password must exist on your FTP server before the transfer process is initiated. In the following examples, the FTP username is joebob, and the FTP password is getmysoftware.

As with TFTP, before you can transfer an IOS image to your device, you need to have the IOS image file on an FTP server. If you do, use the privileged EXEC command **copy ftp:/ /username:password flash** to both specify the username and password for authentication and to initiate the transfer. Substituting our selected username and password, the command would look like **copy ftp://joebob:getmysoftware flash**. In the following example, we copy the IOS image c2500-i-l.120-5.P.bin onto the Singapore router. Note that the Singapore router shows you the current contents of the Flash memory and then asks you for the IP address of the FTP server and for the name of the IOS image before confirming the copy process. Optionally, the FTP server IP address and IOS image name may also be specified as part of the **copy** command, similar to the username and password, as **ftp://username:password@ftpservername/ios-image-name**. As a final step of the transfer process, the device verifies that the file has been loaded without error:

```
Singapore#copy ftp://joebob:getmysoftware flash
System flash directory:
File  Length   Name/status
  1   2980876  c2500-is-mz.111-3.P.bin
[2980876 bytes used, 5407732 available, 8388608 total]
IP address or name of remote host [255.255.255.255]? 131.108.20.45
Name of file to copy ? c2500-i-l.120-5.P.bin
Copy c2500-i-l.120-5.P.bin from 131.108.20.45 into flash memory? [confirm]
Loading from 131.108.20.45:
!!!!!!!!!!!!!!!!!!!!!!!!!!!!!!!!!!!!!!!!!!!!!!!!!!!!!!!!!!!!!!!!!!!!!!!!!
!!!!!!!!!!!!!!!!!!!!!!!!!!!!!!!!!!!!!!!!!!!!!!!!!!!!!!!!!!!!!!!!!!!!!!!!!
!!!!!!!!!!!!!!!!!!!!!!!!!!!!!!!!!!!!!!!!!!!!!!!!!!!!!!!!!!!!!!!!!!!!!!!!!
!!!!!!!!!!!!!!!!!!!!!!!!!!!!!!!!!!!!!!!!!!!!!!!!!!!!!!!!!!!!!!!!!!!!!!!!!
!!!!!!!!!!!!!!!!!!!!!!!!!!!!!!!!!!!!! [OK - 1906676/4194240 bytes]
Verifying via checksum... vvvvvvvvvvvvvvvvvvvvvvvvvvvvvvvvvvvvvvvvvv
vvvvvvvvvvvvvvvvvvvvvvvvvvvvvvvvvvvvvvvvvvvvvvvvvvvvvvvvvvvvvvvvvvvvvv
vvvvvvvvvvvvvvvvvvvvvvvvvvvvvvvvvvvvvvvvvvvvvvvvvvvvvvvvvvvvvvvvvvvvvv
vvvvvvvvvvvvvvvvvvvvvvvvvvvvvvvvvvvvvvvvvvvvvvvvvvvvvvvvvvvvvvvvvvvvvv
vvvvvvvvvvvvvvvvvvvvvvvvvvvvvvvvvvvvvvvvv
Flash verification successful. Length = 1906676, checksum = 0x12AD
```

As discussed previously, the username and password may be defined in the running configuration prior to initiating the IOS image transfer and optionally may be stored in the startup configuration for future use. The FTP username and password are defined using the global configuration commands **ip ftp username** and **ip ftp password**. In the following example, we configure the Singapore router with the FTP username joebob and password getmysoftware and then initiate an IOS image transfer:

```
Singapore#configure terminal
Singapore(config)#ip ftp username joebob
Singapore(config)#ip ftp password getmysoftware
Singapore(config)#^Z
Singapore#copy ftp flash
System flash directory:
File  Length    Name/status
  1   2980876   c2500-is-mz.111-3.P.bin
[2980876 bytes used, 5407732 available, 8388608 total]
IP address or name of remote host [255.255.255.255]? 131.108.20.45
Name of file to copy ? c2500-i-l.120-5.P.bin
Copy c2500-i-l.120-5.P.bin from 131.108.20.45 into flash memory? [confirm]
Loading from 131.108.20.45:
!!!!!!!!!!!!!!!!!!!!!!!!!!!!!!!!!!!!!!!!!!!!!!!!!!!!!!!!!!!!!!!!!!!!!!!!
!!!!!!!!!!!!!!!!!!!!!!!!!!!!!!!!!!!!!!!!!!!!!!!!!!!!!!!!!!!!!!!!!!!!!!!!
!!!!!!!!!!!!!!!!!!!!!!!!!!!!!!!!!!!!!!!!!!!!!!!!!!!!!!!!!!!!!!!!!!!!!!!!
!!!!!!!!!!!!!!!!!!!!!!!!!!!!!!!!!!!!!!!!!!!!!!!!!!!!!!!!!!!!!!!!!!!!!!!!
!!!!!!!!!!!!!!!!!!!!!!!!!!!!!!! [OK - 1906676/4194240 bytes]
Verifying via checksum... vvvvvvvvvvvvvvvvvvvvvvvvvvvvvvvvvvvvvvvvvvvvv
vvvvvvvvvvvvvvvvvvvvvvvvvvvvvvvvvvvvvvvvvvvvvvvvvvvvvvvvvvvvvvvvvvvvvvvv
vvvvvvvvvvvvvvvvvvvvvvvvvvvvvvvvvvvvvvvvvvvvvvvvvvvvvvvvvvvvvvvvvvvvvvvv
vvvvvvvvvvvvvvvvvvvvvvvvvvvvvvvvvvvvvvvvvvvvvvvvvvvvvvvvvvvvvvvvvvvvvvvv
vvvvvvvvvvvvvvvvvvvvvvvvvvvvvvvvvvvvvvvvvv
Flash verification successful. Length = 1906676, checksum = 0x12AD
```

NOTE   A complete discussion of IOS configuration modes and methods is contained in the upcoming section "User Configuration Mode."

As in the previous example, the Singapore router shows you the current contents of the Flash memory and then asks you for the IP address of the FTP server and for the name of the IOS image before confirming the copy process. As a final step of the transfer process, the device verifies that the file has been loaded without error.

As with TFTP, it is possible to perform the reverse of the previous process—namely, to copy an IOS image from the Flash memory on a device to an FTP server—using the EXEC command **copy flash ftp**. As in the previous process, you must specify the username and password needed for the FTP transfer either as part of the **copy** command or by predefining them in the running configuration. Regardless of the transfer protocol, we recommend that you keep a copy of all your IOS images on a server and make backups of these files regularly. When you're upgrading IOS images, it is imperative to have the last known working IOS image for your network on a server. This precaution enables you to revert to a working IOS image by using the **copy ftp flash** command in the event of an unforeseen IOS caveat.

Managing Flash Memory Space

All the commands that transfer IOS software images to Flash memory will evaluate the available space and prompt you to erase and compress the existing Flash memory contents to make additional space, if required. There may be occasions when you would like to erase all or just a portion of the existing contents of Flash memory independent from the transfer process. You can erase the entire contents of Flash memory by using the privileged EXEC command **erase flash**. To delete a specific IOS image from Flash memory, use the **delete** command. For example, to delete the IOS image c2500-i-l.120-5.bin from Flash memory, use the EXEC privileged command **delete c2500-i-l.120-5.bin**. On Cisco devices that have an external Flash memory card (usually located in a slot called slot0), the **delete** command only marks an IOS image file for deletion; it does not actually perform the deletion and thus free the space on Flash memory. You must execute the **squeeze** command to complete the file deletion process.

User Configuration Mode

To configure an IOS device, you must use the EXEC privileged command **configure**. The **configure** command has three options:

- Configure from terminal
- Configure from memory
- Configure from network

TIP

In nonprivileged mode, privileged mode, and user configuration mode, the IOS enables you to repeat commands without retyping them. To do so, move up or down the stack of existing commands until you reach the command you want to repeat. When you reach it, press the Return key. The command is repeated at the current command line. On most terminals, the up arrow key moves up and the down arrow key moves down the stack of previous commands. If the arrow keys do not work on your terminal, you can move up the stack of previous commands with Ctrl+P (previous) and down with Ctrl+N (next).

When you type the **configure** command, the IOS prompts you for which of the three options you want to use, as follows:

```
Singapore#configure
Configuring from terminal, memory, or network [terminal]?
```

The default, which is the first option, enables you to configure the IOS device from your terminal in real time. The commands are executed by the IOS immediately after you enter them:

```
Singapore#configure
```

```
Configuring from terminal, memory, or network [terminal]?
Enter configuration commands, one per line. End with CTRL+Z.
Singapore(config)#
```

The device then changes the prompt to show that you are in configuration mode and allows
you to enter configuration commands. When you are finished entering commands, enter
Ctrl+Z (^Z). In the following example, you change the device name from Singapore to
Seoul using the global configuration command **hostname**:

```
Singapore#configure
Configuring from terminal, memory, or network [terminal]?
Enter configuration commands, one per line. End with CTRL+Z.
Singapore(config)#hostname Seoul
Seoul(config)#^Z
Seoul#
```

As you can see from the prompt, the command takes effect immediately to change the host
name of the device. You do not need to save this new running configuration to the startup
configuration to activate the command.

The second option, configuring from memory, allows you to copy the contents of the
device's startup configuration, which are stored in NVRAM, to the current configuration.
This option is useful if you have changed a configuration parameter in real time and you
want to revert to the previous configuration saved in the startup configuration. This
configure command performs the same function as the **copy startup-config running-
config** command you saw in the previous section:

```
Seoul#configure
Configuring from terminal, memory, or network [terminal]? memory

Singapore#
```

The third option, configuring from the network, enables you to load a configuration file
from a server running the TFTP:

```
Singapore#configure
Configuring from terminal, memory, or network [terminal]? network
Host or network configuration file [host]?
Address of remote host [255.255.255.255]? 131.108.20.45
Name of configuration file [singapore-confg]?
Configure using singapore-confg from 131.108.20.45? [confirm]
Loading singapore-confg !![OK]

Singapore#
```

In the preceding **configure** command, we accepted the IOS defaults shown in brackets ([])
by pressing a carriage return as a reply to the question.

TFTP is a protocol that allows the IOS device to query for a specific file from a host running
a TFTP server. TFTP uses the IP protocol, so you need to have IP routing configured
between the IOS device and the TFTP server for this option to work properly. See Chapter
4 for more information on the configuration of IP routing.

When configuring an IOS device from a TFTP server, the device defaults to trying to load
a file with the name of the device followed by the string **-confg**. In this case, the device
named Singapore tries unsuccessfully to load the file **singapore-confg** by default.

```
Singapore#configure
Configuring from terminal, memory, or network [terminal]? network
Host or network configuration file [host]?
Address of remote host [255.255.255.255]? 131.108.20.45
Name of configuration file [singapore-confg]?
Configure using singapore-confg from 131.108.20.45? [confirm]
Loading singapore-confg ... [timed out]

Singapore#
```

A device can fail to load a configuration file because of problems with IP network connectivity or a TFTP violation.

Configuration Commands

Configuration commands are used to configure an IOS device. As seen in the previous section, the configuration commands can be entered from the terminal, loaded from the startup configuration, or downloaded via a file using TFTP and the EXEC command **configure**. All configuration commands must be entered into the IOS device in configuration mode, not at the EXEC level. A configuration command entered at the device prompt is incorrect:

```
Singapore#hostname Seoul
             ^
% Invalid input detected at '^' marker.
```

A configuration command entered in configuration mode is correct:

```
Singapore#configure
Configuring from terminal, memory, or network [terminal]?
Enter configuration commands, one per line. End with CTRL+Z.
Singapore(config)#hostname Seoul
Seoul(config)#^Z
Seoul#
```

All IOS commands fit into one of three categories:

- Global commands
- Major commands
- Subcommands

A global command is a configuration command that affects the overall IOS configuration. In this chapter, you have seen some global commands in the configuration command script made by the System Configuration Dialog, including **hostname**, **enable secret**, and **ip routing**. Each of these commands changes the IOS configuration without needing additional commands. The **hostname** command sets the name of the device, the **enable secret** command sets the enable secret password used to enter privileged mode, and the **ip routing** command turns on IP routing.

A major command is a command that enables subcommands to configure the device. A major command does not configure the IOS device itself. In the following example, the command **interface Ethernet0** is a major command that tells the IOS that the subsequent subcommands relate specifically to a LAN interface named Ethernet0. In this example, the subcommand **ip address** assigns an IP address to Ethernet0:

```
Singapore#configure
Configuring from terminal, memory, or network [terminal]?
Enter configuration commands, one per line. End with CTRL+Z.
Singapore(config)#interface Ethernet0
Singapore(config-if)#ip address 131.108.1.1 255.255.255.128
Singapore(config-if)#^Z

Singapore#
```

In the previous example, the IOS interprets **interface Ethernet0** as a major command. It shows this by changing the configuration prompt to Singapore(config-if) to reflect that the subsequent commands are subcommands for the interface. The command **interface Ethernet0** does not configure the device itself—it requires subcommands to complete the configuration.

A major command requires the context of a subcommand to configure the device. The subcommand **ip address 131.108.1.1 255.255.255.128** requires an interface to be interpreted properly. The combination of a major command and a subcommand is the proper combination to configure an IOS device.

As of IOS 12.0, some IOS major commands have an additional level of configuration subcommands. For example, on an ATM interface, which we will discuss further in Chapter 3, you specify the interface with the major command **interface atm 0**. You can then specify the permanent virtual path identifier and virtual circuit identifier for this interface to use with the subcommand **pvc [*name*] *vpi/vci***. This subcommand has an additional level of subcommand that enables you to specify the ATM quality of service associated with VPI/VCI. For example, here we set an ATM interface to have VPI/VCI equal to 5/42 with an unspecified bit rate (UBR) quality of service to 384 kbps:

```
Router#configure
Configuring from terminal, memory, or network [terminal]?
Enter configuration commands, one per line. End with CTRL+Z.
Router(config)#interface atm0
Router(config-if)#pvc 5/42
Router(config-if)#ubr 384
Router(config-if)#^Z

Router#
```

This configuration appears in the router as follows (all output except the previous configuration has been truncated):

```
Router#show running-config

Current configuration:
!
interface ATM0
  pvc 5/42
    ubr 384
!
```

As seen in the previous section, you can configure the IOS device from a configuration file loaded via the TFTP protocol by using the **configure** command and selecting the Network option. This configuration file must be a text file that contains the desired global commands, major commands, and subcommands to configure the device. When loading the configuration file, the device interprets the configuration commands immediately and executes them, just as if you had typed in the commands using the **configure** command and the Terminal option.

Configuration Help

The IOS Help system is available while you are configuring a device. Use the question mark (**?**) command to find the available configuration options at any time during device configuration. In the example that follows, this feature finds the global commands available on a device in configuration mode:

```
Singapore(config)#?
Configure commands:
  aaa                          Authentication, Authorization and Accounting.
  access-list                  Add an access list entry
  alias                        Create command alias
  arp                          Set a static ARP entry
  async-bootp                  Modify system bootp parameters
  banner                       Define a login banner
  boot                         Modify system boot parameters
  bridge                       Bridging Group.
  buffers                      Adjust system buffer pool parameters
  busy-message                 Display message when connection to host fails
  cdp                          Global CDP configuration subcommands
  chat-script                  Define a modem chat script
  clock                        Configure time-of-day clock
  config-register              Define the configuration register
  default-value                Default character-bits values
  dialer-list                  Create a dialer list entry
  dnsix-dmdp                   Provide DMDP service for DNSIX
  dnsix-nat                    Provide DNSIX service for audit trails
  downward-compatible-config Generate a configuration compatible with older software
  enable                       Modify enable password parameters
--More--
```

Note that the previous output has been truncated for brevity. You can also use the Help system to find the configuration subcommands available when entering a command. In this example, you find the subcommands that are available for the IP protocol when configuring the Ethernet0 interface:

```
Singapore#configure
Configuring from terminal, memory, or network [terminal]?
Enter configuration commands, one per line. End with CTRL+Z.
Singapore(config)#interface Ethernet0
Singapore(config-if)#ip ?
Interface IP configuration subcommands:
  access-group        Specify access control for packets
  accounting          Enable IP accounting on this interface
  address             Set the IP address of an interface
  bandwidth-percent   Set EIGRP bandwidth limit
  broadcast-address   Set the broadcast address of an interface
  directed-broadcast  Enable forwarding of directed broadcasts
```

```
gdp                 Gateway Discovery Protocol
hello-interval      Configures IP-EIGRP hello interval
helper-address      Specify a destination address for UDP broadcasts
hold-time           Configures IP-EIGRP hold time
irdp                ICMP Router Discovery Protocol
mask-reply          Enable sending ICMP Mask Reply messages
mobile              Mobile Host Protocol
mtu                 Set IP Maximum Transmission Unit
policy              Enable policy routing
probe               Enable HP Probe support
proxy-arp           Enable proxy ARP
rarp-server         Enable RARP server for static arp entries
redirects           Enable sending ICMP Redirect messages
rip                 Router Information Protocol
route-cache         Enable fast-switching cache for outgoing packets
--More--
```

Note that the previous output has been truncated for brevity.

Removing Configuration Commands

To remove a configuration command from an IOS device, add the keyword **no** to the beginning of the configuration command. The following example shows how to remove the IP address from the interface Ethernet0:

```
Singapore#configure
Configuring from terminal, memory, or network [terminal]?
Enter configuration commands, one per line. End with CTRL+Z.
Singapore(config)#interface Ethernet0
Singapore(config-if)#no ip address 131.108.1.1 255.255.255.0
Singapore(config-if)#^Z

Singapore#
```

For the removal of any global command, major command, or subcommand, follow the same procedure.

Default Configuration Commands

Cisco IOS default configuration commands do not appear in **show running-config** or **show startup-config**. If you enter a command that is a default configuration command, the device accepts the command without error. For example, as you will see in the next chapter, all serial interfaces on Cisco routers default to High-Level Data Link Control (HDLC) encapsulation. Entering the interface configuration subcommand **encapsulation hdlc** for a serial interface does not result in a new line of configuration on the router.

All IOS commands also have a default configuration. You can use the **default** configuration command as a precursor to any global command, major command, or subcommand to return the configuration value to its default configuration. Many IOS configuration commands are disabled by default, so the default form is the same as the **no** form, as in the previous section. For example, the following configurations will also remove the IP address from Ethernet0 of the Singapore router:

```
Singapore#configure
Configuring from terminal, memory, or network [terminal]?
Enter configuration commands, one per line. End with CTRL+Z.
Singapore(config)#interface Ethernet0
Singapore(config-if)#default  ip address
Singapore(config-if)#^Z

Singapore#
```

By contrast, some commands are enabled by default with a specific configuration. In these cases, the **default** command enables the command with the default configuration:

```
Singapore#configure
Configuring from terminal, memory, or network [terminal]?
Enter configuration commands, one per line. End with CTRL+Z.
Singapore(config)#default hostname
Singapore(config-if)#^Z

Router#
```

In this example, the **hostname** command is enabled by default with the device name set to Router.

Merging and Superseding of Configuration Commands

A new configuration command may supersede an existing command, in which case the IOS automatically removes the existing command. On the other hand, a new command may merge with an existing command instead of superseding it. As an example of merged commands, it is possible to configure two different **snmp-server** commands on a device. Imagine that you perform the following configuration:

```
Singapore#configure
Configuring from terminal, memory, or network [terminal]?
Enter configuration commands, one per line. End with CTRL+Z.
Singapore(config)#snmp-server community public
Singapore(config)#^Z

Singapore#
```

At this point, you decide to change the **snmp-server** configuration of the device, so you perform the following configuration:

```
Singapore#configure
Enter configuration commands, one per line. End with CTRL+Z.
Configuring from terminal, memory, or network [terminal]?
Singapore(config)#snmp-server community zipnet
Singapore(config)#^Z

Singapore#
```

Because it is possible to have multiple **snmp-server** commands, this second **snmp-server** command is merged into the current configuration, and both commands are active, as shown in the following portion of **show running-config**:

```
!
snmp-server community public
snmp-server community zipnet
!
```

To replace the first **snmp-server** configuration command with the second, do the following:

```
Singapore#configure
Configuring from terminal, memory, or network [terminal]?
Enter configuration commands, one per line. End with CTRL+Z.
Singapore(config)#no snmp-server community public
Singapore(config)#snmp-server community zipnet
Singapore(config)#^Z

Singapore#
```

An example of a command that does not merge is the **hostname** command that sets the name of a device. In the following example, we configure a new name for the Singapore router:

```
Singapore#configure
Configuring from terminal, memory, or network [terminal]?
Enter configuration commands, one per line. End with CTRL+Z.
Singapore(config)#hostname Sing-router
Sing-router(config)#^Z

Sing-router#
```

The **hostname** command immediately supersedes the previous configuration. The running-config shows only one **hostname** command:

```
!
hostname Sing-router
!
```

Remember this IOS issue when adding configuration commands to an existing configuration.

Summary

Now that you understand the basic configuration commands and steps, the next chapter turns to the configuration of interfaces. Keep in mind the following key points about basic device configuration:

- It is recommended that you use the enable secret category of password in defining a privileged password for the IOS.

- The Help system, which is available in EXEC mode, provides information on what EXEC commands are available, what they do, and what their completion options are (see Table 2-1). The Help system is also available while you are configuring a device.

- In nonprivileged mode, you can examine the status of an IOS device but not change its parameters. In privileged mode, you can set and change device parameters.

- The two types of memory that hold IOS configuration commands are RAM and NVRAM. The running configuration is held in RAM. It is erased if the device loses power. The configuration held in NVRAM is not erased when the device is powered off; it is the one that the device reverts to after powering back on.

- You can configure a device from the terminal in real time, from memory (NVRAM), or from the network.

- Add the keyword **no** to the beginning of a configuration command if you want to remove it from the device configuration.

- When added to an existing device configuration, some configuration commands merge with existing commands, while others supersede existing commands (see Table 2-2).

Table 2-1 *Summary of EXEC Commands for Basic Device Configuration*

Command	Description
configure	Configures the IOS device from terminal, network, or memory
copy flash ftp	Copies IOS image file from Flash memory to an FTP server
copy flash tftp	Copies IOS image file from Flash memory to a TFTP server
copy ftp flash	Copies IOS image file from an FTP server to Flash memory
copy running-config startup-config	Saves running configuration to NVRAM
copy startup-config running-config	Makes startup configuration from NVRAM the running configuration
copy tftp flash	Copies IOS image file from TFTP server to Flash memory
delete *IOS image*	Deletes specified IOS image from Flash memory
disable	Exits privileged mode and enters nonprivileged mode
enable	Enters privileged mode
erase flash	Deletes entire contents of Flash memory
erase startup-config	Erases startup configuration
lock	Locks current terminal session
session *module*	Establishes a session to the specified module
show flash	Displays contents of Flash memory
show running-config	Displays the configuration running on the device
show sessions	Displays current user sessions
show startup-config	Displays the configuration saved in NVRAM that the device will use at next startup
squeeze	Erases file marked for deletion on Flash memory

Table 2-2   *Summary of Configuration Commands for Basic Device Configuration*

Command	Description
default *command*	Sets the command to its default value
enable password *password*	Sets a password for entry to privileged mode
enable secret *secret*	Sets a one-way cryptographic password for entry to privileged mode
hostname	Sets the host name of the device
interface *type*	Specifies the interface to configure
ip ftp password	Specifies the password to use for authentication when using FTP for transferring IOS images and other functions
ip ftp username	Specifies the username to use for identification when using FTP for transferring IOS images and other functions
no *command*	Removes the configuration command

References

Specific Cisco documentation can be found at Cisco Systems, Inc. Cisco Product Documentation:
www.cisco.com/univercd/cc/td/doc/product/index.htm

Basic Interface Configuration—The basics of configuring a device interface in the Cisco IOS.

Local-Area Network Technologies—A brief overview of the local-area network technologies found on Cisco devices, including Ethernet/IEEE 802.3, Fast Ethernet, Gigabit Ethernet, Token Ring/IEEE 802.5, and FDDI.

Wide-Area Network and Dialup Network Technologies—A brief overview of the wide-area network and dialup network technologies found on Cisco devices, including HDLC, PPP, X.25, Frame Relay, ATM, DSL, and ISDN.

CHAPTER 3

The Basics of Device Interfaces

This chapter explains the basics of the technology and configuration for the various interface types found on Cisco devices. Both LAN and WAN technologies are considered. We have chosen to cover the five LAN and seven WAN technologies that are widely used.

Basic Interface Configuration

An *interface* is a connection from a Cisco device to a network medium. Each interface has underlying technologies that are used to transfer data across a physical medium, such as copper or fiber. Protocols found on the physical layer of the OSI reference model define the physical characteristics of the interface and the medium. The protocols we describe in this chapter, which all operate on the data link layer (Layer 2) of the OSI reference model, implement the technology to pass data between the network layer and the physical layer.

Each interface on a Cisco device is known as a *port*. Cisco devices label ports in multiple ways. For fixed-configuration Cisco devices, the interfaces are numbered sequentially without a slot designation. For example, on a 2500 series router with one Ethernet and two serial interfaces, the interfaces would be known as ethernet0, serial0, and serial1.

If the device is modular and has interchangeable interface cards, the interfaces are numbered using the syntax type **slot/port**. For example, an Ethernet interface in slot 1, port 2 would be known as ethernet 1/2. To configure interfaces, you must use the major command **interface**. This command, followed by the interface port number or slot/port combination, is used in configuration mode. The following example illustrates the configuration of a Token Ring interface on slot 1, port 0:

```
San-Jose#configure
Configuring from terminal, memory, or network [terminal]?
Enter configuration commands, one per line. End with CTRL+Z.
San-Jose(config)#interface tokenring 1/0
San-Jose(config-if)#^Z
```

NOTE   The IOS changes the configuration mode prompt from **config** to **config-if** to signify that you are configuring an interface. The IOS often changes the configuration mode prompt to give you visual context cues during configuration.

Some Cisco routers have Versatile Interface Processor (VIP) cards. Each VIP card has one or two slots for port adapters. A port adapter is a circuit board with interfaces that inserts into a VIP. Each port adapter can have a number of interfaces. On these types of devices (currently only 7000, 7500, and 12000 series routers), the syntax **type slot/port adapter/ port** is used to specify the interface. For example, if you wanted to reference the second VIP card, first port adapter (number 0), first Token Ring interface, you would use the syntax **token ring 2/0/1**.

The show interfaces Command

The EXEC command **show interfaces** enables you to see the status of all the interfaces on a Cisco device, as shown for an Ethernet interface in the following output:

```
Ethernet0 is up, line protocol is up
  Hardware is QUICC Ethernet, address is 0060.5cbc.0ef9 (bia 0060.5cbc.0ef9)
  MTU 1500 bytes, BW 10000 Kbit, DLY 1000 usec, rely 255/255, load 1/255
  Encapsulation ARPA, loopback not set, keepalive set (10 sec)
  ARP type: ARPA, ARP Timeout 04:00:00
  Last input 00:00:00, output 00:00:01, output hang never
  Last clearing of "show interface" counters never
  Queueing strategy: fifo
  Output queue 0/40, 0 drops; input queue 0/75, 0 drops
  5 minute input rate 1000 bits/sec, 1 packets/sec
  5 minute output rate 1000 bits/sec, 1 packets/sec
     116547 packets input, 13397137 bytes, 0 no buffer
     Received 3402 broadcasts, 0 runts, 0 giants
     0 input errors, 0 CRC, 0 frame, 0 overrun, 0 ignored, 0 abort
     0 input packets with dribble condition detected
     273769 packets output, 84816409 bytes, 0 underruns
     0 output errors, 1 collisions, 1 interface resets
     0 babbles, 0 late collision, 29 deferred
     0 lost carrier, 0 no carrier
     0 output buffer failures, 0 output buffers swapped out
```

We discuss the various types of information in the **show interfaces** output throughout this book. To begin, notice that the first line of the output shows the interface medium type (Ethernet) and the interface number. The interface name is ethernet0, so we can conclude that this is a fixed configuration device; there are no slots, ports, or port adapters. An interface that is shown in the up state is electrically functioning normally and has the proper signaling from the cables connected into it. Other possible states for the interface are down and administratively down. A down interface is operational, but it is not communicating properly with the medium to which it is attached. An administratively down interface is configured to be shut down and is not operational. See the upcoming section "The **shutdown** Command" for information on changing the administrative state of an interface.

The physical hardware type of the interface is shown on the second line of the **show interfaces** command, as is the interface's data link layer address. The fourth line of this output shows the encapsulation type of the interface. The encapsulation of local-area network (LAN) interfaces normally does not require configuration, while the configuration of wide-area network (WAN) interfaces often does. The reason for this difference is that

LAN interfaces typically perform a single data link layer protocol, and WAN interfaces can perform many different data link layer protocols.

The encapsulation Command

The encapsulation of an interface defines the format of the data sent and the data link protocol for the interface. You set the encapsulation of an interface with the **encapsulation** interface configuration subcommand. In the following output, we use the Help system to examine the interface encapsulations available for the WAN interface serial0 and then set the interface to use the High-Level Data Link Control (HDLC) protocol:

```
Singapore#configure
Configuring from terminal, memory, or network [terminal]?
Enter configuration commands, one per line. End with CTRL+Z.
Singapore(config)#interface serial 0
Singapore(config-if)#encapsulation ?
  atm-dxi      ATM-DXI encapsulation
  frame-relay  Frame Relay networks
  hdlc         Serial HDLC synchronous
  lapb         LAPB (X.25 Level 2)
  ppp          Point-to-Point protocol
  smds         Switched Megabit Data Service (SMDS)
  x25          X.25
Singapore(config-if)#encapsulation hdlc
Singapore(config-if)#^Z
```

We explore the other WAN protocol encapsulations later in this chapter.

The shutdown Command

If you want to change the administrative state of an interface from up to down or down to up, use the configuration command **shutdown** or **no shutdown**. A Cisco device does not pass data on an interface that is administratively down. In the following **show interfaces** output, the first line shows that interface serial0 is administratively down:

```
Serial0 is administratively down, line protocol is down
  Hardware is 4T/MC68360
  MTU 1500 bytes, BW 512 Kbit, DLY 20000 usec, rely 137/255, load 1/255
  Encapsulation HDLC, loopback not set, keepalive set (10 sec)
  Last input never, output never, output hang never
  Last clearing of "show interface" counters never
  Input queue: 0/75/0 (size/max/drops); Total output drops: 0
  Queueing strategy: weighted fair
  Output queue: 0/64/0 (size/threshold/drops)
     Conversations  0/1 (active/max active)
     Reserved Conversations 0/0 (allocated/max allocated)
  5 minute input rate 0 bits/sec, 0 packets/sec
  5 minute output rate 0 bits/sec, 0 packets/sec
     0 packets input, 0 bytes, 0 no buffer
     Received 0 broadcasts, 0 runts, 0 giants
     0 input errors, 0 CRC, 0 frame, 0 overrun, 0 ignored, 0 abort
     0 packets output, 0 bytes, 0 underruns
     0 output errors, 0 collisions, 0 interface resets
     0 output buffer failures, 0 output buffers swapped out
     0 carrier transitions
     DCD=down  DSR=down DTR=down RTS=down CTS=down
```

Next, we use the **no shutdown** configuration command to configure the interface to be operational:

```
Singapore#configure
Configuring from terminal, memory, or network [terminal]?
Enter configuration commands, one per line. End with CTRL+Z.
Singapore(config)#interface serial 0
Singapore(config-if)#no shutdown
Singapore(config-if)#^Z
```

NOTE   The IOS configuration command **no shutdown** is often confusing for users. You are telling the device not to shut down the interface, but by using a double negative, you imply that it should be turned on. This is an awkward use of the English language, and it is kept in the Cisco IOS for purely historical (or hysterical) reasons.

Now, if the cables to this interface are providing the proper electrical inputs, the interface is administratively and operationally up. You can use the **shutdown** configuration command to administratively down an interface, as follows:

```
Singapore#configure
Configuring from terminal, memory, or network [terminal]?
Enter configuration commands, one per line. End with CTRL+Z.
Singapore(config)#interface serial 0
Singapore(config-if)#shutdown
Singapore(config-if)#^Z
```

The description Command

You can use the interface subcommand **description** to add a text description to the output of the **show interfaces** command. This text description can be up to 255 characters long.

TIP   We recommend that you add a description to each of your interfaces to document its use. For example, you can add a descriptive name to a LAN interface for the building, floor, or department that is reachable through the interface. On WAN interfaces, you may want to describe the endpoints of the connection and document the circuit identifiers used by the circuit provider.

In the following example, we add a description to interface serial0, the WAN interface from Singapore to Malaysia on the ZIP network. The description shows the encapsulation of the link and the circuit identifier:

```
Singapore#configure
Configuring from terminal, memory, or network [terminal]?
```

```
Enter configuration commands, one per line. End with CTRL+Z.
Singapore(config)#interface serial 0
Singapore(config-if)#description IETF frame relay PVCs on Circuit Z-234987-12-MS-01
Singapore(config-if)#^Z
```

The description appears in the third line of the **show interfaces serial 0** command:

```
Serial0 is administratively down, line protocol is down
   Hardware is 4T/MC68360
   Description: IETF frame relay PVCs on Circuit Z-234987-12-MS-01
   MTU 1500 bytes, BW 512 Kbit, DLY 20000 usec, rely 137/255, load 1/255
   Encapsulation HDLC, loopback not set, keepalive set (10 sec)
   Last input never, output never, output hang never
   Last clearing of "show interface" counters never
   Input queue: 0/75/0 (size/max/drops); Total output drops: 0
   Queueing strategy: weighted fair
   Output queue: 0/64/0 (size/threshold/drops)
     Conversations  0/1 (active/max active)
     Reserved Conversations 0/0 (allocated/max allocated)
   5 minute input rate 0 bits/sec, 0 packets/sec
   5 minute output rate 0 bits/sec, 0 packets/sec
     0 packets input, 0 bytes, 0 no buffer
     Received 0 broadcasts, 0 runts, 0 giants
     0 input errors, 0 CRC, 0 frame, 0 overrun, 0 ignored, 0 abort
     0 packets output, 0 bytes, 0 underruns
     0 output errors, 0 collisions, 0 interface resets
     0 output buffer failures, 0 output buffers swapped out
     0 carrier transitions
     DCD=down  DSR=down  DTR=down  RTS=down CTS=down
```

Local-Area Network Technologies

Cisco devices support multiple LAN technologies. We cover five popular technologies in this chapter:

- Ethernet and IEEE 802.3
- Fast Ethernet
- Gigabit Ethernet
- Token Ring
- Fiber Distributed Data Interface

Each of these protocols operates at the data link layer of the OSI reference model, and each is used in a LAN environment to carry data from point to point at speeds from 4 Mbps to 1 Gbps. This section briefly introduces you to each of these protocols. If you want to learn about these protocols in depth, we have included additional references at the end of the chapter.

All these LAN protocols share a common data link layer addressing scheme. The addresses are 6-byte hexadecimal addresses that are unique in the world. These addresses are called Media Access Control (MAC) addresses, also referred to as hardware, station, or physical addresses. This means that every LAN device in the world has a unique data link layer address. The address is burned into read-only memory (ROM) on the interface card itself.

To ensure that each interface gets a unique address, each manufacturer is assigned a 20-bit prefix of the 6-byte address. For example, Cisco has been assigned the 20-bit prefix of 0060.5 (shown here in hexadecimal format, in which each digit represents 4 bits). The manufacturer can then assign the remaining 28 bits in any manner, as long as each address remains unique.

The unique data link layer address for each Cisco LAN interface is seen in the **show interfaces** command output in the second line of output. The data link address for the Kuala Lumpur router from the ZIP network can be seen in the following output:

```
Kuala-Lumpur>show interface ethernet 0
Ethernet0 is up, line protocol is up
  Hardware is QUICC Ethernet, address is 0060.5cbc.0ef9 (bia 0060.5cbc.0ef9)
  MTU 1500 bytes, BW 10000 Kbit, DLY 1000 usec, rely 255/255, load 1/255
  Encapsulation ARPA, loopback not set, keepalive set (10 sec)
  ARP type: ARPA, ARP Timeout 04:00:00
  Last input 00:00:00, output 00:00:01, output hang never
  Last clearing of "show interface" counters never
  Queueing strategy: fifo
  Output queue 0/40, 0 drops; input queue 0/75, 0 drops
  5 minute input rate 1000 bits/sec, 1 packets/sec
  5 minute output rate 1000 bits/sec, 1 packets/sec
     116547 packets input, 13397137 bytes, 0 no buffer
     Received 3402 broadcasts, 0 runts, 0 giants
     0 input errors, 0 CRC, 0 frame, 0 overrun, 0 ignored, 0 abort
     0 input packets with dribble condition detected
     273769 packets output, 84816409 bytes, 0 underruns
     65959 output errors, 1 collisions, 1 interface resets
     0 babbles, 0 late collision, 29 deferred
     65959 lost carrier, 0 no carrier
     0 output buffer failures, 0 output buffers swapped out
```

NOTE   It is technically possible for the IOS to use a different data link address on a given LAN interface than the burned-in address (bia) found in ROM. The practice of changing the bia for a LAN interface is rare, but it is useful in some complex network configurations.

Ethernet and IEEE 802.3

Ethernet and the Institute of Electrical and Electronic Engineers (IEEE) 802.3 protocol are the most common LAN protocols in use today. Ethernet was developed in the mid-1970s by researchers at the Xerox Palo Alto Research Center (PARC). Xerox, Digital Equipment Corporation, and Intel Corporation standardized it in 1978. Later, the IEEE standardized a similar protocol called IEEE 802.3. The uses of the frame fields between Ethernet and IEEE 802.3 differ slightly.

NOTE   Many IEEE protocols in this book start with the numbering scheme 802, signifying the year and month the original committee was formed.

Both Ethernet and IEEE 802.3 use a network technology called carrier sense multiple access collision detect (CSMA/CD) to allow access to a common 10-Mbps bus on which all devices communicate. Multiple devices on a CSMA/CD bus can sense when there is traffic on the common bus (the *carrier sense*) and detect when two nodes talk at the same time (the *collision detect*). The CSMA/CD protocol also specifies how a device operates in the event of a collision.

Logically, an Ethernet or IEEE 802.3 segment appears to be a single flat wire on which all devices are attached, as shown in Figure 3-1.

Figure 3-1   *An Ethernet Network Segment*

Ethernet or IEEE 802.3 devices can communicate in half-duplex mode, a mode in which the device can either send or receive a frame, but not both at the same time. Common Ethernet or IEEE 802.3 segments operate in half-duplex mode. Full-duplex Ethernet or IEEE 802.3 is where a device can send and receive a frame at the same time. Full-duplex mode is available only in a topology where only two devices are directly connected using Ethernet or IEEE 802.3, such as a device connected to an Ethernet switch.

Cisco bridges and switches can be used to logically connect Ethernet and IEEE 802.3 segments using transparent, translational, or encapsulation bridging. In this environment, the Cisco device connects two or more LAN segments to make a single data link layer segment with separate CSMA/CD physical segments or collision domains. Figure 3-2 shows both the physical and the logical topology for an Ethernet segment, which is bridged and switched with Cisco devices.

Figure 3-2   *An Ethernet Network Segment Shown Physically (a) and Logically (b)*

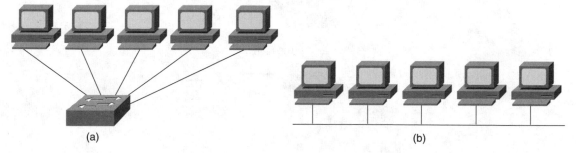

(a)   (b)

You can use Cisco routers to separate Ethernet segments both logically and physically. Each Ethernet interface would have its own address, and the router would route packets based on network layer protocols between the interfaces.

Fast Ethernet

The broad success of Ethernet and CSMA/CD has recently led to the development of Fast Ethernet. Fast Ethernet is a CSMA/CD protocol that operates at 100 Mbps, which is ten times the speed of Ethernet and IEEE 802.3. The success of Fast Ethernet has been primarily due to the fact that the protocol can use the same physical media (copper, twisted-pair, and fiber) as standard Ethernet, making it possible for many networks to migrate from 10 Mbps to 100 Mbps without changing the physical infrastructure.

Because Fast Ethernet is a CSMA/CD protocol, the logical topology of a Fast Ethernet network is exactly the same as that of an Ethernet network. Also like Ethernet, Fast Ethernet can operate in half-duplex or full-duplex mode. Most Fast Ethernet devices can automatically detect whether the segment to which they are connected is Ethernet (10 Mbps) or Fast Ethernet (100 Mbps) and also can detect the appropriate duplex (half-duplex or full-duplex).

Cisco devices have Fast Ethernet interfaces on bridges, switches, and routers. Fast Ethernet is often used on a switch as an uplink for Ethernet interfaces. A common topology would be to have a switch connect ten Ethernet segments to a Fast Ethernet segment, and then to connect the Fast Ethernet segment to a router for access to a WAN, as shown in Figure 3-3.

Figure 3-3   *An Ethernet Switch with a Fast Ethernet Uplink to a Router*

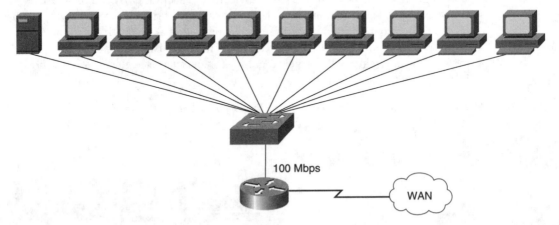

100 Mbps

WAN

Fast Ethernet and Ethernet Interface Configuration Subcommands

On some Cisco 4000 and 7000 series routers, each Ethernet and Fast Ethernet interface has a choice of media types for connecting to the router. Use the interface configuration subcommand **media-type** to tell the router which type of connection is active on the interface. In the following example, we set the media type for the Seoul-1 router:

```
Seoul-1#configure
Configuring from terminal, memory, or network [terminal]?
Enter configuration commands, one per line. End with CTRL+Z.
Seoul-1(config)#interface ethernet 0
Seoul-1(config-if)#media-type 10baseT
Seoul-1(config-if)#^Z
```

Attachment unit interfaces (AUIs) and RJ-45 connectors (called 10BaseT by the IOS to signify twisted-pair wiring) are the valid media types for Ethernet and IEEE 802.3 interfaces. AUIs are 15-pin connectors. Media-independent interfaces (MIIs) and RJ-45 connectors are the valid media types for Fast Ethernet interfaces.

On Fast Ethernet interfaces, you can manually set the duplex using the **full-duplex** interface configuration subcommand. If you remove this command with the **no full-duplex** command, the interface defaults to half-duplex mode. In the following example, we set the Fast Ethernet port on the Seoul-1 router to full-duplex:

```
Seoul-1#configure
Configuring from terminal, memory, or network [terminal]?
Enter configuration commands, one per line. End with CTRL+Z.
Seoul-1(config)#interface ethernet 0
Seoul-1(config-if)#full-duplex
Seoul-1(config-if)#^Z
```

Gigabit Ethernet

Similar to Fast Ethernet, Gigabit Ethernet (or IEEE 802.3z) builds on the IEEE 802.3 Ethernet standard. The main difference, as the name implies, is that Gigabit Ethernet communicates with devices at 1 Gbps. In the same way that Fast Ethernet is ten times faster than Ethernet and IEEE 802.3, Gigabit Ethernet is ten times faster than Fast Ethernet. However, unlike Fast Ethernet, the implementation of Gigabit Ethernet requires that changes are made to the physical interface on a device.

From the data link layer and above on the OSI protocol stack, Gigabit Ethernet operates identically to Ethernet. At the physical layer, Gigabit Ethernet makes use of an interface type already in use by another high-speed LAN technology called Fiber Channel. Gigabit Ethernet combines the Fiber Channel physical layer and the data link layer frame format in use by IEEE 802.3, Ethernet, and Fast Ethernet. Gigabit Ethernet uses the CSMA/CD algorithm and can operate in half-duplex or full-duplex modes. IEEE 802.3x defines the standard for full-duplex Gigabit Ethernet.

Cisco 7500 series routers and Catalyst 5500 series switches support Gigabit Ethernet interfaces. On the 7500 series routers, a single Gigabit Ethernet interface per slot is supported at the present time. If the Gigabit Ethernet interface is in slot 2 of the 7500 series router, it is known as Gigabit Ethernet 2/0/0 (slot/port adapter/port), as seen in the following example:

```
Router>show interface gigabitethernet 2/0/0
GigabitEthernet2/0/0 is up, line protocol is up
Hardware is cyBus GigabitEthernet, address is 0000.0ca4.db61 (bia 0000.0ca4.db61)
Internet address is 10.0.0.2/8
MTU 1500 bytes, BW 1000000 Kbit, DLY 1000 usec, rely 255/255, load 1/255
  Encapsulation ARPA, loopback not set, keepalive set (10 sec)
  ARP type: ARPA, ARP Timeout 04:00:00
  Last input 00:00:00, output 00:00:01, output hang never
  Last clearing of "show interface" counters never
  Queueing strategy: fifo
  Output queue 0/40, 0 drops; input queue 0/75, 0 drops
  5 minute input rate 2300 bits/sec, 2 packets/sec
  5 minute output rate 3000 bits/sec, 3 packets/sec
    116547 packets input, 13397137 bytes, 0 no buffer
    Received 3402 broadcasts, 0 runts, 0 giants
    0 input errors, 0 CRC, 0 frame, 0 overrun, 0 ignored, 0 abort
    0 input packets with dribble condition detected
    273769 packets output, 84816409 bytes, 0 underruns
    65959 output errors, 1 collisions, 1 interface resets
    0 babbles, 0 late collision, 29 deferred
    65959 lost carrier, 0 no carrier
    0 output buffer failures, 0 output buffers swapped out
```

Token Ring

Token Ring is a LAN technology developed by International Business Machines (IBM) and standardized as the IEEE 802.5 protocol. As the name suggests, the Token Ring protocol operates on a logical ring topology, not a bus topology such as Ethernet. Token Ring uses a protocol called token capture to grant access to the physical network medium. The Token Ring protocol has been implemented at two speeds, 4 Mbps and 16 Mbps.

The algorithm is relatively simple to understand. A device on a Token Ring network must capture a special packet called a token. A token traverses the ring in a logical counterclockwise direction. If a device has data to send, and it sees the token pass by on the ring, it can capture the token. After a device has captured the token, it can transmit a frame around the ring. As the frame passes around the ring, the destination system copies the data in the frame. When the frame sent by the device arrives back at the original source, the source removes the frame and puts the token back on the ring. On 16-Mbps Token Ring networks, the source system releases a new token before receiving the data frame back using a feature called *early token release*.

Unlike CSMA/CD, the token capture protocol avoids collisions altogether because only the device that has captured the token can transmit a frame on the Token Ring. Also, it is possible to calculate the maximum time that a device must wait before it can transmit a frame, making the token capture protocol deterministic. For some network applications, such as real-time transactions, this determinism is an important requirement for a LAN protocol. The logical topology of a Token Ring network is shown in Figure 3-4.

Figure 3-4   *Token Ring Topology*

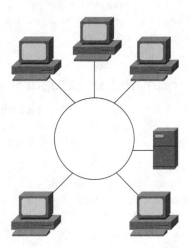

The following output shows the EXEC **show interfaces** command for the Token Ring interface on the San-Jose router, slot 1, port 0:

```
San-Jose#show interfaces tokenring 1/0
TokenRing 1/0 is up, line protocol is up
Hardware is 16/4 Token Ring, address is 5500.2000.dc27 (bia 5500.2000.dc27)
     MTU 8136 bytes, BW 16000 Kbit, DLY 630 usec, rely 255/255, load 1/255
     Encapsulation SNAP, loopback not set, keepalive set (10 sec)
     ARP type: SNAP, ARP Timeout 4:00:00
     Ring speed: 16 Mbps
     Single ring node, Source Route Bridge capable
     Group Address: 0x00000000, Functional Address: 0x60840000
     Last input 0:00:01, output 0:00:01, output hang never
     Output queue 0/40, 0 drops; input queue 0/75, 0 drops
     Five minute input rate 0 bits/sec, 0 packets/sec
     Five minute output rate 0 bits/sec, 0 packets/sec
        16339 packets input, 1496515 bytes, 0 no buffer
        Received 9895 broadcasts, 0 runts, 0 giants
        0 input errors, 0 CRC, 0 frame, 0 overrun, 0 ignored, 0 abort
        32648 packets output, 9738303 bytes, 0 underruns
        0 output errors, 0 collisions, 2 interface resets, 0 restarts
        5 transitions
```

In the previous output, notice that the interface is operationally up, the data link burned-in address (bia) for the Token Ring interface is on the second line, and the 16 Mbps ring speed for the interface is shown on the sixth line.

Token Ring Interface Configuration Subcommands

Use the IOS configuration interface subcommand **ring-speed** to specify whether the Token Ring interface is 4 Mbps or 16 Mbps. All devices on a Token Ring need to operate at the same speed; mixed ring-speed configurations are not permitted by the protocol and may lead to an inoperable ring.

If you choose to use the early token release feature on a 16-Mbps ring, all devices on the Token Ring must have this feature enabled. If any device (Cisco or another manufacturer) on a Token Ring is not enabled to do early token release, the entire ring does not use this feature. The IOS configuration interface subcommand **early-token-release** enables early token release on an interface.

In the following example, we set a Token Ring interface to operate at 16 Mbps and to enable early token release:

```
San-Jose#configure
Configuring from terminal, memory, or network [terminal]?
Enter configuration commands, one per line. End with CTRL+Z.
San-Jose(config)#interface tokenring 1/0
San-Jose(config-if)#ring-speed 16
San-Jose(config-if)#early-token-release
San-Jose(config-if)#^Z
```

Fiber Distributed Data Interface

The Fiber Distributed Data Interface (FDDI) is another token capture LAN protocol. The ANSI X3T9.5 standards committee standardized the FDDI protocol in the mid-1980s. FDDI is similar to Token Ring, but instead of using a single-ring architecture, FDDI uses a dual-fiber ring that transmits data in opposite directions. FDDI uses only one ring, called the primary ring, during normal operation. FDDI uses the second ring, called the backup ring, when there is a failure on the primary ring. When there is a single break in the primary ring, the devices closest to the break enter wrapped mode and use the backup ring to form a loop to ensure that the FDDI ring is still complete, as shown in Figure 3-5.

Figure 3-5   *FDDI Topology in Normal Mode (a) and Wrapped Mode (b)*

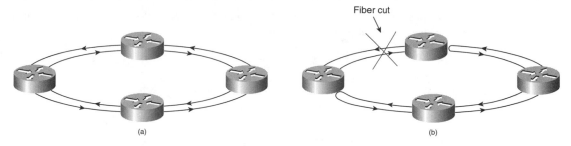

(a)   (b)

Like Fast Ethernet, FDDI operates at 100 Mbps. Because of this high-speed bandwidth and its inherent redundancy, FDDI is often used as a high-speed uplink from a switch to a router backbone or is used as a campus backbone technology. Cisco bridges, switches, and routers support FDDI for transparent and translational bridging, switching, and routing network layer protocols. On the ZIP network, the San Francisco corporate offices are using FDDI to interconnect routers within a multilevel building. The output of **show interfaces** for an FDDI interface on the SF-Core-1 router is as follows:

```
SF-Core-1>show interfaces fddi 0/0
Fddi0/0 is up, line protocol is up
   Hardware is cBus Fddi, address is 0000.0c06.8de8 (bia 0000.0c06.8de8)
   MTU 4470 bytes, BW 100000 Kbit, DLY 100 usec, rely 255/255, load 1/255
   Encapsulation SNAP, loopback not set, keepalive not set
   ARP type: SNAP, ARP Timeout 4:00:00
   Phy-A state is active, neighbor is  B, cmt signal bits 008/20C, status ILS
   Phy-B state is connect, neighbor is unk, cmt signal bits 20C/000, status QLS
   ECM is insert, CFM is c_wrap_a, RMT is ring_op
   token rotation 5000 usec, ring operational 1d01
   Upstream neighbor 0000.0c06.8b7d, downstream neighbor 0000.0c06.8b7d
   Last input 0:00:08, output 0:00:08, output hang never
   Last clearing of "show interface" counters never
   Output queue 0/40, 0 drops; input queue 0/75, 0 drops
   Five minute input rate 5000 bits/sec, 1 packets/sec
   Five minute output rate 76000 bits/sec, 51 packets/sec
      852914 packets input, 205752094 bytes, 0 no buffer
      Received 126752 broadcasts, 0 runts, 0 giants
      0 input errors, 0 CRC, 0 frame, 0 overrun, 0 ignored, 0 abort
      8213126 packets output, 616453062 bytes, 0 underruns
      0 output errors, 0 collisions, 4 interface resets, 0 restarts
      5 transitions, 0 traces
```

In the previous output, notice that the interface is operationally up, the data link burned-in address (bia) for the FDDI interface is on the second line, and the 100-Mbps bandwidth (BW) is shown on the third line. The physical properties of each fiber (Phy-A is the primary ring; Phy-B is the backup ring) are shown on the sixth and seventh lines.

Wide-Area Network and Dialup Network Technologies

Cisco devices support a large number of WAN and dialup technologies. We cover the most popular of these technologies in this chapter:

- High-Level Data Link Control (HDLC)
- Point-to-Point Protocol (PPP)
- X.25
- Frame Relay
- Asynchronous Transfer Mode (ATM)
- Digital Subscriber Line (DSL)
- Integrated Services Digital Network (ISDN)

Like the LAN protocols we have considered in this chapter, these WAN protocols operate at the data link layer of the OSI reference model. The WAN protocols transfer data across an asynchronous or synchronous serial interface from one location to another.

NOTE   Synchronous serial transmissions are digital signals that are transmitted with precise clocking from one device to another. In contrast, asynchronous transmission is not done with precise clocking and relies on control information (called start and stop bits) that signifies the beginning and the end of data.

The first of the synchronous protocols we consider, HDLC, works only in a point-to-point manner, connecting one device to another with minimal encapsulation and addressing. PPP, originally designed for point-to-point serial links, has evolved into working in both synchronous and asynchronous environments. The protocols X.25, Frame Relay, and ATM do not work in a strict point-to-point serial link environment, but instead use virtual circuits to pass data. DSL is a technology that provides encoding for high-speed serial connections over conventional copper wiring for limited distances. ISDN is a WAN technology that uses the telephone network to digitize data. It can operate in a point-to-point or multipoint (one-to-many) environment.

A *virtual circuit (VC)* is a communication mechanism in which the path for the transfer of information is established before the data is sent, a process known as placing a call. All data packets related to the call follow the same route through the network, ensuring that the data arrives at the destination in the same order in which it was sent. At the end of the data transfer, the call is closed. *Switched virtual circuits (SVCs)* are those that can be established and removed as required by the network. *Permanent virtual circuits (PVCs)* are permanently established by the network and are never removed.

As we will see, multiple virtual circuits (SVCs or PVCs) can reside on a single serial interface of a Cisco router. In this case, each virtual circuit can be treated as a separate interface, called a *subinterface*. Subinterfaces can be implemented for any WAN protocol that uses virtual circuits. We examine the advantages and details of subinterfaces in the configuration examples for Frame Relay later in this chapter.

A familiar system that is analogous to a VC is the phone system. Each phone call we make can be thought of as a virtual circuit. Nearly all phone calls we make are analogous to SVCs. But if we placed a call once and left the call active forever, it would be a PVC.

Cisco WAN protocols that use virtual circuits pass data in two different forms, packet switching and cell relay. *Packet switching* is a data transmission method that sends data in variable-length units, or packets. Packet switching on the data link layer takes packets from the network layer and encapsulates them with specific data link layer addressing. As the data-link packets traverse the network, each intermediate packet-switching node between the source and the destination reads the data-link address in the packet and forwards the packet. The packet travels the path of the previously established virtual circuit until the destination data-link address is reached. Frame Relay and X.25 use packet switching.

ATM and Switched Multimegabit Data Service (SMDS—not covered in this book) convert packet data into fixed-length cells and perform cell relay. *Cell relay* is a data transmission method that sends data in small, fixed-size units, or cells, that can be processed by hardware in a fast and efficient manner. The operation of cell relay is similar to packet switching except that the data from the source system is first converted into fixed-length cells rather than packets. Table 3-1 summarizes and compares the transmission methods of the WAN protocols covered in this chapter.

Table 3-1   *WAN Protocol Transmission Characteristics*

Protocol	Point-to-Point	Packet Switching	Cell Relay	Asynchronous	Synchronous
HDLC	yes	no	no	no	yes
PPP	yes	no	no	yes	yes
X.25	yes	yes	no	no	yes
Frame Relay	yes	yes	no	no	yes
ATM	yes	no	yes	no	yes
DSL	yes	no	no	no	yes
ISDN	yes	no	no	yes	yes

It's important to keep in mind the two layers of addressing that are at issue when packet switching or cell relay is transferring network-level data across the network. Packet switching and cell switching addresses are found on the data link layer of the OSI reference model. They should not be confused with network layer addresses, such as those found in IP, IPX, and AppleTalk, which are found on the network layer of the OSI reference model. It is common for Cisco routers to route network layer packets, such as IP packets, over a packet-switching network such as Frame Relay.

In routing these network packets over a packet-switching network, the router uses the IP addresses in the network layer to determine how to route the packet to the next router on the path to the final destination.

The router then encapsulates the entire IP packet in Frame Relay, adding Frame Relay addressing. The packet gets switched across switches in the Frame Relay network as it travels down a single virtual circuit. Each Frame Relay switch uses the packet's Frame Relay addressing to transfer the packet further along the circuit from source to destination router. The routers see themselves directly attached over the Frame Relay network; they do not see the Frame Relay switches as intermediary nodes for network layer traffic.

This same analogy can be used for LAN protocols. Replace the Frame Relay switches with Ethernet switches, and the example is still valid, with the exception that Ethernet does not use virtual circuits.

High-Level Data Link Control

The High-Level Data Link Control (HDLC) protocol is a bit-ordered synchronous protocol developed by the International Organization for Standardization (ISO). HDLC is used to directly connect one Cisco router to another. Cisco routers default to using HDLC encapsulation on all synchronous serial interfaces.

Cisco HDLC is a proprietary version of the protocol; it does not communicate over a serial link with any other vendor's HDLC protocol. The proprietary nature of Cisco HDLC is not unusual. All vendors' HDLC implementations are proprietary because HDLC is a protocol derived from the proprietary Synchronous Data Link Control (SDLC) protocol, which was originally developed by IBM. The following output from the San Jose router on the ZIP network shows the interface serial0/0 using HDLC encapsulation:

```
San-Jose>show interface serial 0/0
Serial0/0 is up, line protocol is up
  Hardware is QUICC Serial
  MTU 1500 bytes, BW 1544 Kbit, DLY 20000 usec, rely 255/255, load 1/255
  Encapsulation HDLC, loopback not set, keepalive set (10 sec)
  Last input 00:00:00, output 00:00:03, output hang never
  Last clearing of "show interface" counters never
  Input queue: 0/75/0 (size/max/drops); Total output drops: 0
  Queueing strategy: weighted fair
  Output queue: 0/64/0 (size/threshold/drops)
     Conversations  0/6 (active/max active)
     Reserved Conversations 0/0 (allocated/max allocated)
  5 minute input rate 28000 bits/sec, 2 packets/sec
  5 minute output rate 1000 bits/sec, 2 packets/sec
     4396629 packets input, 1382566679 bytes, 2 no buffer
     Received 518019 broadcasts, 0 runts, 0 giants, 0 throttles
     1824 input errors, 661 CRC, 542 frame, 0 overrun, 0 ignored, 621 abort
     4674425 packets output, 430814377 bytes, 0 underruns
     0 output errors, 0 collisions, 10 interface resets
     0 output buffer failures, 0 output buffers swapped out
     2 carrier transitions
     DCD=up  DSR=up  DTR=up  RTS=up  CTS=up
```

In the previous output, notice that the serial interface encapsulation is HDLC (the default encapsulation for all Cisco serial interfaces), as shown in the fourth line. (Note also that we've used an unambiguous form of the **show interfaces serial 0/0** command in the previous example.)

Point-to-Point Protocol

The Point-to-Point Protocol (PPP) is another data-link WAN protocol supported by Cisco devices. PPP was designed as an open protocol that would be used to work with several network layer protocols, such as IP, IPX, and AppleTalk. You can think of PPP as the nonproprietary version of HDLC, although the underlying protocol is significantly different. PPP works in both asynchronous and synchronous encapsulation because the protocol uses a flag to signify the beginning or end of a frame. This flag is used in asynchronous encapsulations to signify the start or stop of a frame and is used as a bit-oriented synchronous encapsulation.

PPP relies on the Link Control Protocol (LCP), which establishes, configures, and tests data-link connections for use by PPP. The Network Control Protocol (NCP) is a series of protocols—one for each network layer supported by PPP—for establishing and configuring different network layer protocols to operate over PPP. For IP, IPX, and AppleTalk, the NCP designations are IPCP, IPXCP, and ATALKCP, respectively.

PPP Interface Configuration Subcommands

You can use the IOS interface configuration subcommand **encapsulation ppp** to enable synchronous PPP on a serial interface. In the following example, we configure synchronous PPP on the San Jose router's serial1/1 interface:

```
San-Jose#configure
Enter configuration commands, one per line. End with CTRL+Z.
Configuring from terminal, memory, or network [terminal]?
San-Jose(config)#interface serial 1/1
San-Jose(config-if)#encapsulation ppp
San-Jose(config-if)#^Z
```

Note that we have used an unambiguous form of the **interface serial1/1** major command and an unambiguous form of the **encapsulation ppp** interface subcommand in the preceding example.

The following output from the San Jose router on the ZIP network shows the interface serial1/1 using PPP encapsulation:

```
Serial1/1 is up, line protocol is up
  Hardware is HD64570
  MTU 1500 bytes, BW 1544 Kbit, DLY 20000 usec, rely 255/255, load 1/255
  Encapsulation PPP, loopback not set, keepalive not set
  LCP Open
  Open: IPCP
  Last input 0:00:01, output 0:00:01, output hang never
  Last clearing of "show interface" counters never
```

```
Input queue: 0/75/0 (size/max/drops); Total output drops: 0
Queueing strategy: weighted fair
Output queue: 0/64/0 (size/threshold/drops)
   Conversations  0/4 (active/max active)
   Reserved Conversations 0/0 (allocated/max allocated)
5 minute input rate 0 bits/sec, 0 packets/sec
5 minute output rate 0 bits/sec, 0 packets/sec
   1433 packets input, 117056 bytes, 0 no buffer
   Received 0 broadcasts, 0 runts, 0 giants, 0 throttles
   0 input errors, 0 CRC, 0 frame, 0 overrun, 0 ignored, 0 abort
   714 packets output, 150299 bytes, 0 underruns
   0 output errors, 0 collisions, 11 interface resets
   0 output buffer failures, 0 output buffers swapped out
   0 carrier transitions
```

In the fifth line of the preceding output, you can see that LCP is open. The sixth line shows that IPCP is open as well. We can deduce from the fact that IPCP is open that PPP is configured to encapsulate IP packets across this interface.

X.25

X.25 is a packet-switching protocol that supports both SVCs and PVCs that were first developed in the 1970s. The International Telecommunications Union (ITU) is an agency of the United Nations that administers the X.25 protocol. Because of the international acceptance of X.25, it may be the most widely used WAN protocol in the world today.

Like all packet-switching protocols, X.25 essentially defines a network for data communications similar to that of the telephone network and passes data using virtual circuits. The communication between two devices begins with one device calling the other to establish an SVC or PVC, proceeds with data transfer, and then ends with call termination. The X.25 protocol defines a point-to-point communication between data terminal equipment (DTE) and data circuit-terminating equipment (DCE). DTEs (such as Cisco routers) connect to DCEs (such as modems), which connect to one or more X.25 WAN switches and, ultimately, to another DTE.

NOTE   Data circuit-terminating equipment (DCE) is a device that makes up the network end of the user-to-network interface. The DCE provides a physical connection to the network, forwards traffic, and provides a clocking signal that is used to synchronize data transmission between DCE and DTE devices. Data terminal equipment (DTE) is a device at the user end of a user-network interface that serves as a data source, destination, or both. DTE connects to a data network through a DCE device (for example, a modem) and typically uses clocking signals generated by the DCE.

A call across an X.25 network begins with the origin DTE placing a call with the DCE to which it is connected. The X.25 switches in the network decide how to route the call from origin to destination. All data is then switched from the origin DTE to the destination DTE across the X.25 network, as shown in Figure 3-6.

Figure 3-6   *An X.25 Network*

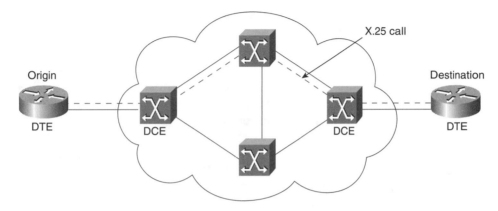

The X.25 protocol uses an addressing scheme called X.121. ITU-T Recommendation X.121 specifies the source and the destination address formats for the X.25 protocol on the data link layer. X.25 switches route calls along the path of a virtual circuit based on source and destination X.121 addresses.

X.121 addresses vary in length and can be up to 14 decimal digits long. The first four digits of the X.121 address are called the data network identification code (DNIC). After the DNIC, the remaining digits of the address can be used however the network administrator decides to utilize them.

X.25 Interface Configuration Subcommands

The first step to using X.25 on a Cisco serial interface is to set up the interface so that it can use X.25 encapsulation with the **encapsulation x25** command.

The X.25 data link X.121 addresses are not burned into ROM as are LAN addresses. This means that the network administrator needs to tell a Cisco router the local X.121 address on an X.25 serial interface, which is accomplished with the interface configuration subcommand **x25 address**. Some vendors' X.25 switches require you to set a maximum packet size for input and output packets (the default is 128 bytes). You may need to configure your Cisco router with the proper input packet size (ips) and output packet size (ops) on the serial interface with the commands **x25 ips** and **x25 ops** to operate properly on your X.25 network.

X.25 networks have a default input and output window size for packets that are used by flow control mechanisms. You may need to set up the default input window size (win) and output window size (wout) for your X.25 network to work properly, just as you may need to set a maximum packet size. (The default input and output window size is 2 packets.) The IOS interface configuration subcommands **x25 win** and **x25 wout** set the input and output window size.

You should check with your X.25 switch vendor for recommendations for the maximum packet size and maximum window size parameters. Coordination of these parameters between the DTE and the DCE is often required to enable the X.25 data link layer to operate properly.

In the following example, we set up the San Jose router with X.25 encapsulation and an X.121 data link address of 537000000001. We also specify an input and output packet size of 256 bytes. We specify the input and output window size as 7 packets.

```
San-Jose#configure
Configuring from terminal, memory, or network [terminal]?
Enter configuration commands, one per line. End with CTRL+Z.
San-Jose(config)#interface serial 1
San-Jose(config-if)#encapsulation x25
San-Jose(config-if)#x25 address 537000000001
San-Jose(config-if)#x25 ips 256
San-Jose(config-if)#x25 ops 256
San-Jose(config-if)#x25 win 7
San-Jose(config-if)#x25 wout 7
San-Jose(config-if)#^Z
```

Notice the many interface configuration subcommands that are needed to configure the router in this example.

The following **show interfaces** output shows a router interface using X.25 encapsulation:

```
Serial 0 is up, line protocol is up
  Hardware is MCI Serial
  MTU 1500 bytes, BW 512 Kbit, DLY 20000 usec, rely 255/255, load 1/255
  Encapsulation X25-DTE, loopback not set, keepalive set
  LAPB state is CONNECT, T1 3000, N1 12000, N2 20, K7, TH 3000
  Window is closed
  IFRAMEs 12/28 RNRs 0/1 REJs 13/1 SABMs 1/13 FRMRs 3/0 DISCs 0/11
  Last input 0:00:00, output 0:00:00, output hang never
  Output queue 0/40, 0 drops; input queue 0/75, 0 drops
  5 minute input rate 0 bits/sec, 1 packets/sec
  5 minute output rate 1000 bits/sec, 1 packets/sec
     261 packets input, 13212 bytes, 0 no buffer
     Received 33 broadcasts, 0 runts, 0 giants
     0 input errors, 0 CRC, 0 frame, 0 overrun, 0 ignored, 0 abort
     238 packets output, 14751 bytes, 0 underruns
     0 output errors, 0 collisions, 0 interface resets, 0 restarts
```

In the previous output, notice that the interface encapsulation is X.25 DTE in the fourth line. The following three lines give Link Access Procedure, Balanced (LAPB) statistics. LAPB is the data link layer protocol used by the X.25 protocol stack that is based on HDLC. If you want to see the status of the X.25 virtual circuits on a Cisco device, you can use the EXEC command **show x25 vc**.

Frame Relay

Frame Relay is a WAN packet-switching protocol that was first developed for use over Integrated Services Digital Network (ISDN, discussed later in this chapter). The initial proposals for Frame Relay standards were presented to CCITT in 1984. Although the standard existed, there were problems with vendor interoperability, and the technology received little industry support until late in the 1980s.

Like X.25, Frame Relay is a packet-switching protocol that has PVCs and SVCs. Most Frame Relay networks today use PVCs because SVCs are just beginning to be implemented. Frame Relay uses the call setup, data transfer, and call termination process, as discussed previously with X.25. End devices, such as routers, place calls across the Frame Relay network. After the call is established, the router transfers data and then closes the call. In the case of a PVC, the call is always active, allowing the router to send data without placing the call.

In the same way that X.25 uses X.121 addresses, Frame Relay uses addresses called data-link connection identifiers (DLCI). Each DLCI can have local or global significance throughout the Frame Relay network. The most common use today is for each DLCI to have local significance only. This means that to a device such as a router, the DLCI number on each side of a virtual circuit may be the same because Frame Relay maps a local DLCI number to a virtual circuit at each switch in the WAN. A Frame Relay network example is shown in Figure 3-7.

Figure 3-7   *A Frame Relay Network with PVCs*

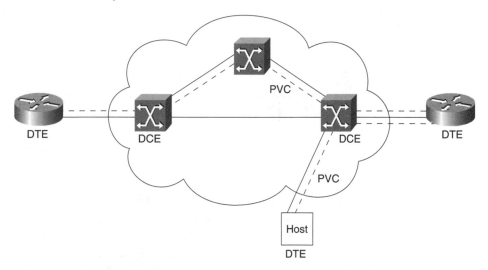

In 1990, Cisco, Digital Equipment Corporation, Northern Telecom, and StrataCom formed a consortium to focus on Frame Relay development and interoperability. This group of vendors took the basic Frame Relay protocol from CCITT and added extensions to the protocol features that allow internetworking devices to communicate easily with a Frame Relay network.

These features, which are called Local Management Interface (LMI), allow Frame Relay DTE devices such as routers to communicate with Frame Relay DCE devices and to exchange the information that is used to pass internetwork traffic over a Frame Relay WAN. LMI messages provide information about the current DLCI values, the global or local significance of the DLCI values, and the status of virtual circuits.

NOTE   The consortium LMI developed by Cisco, DEC, NT, and StrataCom is now known as *the Gang-of-Four LMI*, or *Cisco LMI*. In addition to the consortium LMI, the American National Standards Institute (ANSI) has developed a standard LMI called Annex-D that is used throughout the world on Frame Relay networks.

Frame Relay Interface Configuration Subcommands

To configure Frame Relay on a Cisco serial interface, you must begin by using the **encapsulation frame-relay** interface subcommand. You can then use the **frame-relay interface-dlci** subcommand to set the DLCI on the interface. Cisco devices default to using the Cisco LMI on Frame Relay interfaces. You can set the LMI type using the **frame-relay lmi-type** interface subcommand.

Using the ZIP network as an example, we can configure Frame Relay on the Singapore router as follows:

```
Singapore#configure
Configuring from terminal, memory, or network [terminal]?
Enter configuration commands, one per line. End with CTRL+Z.
Singapore(config)#interface serial 0
Singapore(config-if)#encapsulation frame
Singapore(config-if)#frame-relay interface-dlci 100
Singapore(config-if)#frame-relay lmi-type ansi
Singapore(config-if)#^Z
```

The preceding Frame Relay configuration is a basic configuration for a single virtual circuit on a Cisco serial interface. As mentioned earlier, you can also have multiple virtual circuits on a single serial interface and treat each as a separate interface, which is called a subinterface. Think of a subinterface as a hardware interface defined by the IOS software.

The advantage to using subinterfaces is that you can assign different network layer characteristics to each subinterface and virtual circuit, such as IP routing on one virtual circuit and AppleTalk routing on another. You can define virtual interfaces with the **interface serial slot/port.number** command. The **number** parameter specifies the subinterface number associated with the **slot/port**.

The two types of subinterfaces are *point-to-point* and *multipoint*. Point-to-point subinterfaces are used when a single virtual circuit connects one router to another. Think of a point-to-point subinterface as a virtual circuit that emulates a dedicated serial link. Multipoint subinterfaces are used when the router is the center of a star of virtual circuits, as shown in Figure 3-8.

Figure 3-8   *Point-to-Point (a) and Multipoint (b) Frame Relay Networks*

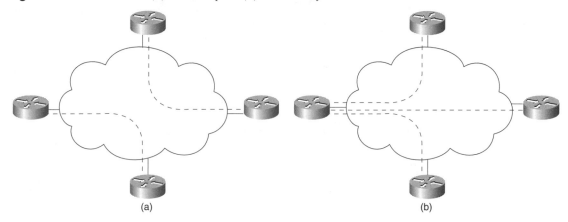

(a)   (b)

You can define a limitless number of subinterfaces on a given physical interface. (Router memory is the only exception.) In the following example, we define subinterface serial 0.100 on the Singapore router:

```
Singapore#configure
Configuring from terminal, memory, or network [terminal]?
Enter configuration commands, one per line. End with CTRL+Z.
Singapore(config)#interface serial 0
Singapore(config-if)#encapsulation frame
Singapore(config-if)#interface serial 0.100 point-to-point
Singapore(config-subif)#frame-relay interface-dlci 100
Singapore(config-subif)#frame-relay lmi-type ansi
Singapore(config-subif)#^Z
```

TIP

We suggest that you adhere to a numbering scheme for the subinterface numbers you choose. We recommend making the subinterface number match the virtual circuit DLCI number.

To view the status of a Frame Relay interface, you can use the **show interfaces** command. Following is the output from the **show interfaces s 0** command on the Singapore ZIP network router:

```
Serial0 is up, line protocol is up
  Hardware is HD64570
  MTU 1500 bytes, BW 256 Kbit, DLY 20000 usec, rely 255/255, load 1/255
  Encapsulation FRAME-RELAY, loopback not set, keepalive set (10 sec)
```

```
LMI enq sent  459618, LMI stat recvd 459618, LMI upd recvd 0, DTE LMI up
LMI enq recvd 0, LMI stat sent  0, LMI upd sent  0
LMI DLCI 100  LMI type is CISCO  frame relay DTE
Broadcast queue 0/64, broadcasts sent/dropped 121505/0, interface broadcasts 121505
Last input 00:00:00, output 00:00:00, output hang never
Last clearing of "show interface" counters never
Input queue: 0/75/0 (size/max/drops); Total output drops: 0
Queueing strategy: weighted fair
Output queue: 0/64/0 (size/threshold/drops)
   Conversations  0/9 (active/max active)
   Reserved Conversations 0/0 (allocated/max allocated)
5 minute input rate 1000 bits/sec, 1 packets/sec
5 minute output rate 0 bits/sec, 1 packets/sec
   34278826 packets input, 2790079482 bytes, 0 no buffer
   Received 0 broadcasts, 0 runts, 0 giants
   17 input errors, 7 CRC, 9 frame, 0 overrun, 0 ignored, 1 abort
   29613202 packets output, 1145345093 bytes, 0 underruns
   0 output errors, 0 collisions, 1 interface resets
   0 output buffer failures, 0 output buffers swapped out
   0 carrier transitions
   DCD=up  DSR=up  DTR=up  RTS=up  CTS=up
```

You can see the encapsulation of the interface set to Frame Relay in the fourth line of the previous code. LMI information follows on subsequent lines. The following is the output of **show interfaces s 0.100**, which examines subinterface status:

```
Serial0.100 is up, line protocol is up
  Hardware is HD64570
  MTU 1500 bytes, BW 256 Kbit, DLY 20000 usec, rely 255/255, load 1/255
  Encapsulation FRAME-RELAY
```

The previous output is much shorter than a normal **show interfaces** command because a subinterface inherits all the diagnostic counters of the major interface it is associated with—in this case, interface serial0.

You can examine the status of the Frame Relay virtual circuits using the EXEC command **show frame pvc** or **show frame svc** *maplist*. SVCs require the *maplist* option, which lists the mapping from the current device to the other devices to call and establish SVCs. Sample output for the PVC with DLCI 100 on the Singapore ZIP network router is as follows:

```
PVC Statistics for interface Serial 0 (Frame Relay DTE)

DLCI = 100, DLCI USAGE = LOCAL, PVC STATUS = ACTIVE, INTERFACE = Serial0.100

   input pkts 34263984 output pkts 29648752 in bytes 3135739012
   out bytes 1083480465 dropped pkts 93 in FECN pkts 170
   in BECN pkts 11741 out FECN pkts 0 out BECN pkts 0
   in DE pkts 15741022 out DE pkts 0
   pvc create time 7w5d, last time pvc status changed 1d10h
```

Asynchronous Transfer Mode

The Asynchronous Transfer Mode (ATM) is a standard defined by the ITU-T for cell relay. In the case of ATM, all cells are 53 bytes long.

Using cell relay, ATM is designed to handle multiple types of network services, including voice, video, and data. An ATM network comprises ATM switches (DCE devices) and ATM endpoints (DTE devices). The endpoints send information to the ATM switches, which segment the information into cells and switch the cells through the network. This process is the same for all three types of traffic handled by the ATM network.

The ITU-T based ATM on the Broadband Integrated Services Digital Network (BISDN) standard, which was initially designed for sending voice, video, and data over a public network. A coalition of companies formed the ATM Forum, which has released specifications for multiple vendor interoperability and extensions of ATM for public and private networks. To date, the ATM Forum has written three versions of User-Network Interface (UNI), a protocol similar in concept to Frame Relay LMI that standardizes communication between ATM devices and switches. The ATM Forum has also released documents defining standard communications between ATM switches (called the Private Network-to-Network Interface, or PNNI) and a method to emulate classic LAN architectures over an ATM network, which is called LAN Emulation (LANE).

Like the packet-switching technologies we have seen in previous sections of this chapter, ATM provides two types of connection-oriented virtual circuits: PVCs and SVCs. ATM also has a connectionless service that allows it to operate similarly to a LAN technology. ATM provides both connection-oriented and connectionless services using virtual channels. A virtual channel is similar to a virtual circuit in X.25 or Frame Relay.

The ATM network defines connections through the ATM network as virtual paths, which are identified by virtual path identifier (VPI) numbers. A virtual path is a bundle of virtual channels that are all switched across the ATM network based on the same VPI. You can think of a virtual path as a grouping mechanism to define the route for a series of virtual channels.

A virtual channel is identified by the combination of a VPI and a virtual channel identifier (VCI). The VPI defines the path that the virtual channel takes through the network, and the VCI is unique for each connection in the VPI. VPI and VCI numbers have only local significance, just as DLCI numbers for Frame Relay often have only local significance. ATM switches map the VPI/VCI numbers across a particular link to the next device in the connection (in the direction of the destination).

ATM networks bundle virtual paths into groups called transmission paths. A transmission path contains virtual paths, which in turn contain virtual channels, as shown in Figure 3-9.

Figure 3-9   *The Relationship Between ATM Virtual Channels, Virtual Paths, and Transmission Paths*

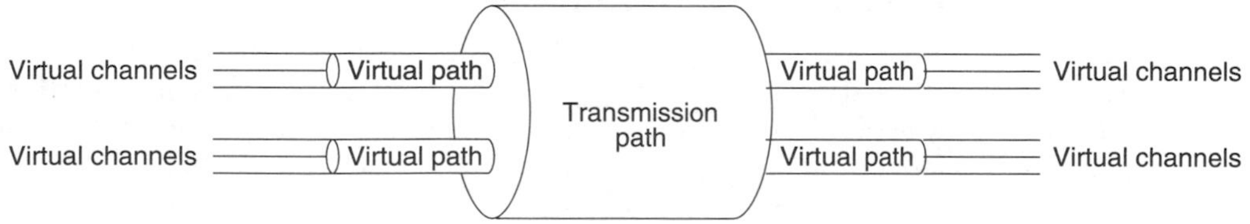

ATM networks can use two different types of addressing, one based on E.164 addressing (an addressing scheme similar to phone numbers) and another based on OSI network service access point (NSAP) addresses. The E.164 addressing scheme was developed by the ITU-T, and the NSAP addressing scheme was added by the ATM Forum. It is common to use E.164 addressing on public ATM networks that are provided by telecommunications carriers and to use NSAP addressing on private ATM networks, such as one connecting ATM switches and internetworking devices.

As noted earlier, ATM is designed to handle voice, video, and data services. To hide some of the complexities of the ATM protocol from these upper-layer services, ATM has defined three ATM adaptation layers. ATM adaptation layers (AAL) are protocols that sit on the OSI reference model at the top of the data link layer. These layers, each called an AAL, are responsible for providing the various ATM services to network layer protocols. AAL1 is a connection-oriented service that is commonly used to emulate dedicated circuits through the ATM network. Common AAL1 applications are voice or video connections. The next AAL, AAL3/4, supports both connection-oriented and connectionless data. Many AAL3/4 connections are used by network service providers for connectionless data. AAL3/4 is designed to integrate easily into a Switched Multimegabit Data Service (SMDS) network, another standard cell relay technology. AAL5, the third AAL, also supports both connection-oriented and connectionless service. AAL5 is used to transfer information that does not need to integrate easily with SMDS, such as data across a private LAN or WAN. Today, most ATM connections on private internetworks use AAL5.

Another feature of ATM is that it supports quality of service (QoS) guarantees across the network. Each ATM device interacts with the ATM network to provide a certain quality of service for each virtual path based on a traffic contract, traffic shaping, and traffic policing. A traffic contract specifies the requirements of the virtual channel, such as peak bandwidth, average sustained bandwidth, and burst size. Traffic shaping controls the flow of traffic to fit within the traffic contract by constraining data bursts, passing cells in a consistent flow, and limiting peak data rates. Traffic policing enforces the traffic contract by examining the actual traffic flow and comparing it to the traffic contract. Traffic policing procedures may enable switches to discard cells if they violate the traffic contract in a congestion situation. These QoS features of ATM make the protocol powerful in dealing with the various data requirements of a combined voice, video, and data network.

ATM Interface Configuration Subcommands

Cisco ATM interfaces are dedicated interface processors (or port adapters on a VIP card). This means that you do not need to specify the interface subcommand **encapsulation** for ATM interfaces; ATM encapsulation is all that is supported by the hardware. You do need to specify the virtual circuits that exist on a given interface using the **atm pvc** interface subcommand. The following output shows the configuration of PVC 1 using VPI 0 and VCI 100 for an AAL5 virtual channel:

```
Router#configure
Configuring from terminal, memory, or network [terminal]?
Enter configuration commands, one per line. End with CTRL+Z.
Router(config)#int atm2/0
Router(config-if)#atm pvc 1 0 100 aal5snap
Router(config-if)#^Z
```

You can examine the status of an ATM interface using the **show interfaces** command. Following is the output from **interface atm2/0** for the preceding configuration:

```
ATM2/0 is up, line protocol is up
  Hardware is cxBus ATM
  MTU 4470 bytes, BW 100000 Kbit, DLY 100 usec, rely 255/255, load 1/255
  Encapsulation ATM, loopback not set, keepalive set (10 sec)
  Encapsulation(s): AAL5, PVC mode
  256 TX buffers, 256 RX buffers, 1024 Maximum VCs, 1 Current VCs
  Signalling vc = 1, vpi = 0, vci = 100
  ATM NSAP address: BC.CDEF.01.234567.890A.BCDE.F012.3456.7890.1234.13
  Last input 0:00:05, output 0:00:05, output hang never
  Last clearing of "show interface" counters never
  Output queue 0/40, 0 drops; input queue 0/75, 0 drops
  Five minute input rate 0 bits/sec, 0 packets/sec
  Five minute output rate 0 bits/sec, 0 packets/sec
     144 packets input, 3148 bytes, 0 no buffer
     Received 0 broadcasts, 0 runts, 0 giants
     0 input errors, 0 CRC, 0 frame, 0 overrun, 0 ignored, 0 abort
     154 packets output, 4228 bytes, 0 underruns
     0 output errors, 0 collisions, 1 interface resets, 0 restarts
```

In the preceding output, you can see the ATM encapsulation set on the fourth line, the AAL5 encapsulation and PVC mode on the fifth line, and the VC, VPI, and VCI numbers on the seventh line. This interface is also configured for an ATM NSAP address, as you can see in the eighth line.

Digital Subscriber Line

Digital Subscriber Line (DSL) is a technology that has become popular in recent years and has the capability to provide dedicated high-capacity bandwidth to end users. DSL employs a star network topology, with the center of the star having dedicated connections to the leaf nodes with twisted-pair copper wire. The bandwidth between the leaf nodes and the center of the star can range from 64 Kbps to 8 Mbps, depending on the characteristics of the twisted-pair copper wire, the physical interconnections, the distance the signal travels, environmental conditions, and the specific DSL technology used. Shorter distances, minimum interconnections, and large-gauge copper wire can yield faster data transmission rates.

Many different DSL technologies are in use in the market today. In the industry, the term *xDSL* refers to a number of different forms of DSL, such as Asymmetric Digital Subscriber Line (ADSL), Symmetric Digital Subscriber Line (SDSL), and Very High Data Rate Digital Subscriber Line (VDSL).

ADSL technology provides asymmetrical bandwidth between the center of the star and a leaf node. Data transmission from the center of the star to the leaf node is faster (often at least three times as fast) than the opposite path. ADSL is an attractive service for an Internet service provider (ISP) to offer end users because Internet users typically download more data than they transmit. The ISP is the center of the DSL star topology, and users represent the leaf nodes in this configuration. The ISP connects the twisted-pair wire with an ADSL modem on each end to form a circuit. On the twisted-pair wire, an ADSL modem makes three separate channels: 1) the downstream channel, 2) the duplex channel, and 3) a basic telephone service channel. An ADSL service provider can use all three of these channels to provide data and telephone service to an end user.

Network equipment, such as routers and bridges, typically connects to an ADSL modem using WAN technology such as ATM or Frame Relay. Each end user, or sometimes each channel per end user, appears to the network equipment as a separate virtual circuit. On a high-speed WAN interface to an ADSL modem, a router may support a large number of virtual circuits and corresponding users, as shown in Figure 3-10.

Figure 3-10   *An ADSL Network Connected to a Cisco ATM Interface with Separate Virtual Circuits for each DSL Device*

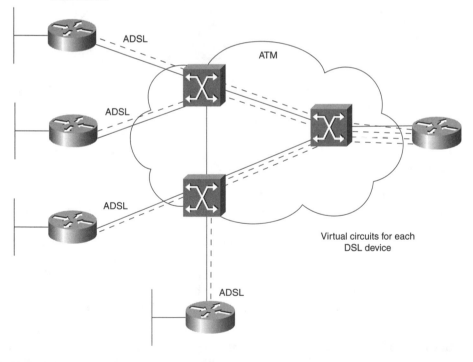

In today's market, ISPs are offering only asymmetrical data services to end users using ADSL, but it is predicted that ISPs may begin to offer local telephone service in the near future. Many factors, including regulatory issues, may affect this future dramatically.

SDSL gives the same amount of bandwidth in both directions (similar to any other full-duplex circuit) between the center of the star and the leaf nodes. SDSL is a technology that many small businesses are using for interoffice connections and connections to the Internet. ISPs and other providers provision and connect to SDSL circuits in a similar manner to ADSL. The main difference is that the modems on either end of the twisted-pair wiring provide a symmetrical data channel.

VDSL, the Very High Data Rate Digital Subscriber Line, enables high-bandwidth connections over short distance of twisted-pair copper telephone lines. Like other forms of DSL, the actual speed varies with the length of the twisted-pair copper between the DSL modems. At this time, VDSL is still a technology being developed, but high data rates would enable a wealth of new services for DSL providers. The developers of VDSL envision that bandwidth rates between 13 Mbps and 55 Mbps are a possibility. Initial development of VDSL will most likely be asymmetrical like ADSL, with upstream bandwidth between 1.6 Mbps and 2.3 Mbps.

Cisco makes a series of routers, the 600 series, that have DSL interfaces. The Cisco 600 series routers can act as Ethernet to DSL bridges and routers or can be modems for both ADSL and SDSL connections. At this time, the Cisco 600 series operates using an IOS variant called the Cisco Broadband Operating System (CBOS). The configuration of the CBOS is different than configuring IOS, but Cisco plans to change the user interface of the CBOS to be compatible with the IOS. Using a combination of the IOS and CBOS products enables you to build a network in a variety of environments.

Integrated Services Digital Network

The Integrated Services Digital Network is a connection-oriented WAN technology that uses digital telephony to digitize voice, data, video, and other information over existing telephone wires. Currently, many telephone carriers throughout the world offer ISDN as a digital subscription service to users for Internet access, voice telephone calls, and videoconferencing. The result of setting up an ISDN network is the capability for ISDN devices to place phone calls over the telephone carrier network that carry many types of data. Conceptually, you may want to think of ISDN as a digital modem that can carry multiple types of data.

Devices that connect to the ISDN network are terminals. The two types of terminals are those that understand ISDN standards, which are called terminal equipment type 1 (TE1), and those that predate ISDN standards, which are called terminal equipment type 2 (TE2). TE2s connect to the ISDN network using a terminal adapter (TA). TE1s do not need a TA.

The next step in talking to the ISDN network is to connect to a network termination type 1 (NT1) or network termination type 2 (NT2) device. Both types of network termination devices convert wiring used within the telephone carrier (four-wire) network to the wiring most often found in homes and businesses throughout the world (two-wire local loop).

In North America, it is common to find an NT1 at a user location and inside a networking device. Most ISDN connections in North America from ISDN cards in PCs or from ISDN routers use a built-in NT1. Elsewhere, the telephone carrier provides the NT1; it is not part of the ISDN device at the user location. The NT2, which adds data link layer and network layer functionality to an NT1, usually is used with connecting private branch exchange (PBX) devices. The relationship between these ISDN components is shown in Figure 3-11.

Figure 3-11   *The Components of an ISDN Network*

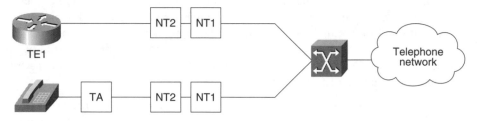

ISDN provides two types of services to devices: Basic Rate Interface (BRI) and Primary Rate Interface (PRI). An ISDN BRI interface offers two *B channels* and one *D channel* (2B+D). BRI B channel service, which operates at 64 Kbps, is used to carry user data. BRI D channel service, which operates at 16 Kbps, is normally used to transfer ISDN control information. The BRI D channel can be set up to carry user data under some circumstances. (It is often used to carry X.25 traffic in Europe.) Using a single B channel, a BRI interface can transfer data at 64 Kbps, but using both B channels, ISDN can achieve transfer rates of 128 Kbps.

An ISDN PRI offers 23 B channels at 64 Kbps each and one D channel, also operating at 64 Kbps, in North America and Japan. This means that a PRI interface can be used to place 23 different digital phone calls. In Europe, Australia, and other parts of the world, ISDN PRI provides 30 B channels and 1 D channel at 64 Kbps each.

A service profile identifier (SPID) is a number that some telephone carriers use to define the services available to an ISDN device. In many cases, the SPID number is the equivalent of the ISDN device's phone number. The ISDN device gives the SPID to the ISDN switch, which then allows the device to access the network for BRI or PRI service. Without providing a valid SPID, many ISDN switches do not allow an ISDN device to place a call on the network.

ISDN Interface Configuration Subcommands

The configuration of ISDN on Cisco IOS devices requires you to tell the device the ISDN switch type to which it is connected. This requirement is needed because the ISDN terminal needs to talk to each different vendor's ISDN switch in a proprietary manner.

NOTE   You can find all the ISDN switch types available for the IOS device you are using by invoking the IOS Help system with the configuration command **isdn switch-type ?**. Your telephone carrier should tell you the switch type you are connected to when you order ISDN service.

You can configure the ISDN switch type to which the IOS device is connected with the **isdn switch-type** major command. The Cisco device needs to know the manufacturer of the ISDN switch it will talk to, because each manufacturer has a proprietary protocol for signaling. Without the proper ISDN switch type configured, the Cisco device cannot communicate with the ISDN switch at the telephone carrier facility.

For each ISDN BRI interface, you need to specify the SPIDs using the **isdn spid1** and **isdn spid2** interface subcommands. Each SPID identifies a unique B channel to the ISDN switch. We need to specify the two different SPIDs for a BRI interface.

To use ISDN PRI on a Cisco device, you need an ISDN PRI interface. Currently, this type of interface is supported on the high-end and midrange routers and access servers, such as the Cisco 3600, Cisco 4000, and Cisco 7000 series routers, and the Cisco 5300 access servers.

The PRI communicates with the ISDN switch via a T1 controller. A T1 controller is a set of data link software that handles the data link signaling on the interface. You need to specify the data link-specific information for the T1 controller, such as the framing method and line coding method. In the following example, we configure a T1 controller on **interface serial 1/0** for Extended Superframe (ESF) framing, binary 8-zero substitution (B8ZS) line coding, and an ISDN PRI using 24 timeslots. ESF is a framing type used on T1 circuits. It consists of 24 frames of 192 data bits each, with the 193rd bit providing timing and other functions. B8ZS is a line-coding mechanism that guarantees ones density over a link by substituting a special code whenever 8 consecutive zeros are sent and then removes the special code at the remote end of the connection.

```
Router#configure
Configuring from terminal, memory, or network [terminal]?
Enter configuration commands, one per line. End with CTRL+Z.
Router(config)#controller T1 1/0
Router(config-if)#framing esf
Router(config-if)#linecode b8zs
Router(config-if)#pri-group timeslots 1-24
Router(config-if)#^Z
```

In the following example, we configure the interface BRI0 on the ZIP network access server in Seoul to talk to the Northern Telecom DMS100 switch to which it is attached. We also configure the ISDN interface to encapsulate data in PPP after the digital call is placed. We need to specify PPP encapsulation because ISDN specifies the method used to establish the digital phone call, not the data link layer encapsulation for packets across this technology:

```
Seoul-AS1#configure
Configuring from terminal, memory, or network [terminal]?
Enter configuration commands, one per line. End with CTRL+Z.
Seoul-AS1(config)#isdn switch-type basic-dms100
Seoul-AS1(config)#interface bri0
Seoul-AS1(config-if)#encapsulation ppp
Seoul-AS1(config-if)#isdn spid1 8864567832
Seoul-AS1(config-if)#isdn spid2 8864567833
Seoul-AS1(config-if)#^Z
```

You can view the status of an ISDN interface with the **show interfaces** command. In the following example, we examine the status of the BRI0 interface on the Seoul-AS1 access server:

```
BRI0 is up, line protocol is up (spoofing)
  Hardware is BRI with U interface and external S bus interface
  MTU 1500 bytes, BW 64 Kbit, DLY 20000 usec, rely 255/255, load 1/255
  Encapsulation PPP, loopback not set
  Last input 00:00:02, output never, output hang never
  Last clearing of "show interface" counters never
  Queueing strategy: fifo
  Output queue 0/40, 0 drops; input queue 0/75, 0 drops
  5 minute input rate 0 bits/sec, 0 packets/sec
  5 minute output rate 0 bits/sec, 0 packets/sec
     644807 packets input, 2938029 bytes, 0 no buffer
     Received 0 broadcasts, 0 runts, 0 giants
     0 input errors, 0 CRC, 0 frame, 0 overrun, 0 ignored, 0 abort
     700200 packets output, 3329945 bytes, 0 underruns
     0 output errors, 0 collisions, 5 interface resets
     0 output buffer failures, 0 output buffers swapped out
     3 carrier transitions
```

Note in the first line of this output that the interface BRI0 is shown as *spoofing*. Spoofing means that the ISDN interface always pretends to be up for routing packets, even though it may not have a valid digital call placed. The ISDN interface spoofs the routing protocol and other software in the IOS device into believing that the interface is up and running so that the ISDN interface receives packets and then places the digital call with the ISDN network. After the call is made, the interface stays up (and is not spoofing) for a period of time until the call is idle. The interface then hangs up the call and returns to the spoofing mode until it needs to place another digital call to route data. This mechanism—spoofing that the interface is up, dialing the digital call to pass the data, and then hanging up the call when idle—is called *dial-on-demand routing*. In the fourth line of the previous output, you can see that the ISDN interface is using PPP encapsulation.

Summary

The basic IOS configuration commands for each LAN and WAN protocol discussed in this chapter are summarized in Table 3-2 and in the following list. Now that you understand the LAN and WAN technologies that operate on the data link layer of the OSI reference model, we move on to discussing the network layer and configuring the Cisco IOS devices for the Internet Protocol (IP).

- The **interface** major command is used to identify an interface by name and to begin configuring it. Naming conventions exist for fixed devices, devices with interchangeable interface cards, and devices with VIP cards.

- Adding a description of each interface with the **description** subcommand is recommended for efficient administration and record keeping. The description appears in the **show interfaces** output for an interface.

- The **shutdown** command causes an interface to be administratively down.

- The **encapsulation** subcommand specifies the format of the data sent and the data-link protocol for an interface. LAN interfaces don't require this configuration usually, but WAN interfaces often do.

Table 3-2   *Summary of IOS Configuration Commands for LAN and WAN*

Protocol	Relevant Commands	Description/Purpose
Ethernet and Fast Ethernet	**media-type {aui, 10baseT, mii, 100basex}**	Tells the router which connection is active on the interface: AUI, RJ-45, or MII.
Fast Ethernet and Gigabit Ethernet	**full-duplex**	Enables full-duplex communication on an interface.
Token Ring	**ring-speed {4 | 16}**	Specifies ring speed as 4 Mbps or 16 Mbps.
	early-token-ring	Enables early token release on an interface.
X.25	**x25 address** *x121 address*	Defines the local X.121 address on an X.25 serial interface.
	x25 ips; **x25 ops**	Configures, respectively, the input packet size and output packet size on the serial interface.
	x25 win; **x25 wout**	Configures, respectively, the input window size and output window size.
Frame Relay	**frame-relay interface-dlci**	Sets the address DLCI on the interface.
	frame-relay lmi-type	Sets the LMI type on the interface.
ATM	**atm pvc**	Specifies the permanent virtual circuits that exist on a given interface.

continues

Table 3-2 *Summary of IOS Configuration Commands for LAN and WAN (Continued)*

Protocol	Relevant Commands	Description/Purpose
DSL	**set bridging**	Sets the bridging options on a Cisco600 (CBOS only).
	set interface	Sets interface parameters on a Cisco600 (CBOS only).
ISDN	**isdn switch-type**	Specifies the type of switch to which the IOS device is connected.
	isdn spid1; **isdn spid2**	Specifies the SPID numbers for each BRI interface.
	pri-group timeslots	Specifies relevant time slots for the controller interface.
T1	**framing**	Specifies the framing protocol for channels on the controller interface.
	linecode	Specifies the line-encoding protocol for channels on the controller interface.

Table 3-3 *Summary of EXEC Commands for LAN and WAN*

Command	Description
show frame pvc	Displays statistics for Frame Relay permanent virtual circuits.
show frame *svc maplist***:**	Displays statistics for Frame Relay switched virtual circuits.
show interfaces	Displays statistics for device interfaces.
show x25 vc	Displays statistics for X.25 virtual circuits.

References

The following references explore the subjects in this chapter further:

Cisco Systems, at al. *Internetworking Technologies Handbook,* Third Edition. Indianapolis, Indiana: Cisco Press, 2001.

Stallings, W. *Networking Standards: A Guide to OSI, ISDN, LAN, and MAN Standards.* Reading, Massachusetts: Addison-Wesley Publishing Company, 1993.

TCP/IP Addressing—Fundamentals of the address structure and the network classes of the IP protocol.

Configuring IP Addresses—Overview of selecting and organizing an address space. Also gives address configuration examples for different LAN and WAN types.

IP Routing Configuration—Basics of routing configuration, including static routes, classless routing, summary and default routes, and related **show** commands.

Configuring IP Routing Protocols—Characteristics of the major dynamic routing protocols, and basic configuration examples for each. In addition, the **distribute-list**, **passive-interface**, and **no auto-summary** commands are introduced.

Configuring IP Filtering via Access Lists—How to control network access and security through the use of the **access-list**, **ip access list**, and **access-group** commands.

Configuring Basic IP Dialup Services—How to configure remote access for asynchronous and ISDN connections.

Verifying IP Connectivity and Troubleshooting—How to identify connectivity problems through the use of the **show**, **ping**, **trace**, and **debug** commands.

Configuring Other IP Options—Configuration examples for domain name services, broadcast forwarding, IOS DHCP Server, and Hot Standby Router Protocol.

CHAPTER 4

TCP/IP Basics

In this chapter, we examine the configuration and setup of the popular Transmission Control Protocol/Internet Protocol, commonly referred to as TCP/IP, for Cisco IOS devices. Developed in the mid-1970s as a Defense Advanced Research Projects Agency (DARPA) project to provide nationwide communication services to research facilities and universities, TCP/IP has emerged as the de facto protocol standard for networking dissimilar computer systems.

This chapter begins with a brief overview of some fundamentals of TCP/IP, including addressing, network classes, and organization of your network's address space. However, the focus of this chapter is on configuring TCP/IP for the Cisco IOS. For a more comprehensive treatment of TCP/IP, we recommend that you consult one of several good volumes currently available (see the "References" section at the end of this chapter).

TCP/IP Addressing

This section introduces the structure of the IP address, including the network, subnetwork, and host portions. We explain how a user determines what IP addressing to use and what configuration commands are required to implement the desired address scheme.

Address Structure

TCP/IP is a collection of communication protocols that define how different computers are addressed on the network, what methods are used to move information from one computer to another, and some services that are available between computers. The router primarily deals with the network layer (IP) and the transport layers (UDP and TCP) in performing its routing and switching functions.

TCP/IP Standards

TCP/IP is often described as an *open standard*, which means that no one company or person controls the specifications of the protocol or the way in which it operates. Instead, a governing body called the Internet Engineering Task Force (IETF), consisting of networking industry experts and company representatives, guides the evolution of the protocol. Working groups within IETF review, discuss, recommend, and approve proposed changes to the standards by means of vehicles called Request For Comments (RFC).

All of the concepts and many of the topics covered in this chapter are defined by the hundreds of RFCs that make up the standards for TCP/IP. Though often dry reading and technical in nature, the RFCs provide the most complete definitions of the TCP/IP protocols. As of this writing, RFC documents can be obtained from the Information Sciences Institute of the University of Southern California (ISI) web site, at www.rfc-editor.org/rfc.html.

Internet Protocol (IP), the addressing component of TCP/IP, operates at Layer 3 of the OSI model. Each station that wants to communicate with another has a unique IP address, in the same way that each house on a street has an individual address. The IP address is a little more complex than a street address (computers like those 0s and 1s), but after a little examination, it won't seem so mysterious.

At Layer 4 of the OSI model for TCP/IP are the two primary transport protocols, User Datagram Protocol (UDP) and TCP. As mentioned previously, the transport protocols are responsible for basic transfer mechanisms, flow control, reliability, and error checking of communications between stations. UDP is considered unreliable because packets sent using this protocol are not acknowledged by the receiving station. It is considered connectionless because a sending station is not required to advise a receiving station of its desire to form a communications channel over which to pass data. In contrast, TCP is considered a connection-oriented protocol because a sending station must advise the receiving station of its desire to form the communications channel. Packets sent via TCP are tagged with sequence numbers, and the sending and receiving stations each acknowledge the receipt of one another's packets.

The IP address is a 32-bit binary address written in four groups of 8 bits called octets. The complete address represents the three components of the addressing model of IP—namely, the network, subnetwork, and host portions of the address. First, let's look at the address numbering itself.

A typical IP address written in 32-bit binary might look like the following:

```
10101100.00010000.00000001.00000001
```

Each of the 8 bits in an octet can take on the value of 0 or 1. Therefore, the values can range from 00000000 to 11111111 in each octet. You can already see that managing 32-bit addresses in binary can be cumbersome and prone to errors. Recognizing that fact, the developers of TCP/IP decided that the binary should be reserved for computers and that IP addresses should be converted to decimal form (the common way people look at numbers) for easier human interaction. Therefore, an octet in which all bit positions are set to 1 is equivalent to 255 in decimal form:

```
 1   1   1   1  1   1   1    1  = Binary Positions
128  64  32  16  8   4   2    1  = Decimal Equivalent
```

Adding up the decimal equivalent of the binary number, we have the following:

```
128+64+32+16+8+4+2+1  =  255
```

Now, let's convert an address example:

```
  1   0  1  01 1 0 0.  0  0   0  1 0 0 0 0.  0   0   0   0 0 0 0 1.  0   0   0   0 0 0 0 1
 128 64 32 16 8 4 2 1.128 64 32 16 8 4 2 1 . 128 64 32 16 8 4 2 1. 128 64 32 16 8 4 2 1
128+0+32+0+8+4+0+0=172  . 0+0+0+16+0+0+0+0=16  . 0+0+0+0+0+0+0+1 = 1 . 0+0+0+0+0+0+0+1 = 1
```

Therefore, the decimal notation for this IP address is 172.16.1.1.

The IP address represents the three components of the IP addressing model: the network component, the subnetwork (often shortened to subnet) component, and the host component. The three components describe the different levels of entity specificity within a collection of networked systems. The host component is most specific, describing the address of a single workstation or server. The network component is most general, describing the address of a collection of hosts within the same logical computer network. The subnet component falls between the network and host components. It describes the address of a subset of the hosts within the overall network address space.

The subnet is created by "borrowing" a portion of the host component to make address subgroupings within the same logical network. The subnet component typically identifies a collection of systems within a LAN or WAN segment. Read from left to right, an IP address moves from the least-specific portion of the address (the network portion) to the next most specific portion (the subnet) to the most specific portion (the host). Where the breaks between the three levels occur in the address depends on the address class and how the address has been subnetted.

As originally specified in the RFCs, five classes of network addresses exist, each distinguished by how many initial bits of the address are set to 1:

- Originally Class A network addresses were intended mainly for very large networks. With Class A addresses, the first bit of the first octet is reserved and set to 0, and the next seven bits are used to identify the network component. The three remaining octets make up the host component. Given these groupings, Class A addresses provide relatively few networks, but each network can accommodate many hosts within the given address space.

- In Class B network addresses, the first two bits of the first octet are reserved; the first bit is set to 1, with the second bit set to 0. This construction gives Class B addresses 14 bits for the network component and 16 bits for the host component. Class B network addresses allow for roughly equal numbers of networks and the hosts on those networks.

- In Class C network addresses, the first three bits for the first octet are reserved; the first two bits are set to 1, and the third is set to 0. This construction gives Class C addresses 22 bits for the network component and only eight bits for the host components. There can be millions of Class C networks; however, each one can support only 255 hosts.

- Class D addresses are reserved for multicast groups. In Class D addresses, the first four bits of the first octet are reserved, and the first three bits are set to 1. A multicast address does not represent a single station address, but rather a group of stations that want to receive information. With multicasting, a station can send a single stream of information to a specific multicast IP address. The network devices—such as routers and switches—then replicate the stream, sending it to multiple stations that have to receive the data stream.

- Class E addresses are defined by IP. Although they are unused at this time, they are reserved for future use. In Class E addresses, the first four bits of the first octet are all set to 1.

Figure 4-1 illustrates the address structure of network Classes A, B, and C.

Figure 4-1   *Classes A, B, and C Address Structure*

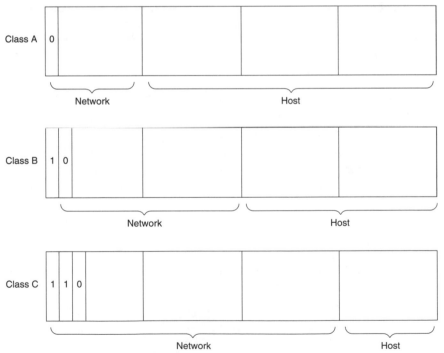

When converting an IP address from decimal to binary and determining how many of the high-order bits are set to 1, it is easy to see to which network class an address belongs. Assuming that there is no subnetting, knowing the class to which the address belongs tells us what portion of the address to read as the network portion and what portion to read as the host portion. Devices such as routers need to decipher this information to deliver data to the appropriate destination.

If a network is subnetted, however, it is not possible to tell at a glance how much of the host portion of the address has been borrowed to make the subnet. To solve this dilemma, IP addresses also have a subnet mask (commonly referred to as the network mask). Like the IP address, the network mask is a 32-bit binary number, grouped into four octets, that can be expressed in decimal notation. Unlike the IP address, however, the network mask has bits set to 1 in all positions except for the host portion of the IP address.

For example, a Class B network with no subnetting defined has a mask of 255.255.0.0, in which the upper 16 bits of the mask denote the network portion of the IP address and the lower 16 bits denote the host portion of the IP address. A Class B network in which seven bits of the host portion of the address have been used for subnetting would have a mask of 255.255.254.0. A Class C network with four bits of subnetting would have a mask of 255.255.255.240. Figure 4-2 shows the relationship between the network mask and the IP address.

Subnetting gives network administrators the flexibility to assign a unique network identifier to each LAN and WAN segment without having to obtain a separate network address space for each. For example, instead of a single Class B network address having one logical network segment of more than 65,000 hosts, a subnetting scheme that borrows eight bits from the host component allows for 255 logical network segments of 255 hosts each. By pairing an IP address with its network mask, it is possible to determine exactly which bits of the address correspond to the network, subnet, and host components. For example, an IP address of 131.108.3.4 with a network mask of 255.255.0.0 has a network component of 131.108.0.0, a host component of 3.4, and no subnet component. An IP address of 131.108.3.4 with a network mask of 255.255.255.0 has a network component of 131.108.0.0, a subnet component of 3, and a host component of 4.

With today's routing protocols carrying network mask information as well as network information in their updates, you can use multiple network masks within a single logical IP network to increase the efficiency of IP address utilization.

The concept of the network mask has been extended beyond its original subnet usage. In response to the explosive growth of the Internet, the number of IP network addresses requested, the shortage of IP address space, and the size of the global IP routing table, the agencies that issue IP addresses might not issue IP addresses along the specified class boundaries described thus far. Instead, they might choose to group multiple IP network addresses of a given class into what is called a supernet, or a classless interdomain route (CIDR) block.

Figure 4-2   *Sample Network Masks*

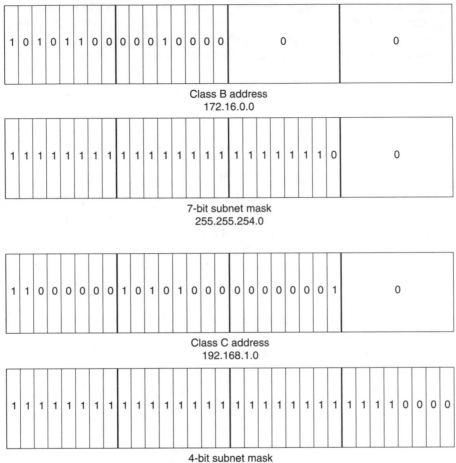

Class B address
172.16.0.0

7-bit subnet mask
255.255.254.0

Class C address
192.168.1.0

4-bit subnet mask
255.255.255.240

Additionally, some of the former Class A networks have been subdivided and issued as smaller CIDR blocks to companies and ISPs. In the past, a company or ISP might have been issued a Class B network. Today, it might be issued 255 Class C addresses, ranging from 209.32.0.0 to 209.32.255.0. The natural network mask of these Class C networks—with no subnetting within the block of addresses—is 255.255.255.0. However, by shortening the mask and creating a supernet of these addresses, the same group of addresses can be represented by the network address 209.32.0.0 and network mask 255.255.0.0. The organization that receives an allocation of a CIDR block is then free to further subdivide that network address space as either subnets within their logical network or as allocations to their customers.

This same method can be applied to the Class A addresses in reverse. Formerly, the network address 12.0.0.0 with a natural network mask of 255.0.0.0 would have to be assigned to one company or ISP. Now, this network address can be treated as a block of addresses, and smaller pieces can be allocated to multiple entities. For example, the group of addresses from 12.1.0.0 through 12.1.255.0 can be represented as a single CIDR block with network address 12.1.0.0 and a network mask of 255.255.0.0. By subdividing these formerly large network address blocks, larger numbers of IP network addresses have been made available, and address exhaustion has been slowed.

Writing and describing network addresses as four dotted-decimal octets followed by a four-dotted-decimal octet network mask has always been somewhat cumbersome. A more precise and compact way of describing the address space was desired when assigning CIDR blocks of addresses. The creation of the classless IP network address system provided the network community with a new shorthand for writing IP network masks.

In this shorthand, a forward slash, /, followed by the number of bits set to 1 in the network mask, is used instead of the four-octet dotted-decimal mask. A network mask of 255.255.0.0 has 16 bits of ones, so it can be written as /16 (pronounced "slash sixteen"). A network mask of 255.255.252.0 has 22 bits of ones, so it can be written as /22. This type of mask is known as a bit-count mask. Combined with an IP network address, the network shorthand of 131.108.0.0/16 can be used to represent 131.108.0.0 mask 255.255.0.0. Likewise, 206.220.224.0/22 can be used to represent 206.220.224.0 mask 255.255.252.0 (which itself is a CIDR block representing the Class C addresses 206.220.224.0 through 206.220.227.0, each with mask 255.255.255.0).

NOTE   During the system configuration dialog described in Chapter 2, "The Basics of Device Configuration," it is assumed that all network addresses fall along the classful network boundaries described earlier. The *Number of bits in subnet field [0]:* question that is posed to the user is asking how many bits of the host component should be used for subnetting based on the class of the network number the user entered. If the network number is a Class A network, such as 17.0.0.0, 24 bits of the host field could be used for subnetting. If the user indicates that nine bits are used for subnetting, the IOS calculates the appropriate network mask—in this case, 255.255.128.0.

Configuring IP Addresses

Before any addresses can be assigned, you must decide what address space to use for the devices in your network and how to allocate that address space. This decision is important—the way in which you assign addresses now may have a serious impact on your network in the future. Answering the following questions helps you determine what address space to use:

- Will my network connect to the Internet via an Internet service provider (ISP) or a network service provider (NSP)? If it does, will there be more than one ISP or NSP connection?

- Will my network connect directly with another company's network (such as a parent company)?

- How many unique LAN and WAN segments will I need in my network?

- How many unique hosts will reside on a typical LAN segment? What is the maximum number? What is the minimum number?

If your network will connect to the Internet or to another company's network, it is important for it to have a unique network address space. If you choose network addresses that are the same as those used in another network, routers within the Internet cannot properly distinguish the duplicate addresses. If your network connects to the Internet via a single ISP or NSP, that provider normally provides you with unique address space from a large pool that has been allocated to it by one of a number of network address registries. These registries include the American Registry for Internet Numbers (ARIN), Réseaux IP Européens (RIPE), and Asia Pacific Network Information Center (APNIC). The ISP allocates your network address space based on factors such as the number of hosts in your network, the number of physical LAN and WAN segments, and the expected growth of your network.

In cases in which your network is connected to multiple service providers, there are two options for obtaining address space. With the first option, your network has IP addresses assigned by one ISP. Because these addresses are assigned out of the ISP's address space, traffic coming to your network follows a path through that service provider's network. However, your network is connected to multiple service providers, so traffic leaving your network can take a different path from inbound traffic, a situation known as asymmetric routing. This scenario may be fine for your network if the predominant traffic flow is outbound and the desire is to load-share. This scenario might also be okay if the additional ISP connection is simply for redundancy (in case of failure). But this scenario may be less than optimal if your predominant traffic flow is inbound to your network and the desire is to load-share across the multiple ISPs.

The second scenario for obtaining address space when the network is connected to multiple ISPs is to request it directly from the registry for your region. Generally speaking, the registries discourage this practice and have set up stringent guidelines for IP address assignments directly to end user networks. The explosive growth in the number of unique networks on the Internet has resulted in a lack of available address space and an exponential growth in the size of the routing tables for the complete Internet. These challenges have prompted the registries to adopt their stringent policies for distributing IP addresses.

Requesting addresses directly from a registry is appropriate in situations in which the predominant traffic flow to your network is inbound and there is a desire to share that load across multiple service providers. The disadvantage of requesting address space directly from a registry is that the issuing body may grant your network only a very small address allocation. As a result of this limited allocation, not all service providers on the Internet will propagate information about your network globally. If information about your network is not available globally, there will be networks that cannot reach your network, and vice versa.

NOTE	Guidelines for requesting IP address space from the registries can be found on each of the respective registries' web sites: • **ARIN**—www.arin.net • **RIPE**—www.ripe.net • **APNIC**—www.apnic.net

If your network has no plans to connect to the Internet, or if you intend to use advanced firewall and Network Address Translation (NAT) techniques found in products such as the Cisco Systems Private Internet Exchange (PIX) product, it is highly desirable to use IP addresses from a class of addresses that have been designated as private addresses by the IETF. The addresses in this set are considered private because information about these networks is not propagated on the Internet by any ISP or NSP. Because information about these addresses is not propagated, they can be used repeatedly by multiple companies, thereby conserving the amount of public addresses available. The set of private IP addresses is defined in RFC 1918, "Address Allocation for Private Internets," as follows:

```
10.0.0.0-10.255.255.255
172.16.0.0-172.31.255.255
192.168.0.0-192.168.255.255
```

After IP addresses have been assigned by your ISP or registry, or after private address space has been selected, that address space must be allocated across the whole of your network. The way that address space is allocated depends primarily on how many hosts will be connected to a given LAN segment, how many LAN/WAN segments are in your network, and how much address space is available for your network. If the network is using private IP addresses, the amount of address space available is not as big of a concern. Private IP network 10.0.0.0 can support as many as four million hosts or LAN/WAN segments, depending on the subnet allocation scheme. Here, a network administrator may choose to assign 24-bit subnets from network 10.0.0.0 to all LAN and WAN segments. This allows for 255 hosts on a given segment, which is more than suitable for most LAN segments and is overkill for point-to-point WAN segments with only two devices.

In situations in which IP address space has been assigned by an ISP or registry and may be at a premium, the network administrator may choose to assign subnets of varying length to LAN and WAN segments. For example, on point-to-point WAN segments, assign a network address with a 30-bit mask instead of assigning a network address that can support more than two devices. A single Class C address space that can support 255 devices can then be configured to support 64 point-to-point WAN segments when subnetting to a 30-bit mask. Likewise, with LAN segments, choose a subnetting scheme and network masks that support only the number of devices that will actually reside on that segment. For example, a small remote office with only 10 people does not need a network address that can support 128.

If you use multiple network masks to create subnets that support varying numbers of hosts, the address space allocated to your network is probably more effectively utilized and less quickly exhausted.

TIP   We recommend that an efficient subnetting scheme be used that does not overallocate addresses to segments such as WAN point-to-point interfaces, regardless of the address space that is allocated to your network. As of this writing, the Cisco Systems Technical Assistance Center has created an IP Subnet Design Calculator that is available to registered CCO users at www.cisco.com/techtools/ip_addr.html to aid in the selection and design of IP numbering schemes.

LAN Interface Configuration

Devices such as routers have a unique IP address on each of the LAN segments attached to them. Thus, the router knows which networks are connected to each interface and where packets for those networks should be sent. In contrast, devices such as bridges and switches have only a single IP address for the entire system. Typically, this IP address is used solely for the purposes of remote administration and network management.

Each of the five LAN types described in Chapter 3, "The Basics of Device Interfaces" (Ethernet, Token Ring, Fast Ethernet, Gigabit Ethernet, and FDDI), supports the concept of dynamically mapping the data link address (commonly referred to as the MAC address) found on the LAN adapter to the IP address assigned to the interface. This process, which is called address resolution, is supported by a protocol called the Address Resolution Protocol (ARP).

When an IP station needs to contact another IP station on the same logical network and doesn't know that station's data link address, it sends a broadcast requesting that a data link address be supplied for the desired IP address. This process is illustrated in Figure 4-3. Each station in that logical network examines the request and, if the requested IP address matches that station, responds with its MAC address. Therefore, a station does not need to know which specific MAC addresses reside on its logical network to communicate with them. In contrast, many of the WAN protocols do not support a dynamic mapping of the data link address to the IP address and require additional IP address configuration to communicate with other stations across a WAN interface.

Figure 4-3   *An IP Router Sends an ARP Request for the Unknown MAC Address of an IP Destination*

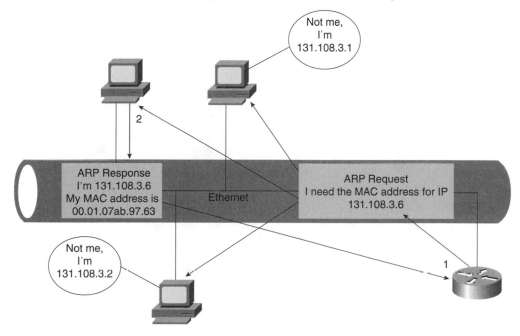

To examine LAN interface configuration, we utilize the IP network addresses that were selected for the ZIP network, which are summarized in Table 4-1.

Table 4-1   *ZIP Network IP Network Address Allocation*

Network Segment	Assigned IP Network Address and Mask
Network summary route	131.108.0.0/16
Singapore Ethernet LAN	131.108.1.0/25
Kuala Lumpur Ethernet LAN	131.108.2.0/25
Seoul Ethernet LAN	131.108.3.0/25
San Francisco Fast Ethernet LAN	131.108.20.0/22
San Jose Token Ring LAN	131.108.100.0/24
SF-1 Ethernet LAN	131.108.101.0/24

continues

Table 4-1   *ZIP Network IP Network Address Allocation (Continued)*

Network Segment	Assigned IP Network Address and Mask
SF-2 first Ethernet LAN	131.108.110.0/24
SF-2 second Ethernet LAN	131.108.120.0/24
SF-Core-1->San-Jose point-to-point HDLC WAN	131.108.240.0/30
SF-Core-2->Seoul-2 point-to-point HDLC WAN	131.108.240.4/30
San-Jose->Seoul-1 point-to-point HDLC WAN	131.108.241.0/30
Seoul-1->Kuala Lumpur point-to-point Frame Relay WAN	131.108.242.0/30
Seoul-1->Singapore point-to-point Frame Relay WAN	131.108.242.4/30
Loopback interfaces on individual routers	131.108.254.0/32
ZIPnet->ISP point-to-point HDLC Internet connection in San Francisco	192.7.2.0/30 (assigned by ISP)
ZIPnet->ISP point-to-point HDLC Internet connection in Seoul, Korea	211.21.2.0/30 (assigned by ISP)

Figure 4-4 shows the logical IP address topology for the complete ZIP network.

In addition to the assignment of IP network addresses, the following IP addresses have been assigned to workstations that perform the indicated function for the ZIP network:

- 131.108.20.45: SNMP management station
- 131.108.21.70: Corporate DHCP server and WINS server
- 131.108.101.34: Primary SMTP mail and DNS server
- 131.108.101.35: Secondary SMTP mail and DNS server
- 131.108.101.100: WWW and FTP server
- 131.108.110.33: Syslog, TACACS+, and RADIUS server

Assigning IP addresses to both LAN and WAN interfaces is accomplished with the Cisco IOS interface configuration subcommand **ip address**. This command requires that you supply both the IP address and the network mask for that IP address.

Figure 4-4   *ZIP Network's IP Address Topology*

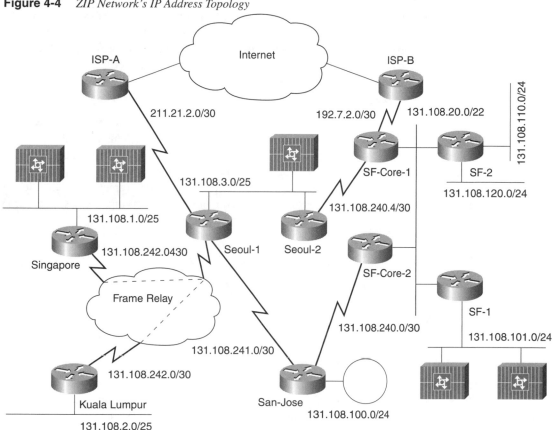

In the following example, we configure the SF-2 router with IP addresses on each of its three LAN interfaces. In each case, we preface the **ip address** subcommand with the major configuration command **interface** to reference the LAN interface to which **the ip address** command should be applied:

```
SF-2#configure
Configuring from terminal, memory, or network [terminal]?
Enter configuration commands, one per line.  End with CNTL/Z.
SF-2(config)#interface ethernet  0
SF-2(config-if)#ip address 131.108.110.1 255.255.255.0
SF-2(config-if)#interface ethernet 1
SF-2(config-if)#ip address 131.108.120.1 255.255.255.0
SF-2(config-if)#interface fastethernet 0
SF-2(config-if)#ip address 131.108.20.2 255.255.252.0
SF-2(config-if)#^Z
```

TIP   We recommend that you reserve some IP addresses at either the start or the end of each
            LAN network address space for routers and other network infrastructure devices. Having a
            consistent group of addresses for various network devices across all LAN segments aids in
            the troubleshooting process by providing quicker recognition of specific IP addresses.

In some instances, the amount of IP address space allocated to your network may require
the use of a subnetwork that is the first subnet in an address range. This first subnet is
generally referred to as *subnet zero* because all the bits of the subnet portion of the network
mask are 0. Older routing protocols have trouble distinguishing between a major network
such as 131.108.0.0 and the subnet 131.108.0.0; therefore, routers typically do not allow
the use of the first subnet. The following is an example of a user trying to use subnet zero
on the SF-1 router:

```
SF-1#configure
Configuring from terminal, memory, or network [terminal]?
Enter configuration commands, one per line.  End with CNTL/Z.
SF-1(config)#interface ethernet 1
SF-1(config-if)#ip address 131.108.0.1 255.255.255.128
Bad mask 255.255.255.128 for address 131.108.0.1
SF-1(config-if)#^Z
```

In this example, the router warns the user that the network mask is bad because the user
tried to use subnet zero. In the ZIP network, sufficient IP address space is available, so the
first subnet of the assigned address space, 131.108.0.0/25, was not used.

Newer routing protocols are more adept at recognizing the differences between a major
network and subnet zero; therefore, the router has configuration commands to allow the
user to make use of subnet zero. If in the future it is necessary to use subnet zero on the
SF-1 router, the IOS global configuration command **ip subnet-zero** would be required
before entering the **ip address** command:

```
SF-1#configure
Configuring from terminal, memory, or network [terminal]?
Enter configuration commands, one per line.  End with CNTL/Z.
SF-1(config)#ip subnet-zero
SF-1(config)#interface ethernet 1
SF-1(config-if)#ip address 131.108.0.1 255.255.255.128
SF-1(config-if)#^Z
```

WAN Interface Configuration

IP addressing of WAN interfaces is similar in many ways to LAN interfaces, with the
following exceptions:

- Point-to-point WAN interfaces may be unnumbered.
- Multipoint WAN interfaces, such as Frame Relay, X.25, ISDN, and ATM, require a
  mapping of the data link addresses to IP addresses.

Point-to-Point WAN Interface Addressing

A point-to-point WAN interface is simply an interface in which exactly two devices are connected—one at each end of the line. These types of interfaces are usually found when using dedicated leased data circuits or when two routers are connected back to back via cables or modem-eliminators. Point-to-point connections can also be emulated on a multipoint medium such as Frame Relay or ATM through the use of subinterfaces. There is exactly one device at the opposite end of the line, so there is no question as to what address or which station a packet is sent when it is placed on the point-to-point interface. Given this property, this type of interface (or subinterface) does not require IP addresses as LAN or multipoint WAN interfaces do. In most cases, network administrators prefer to address their point-to-point WAN interfaces for the purposes of network management and ease of troubleshooting. However, if network address space is in short supply, unnumbered interfaces are a definite plus.

If a point-to-point WAN interface, such as a PPP, HDLC, ATM, or Frame Relay subinterface, is assigned an IP address, the **ip address** command is used (which is similar to the addressing of LAN interfaces). As with the LAN interfaces, the **ip address** command requires you to supply the network mask and the actual IP address. You must assign each separate point-to-point WAN connection (or point-to-point subinterface) a separate IP network address. Again, note that the IOS major configuration command **interface** precedes the use of the **ip address** command to denote which WAN interface is being addressed. The following is an example of IP addressing for an HDLC point-to-point interface and for two Frame Relay point-to-point subinterfaces on the ZIP Seoul-1 router:

```
Seoul-1#configure
Configuring from terminal, memory, or network [terminal]?
Enter configuration commands, one per line.  End with CNTL/Z.
Seoul-1(config)# interface serial 0.16 point-to-point
Seoul-1(config-if)#ip address 131.108.242.1 255.255.255.252
Seoul-1(config-if)#interface serial 0.17 point-to-point
Seoul-1(config-if)#ip address 131.108.242.5 255.255.255.252
Seoul-1(config-if)#interface serial 1
Seoul-1(config-if)#ip address 131.108.241.2 255.255.255.252
Seoul-1(config-if)#^Z
```

Although no unnumbered interfaces are currently used in the ZIP network, let's examine the configuration if a WAN interface were added to the Seoul-2 router in the future. An unnumbered IP point-to-point WAN interface is configured using the IOS interface subcommand **ip unnumbered**. The command requires that a reference interface parameter is supplied so that IP routing protocols have an actual IP address to use when running over the unnumbered interface. This reference interface can be a physical interface, such as an Ethernet or Token Ring, or a virtual interface, such as the loopback interface. Each end of the WAN link must be unnumbered—that is, one end cannot be assigned an address and the other be unnumbered. The following is an example of adding the future unnumbered interface to the ZIP Seoul-2 router:

```
Seoul-2#configure
Configuring from terminal, memory, or network [terminal]?
Enter configuration commands, one per line.  End with CNTL/Z.
```

```
Seoul-2(config)#interface serial 1
Seoul-2(config-if)#ip unnumbered loopback 0
Seoul-2(config-if)#^Z
```

IP unnumbered interfaces have two drawbacks. First, you cannot form a virtual terminal connection (via the Telnet protocol, for instance) directly to the serial interface or use SNMP to query the router via the serial interface. (SNMP is a network management protocol; it is discussed in more detail in Chapter 7, "Basic Administrative and Management Issues.") You can make a connection to the IP address of the LAN or virtual interface on the device and query that address for network management. Second, if the unnumbered interface is referenced to a LAN interface and that interface is placed in shutdown or has a fault, you may be unable to reach the device. For this reason, we recommend that unnumbered interfaces be referenced to virtual interfaces, such as the loopback interface.

Multipoint WAN Interface Addressing

A multipoint WAN interface is an interface on which multiple devices can be reached via a single connection to the WAN medium. A packet sent out to a multipoint WAN interface does not know which station it is destined for, so multipoint WAN interfaces must be addressed for IP communications. Furthermore, multipoint WAN technologies, such as X.25, ISDN, ATM, and Frame Relay, have data-link addressing methodologies to distinguish between stations on the WAN, so there must be a mapping of the IP address to the data-link address—in much the same way that IP addresses are mapped to MAC addresses on LAN interfaces. Most of the multipoint WAN technologies have no dynamic method by which to map the IP address to the data-link address. Thus, additional commands are required to provide proper addressing on this type of interface. The exception to this is that Frame Relay does have a dynamic mapping method called Inverse ARP.

Although there are multipoint Frame Relay interfaces in the ZIP network, they are configured to operate as point-to-point connections using subinterfaces. No X.25, ISDN, or ATM is in the ZIP network. Let's examine how multipoint WAN interfaces might be addressed if they were added to the ZIP network device SF-Core-1.

As described in Chapter 3, Frame Relay makes use of the DLCI to distinguish between different virtual circuits on the Frame Relay network. Multiple virtual circuits terminate on a multipoint Frame Relay interface, so multiple DLCIs are associated with it as well. For the IP devices at the ends of those virtual circuits to communicate, their IP addresses must be mapped to the DLCIs. This mapping allows the multipoint device to identify to the Frame Relay network the proper destination virtual circuit for each packet sent out the single physical interface. The packets can then traverse the Frame Relay network. On a multipoint Frame Relay interface, you can perform the mapping manually via the IOS interface configuration **frame relay map** subcommand or rely on the Inverse ARP function. When you are addressing multipoint WAN interfaces, you should assign all devices in the same multipoint network addresses from the same logical IP network number. The following is an example of configuring a multipoint Frame Relay interface using the **frame-relay map** command on the SF-Core-1 router:

```
SF-Core-1#configure
Configuring from terminal, memory, or network [terminal]?
Enter configuration commands, one per line.  End with CNTL/Z.
SF-Core-1(config)#interface serial 1/1
SF-Core-1(config-if)#encapsulation frame-relay ietf
SF-Core-1(config-if)#no inverse-arp
SF-Core-1(config-if)#ip address 131.108.130.1 255.255.255.0
SF-Core-1(config-if)#frame-relay map ip 131.108.130.17 30 cisco broadcast
SF-Core-1(config-if)#frame-relay map ip 131.108.130.20 50 broadcast
SF-Core-1(config-if)#frame-relay map ip 131.108.130.35 62 broadcast
SF-Core-1(config-if)#^Z
```

In the preceding example, the dynamic mapping function Inverse ARP is disabled by the IOS interface configuration subcommand **no inverse-arp**. Three IP addresses are mapped to three virtual circuits and their corresponding DLCI numbers. Additionally, the virtual circuit on DLCI 30 with IP address 131.108.101.17 uses the Cisco "gang of four" encapsulation method rather than the default for the interface. (The default encapsulation is defined as IETF by using the IOS interface configuration subcommand **encapsulation frame-relay ietf**.) The **broadcast** keyword at the end of the **frame-relay map** command instructs the router to forward broadcasts for this interface to this specific virtual circuit.

Optional Keywords and Commands

Like most IOS software commands, all of the IP-to-data link-mapping commands have optional keywords that change the behavior of a virtual circuit or enable/disable special features on that virtual circuit, such as compression. We highlight only the most widely used of those keywords. For a complete explanation of all optional keywords and IOS software commands, refer to the Cisco Connection Documentation CD-ROM or online version at www.cisco.com/univercd/home/home.htm.

If we allowed the Inverse ARP function to perform a dynamic mapping of the IP addresses to DLCI numbers in the preceding example, there would be no need for the **frame-relay map** commands. Instead, the interface would send Inverse ARP queries to each of the virtual circuits identified as active by the Frame Relay network on this interface. Those queries would result in the far-end devices responding with their IP addresses for the particular virtual circuit and DLCI queried. Using Inverse ARP would reduce the example to the following:

```
SF-Core-1#configure
Configuring from terminal, memory, or network [terminal]?
Enter configuration commands, one per line.  End with CNTL/Z.
SF-Core-1(config)#interface serial 1/1
SF-Core-1(config-if)#encapsulation frame-relay ietf
SF-Core-1(config-if)#ip address 131.108.130.1 255.255.255.0
SF-Core-1(config-if)#^Z
```

TIP Frame Relay configuration requires some care. When you rely on Inverse ARP to provide mapping of IP addresses to DLCIs, configuration errors can result in unexpected virtual circuits being dynamically mapped to unknown devices. Also, mixing the IETF and Cisco "gang of four" encapsulations on the same Frame Relay interface requires the use of the **frame-relay map** command.

Static addressing of X.25 WAN interfaces is performed in much the same manner as static addressing of Frame Relay interfaces—that is, with the **static map** command. X.25 interfaces' IP addresses must be mapped to the X.121 addresses that are used to set up the virtual circuits between systems on the X.25 network. Each virtual circuit is identified by the X.121 address used to set up the connection. The following is an example of configuring a new X.25 interface on the ZIP SF-Core-1 router using the IOS interface configuration subcommand **x25 map**:

```
SF-Core-1#configure
Configuring from terminal, memory, or network [terminal]?
Enter configuration commands, one per line.  End with CNTL/Z.
SF-Core-1(config)#interface serial 1/2
SF-Core-1(config-if)#encapsulation x25
SF-Core-1(config-if)#x25 address 44598631
SF-Core-1(config-if)#ip address 131.108.102.1 255.255.255.0
SF-Core-1(config-if)#x25 map ip 131.108.102.15 44593389 broadcast
SF-Core-1(config-if)#x25 map ip 131.108.102.29 44591165 broadcast
SF-Core-1(config-if)#x25 map ip 131.108.102.176 44590712 broadcast
SF-Core-1(config-if)#^Z
```

Addressing ISDN interfaces requires mapping commands similar to those of Frame Relay and X.25. However, the mapping commands are required only when a device wants to establish a call to another device. If a device receives only inbound calls, IP addresses can be dynamically mapped to the incoming device and phone number. The IOS interface configuration subcommand **dialer map** is used to provide the mapping between IP addresses and the system names and phone numbers that are used to set up calls over ISDN. The **name** keyword for the **dialer map** command must be supplied to properly relate the IP address and telephone number to the remote system. Additionally, the **name** keyword is used as part of the authentication process when a connection is established with the remote system. The following is an example of configuring a new ISDN BRI interface on the ZIP Seoul-1 router:

```
Seoul-1#configure
Configuring from terminal, memory, or network [terminal]?
Enter configuration commands, one per line.  End with CNTL/Z.
Seoul-1(config)# interface bri 0
Seoul-1(config-if)# ip address 131.108.103.3 255.255.255.0
Seoul-1(config-if)# dialer map ip 131.108.103.1 name SF-Core-1 broadcast 14085551212
Seoul-1(config-if)# dialer map ip 131.108.103.2 name SF-Core-2 broadcast 14085551313
Seoul-1(config-if)# ^Z
```

Addressing ATM interfaces requires the basic **ip address** command, just like the other types of interfaces that we have explored so far. With ATM interfaces, however, the type of commands used to map IP addresses to the data link layer depends on the type of ATM protocols used, as well as on the type of virtual circuits used. The three possible protocol variations are as follows:

- **Logical link control/Subnetwork Access Protocol (LLC/SNAP) encapsulation with PVCs**—In this model, a permanent virtual circuit is established through the ATM network. Packets are identified as being destined to an IP address at the other end of the specific virtual circuit.

- **LLC/SNAP encapsulation with SVCs**—In this model, IP packets are identified as being destined to a specific statically defined ATM link layer address. ATM switches establish the virtual circuit on demand when the router requests a connection to the ATM address for a specific IP address.

- **IP with ARP**—In this model, the ATM link layer address for a specific IP address is dynamically supplied by a station called the ATM ARP server.

LLC/SNAP encapsulation with PVCs makes use of the IOS interface configuration subcommand **map-group** and the IOS global configuration command **map-list** to map IP addresses to specific PVCs. The following is a configuration example for addressing a new ATM interface with LLC/SNAP and PVCs on the SF-Core-1 router:

```
SF-Core-1#configure
Configuring from terminal, memory, or network [terminal]?
Enter configuration commands, one per line.  End with CNTL/Z.
SF-Core-1(config)#interface atm 1/0
SF-Core-1(config-if)#atm pvc 3 0 21 aal5snap
SF-Core-1(config-if)#atm pvc 5 0 22 aal5snap
SF-Core-1(config-if)#ip address 131.108.104.1 255.255.255.0
SF-Core-1(config-if)#map-group zip1
SF-Core-1(config-if)#map-list zip1
SF-Core-1(config-map-list)#ip 131.108.104.2 atm-vc 3 broadcast
SF-Core-1(config-map-list)#ip 131.108.104.7 atm-vc 5 broadcast
SF-Core-1(config-map-list)# ^Z
```

LLC/SNAP encapsulation with SVCs makes use of the IOS interface configuration subcommand **map-group** and the IOS global configuration command **map-list** to map IP addresses to the network service access point (NSAP) addresses used to identify the remote devices on the ATM network. The following is a configuration example for addressing a new ATM interface with LLC/SNAP and SVCs on the SF-Core-1 router:

```
SF-Core-1#configure
Configuring from terminal, memory, or network [terminal]?
Enter configuration commands, one per line.  End with CNTL/Z.
SF-Core-1(config)#interface atm 1/0
SF-Core-1(config-if)#atm nsap FE.DCBA.01.987654.3210.ABCD.EF12.3456.7890.1234.12
SF-Core-1(config-if)#ip address 131.108.104.1 255.255.255.0
SF-Core-1(config-if)#map-group zip1
SF-Core-1(config-if)#map-list zip1
SF-Core-1(config-map-list)#ip 131.108.104.2 atm-nsap A1.9876.AB.123456.7890.FEDC.BA.1234.5678.ABCD.12
SF-Core-1(config-map-list)#ip 131.108.104.7 atm-nsap B2.9876.AB.123456.7890.FEDC.BA.1234.5678.AB12.12
SF-Core-1(config-map-list)# ^Z
```

Classical IP with ARP requires the **ip address** subcommand to configure IP addresses for the interface. The ATM interface configuration subcommand **atm arp-server** identifies the ATM ARP server address that can resolve IP addresses to ATM NSAP addresses, which is required to establish the virtual circuits. The following is a configuration example for addressing a new ATM interface with Classical IP and ARP on the SF-Core-1 router:

```
SF-Core-1#configure
Configuring from terminal, memory, or network [terminal]?
Enter configuration commands, one per line.  End with CNTL/Z.
SF-Core-1(config)#interface atm 1/0
SF-Core-1(config-if)#atm nsap FE.DCBA.01.987654.3210.ABCD.EF12.3456.7890.1234.12
SF-Core-1(config-if)#ip address 131.108.104.1 255.255.255.0
SF-Core-1(config-if)#atm arp-server nsap 01.ABCD.22.030000.0000.0000.0000.0000.0000.0000.00
SF-Core-1(config-if)#^Z
```

Verifying IP Address Configuration

Verifying the IP addresses and other IP attributes that have been assigned to your interfaces can be accomplished via one of three EXEC commands. The IOS EXEC **show interface** command provides general information about an interface, including the IP address and network mask assigned to it. When a specific interface is supplied as a command parameter, only that interface is displayed. When no interface is specified, all interfaces are shown. The following is output from **the show interface ethernet 0** command executed on the ZIP SF-2 router:

```
SF-2#show interface ethernet 0
Ethernet0 is up, line protocol is up
  Hardware is Lance, address is 0000.0c07.b627 (bia 0000.0c07.b627)
  Internet address is 131.108.110.1 255.255.255.0
  MTU 1500 bytes, BW 10000 Kbit, DLY 1000 usec, rely 255/255, load 1/255
  Encapsulation ARPA, loopback not set, keepalive set (10 sec)
  ARP type: ARPA, ARP Timeout 04:00:00
  Last input 00:00:00, output 00:00:00, output hang never
  Last clearing of "show interface" counters never
  Queuing strategy: fifo
  Output queue 0/40, 0 drops; input queue 0/75, 0 drops
  5 minute input rate 0 bits/sec, 0 packets/sec
  5 minute output rate 1000 bits/sec, 1 packets/sec
     716895 packets input, 69741733 bytes, 0 no buffer
     Received 76561 broadcasts, 0 runts, 0 giants, 0 throttles
     0 input errors, 0 CRC, 0 frame, 0 overrun, 0 ignored, 0 abort
     0 input packets with dribble condition detected
     5148972 packets output, 750393298 bytes, 0 underruns
     0 output errors, 68 collisions, 5 interface resets
     0 babbles, 0 late collision, 286 deferred
     0 lost carrier, 0 no carrier
     0 output buffer failures, 0 output buffers swapped out
```

The IOS EXEC **show ip interface** command provides a complete look at all the parameters associated with the IP configuration of an interface. If a specific interface is supplied as a parameter to the command, only the information about that interface is displayed. When no specific interface is supplied, information about all interfaces is supplied. The following is the output of the **show ip interface ethernet 0** command executed on the ZIP SF-2 router:

```
SF-2#show ip interface ethernet 0
Ethernet0 is up, line protocol is up
  Internet address is 131.108.110.1 255.255.255.0
  Broadcast address is 255.255.255.255
  Address determined by non-volatile memory
  MTU is 1500 bytes
  Helper address is not set
  Directed broadcast forwarding is enabled
  Multicast reserved groups joined: 224.0.0.1 224.0.0.2 224.0.0.10
  Outgoing access list is not set
  Inbound  access list is not set
  Proxy ARP is enabled
  Security level is default
  Split horizon is enabled
  ICMP redirects are always sent
  ICMP unreachables are always sent
  ICMP mask replies are never sent
  IP fast switching is enabled
  IP fast switching on the same interface is disabled
  IP multicast fast switching is enabled
  Router Discovery is disabled
  IP output packet accounting is disabled
  IP access violation accounting is disabled
  TCP/IP header compression is disabled
  Probe proxy name replies are disabled
  Gateway Discovery is disabled
  Policy routing is disabled
  Network address translation is disabled
```

The IOS EXEC **show ip interface** command has an optional form that enables you to see a brief summary of IP address information and interface status for all available interfaces on the device. This summarized version is obtained using the **show ip interface brief** command.

The following is the output of the **show ip interface brief** command executed on the ZIP SF-2 router:

```
SF-2#show ip interface brief
Interface       IP-Address      OK? Method Status    Protocol
Ethernet0       131.108.110.1   YES NVRAM  up          up
Ethernet1       131.108.120.1   YES NVRAM  up          up
FastEthernet    0131.108.20.2    YES NVRAM  up          up
```

In addition to verifying the IP configuration on the interface itself, you can view both the static and the dynamic mappings of IP addresses to data-link addresses on the various WAN multipoint media. To do so, use the IOS EXEC commands **show frame-relay map**, **show atm map**, **show x25 map**, and **show dialer maps**. The following is an example of the output from the **show frame-relay map** command from the ZIP router Seoul-1:

```
Seoul-1#show frame-relay map
Serial0.16 (up): point-to-point dlci, dlci 16(0x10,0x400), broadcast, status
defined, active
Serial0.17 (up): point-to-point dlci, dlci 17(0x11,0x410), broadcast, status
defined, active
Seoul-1#
```

The other WAN protocol mapping commands have output similar to that of the **show frame-relay map** command.

As discussed in the section "TCP/IP Addressing," network masks can be represented in both dotted-decimal and bit-count, or slash, format. The router defaults to use the bit-count format. If you are more comfortable with the dotted-decimal format for verifying network masks, the IOS EXEC command **terminal ip netmask-format decimal** can be used to switch formats. This command is in effect only for the current virtual terminal or console session. The following is an example of using the command on the ZIP Seoul-1 router:

```
Seoul-1#terminal ip netmask-format decimal
Seoul-1#
```

To preserve this format for all virtual terminal or console sessions, you must apply the IOS line configuration subcommand **ip netmask-format decimal** to the desired lines in configuration mode. The following is an example of changing the network mask format for all virtual terminal sessions on the ZIP router Seoul-1:

```
Seoul-1#configure
Configuring from terminal, memory, or network [terminal]?
Enter configuration commands, one per line.  End with CNTL/Z.
Seoul-1(config)#line vty 0 4
Seoul-1(config-line)#ip netmask-format decimal
Seoul-1(config-line)#^Z
```

IP Routing Configuration

Assigning a unique IP address to every device in the network is necessary but not sufficient to enable them to communicate with one another. Devices in an IP network must also know the path or the route to other devices within the same autonomous network or within the Internet to send data packets between one another. Rather than every device in a network having a complete list of all other devices and where they reside on that network, the router acts as a sort of traffic director, performing two functions for the IP network.

First, the router receives packets from a station, determines the optimal path to the destination, and then places the packet on the next LAN or WAN segment that leads to that destination. This process may be repeated several times as a data packet moves from one router to the next in a complex intranetwork or in the Internet itself. This process is described as routing or switching packets. Second, a router must learn where other IP network and subnetworks are, both within the same autonomous network and outside that network—such as within the Internet. To determine where other networks are, routers employ the use of a routing table, which is created by routing algorithms or routing protocols.

Routing protocols can be either static or dynamic in nature. In static protocols, a network administrator manually configures the routing table with the network path information. Static protocols are not robust because they are incapable of reacting to changes in the network and must be reconfigured manually for every change. Dynamic routing protocols rely on the routers themselves to advertise information about the different networks and subnetworks to which they are attached. The numerous different dynamic routing protocols are examined in the section "Configuring IP Routing Protocols," later in this chapter.

Before delving into dynamic routing protocols, however, we examine several more general aspects of IP routing configuration and static routing configuration.

Configuring IP Routing Commands

To enable IP routing, the IOS global configuration command **ip routing** is used. By default, the IOS software is configured for IP routing on devices such as standalone routers. However, if the IP routing has been disabled on such a device, you must re-enable it before switching packets and enabling routing protocols. Some Cisco-integrated router devices do not have IP routing enabled by default. Again, you must use the **ip routing** command to perform the packet switching and routing protocol processes on these devices. In this example, IP routing is enabled on the ZIP router Seoul-1:

```
Seoul-1#configure
Configuring from terminal, memory, or network [terminal]?
Enter configuration commands, one per line.  End with CNTL/Z.
Seoul-1(config)#ip routing
Seoul-1(config)#^Z
```

After IP routing is enabled, the routing table used for switching packets can be built. By default, when an IP address is configured on an interface and that interface is placed in an operational state, the network address for that interface is placed in the routing table. All operational interfaces connected to the router are placed in the routing table. Therefore, if only one router is in your network, it has information about all the different networks or subnets, and there is no need to configure static or dynamic routing. Only when two or more routers exist in the network are static or dynamic routing table entries needed.

To view the IP routing table, use the IOS EXEC command **show ip route**. When entered with no parameters, the entire routing table is displayed. The following is an example of the routing table on the ZIP Seoul-1 router with only the connected interfaces operational and no additional routing table entries configured or learned:

```
Seoul-1#show ip route
Codes: C - connected, S - static, I - IGRP, R - RIP, M - mobile, B - BGP
       D - EIGRP, EX - EIGRP external, O - OSPF, IA - OSPF inter area
       N1 - OSPF NSSA external type 1, N2 - OSPF NSSA external type 2
       E1 - OSPF external type 1, E2 - OSPF external type 2, E - EGP
       i - IS-IS, L1 - IS-IS level-1, L2 - IS-IS level-2, * - candidate default
       U - per-user static route, o - ODR

Gateway of last resort is not set

     131.108.0.0/16 is variably subnetted, 4 subnets, 2 masks
C        131.108.3.0/25 is directly connected, Ethernet0
C        131.108.242.0/30 is directly connected, Serial0.16
C        131.108.242.4/30 is directly connected, Serial0.17
C        131.108.241.0/30 is directly connected, Serial1
```

The **show ip route** command provides an immense amount of data to the network administrator. It is the key tool used to determine what path a packet follows through the network. The first section of output is the legend for the first column of the table itself. It tells us where a route was derived from. In this example, a C tells us that the route is from a directly connected operational interface. The gateway of last resort is the network address of the router to which packets destined for outside this network should be sent when there is no specific routing information on how to reach the destination. In this example, the router has not learned a gateway of last resort because no static routes have been configured and no dynamic routing protocols are running.

The last section of output is the routing table itself. From the notation variably subnetted in this example, we can see that the ZIP Class B network 131.108.0.0 has been configured with multiple network masks. The output also shows that this router has learned four subnet routes and that those four subnet routes have only two different network masks associated with them. Each of the network numbers associated with the IP addresses that were entered on the respective interfaces is listed, along with the bit-count network mask and the associated interface name. It is important to note that the network and subnetwork addresses, not the IP addresses of the individual devices, are listed in the routing table. The network address may represent the route to as few as two hosts (as with a network that has a /30 network mask) or to as many 65536 hosts (as with a network that has a /16 network mask), or to even greater numbers of hosts, depending on the network mask.

The **show ip route** command also has optional parameters that can be used to request only certain types of routes. For example, if the routing table is fully populated with connected, static, and dynamically learned routes, the IOS EXEC command **show ip route connected** can be used to show only those routes learned from operational directly connected interfaces. Likewise, the **show ip route static** command displays only those routes derived from manually configured network path commands. By entering a specific network address as a parameter to the command, only information regarding that specific route is displayed. The following is an example of entering a specific route parameter via the **show ip route 131.108.3.0** command on the ZIP Seoul-1 router:

```
Seoul-1#show ip route 131.108.3.0
Routing entry for 131.108.3.0/25
  Known via "connected", distance 0, metric 0 (connected)
Routing Descriptor Blocks:
  * directly connected, via Ethernet0
      Route metric is 0, traffic share count is 1
```

We explore more optional parameters of the **show ip route** command and explain the meaning of the route metric in the section "Configuring IP Routing Protocols," later in this chapter.

Configuring Static Routing

As noted previously, both static and dynamic routing information can be used to build up the routing table and, therefore, the network path information. Historically, static routes were the first available way for network administrators to build network path tables for routers and some end devices. Static routes do have drawbacks, such as the inability to adapt when a data circuit goes down or when the network topology changes. However, many situations still exist in which the static route is needed and desired. The following are a few examples in which static routes are appropriate:

- A data circuit is particularly unreliable and constantly flaps. In these circumstances, a dynamic routing protocol may inject too much instability, whereas a static route does not change.

- A network is reachable over a dialup connection. Such a network is not capable of providing the constant updates required by a dynamic routing protocol.

- A single connection exists to a single ISP. Rather than learning all the global Internet routes, a single static default route is used. The same is true of a corporate remote office with a single connection back to the corporate intranet.

- A customer or other attached network does not want to exchange dynamic routing information. A static route can be used to provide reachability information for that network.

Configuring static routes is performed by the IOS global configuration command **ip route**. The command takes several parameters, including the network address and the associated network mask, as well as information on where the router should send packets destined for that network. The destination information can take one of several forms:

- A specific IP address of the next router in the path

- The network address of another route in the routing table to which packets should be forwarded

- A directly connected interface where the destination network resides

The first option is fairly straightforward, and it is the predominant way in which static routes are entered. The following is an example of entering a static route on the ZIP SF-Core-1 router. This route directs packets destined to the network address 131.108.230.0/24 over the serial connection to the San-Jose router, which has an address of 131.108.240.2:

```
SF-Core-1#configure
Configuring from terminal, memory, or network [terminal]?
Enter configuration commands, one per line.  End with CNTL/Z.
SF-Core-1(config)#ip route 131.108.230.0 255.255.255.0 131.108.240.2
SF-Core-1(config)#^Z
```

The second option, specifying another network route as the destination, is useful when there are multiple paths for reaching the desired network address. One benefit is the load sharing of traffic across multiple equal-cost paths. Another benefit is that a failure of one of the paths results in traffic being rerouted onto one of the alternative paths. The following is an example on the ZIP SF-Core-1 router. Packets destined to the network address 131.108.231.0/24 are directed to follow the route to the San Jose network 131.108.100.0/24:

```
SF-Core-1#configure
Configuring from terminal, memory, or network [terminal]?
Enter configuration commands, one per line.  End with CNTL/Z.
SF-Core-1(config)#ip route 131.108.231.0 255.255.255.0 131.108.100.0
SF-Core-1(config)#^Z
```

Note that for packets to reach the 131.108.231.0/24 network, a route to the 131.108.100.0/24 network must be in the routing table. Packets for 131.108.231.0/24 are forwarded out the same interface from which packets destined to 131.108.100.0/24 are forwarded.

The last option for specifying a destination—a directly connected interface—is perhaps the least used of the various options. By specifying a directly connected interface as the destination for a route, the network administrator is in effect saying that devices addressed with IP addresses from that network reside on the specified interface. The result is that packets destined to IP addresses for that network must have their IP addresses resolved to the data link layer address for that particular interface type (and the route will appear directly connected in the routing table). In the case of Ethernet, an IP address would have to resolve to a MAC address. In the case of Frame Relay, there would have to be a static Frame Relay map or Inverse ARP mapping that provided DLCI information to IP address mapping. In the case of ISDN, there would have to be a dialer map that maps the IP address to a system name and a phone number.

TIP

Specifying an interface as the destination for a static route is one of the top configuration mistakes made when using the **ip route** command. Some network administrators mistakenly believe that packets are forwarded properly to the next router in a path by simply pointing the route toward a particular interface. Packets are forwarded to the next-hop router only if the IP address for that router is specified or another network route that traverses the next-hop router is specified.

The following is an example of specifying a directly connected interface as the destination in the **ip route** command. In this example, the network address 131.108.232.0/24 is configured to be reachable directly on the Fast Ethernet interface of the ZIP SF-Core-1 router:

```
SF-Core-1#configure
Configuring from terminal, memory, or network [terminal]?
Enter configuration commands, one per line.  End with CNTL/Z.
SF-Core-1(config)#ip route 131.108.232.0 255.255.255.0 fastethernet 0/0
SF-Core-1(config)#^Z
```

Let's verify the routing table on the SF-Core-1 router with the directly connected interfaces and the new static route entries:

```
SF-Core-1#show ip route
Codes: C - connected, S - static, I - IGRP, R - RIP, M - mobile, B - BGP
       D - EIGRP, EX - EIGRP external, O - OSPF, IA - OSPF inter area
       N1 - OSPF NSSA external type 1, N2 - OSPF NSSA external type 2
       E1 - OSPF external type 1, E2 - OSPF external type 2, E - EGP
       i - IS-IS, L1 - IS-IS level-1, L2 - IS-IS level-2, * - candidate default
       U - per-user static route, o - ODR

Gateway of last resort is not set

131.108.0.0/16 is variably subnetted, 5 subnets, 3 masks
```

```
C       131.108.20.0/22 is directly connected, FastEthernet0/0
C       131.108.240.0/30 is directly connected, Serial1/0
S       131.108.230.0/24 [1/0] via 131.108.240.2
S       131.108.231.0/24 [1/0] via 131.108.100.0
S       131.108.232.0/24 [1/0] is directly connected, FastEthernet0/0
```

As packets traverse the router and the destination networks are looked up in the routing table, the router's default behavior matches the most specific network address/network mask pair within the network class for the destination IP address. For example, if a packet is destined to IP address 131.108.21.6 and there is a route to network 131.108.20.0/22, the packet is forwarded out the interface for this route. If for the same destination there are routes to 131.108.20.0/22 and 131.108.21.0/24, the packet is forwarded out the interface for the route to 131.108.21.0/24 because it is a more specific route (with a longer network mask) than the 131.108.20.0/22 route. In the case of the ZIP network, the least-specific route is 131.108.0.0/16; the most-specific routes are the network addresses that are /30.

Configuring for Classless Routing

The ZIP network was assigned a Class B network, as specified by the legacy classful addressing system. However, if it had been assigned a CIDR block of addresses, additional commands would be required to allow the router to match routes in the routing table that are beyond the classful boundaries. Assume that a network was assigned the CIDR block 206.220.224.0/22 (which is composed of the Class C addresses 206.220.224.0/24 through 206.220.227.0/24) and was subnetted and allocated on a router's interface as follows:

- Ethernet 0 is assigned address 206.220.224.0/24.
- Ethernet 1 is assigned address 206.220.225.0/24.
- Ethernet 2 is assigned address 206.220.226.0/23.

The router operates in classful mode by default. Packets destined to 206.220.224.5 are properly routed to Ethernet 0 because the network address is a Class C address and matches the destination IP address. The same is true of Ethernet 1 and a packet destined to 206.220.225.9. However, a packet that is destined to 206.220.226.8 or 206.220.227.12 does not match the route 206.220.226.0/23 for Ethernet 2, and those destination addresses are unreachable. This occurs because the network address of Ethernet 2 is a CIDR block of two Class C addresses. For the router to operate in a classless manner and match destination IP addresses to this CIDR network address, the IOS global configuration command **ip classless** must first be configured. The following is an example of configuring the **ip classless** command on the ZIP SF-Core-1 router:

```
SF-Core-1#configure
Configuring from terminal, memory, or network [terminal]?
Enter configuration commands, one per line.  End with CNTL/Z.
SF-Core-1(config)#ip classless
SF-Core-1(config)#^Z
```

Configuring Summary and Default Routes

In many situations, it is undesirable to carry the entire routing table for an intranet or for the Internet. These situations include a small office with a single connection to the corporate intranet, a router that is configured with insufficient memory, or a single connection to a single ISP. In these situations, end users want to reach certain destination addresses that are not specifically found in the routing table. Under normal circumstances, these packets would be discarded as unreachable destinations. However, through the use of summary routes and default network routes, a router can still have reachability information. A summary route and a default route both provide alternative path information when no route specifically matches a destination IP address.

A summary route provides default reachability information within a given address space. The summary route, which normally follows classful network boundaries, is typically used to provide default reachability information about subnets that are not specifically found in the routing table but that exist within the intranet. In the ZIP network, for example, the route 131.108.0.0/16 would be considered a summary route. If a router in the ZIP network encounters a packet destined to 131.108.99.5 but does not find a specific route—such as 131.108.99.0/24—it usually discards the packet. If in this situation there were a summary route 131.108.0.0/16 in the routing table, the packet would be forwarded out the interface toward the next-hop destination for the summary route.

The summary route usually points to another subnet route within the intranet, but it can also point to a specific next-hop IP address. In either case, the goal of the summary route is to direct packets toward other routers within the intranet that have more complete routing information. The summary route can be configured using the IOS global configuration commands **ip default-network** or **ip route**.

When using the **ip default-network** command, a nonconnected subnet that exists within the intranet is supplied as a parameter to the command. When the **ip route** command is used, the summary route, the network mask, and the nonconnected subnet are supplied as parameters. The following are examples of both commands as configured on the ZIP Singapore router. In these examples, the summary route is 131.108.0.0/16, and the nonconnected subnet used for default reachability is 131.108.20.0, which is found on the SF-Core-1 and SF-Core-2 routers:

```
Singapore#configure
Configuring from terminal, memory, or network [terminal]?
Enter configuration commands, one per line.  End with CNTL/Z.
Singapore(config)#ip default-network 131.108.20.0
Singapore(config)#^Z
Singapore#configure
Configuring from terminal, memory, or network [terminal]?
Enter configuration commands, one per line.  End with CNTL/Z.
Singapore(config)#ip route 131.108.0.0 255.255.0.0 131.108.20.0
Singapore(config)#^Z
```

After it is configured, the summary route appears in the routing table as a less-specific network route with a bit-count mask smaller than the other network and subnetwork routes in the table. In the following **show ip route** example from the ZIP Singapore router,

131.108.0.0/16 is the summary route that was configured in the previous example. Note that the summary route destination of 131.108.20.0 is learned from the ZIP Seoul-1 router:

```
Singapore#show ip route
Codes: C - connected, S - static, I - IGRP, R - RIP, M - mobile, B - BGP
       D - EIGRP, EX - EIGRP external, O - OSPF, IA - OSPF inter area
       N1 - OSPF NSSA external type 1, N2 - OSPF NSSA external type 2
       E1 - OSPF external type 1, E2 - OSPF external type 2, E - EGP
       i - IS-IS, L1 - IS-IS level-1, L2 - IS-IS level-2, * - candidate default
       U - per-user static route, o - ODR

Gateway of last resort is not set

     131.108.0.0/16 is variably subnetted, 4 subnets, 4 masks
C       131.108.1.0/25 is directly connected, Ethernet0
C       131.108.242.4/30 is directly connected, Serial0.100
D       131.108.20.0/22 [1/0] via 131.108.242.5, 20:10:45, Serial0.100
S       131.108.0.0/16 [1/0] via 131.108.20.0
```

NOTE   The IOS software replaces the **ip default-network** command with the summary route version of the **ip route** command when the nonconnected subnet is contained within the same classful network address space of a directly connected interface on the router.

When an IP station is communicating with another company, university, or other entity—either through private network connections or via the Internet—it sends packets that need to reach stations residing in an IP address space other than its own. For example, if a station in the ZIP network is communicating with the popular web site www.yahoo.com, packets originating from the ZIP network address space of 131.108.0.0/16 are destined for Yahoo!'s network address space of 216.32.74.55/22. To forward packets properly, the ZIP network routers need either a route to 216.32.74.55/22 or a less-specific CIDR route giving them the general direction of the Yahoo! network.

As explained earlier, it is unlikely that every router in the ZIP network or even the ZIP Internet connection router has this route in its routing tables. Unless the ZIP network has multiple ISPs or is exchanging dynamic routing information with its sole ISP, the ZIP network routers probably rely on a default network route to provide reachability information for the Yahoo! site, as well as for other sites on the Internet (or potentially within their own intranet).

The basic concept of the default route is that when a router does not have specific routing information for a destination, it will use the default path to a specified network where there are routers with more complete information. Although the default route is similar to the summary route, it is used to direct packets to IP destinations that are outside both the autonomous intranet and the classful address boundaries for a given entity. In the case of the Internet, a company's ISP or the ISP's upstream provider is likely exchanging dynamic routing information with other ISPs about the location and reachability of all networks on the Internet. Using an IP network address in the ISP's network as a default route, a company's Internet connection router forwards packets to unknown destinations toward the ISP and ultimately to routers with more complete routing tables and pictures of the Internet.

We will now discuss some of the many methods for configuring a default network using the IOS software:

- Configuring a default network using a dynamic learned external route
- Configuring a default network using a statically configured external route
- Configuring a default network using the reserved address 0.0.0.0

The primary difference between methods of configuring a default network is whether any dynamic routing information is learned from an external source, such as an ISP. When routes to external network addresses are learned from an external source, simply denote one of these external addresses as the default network by using the IOS global configuration command **ip default-network**. The parameter to this command is a route that has the following characteristics: It exists in the routing table, it is not connected to the router being configured, and it falls outside the classful address space configured on any of the router's interfaces. The following is an example of configuring the **ip default-network** command on the ZIP SF-Core-1 router to the network 140.222.0.0, which is being learned from the ZIP network's ISP:

```
SF-Core-1#configure
Configuring from terminal, memory, or network [terminal]?
Enter configuration commands, one per line.  End with CNTL/Z.
SF-Core-1(config)#ip default-network 140.222.0.0
SF-Core-1(config)#^Z
```

After it is configured, the router shows that it has accepted this network as a default and that the route is reachable by signifying it as the gateway of last resort in the output of **show ip route**. The router places an asterisk next to the route to denote that the route is a candidate for the default network because multiple defaults may be configured. The following is an example of the gateway of last resort set on the ZIP SF-Core-1 router:

```
SF-Core-1#show ip route
Codes: C - connected, S - static, I - IGRP, R - RIP, M - mobile, B - BGP
       D - EIGRP, EX - EIGRP external, O - OSPF, IA - OSPF inter area
       N1 - OSPF NSSA external type 1, N2 - OSPF NSSA external type 2
       E1 - OSPF external type 1, E2 - OSPF external type 2, E - EGP
       i - IS-IS, L1 - IS-IS level-1, L2 - IS-IS level-2, * - candidate default
       U - per-user static route, o - ODR

Gateway of last resort is 192.72.2.1 to network 140.222.0.0

131.108.0.0/16 is variably subnetted, 5 subnets, 3 masks
C       131.108.20.0/22 is directly connected, FastEthernet0/0
C       131.108.240.0/30 is directly connected, Serial1/0
S       131.108.230.0/24 [1/0] via 131.108.240.2
S       131.108.231.0/24 [1/0] via 131.108.100.0
S       131.108.232.0/24 [1/0] is directly connected,
        FastEthernet0/0
C       192.7.2.2/30 is directly connected, Serial1/1
B*      140.222.0.0/16 [20/19] via 192.7.2.1, 3d08h
```

When dynamic routing is not exchanged with your external provider, it is possible to use a static route to point to the external network address that is used as a default. The following is the previous example again, but this time a static route is used to provide reachability information about the default network address through the ISP connection:

```
SF-Core-1#configure
Configuring from terminal, memory, or network [terminal]?
Enter configuration commands, one per line.  End with CNTL/Z.
SF-Core-1(config)#ip route 140.222.0.0 255.255.0.0 192.7.2.1
SF-Core-1(config)#ip default-network 140.222.0.0
SF-Core-1(config)#^Z
```

As in the previous example, verifying the output of **show ip route** indicates that the router has installed the default network, but note that the route to 140.222.0.0 now shows S as the origin because it was configured manually:

```
SF-Core-1#show ip route
Codes: C - connected, S - static, I - IGRP, R - RIP, M - mobile, B - BGP
       D - EIGRP, EX - EIGRP external, O - OSPF, IA - OSPF inter area
       N1 - OSPF NSSA external type 1, N2 - OSPF NSSA external type 2
       E1 - OSPF external type 1, E2 - OSPF external type 2, E - EGP
       i - IS-IS, L1 - IS-IS level-1, L2 - IS-IS level-2, * - candidate default
       U - per-user static route, o - ODR

Gateway of last resort is 192.72.2.1 to network 140.222.0.0

131.108.0.0/16 is variably subnetted, 5 subnets, 3 masks
C        131.108.20.0/22 is directly connected, FastEthernet0/0
C        131.108.240.0/30 is directly connected, Serial1/0
S        131.108.230.0/24 [1/0] via 131.108.240.2
S        131.108.231.0/24 [1/0] via 131.108.100.0
S        131.108.232.0/24 [1/0] is directly connected, FastEthernet0/0
C        192.7.2.2/30 is directly connected, Serial1/1
S*       140.222.0.0/16 [20/19] via 192.7.2.1
```

The last configuration method for the default network should be familiar to those who have worked within the UNIX (or its derivatives) operating system environment or with the Routing Information Protocol (RIP). This method involves installing a static route to a special network address—namely, 0.0.0.0. This address is considered reserved. Within the UNIX and RIP environments, it denotes the route to all unknown IP destinations.

Within the IOS software on the router, the 0.0.0.0 network address is the least-specific network address possible. With its implied mask of 0.0.0.0 or 0 bits, this route matches any IP destination outside of a classful address. When the **ip classless** command is configured, the route matches any unknown IP destination address both inside and outside a classful address space. The following is an example of using the **ip route** command to configure the ZIP SF-Core-1 router with a default network of 0.0.0.0/0 and with the ISP connection as the next-hop IP address:

```
SF-Core-1#configure
Configuring from terminal, memory, or network [terminal]?
Enter configuration commands, one per line.  End with CNTL/Z.
SF-Core-1(config)#ip route 0.0.0.0 0.0.0.0 192.7.2.1
SF-Core-1(config)#^Z
```

The output of **show ip route** indicates that the router has installed the default network route to 0.0.0.0/0. As with the previous method, the route 0.0.0.0 shows an S as the origin because it was configured manually:

```
SF-Core-1#show ip route
Codes: C - connected, S - static, I - IGRP, R - RIP, M - mobile, B - BGP
       D - EIGRP, EX - EIGRP external, O - OSPF, IA - OSPF inter area
       N1 - OSPF NSSA external type 1, N2 - OSPF NSSA external type 2
       E1 - OSPF external type 1, E2 - OSPF external type 2, E - EGP
```

```
i - IS-IS, L1 - IS-IS level-1, L2 - IS-IS level-2, * - candidate default
U - per-user static route, o - ODR

Gateway of last resort is 192.72.2.1 to network 0.0.0.0

     131.108.0.0/16 is variably subnetted, 5 subnets, 3 masks
C          131.108.20.0/22 is directly connected, FastEthernet0/0
C          131.108.240.0/30 is directly connected, Serial1/0
S          131.108.230.0/24 [1/0] via 131.108.240.2
S          131.108.231.0/24 [1/0] via 131.108.100.0
S          131.108.232.0/24 [1/0] is directly connected, FastEthernet0/0
C          192.7.2.2/30 is directly connected, Serial1/1
S*         0.0.0.0 [1/0] via 192.7.2.1
```

NOTE   Both a classful summary route and a default network route must be configured if **the ip classless command** is not configured and if all IP destination routes within and outside the intranet are not known. This requirement derives from the assumption that all routers within a classful IP address space have complete knowledge of the subnets within that address space. When operating in **ip classless mode**, the single default route to network 0.0.0.0/0 suffices as the default for both internal subnets and external network destinations because it matches all unknown IP destinations.

When configuring a default network route for your network, follow these important guidelines:

- When dynamic routing information is not exchanged with an outside entity such as an ISP, using a static route to 0.0.0.0/0 is usually the easiest way to generate a default route.

- When dynamic routing information is exchanged with one or more ISPs, using the **ip default-network command** is the most appropriate way to designate one or more possible default network routes.

- When there are one or more Internet connections via an ISP, the Internet connection router(s) should propagate the default network throughout the intranet via a dynamic routing protocol.

- It is acceptable to configure multiple routers in the intranet with the **ip default-network** command to denote a dynamically learned route as the default. It is inappropriate to configure more than one router in the intranet with a default route to 0.0.0.0/0 if that router does not provide an Internet connection via an ISP. Doing so can cause routers without connectivity to unknown destinations to draw packets toward themselves, resulting in unreachability. The exception is those routers that do not exchange dynamic routing information or that have only occasional connections to the intranet over such media as dialup ISDN or Frame Relay SVCs.

- Routers that do not exchange dynamic routing information or that reside on dialup connections, such as ISDN or Frame Relay SVCs, should be configured with a route to the default network or to 0.0.0.0/0, as noted previously.

- When an intranet is not connected to any outside networks, such as the Internet, the default network configuration should be placed on a router or routers that reside at the core of the network and that have the complete network routing topology for the given intranet.

TIP   When a default network is configured using a static route to 0.0.0.0/0 and the router is operating in IP classless mode via the **ip classless** command, it is very easy to create a routing loop between an ISP and your network if all the network addresses in your network are not allocated. For example, if the network address 131.108.227.1 in the ZIP address space has not been assigned to any particular network segment and device, routers forward the packets for this destination toward the default network. The Internet connection router does not know about this address because it is unassigned. However, the destination address matches the route 0.0.0.0/0, so the router forwards the packets to the ISP.

In turn, the ISP recognizes that the address 131.108.227.1 resides in the ZIP network (probably via a route to 131.108.0.0/16) and forwards the packet back to the ZIP Internet connection router. Again, this router does not find a specific route, but it matches the route to 0.0.0.0/0 and forwards the packet back to the ISP. The ISP repeats the previous step.

This process repeats itself until the Time To Live on the packet expires. If such a loop occurs for many packets, the result can be an unnecessary consumption of the Internet connection bandwidth and huge amounts of congestion for ZIP users trying to reach the Internet. Figure 4-5 depicts this undesirable situation.

Figure 4-5   *A Routing Loop Has Occurred Because an Unassigned Address Was Sent to a Default Address in a Classless IP Network*

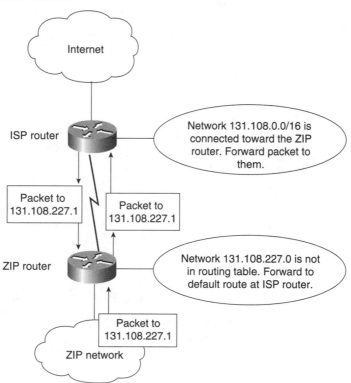

TIP   To avoid such a loop, you need to provide a summary route for the ZIP address space that discards packets addressed to unassigned IP addresses within the ZIP network address space. To achieve this, set a route's destination to the nonexistent interface Null 0. A summary route for the ZIP network that would discard packets to unassigned destinations would be IP route 131.108.0.0 255.255.0.0 Null 0. This route would be installed on the Internet connection router, which is the last router to receive the packets before they are forwarded to the ISP.

Verifying IP Routing Configuration

As we saw earlier in this chapter, the primary command for verifying IP routing config-uration is the IOS EXEC command **show ip route**. In this section, we explore several other commands that aid in verifying and managing IP route table configuration.

The **show ip route** command is the tool used to view the state of the IP routing table. Whether there are static routes configured or dynamic routing protocols running, this command shows whether the routes that have been configured or that are expected to be learned are actually present on the router. The following is an excerpt from the output of the **show ip route** command on the ZIP SF-Core-1 router:

```
SF-Core-1#show ip route
Codes: C - connected, S - static, I - IGRP, R - RIP, M - mobile, B - BGP
       D - EIGRP, EX - EIGRP external, O - OSPF, IA - OSPF inter area
       N1 - OSPF NSSA external type 1, N2 - OSPF NSSA external type 2
       E1 - OSPF external type 1, E2 - OSPF external type 2, E - EGP
       i - IS-IS, L1 - IS-IS level-1, L2 - IS-IS level-2, * - candidate default
       U - per-user static route, o - ODR

Gateway of last resort is 192.72.2.1 to network 0.0.0.0

     131.108.0.0/16 is variably subnetted, 8 subnets, 3 masks
C       131.108.20.0/22 is directly connected, FastEthernet0/0
C       131.108.240.0/30 is directly connected, Serial1/0
S       131.108.230.0/24 [1/0] via 131.108.240.2
S       131.108.231.0/24 [1/0] via 131.108.100.0
S       131.108.232.0/24 [1/0] is directly connected, FastEthernet0/0
C       192.7.2.0/30 is directly connected, Serial1/1
D       131.108.240.4/30 [90/307200] via 131.108.20.4, 1d00h, FastEthernet0/0
D       131.108.241.0/30 [90/3182080] via 131.108.240.2, 1d00h, Serial1/0
D       131.108.100.0/24 [90/3182080] via 131.108.240.2, 1d00h, Serial1/0
S       131.108.0.0/16 is directly connected, Null0
S*      0.0.0.0 [1/0] via 192.7.2.1
```

This output provides the following information:

- A list of all of the network routes and masks currently in the routing table.

- The next-hop IP address and output interface for those routes (or just the output interface, in the case of directly connected routes).

- If the route is dynamically learned, the length of time (in seconds) the route has been in the table or the length of time since the last update, depending on the particular routing protocol.

- The administrative distance and routing protocol metric for all but directly connected routes. The administrative distance is the number on the left of the slash that is inside the brackets and that follows the network route and bit-count mask. The routing protocol metric is the number to the right of the slash that is inside the brackets.

The administrative distance is a numeric value that represents the trustworthiness of the routing update source. Each type of route and routing protocol is assigned a particular administrative distance. The lower the value, the more trusted the source. Table 4-2 shows the current IOS software administrative distances. The routing protocol metric is a number used to rank routes by preference when more than one route to the same destination exists. The metric is often a composite number reflecting multiple route characteristics, such as path length and path cost. Each dynamic routing protocol has a different algorithm for determining the metric number.

Table 4-2   *Default Administrative Distances*

Route Source	Default Distance
Connected interface	0
Static route	1
Enhanced IGRP summary route	5
External BGP	20
Internal Enhanced IGRP	90
IGRP	100
OSPF	110
IS-IS	115
RIP	120
EGP	140
Internal BGP	200
Unknown	255

Another tool that gives a quick glimpse into the state of the routing table is the IOS EXEC command **show ip masks**. Given a network address as a parameter, this command lists the masks that have been applied to a particular network address and the number of routes that have each of those masks. This command is often useful in identifying addressing errors and static route configuration errors by highlighting missing or unexpected network masks that appear in the routing table. The following is an example of the **show ip masks**

131.108.0.0 command on the ZIP SF-Core-1 router, which shows six different networks for the 131.108.0.0 network:

```
SF-Core-1#show ip masks 131.108.0.0
 Mask                    Reference count
 255.255.255.255         9
 255.255.255.252         5
 255.255.255.128         3
 255.255.255.0           4
 255.255.252.0           1
 255.255.0.0             1
SF-Core-1#
```

Most dynamic routing protocols automatically send refreshes of routing information held by routers. These refreshes include updates to add or remove routes from the routing table and information to keep routes currently in the table fresh. However, occasionally you might want to clear a particular routing table entry or the entire table itself manually. For example, you might want to clear a dynamic route that has been marked as no longer valid but that has not yet aged out of the routing table naturally. Alternatively, you might want to refresh a particular route or the entire routing table for debugging purposes. You can use the IOS EXEC command **clear ip route** to clear either one particular route or the entire routing table. The command takes either an asterisk, which causes the entire routing table to be cleared, or a network address and mask pair, which clears only that particular route.

Use caution when deciding whether to clear the entire routing table. Refreshing all its information can take a few seconds to a few minutes. During this interval, lack of connectivity can occur for packets through the router and to the router via a virtual terminal session. Furthermore, clearing the entire table can cause excessive CPU utilization, depending on the particular dynamic routing protocol in use and the size of the routing table itself. The following is an example of clearing the entire routing table on the ZIP SF-Core-1 router:

```
SF-Core-1#clear ip route *
SF-Core-1#
```

The following is an example of clearing the route 131.108.3.0/25 from the ZIP SF-Core-1 router:

```
SF-Core-1#clear ip route 131.108.3.0 255.255.255.128
SF-Core-1#
```

Configuring IP Routing Protocols

In the previous section, we explored establishing the routing environment and creating the routing table via static routes. Although entire networks could be run using static routes, they would be tedious to manage and would not be very responsive to outages and topology changes that could occur on a frequent basis.

To address these concerns, dynamic routing protocols were developed. Dynamic routing protocols are algorithms that enable routers to advertise the existence of the IP network path information required to build the routing table. These algorithms also determine the selection criteria of the route that a packet follows when it is presented to the router for a switching decision. The goals of the routing protocol are to provide the user with the ability to select the optimum path through the network, to react rapidly to changes in the network, and to do these tasks in the simplest manner with the least overhead on the router.

Routing protocols fall into two major classes: Interior Gateway Protocols (IGP) and Exterior Gateway Protocols (EGP). IGPs are designed to exchange network and subnetwork information among routers within the same autonomous system—that is, among routers running a common routing protocol under one administrative domain. EGPs are designed to exchange only network information between routers in different autonomous systems.

The most common EGP used today is the Border Gateway Protocol version 4 (BGP-4). It is the predominant routing protocol used to exchange network path information between companies, ISPs, and NSPs on the Internet. A basic BGP-4 configuration is described in the section "Configuring the Border Gateway Protocol," later in this chapter.

Among the IGPs, the two major attributes that distinguish one protocol from another are the propagation methodology and whether the protocol is classful or classless. The two common propagation methodologies are the distance vector and the link-state methodologies. In the distance vector method, each router sends all or a portion of its routing table in update messages at regular intervals to neighboring routers. As routing information is spread through the network, routers can calculate distances to all networks and subnetworks within the intranetwork.

With the link-state method, each router sends complete local connection information to all other routers in the intranetwork. Because each router receives all the local connection information, it can build a complete view of the entire intranetwork by running a complex algorithm called Shortest Path First (SPF) against the connection information.

The IGPs are also distinguished by whether they are classful or classless. Classful routing protocols do not have the capability to exchange network mask information between routers. For this reason, these protocols must assume that a uniform network or subnetwork mask is applied throughout a common network address space. This limitation prohibits the use of variable-length subnet masking (VLSM) and so usually results in suboptimal network address space utilization. Furthermore, network mask information cannot be passed from router to router, so network address information must be summarized at the classful network address boundaries. For example, subnet information from network 131.108.0.0 could not be shared with network 172.16.0.0. Only the classful network route 131.108.0.0 could be propagated through the 172.16.0.0 network address space. The routing protocols that are considered classful include Routing Information Protocol (RIP) version 1 and Cisco Systems Interior Gateway Routing Protocol (IGRP).

Classless routing protocols are distinguished from the classful protocols by their capability to carry network mask information along with the network route information. For this reason, the classless protocols can support multiple subnet masks within a network address space and can therefore implement VLSM. By carrying network mask information, classless protocols can also implement supernet or CIDR block addressing.

Furthermore, classless protocols do not require the summarization of subnets at major network boundaries, as do the classful protocols (although the default behavior is to summarize). More detailed subnet information from one major network address space can be propagated into another major network address space because network masks give specific information about which subnetworks are available. The capability of classless routing to propagate subnet information from one major network address space to another facilitates the use of discontiguous networks. A discontiguous network occurs when a major network address space is broken into two or more pieces by a second major network address space, as depicted in Figure 4-6. The routing protocols that are considered classless include RIP version 2, Cisco Systems Enhanced IGRP (EIGRP), the IETF Open Shortest Path First (OSPF), and the ISO Intermediate System-to-Intermediate System Intradomain Routing Exchange Protocol (IS-IS).

Figure 4-6   *Classless Routing Protocols Allow for Discontiguous Network Address Space*

The selection of which dynamic routing protocol to use in a network is influenced by many variables. Although an entire book could be devoted to the design of the network and the selection of a routing protocol, the following are some of the key points that influence the network administrator's decision:

- **Network topology**—Some routing protocols rely on a logical hierarchy to properly scale and distribute network path information. Protocols such as OSPF and IS-IS require the establishment of a backbone and logical areas, as depicted in Figure 4-7. These protocols may require you to redesign your physical network topology or to engineer initial network design to operate optimally.

- **Address and route summarization**—In a large intranetwork, the benefits of reducing the number of routing table entries maintained by routing nodes include the reduction of the relative complexity of the network as well as a reduction in the routers' loads. Summarization requires that a routing protocol support VLSM and that it have the capability to propagate network mask information with the network routes. Classless protocols, such as OSPF and EIGRP, are well-suited to summarization.

- **Convergence speed**—The speed with which a routing protocol identifies that a path is not available, selects a new path, and propagates the new path information can be one of the most important criteria. If the network supports mission-critical applications, the network administrator likely desires a fast converging routing protocol. Distance vector protocols typically require more time to converge than link-state protocols because new path information must be passed hop by hop to each successive router in the intranetwork. RIP version 1 and IGRP are typically slower to converge than EIGRP and OSPF.

- **Route selection criteria**—The individual route attributes that a routing protocol uses to create its route metric play a key role in determining the proper dynamic routing protocol to implement. A protocol that relies strictly on the number of router hops to determine the route selection—such as RIP—may not be ideal when multiple paths in the intranetwork are composed of different types of LAN or WAN media. RIP views the router hop across a Fast Ethernet segment as being the same relative cost as a router hop across a 56-kbps WAN link. Some of the network path attributes used by various protocols to compute their metric include path length, reliability, delay, bandwidth, and load.

- **Scalability**—Depending on the types of routers in the intranetwork and the size of the network, the relative scalability of the routing protocol is very important. Distance vector protocols consume fewer CPU cycles than link-state protocols, with their complex SPF algorithms. Link-state protocols consume less LAN and WAN bandwidth than distance vector protocols because only change information is propagated instead of the complete routing table.

- **Ease of implementation**—If the network is not overly complex, protocols that do not require network re-engineering or well-structured and organized topologies are easier to implement. For example, RIP, IGRP, and EIGRP do not require much planning or organization within the topology to be run effectively. OSPF and IS-IS require that the network topology and addressing schemes be well thought-out before deployment.

- **Security**—If your network might exchange IGP information with a partner company or with divisions within a corporation, you might want to be able to authenticate the source of the routing information. Protocols such as OSPF and EIGRP support strong authentication methods, such as MD5 key authentication.

NOTE   A complete evaluation of the operation and features of the various protocols is available in *Technology Overview Briefs*, which is located on CCO at www.cisco.com/univercd/cc/td/doc/cisintwk/ito_doc/index.htm.

Figure 4-7 *A Hierarchical Network Topology*

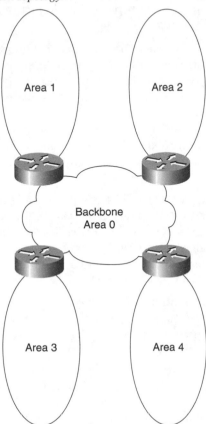

The selection of a routing protocol for any one network greatly depends on the following factors:

- Whether a router is being added to an existing network topology
- The design of the network
- The presence of existing routers and routing protocols
- The administrator's relative comfort and experience with TCP/IP routing
- The necessity to exchange routing information with end system devices, such as a server

If you are unsure about what routing protocol is appropriate for your network environment, we recommend that you discuss different options with technical sales engineers, outside network consultants, or other individuals who have experience in deploying IP networks. Additionally, Cisco Systems has documented in detail the design and selection criteria for deploying dynamic routing protocols in a design guide called *Designing Large-Scale IP Internetworks*. This guide is available on CCO at www.cisco.com/univercd/cc/td/doc/cisintwk/idg4/nd2003.htm.

For the ZIP network, the EIGRP routing protocol was selected because of its effective balance of the distance vector and link-state protocols' features. It is relatively easy to configure, does not require a specific physical topology, supports summarization and VLSM, and offers fast convergence. The basic configuration of EIGRP is discussed in the section "Configuring the Cisco IP Enhanced Interior Gateway Routing Protocol," later in this chapter. Although other popular IGPs are not implemented in the ZIP network, their basic configuration is covered in the following sections. Throughout the following discussions, we stick to basic configuration steps for each protocol. Additional commands for controlling dynamic routing protocol information are covered later, in the section "Managing Dynamic Routing Protocol Information."

Configuring the Routing Information Protocol

The Routing Information Protocol (RIP) is one of the oldest routing protocols used by IP-based devices. Its original implementation was for the Xerox PUP protocol in the early 1980s. RIP gained popularity when it was distributed with the Berkeley Systems Distribution (BSD) version of UNIX as the routing protocol for that TCP/IP implementation. Formal specification of RIP as a TCP/IP routing protocol can be found in RFC 1058.

RIP is a distance vector protocol that uses a router hop count as its metric. The maximum hop count in RIP is 15. Any route farther than 15 is tagged as unreachable by setting the hop count to 16. Routing information in RIP is propagated from a router to its neighbor routers via an IP broadcast using the UDP protocol and port 520.

RIP version 1 is a classful routing protocol that did not support the advertisement of network mask information. RIP version 2 is a classless protocol that can support CIDR, VLSM, route summarization, and security via plain text and MD5 authentication.

Although RIP is not implemented in the ZIP network, let's examine how it would be configured on a router that we'll call RIProuter. Configuring the RIP routing protocol consists of three basic steps: enabling the router to run the RIP protocol, deciding which RIP version to run, and configuring which network addresses and interfaces are included in routing updates. To enable the router to run RIP, the IOS major configuration command

router rip is used. To select the RIP version to run, the IOS routing configuration sub-command **version** is used. The **version** command takes a parameter of either 1 or 2 to specify which RIP version to use. If no version is specified, the IOS software defaults to sending RIP version 1 but receives both version 1 and version 2 updates. In this example, we enable the RIP routing protocol and select RIP version 2:

```
RIProuter#configure
Configuring from terminal, memory, or network [terminal]?
Enter configuration commands, one per line.  End with CNTL/Z.
RIProuter(config)#router rip
RIProuter(config-router)#version 2
RIProuter(config-router)#^Z
```

Specifying which interfaces and network addresses to include in RIP routing advertisements is accomplished with the IOS routing configuration subcommand **network**. This command takes as a parameter the classful network address that should be included in routing updates. The **network** command should be used to identify only those IP network addresses that are directly connected to the router being configured and that are meant to be included in the RIP routing process. Only interfaces having IP addresses in the identified network are included in routing updates.

For example, suppose that a router has two interfaces with IP addresses 131.108.4.5 and 131.108.6.9, respectively, and a third interface with the IP address 172.16.3.6. The subcommand **network 131.108.0.0** causes routing advertisements to be sent only about the subnets of network 131.108.0.0 and only to the interfaces that are addressed in the 131.108.0.0 network. To include routing updates for the interface in the 172.16.0.0 address space, an additional command **network 172.16.0.0** must be configured.

The following is an example of configuring the **network** command to include the subnets and interfaces of the 131.108.0.0 network:

```
RIProuter#configure
Configuring from terminal, memory, or network [terminal]?
Enter configuration commands, one per line.  End with CNTL/Z.
RIProuter(config)#router rip
RIProuter(config-router)#network 131.108.0.0
RIProuter(config-router)#^Z
```

NOTE   It is possible to mix RIP version 1 and RIP version 2 in the same network, even though version 1 cannot support many of the features of version 2. Mixing the versions can result in interoperability problems. Overriding the globally configured version and specifying the version on a per-interface basis is accomplished with the IOS interface configuration subcommands **ip rip send version** and **ip rip receive version**.

Configuring the Cisco Interior Gateway Routing Protocol

The Cisco Interior Gateway Routing Protocol (IGRP) is an enhanced distance vector protocol that was developed by Cisco Systems in the mid-1980s. It was designed to address some of the shortcomings of RIP and to provide better support for larger networks with multiple bandwidth link characteristics.

IGRP calculates its metric based on several user-configurable network path attributes, which include the internetwork delay, bandwidth, reliability, and load. Each WAN and LAN interface has preconfigured values for bandwidth and delay based on the relative speed and capabilities of the interface. The reliability and load attributes are calculated based on the performance of the interface in handling actual network traffic, although they are not enabled by default for routing decisions in the Cisco IOS.

Like RIP, IGRP uses IP broadcasts to communicate routing information to neighbor routers. However, IGRP is designated as its own transport layer protocol. It does not rely on UDP or TCP to communicate network route information. (Because IGRP has no feedback mechanisms, it operates in a manner similar to UDP.)

IGRP offers three major enhancements over the RIP protocol. First, the metric for IGRP can support a network with up to 255 router hops. Second, the metric for IGRP can distinguish between different types of connection media and their associated costs. Third, IGRP offers faster convergence through the use of flash updates. Flash updates send network change information as it becomes available instead of waiting for the regularly scheduled update time.

Let's examine the configuration of IGRP on a router that we'll call IGRProuter. Configuring the IGRP routing process consists of two steps: enabling the router to run IGRP, and identifying which network addresses and interfaces are included in routing updates. To enable the router to run IGRP, use the IOS major configuration command **router igrp**. This command requires a parameter known as a process-id. The process-id can be an integer in the range from 1 to 65535. Because multiple IGRP processes can run on the same router, process-id numbers are needed to distinguish them. Multiple IGRP processes might be run on a router that interconnects two divisions of a company, both of which want to separate the network administration between them. All routers in one division would share the same IGRP process-id with the other routers within that division.

As with RIP, specifying which interfaces and network addresses to include in IGRP routing advertisements is accomplished with the IOS routing configuration subcommand **network**. This command takes as a parameter the classful network address, which should be included in routing updates. The **network** command should be used to identify only those IP network addresses that are directly connected to the router being configured and that are meant to be included in the IGRP routing process. Only interfaces having IP addresses in the identified network are included in routing updates.

For example, if two interfaces have IP addresses 131.108.4.5 and 131.108.6.9, respectively, and a third interface has the IP address 172.16.3.6, the command **network 131.108.0.0** results in routing advertisements being sent only about the subnets of network 131.108.0.0 and only to the interfaces that are addressed in the 131.108.0.0 network. To include routing updates for the interface in the 172.16.0.0 address space, the additional command **network 172.16.0.0** must be configured.

The following is an example of configuring the IGRP routing process for network 131.108.0.0:

```
IGRProuter#configure
Configuring from terminal, memory, or network [terminal]?
Enter configuration commands, one per line.  End with CNTL/Z.
IGRProuter(config)#router igrp 25000
IGRProuter(config-router)#network 131.108.0.0
IGRProuter(config-router)#^Z
```

Configuring the Open Shortest Path First Protocol

Open Shortest Path First (OSPF) was designed in the late 1980s by the OSPF Working Group of the IETF. It was designed to address the needs of IP-based networks, including VLSM, route source authentication, fast convergence, tagging of routes learned via external routing protocols, and multicast route advertisements. OSPF version 2, the most current implementation, is specified in RFC 1583.

OSPF operates by dividing a large intranet or an autonomous system into smaller hierarchical units. Each of these areas is attached to a backbone area via an Area Border Router, as shown previously in Figure 4.7. All packets addressed from a workstation address in one area to a workstation address in another area traverse the backbone area, regardless of whether there is a direct connection from one area to another. Although it is possible to operate an OSPF network with only the backbone area, OSPF scales well only when the network is subdivided into a number of smaller areas.

As described previously, OSPF is a link-state routing protocol. Unlike RIP and IGRP, which advertise their routes only to neighboring routers, OSPF routers send link-state advertisements (LSAs) to all other routers within the same hierarchical area via an IP multicast. The LSA contains information on attached interfaces, metrics used, and other information needed to compute network path and topology databases. OSPF routers accumulate link-state information and run the SPF algorithm (also known as the Dijkstra algorithm, after the person credited with its creation) to calculate the shortest path to each node.

To determine which interfaces receive link-state advertisements, routers run the OSPF Hello protocol. Neighboring routers exchange hello messages to determine which other routers exist on a given interface and to serve as keepalives to indicate that those routers are still accessible.

When a neighbor router is detected, OSPF topology information is exchanged. After the routers are in sync, they are said to have formed an adjacency. LSAs are sent and received only on adjacencies.

LSA information is carried in packets via the OSPF transport layer. The OSPF transport layer defines a reliable advertisement, acknowledgment, and request process to ensure that LSA information is properly flooded to all routers within an area. LSAs are divided into four types. The most common types are those that advertise information about a router's connected network links and those that advertise networks available outside the OSPF areas.

OSPF's routing metric is calculated as the sum of the OSPF costs across the path to reach a network. The OSPF cost for a link is calculated based on the bandwidth of the interface and is user-configurable.

We consider the basic configuration of OSPF on a router called OSPFrouter. Configuring the OSPF routing process consists of two steps: enabling the router to run OSPF, and identifying which network addresses and interfaces are included in routing updates and to which areas the interfaces belong.

To enable the router to run OSPF, use the IOS major configuration command **router ospf**. This command requires as a parameter a process-id integer in case multiple OSPF processes are run on the same router. As with other routing protocols, you need to configure which interfaces and network addresses are included in OSPF routing advertisements. Additionally, you must identify which OSPF area an interface resides within.

Use the IOS routing configuration subcommand **network area** to identify the network addresses and interfaces to include in OSPF and to identify the areas to which they belong. This command takes two parameters. The first parameter is the network address and the wildcard mask used to compare against IP addresses assigned to interfaces. The wildcard mask is a method for matching IP addresses or ranges of IP addresses. It is described in the section "Configuring IP Filtering via Access Lists," later in this chapter. When the wildcard mask is applied to the IP address of an interface and the resulting network address matches the network address in the **network area** command, the interface is included in the OSPF routing process for the specified area. The second parameter, which is referred to as the area id, is used to identify the area to which the interface belongs. The area id can be an integer or a dotted-decimal number, such as an IP address.

Let's assume that our example router, called OSPFrouter, has three interfaces. The interfaces are assigned IP addresses 131.108.200.1, 131.108.201.1, and 131.108.202.1, respectively. The first two interfaces are assigned to Area 1, and the third is assigned either to Area 0 or to the backbone area. Based on these assumptions, the following is an example of configuring OSPF:

```
OSPFrouter#configure
Configuring from terminal, memory, or network [terminal]?
Enter configuration commands, one per line.  End with CNTL/Z.
OSPFrouter(config)#router ospf 25000
OSPFrouter(config-router)#network 131.108.200.0 0.0.1.255 area 1
OSPFrouter(config-router)#network 131.108.202.0 0.0.0.255 area 0
OSPFrouter(config-router)#^Z
```

As with the previously discussed routing protocols, only those network addresses and interfaces that match the addresses in the **network area** commands are included in OSPF routing updates.

OSPF operates on the principle that LSAs can be multicast to all routers within an autonomous system. However, many WAN media—such as point-to-point serial lines, point-to-point Frame Relay, and multipoint Frame Relay—are non-broadcast media and do not support multicasting. Without the capability to multicast the LSA routing information, the network administrator is forced to manually configure the neighbor relationships between routers on the point-to-point and multipoint network interfaces. However, one solution eliminates this manual configuration of neighbors. OSPF can be instructed to treat a point-to-point interface as a broadcast medium and a multipoint interface as a partial broadcast network. The IOS interface configuration subcommand **ip ospf network** controls the network type that OSPF believes is connected to the interface. The command takes as a parameter one of the following options:

- **broadcast**—Treat this medium as a broadcast medium, assuming that multicasts can be transmitted and received.

- **non-broadcast**—Treat this medium as a non-broadcast medium. This option requires the administrator to manually configure neighbor relationships via the IOS routing configuration subcommand **neighbor**.

- **point-to-multipoint**—Treat this medium as a partial broadcast medium. The router at the hub of a point-to-multipoint topology has virtual circuits to the multiple remote routers, and it serves as the relay for LSAs and routing between the routers that are not directly connected.

The following is an example of configuring a point-to-point Frame Relay subinterface as an OSPF broadcast type and a multipoint Frame Relay interface as an OSPF point-to-multipoint type:

```
OSPFrouter#configure
Configuring from terminal, memory, or network [terminal]?
Enter configuration commands, one per line.  End with CNTL/Z.
OSPFrouter(config)#interface serial 0.1 point-to-point
OSPFrouter(config-int)#ip ospf network broadcast
OSPFrouter(config-int)#interface serial 1
OSPFrouter(config-int)#ip ospf network point-to-multipoint
OSPFrouter(config-int)#^Z
```

Unlike other IGP routing protocols, OSPF does not generate a default route when configured with the **ip default-network** command. For OSPF, the autonomous system boundary router must be configured manually to force it to generate the default route into the rest of the OSPF domain. The IOS routing configuration subcommand **ip default-information originate** causes OSPF to generate the default route. The following is an example of configuring the **ip default-information originate** command in conjunction with the **ip default-network** command to force an autonomous system boundary router to generate a default route:

```
OSPFrouter#configure
Configuring from terminal, memory, or network [terminal]?
```

```
Enter configuration commands, one per line.  End with CNTL/Z.
OSPFrouter(config)#ip default-network  140.222.0.0
OSPFrouter(config-router)#router ospf  25000
OSPFrouter(config-router)#ip default-information originate
OSPFrouter(config-router)#^Z
```

Configuring the Cisco IP Enhanced Interior Gateway Routing Protocol

The Enhanced Interior Gateway Routing Protocol (EIGRP) is an improved version of the original IGRP developed by Cisco Systems. EIGRP retains the same distance vector algorithm and metric information as the original IGRP; however, the convergence time and other scalability aspects have been significantly improved. EIGRP offers features not found in its predecessor, IGRP, such as support for VLSM and arbitrary route summarization. Additionally, EIGRP offers features found in protocols such as OSPF, including partial incremental updates and decreased convergence time. EIGRP combines the advantages of link-state protocols with the advantages of distance vector protocols.

As with IGRP, EIGRP advertises routing table information only to neighbor routers. However, unlike IGRP, these neighbors are discovered via a simple Hello protocol exchanged by routers on the same physical network. After neighbors are discovered, EIGRP uses a reliable transport protocol to ensure the accurate and ordered delivery of routing table information and updates. A router keeps track not only of its own connected routes, but also of all routes advertised by its neighbors. Based on this information, EIGRP can quickly and efficiently select the least-cost path to a destination and guarantee that the path is not part of a routing loop. By storing the routing information of its neighbors, the algorithm can more quickly determine a replacement route or feasible successor in case of a link failure or other topology change event.

EIGRP hello and routing information are carried in the EIGRP transport protocol. The EIGRP transport defines a reliable advertisement, acknowledgment, and request process to ensure that hello and routing information is properly transmitted to all neighbor routers.

EIGRP is the dynamic routing protocol of the example ZIP network, so let's examine its configuration in that context. Configuring the EIGRP routing process consists of two steps: enabling the router to run EIGRP, and identifying which network addresses and interfaces are included in routing updates.

To enable the router to run EIGRP, use the IOS major configuration command **router eigrp**. This command requires as a parameter a process-id integer in case multiple EIGRP processes are run on the same router. As with IGRP, specifying which interfaces and network addresses are included in EIGRP routing advertisements is accomplished with the IOS routing configuration subcommand **network**. This command takes as a parameter the classful network address, which should be included in routing updates. The **network** command should be used to identify only those IP network addresses that are directly connected to the router being configured and that are meant to be included in the EIGRP routing process. Only interfaces having IP addresses in the identified network are included in routing updates.

For example, on the ZIP SF-Core-1 router, there are interfaces in the 131.108.0.0 network and in the 192.7.2.0 network. The command **network** 131.108.0.0 stipulates that routing advertisements are sent about the subnets of network 131.108.0.0 and to the interfaces that are addressed in the 131.108.0.0 network. To include routing updates for the interface in the 192.7.2.0 address space, an additional command, **network 192.7.2.0**, would need to be configured. In this case, the 192.7.2.0 network is the connection to the ISP. It is not included in the EIGRP routing process because the ISP does not use EIGRP.

The following is an example of configuring EIGRP on the ZIP SF-Core-1 router for the 131.108.0.0 network:

```
SF-Core-1#configure
Configuring from terminal, memory, or network [terminal]?
Enter configuration commands, one per line.  End with CNTL/Z.
SF-Core-1(config)#router eigrp 25000
SF-Core-1(config-router)#network 131.108.0.0
SF-Core-1(config-router)#^Z
```

Configuring the Border Gateway Protocol

The Border Gateway Protocol (BGP) is an Exterior Gateway Protocol (EGP). Unlike IGPs, which exchange information about networks and subnetworks within the same routing domain or autonomous system, EGPs are designed to exchange routing information between routing domains or autonomous systems. BGP is the primary method for exchanging network information between companies, ISPs, and NSPs for the global Internet. BGP offers advantages over its predecessor, the Exterior Gateway Protocol (EGP). The most notable advantage is that it guarantees the loop-free exchange of routing information between autonomous systems. BGP version 4 is the most current revision of BGP. It offers advantages over previous versions, such as handling CIDR blocks. BGP, which has been adopted by the IETF, is specified in RFCs 1163, 1267, and 1771. These RFCs define BGP versions 2, 3, and 4, respectively.

BGP routers are configured with neighbor information so that routers may form a reliable TCP connection over which to transport network route and autonomous system path information. Unlike some of the IGPs, BGP uses TCP as its transport protocol instead of defining its own. After a neighbor BGP session is established, it remains open unless it is specifically closed or unless there is a link failure. When two neighbor routers are exchanging BGP session and route information, they are said to be BGP peers. The route information exchanged between peers includes the network number/autonomous system path pair and other route attributes. The autonomous system path is a string of autonomous system numbers through which the advertised route can be reached.

Initially, BGP peers exchange the entire contents of their BGP routing tables. Subsequently, only incremental updates are sent between the peers to advise them of new or deleted routes. Unlike IGP route tables, the BGP route table does not require periodic refreshing. Instead, each BGP router retains the latest version number of the table that it has advertised to its peers, as well as its own internal table version. When a change is received from a peer, the internal table version is incremented and compared to the advertised table versions of the peers. This process ensures that each of the router's peers is kept in sync with all changes that are processed. BGP also keeps a separate BGP route table that contains all possible paths to the advertised networks. Only the optimal path is stored in the primary route selection table of the router, and only the optimal path is advertised to other BGP peers.

BGP peers are divided into two categories, external BGP peers (EBGP) and internal BGP peers (IBGP). BGP peers that are in different administrative domains or autonomous systems and that exchange routing information are said to be EBGP peers. EBGP peers are typically other organizations, ISPs, or NSPs with whom an autonomous system wants to share information regarding routes within the autonomous system or that were learned from other external sources.

BGP peers that are in the same administrative domain or autonomous system and that exchange routing information are said to be IBGP peers. IBGP peers are routers within the same autonomous system that need to share the externally learned BGP routes to have a complete picture of all possible routes to external destinations and for readvertisement to other EBGP peers. IBGP peering is typical when an autonomous system has more than one external BGP peering relationship, such as two ISP or NSP connections to the global Internet. IBGP peering is a simpler and more flexible method to share routes derived from EBGP peers.

The alternative to IBGP peering is to redistribute the EBGP learned routes into an IGP (such as EIGRP or OSPF) to be transported through the autonomous system and then to redistribute the routes from the IGP back into BGP to be advertised via EBGP to other external BGP peers. As described in the following section, "Managing Dynamic Routing Protocol Information," route redistribution can result in loss of routing metric information and potential routing loops. In addition to protection from the hazards of route redistribution, IBGP peering offers all the administrative controls, weights, and filtering capabilities associated with the BGP protocol, and it maintains a consistent view of routing information advertised to the external world via BGP.

Figure 4-8 demonstrates the difference between IBGP and EBGP peers as seen in the ZIP network. EBGP peers exist between the router pairs Seoul-1 and ISP-A, and SF-Core-1 and ISP-B. IBGP peers exist between the router pair Seoul-1 and SF-Core-1. As IBGP peers, Seoul-1 and SF-Core-1 will share routing information learned from ISP-A and ISP-B to determine the best route to destinations outside the ZIP network.

Figure 4-8 *EBGP and IBGP Peers in the ZIP Network*

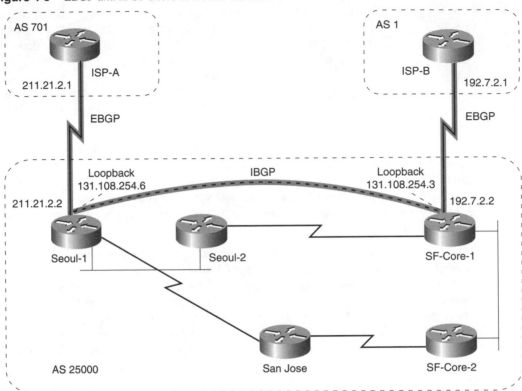

Without applying administrative controls and weights, BGP optimal route selection is based on the length of the autonomous system path for a network route. The length is defined as the number of distinct autonomous systems required to reach the network. The shorter the length, the more desirable the path. Through its use of administrative controls, BGP is one of the most flexible and highly configurable routing protocols available. It gives the network administrator the ability to implement a wide variety of routing policies through route attributes such as the Multi-Exit Discriminator (MED) metric and the Local Preference attribute and filtering features such as distribution lists.

TIP
Before implementing BGP routing policies through the use of MEDs, Local Preference, and other attributes, make sure that you have a complete understanding of the effects of these modifiers. We recommend reviewing the text *Internet Routing Architectures,* Second Edition, and the Cisco Systems case study *Using the Border Gateway Protocol for Interdomain Routing.* The case study can be found on CCO at www.cisco.com/univercd/cc/td/doc/cisintwk/ics/icsbgp4.htm.

When a network has multiple ISP connections, BGP normally is run to allow the selection of the best path to external networks. Running BGP when there is only one ISP connection generally is not required, because all external network paths are reached through only the one provider. However, some providers like to exchange BGP to learn the path to their customer networks and to provide network routes for default routing.

Let's examine the configuration of BGP on the ZIP SF-Core-1 and the Seoul-1 router, each of which has a connection to the Internet through an ISP. Configuring the BGP routing process consists of three steps: enabling the router to run BGP, identifying the peer routers, and identifying what network addresses to advertise to the peer routers.

To enable the router to run BGP, use the IOS global configuration command **router bgp**. This command takes as a parameter an integer, which is the autonomous system number (ASN) assigned to this network by one of the network address registries (RIPE, APNIC, or ARIN). Each independent autonomous system that is connected to the Internet must be assigned a unique ASN by one of the registries to prevent accidental duplication. Duplication of ASN could result in a network not being advertised because of an erroneous loop detection. If BGP is run on a completely private network that is not connected to the Internet, selection of an ASN should be from the block of private ASNs in the range from 32768 through 64511.

| NOTE | Many network administrators use the ASN as the process-id for other dynamic routing protocols such as EIGRP. The ZIP network follows this convention. |

Identifying peer routers is accomplished through the use of the IOS routing configuration subcommand **neighbor remote-as**. This command takes two parameters, the IP address of the neighbor router and an ASN. When the ASN specified as the **remote-as** is different from the ASN specified in the **router bgp** global configuration command, that neighbor is considered an external BGP (EBGP) peer. The IP address of a neighbor router that is an EBGP peer is usually an address on a directly connected network interface.

When the ASN specified as the **remote-as** is the same as the ASN specified in the **router bgp** global configuration command, that neighbor is considered an internal BGP (IBGP) peer. The IP address of a neighbor router that is an IBGP peer is any valid and reachable IP address for that peer. IBGP peers can be located on a directly connected network interface (as with multiple ISP connections in one location) or a nonconnected network attached to a distant router within the autonomous system (as with multiple ISP connections at different locations).

Because IBGP peer IP addresses need not be found on a directly connected network interface, it is often desirable to use the loopback interface address as the source and destination address for IBGP peering. Because the loopback interface is not associated with any physical interface, it is always up and reachable as long as there is a path to its associated IP address through IGP routing or static routes. To configure a loopback interface as the source IP address for IBGP peering, use the IOS routing configuration subcommand **neighbor** with the **update-source** keyword. The **update-source** keyword should be followed by the name and number of a properly addressed and configured loopback interface of the router being configured.

When a router has many BGP peering neighbors, it is often difficult to remember which IP addresses and ASNs belong to which peers. Using the **description** keyword parameter of the IOS routing configuration subcommand **neighbor**, comments can be added that can help provide information to the network administrator.

Identifying which networks within the autonomous system to advertise to the EBGP peers is accomplished through the use of the IOS routing configuration subcommand **network**. This command takes as a parameter the network address to be advertised to the peer routers and the optional keyword **mask**, followed by a network mask for that address. If no network mask is supplied, the classful network address is assumed. Through the use of the network mask, BGP can advertise both subnets and CIDR blocks to peer routers. Networks learned from other autonomous systems via EBGP will be exchanged between the IBGP peers within the autonomous system.

NOTE
Keep in mind that a BGP router advertises routes learned from a BGP peer to all its other BGP peers. For example, routes learned via EBGP with one ISP will be readvertised to IBGP peers, which in turn will readvertise to other ISPs via EBGP. By readvertising routes, your network may become a transit network between the providers to which you connect. This result could upset the providers as well as cause massive network congestion. If creation of such transit networks is not desired, use the route filtering capabilities of **distribute-lists** and **route-maps** to control the readvertising of learned routes. Distribute lists are discussed in more detail in the next section.

Finally, because the ZIP network will not be transmitting traffic between ISP-A and ISP-B, and because BGP routes will not be redistributed into the IGP routing process, BGP synchronization will be disabled via the IOS route configuration subcommand **no synchronization**. With synchronization enabled, a route will not be advertised to an EBGP peer unless that route appears in the primary route selection table for the peer and is learned via the IGP routing process. Because the ZIP network wants to advertise only routes for its own autonomous system, disabling synchronization will result in faster BGP convergence times.

The following is an example of configuring BGP routing on the ZIP SF-Core-1 router to advertise the network 131.108.0.0 to its ISP via EBGP. The ZIP SF-Core-1 router has an ASN of 25000. The ISP has an ASN of 1, with a peer IP address of 192.7.2.1. Additionally, the Seoul-1 router is configured as an IBGP peer to the SF-Core-1 router with a peer IP address of 131.108.254.6, using the IP address of interface loopback 0 as the source address for the peering connection:

```
SF-Core-1#configure
Configuring from terminal, memory, or network [terminal]?
Enter configuration commands, one per line.  End with CNTL/Z.
SF-Core-1(config)#router bgp 25000
SF-Core-1(config-router)#no synchronization
SF-Core-1(config-router)#network 131.108.0.0
SF-Core-1(config-router)#neighbor 192.7.2.1 remote-as 1
SF-Core-1(config-router)#neighbor 192.7.2.1 description Internet Connection to ISP-B
SF-Core-1(config-router)#neighbor 131.108.254.6 remote-as 25000
SF-Core-1(config-router)#neighbor 131.108.254.6 description IBGP to Seoul-1
SF-Core-1(config-router)#neighbor 131.108.254.6 update-source loopback 0
SF-Core-1(config-router)#^Z
```

The following is an example of configuring BGP routing on the ZIP Seoul-1 router to advertise the network 131.108.0.0 to its ISP via EBGP. The ZIP Seoul-1 router has an ASN of 25000. The ISP has an ASN of 701, with a peer IP address of 211.21.2.1. Additionally, the SF-Core-1 router is configured as an IBGP peer to the Seoul-1 router with a peer IP address of 131.108.254.3, using the IP address of interface loopback 0 as the source address for the peering connection:

```
Seoul-1#configure
Configuring from terminal, memory, or network [terminal]?
Enter configuration commands, one per line.  End with CNTL/Z.
Seoul-1(config)#router bgp 25000
Seoul-1(config-router)#no synchronization
Seoul-1(config-router)#network 131.108.0.0
Seoul-1(config-router)#neighbor 211.21.2.1 remote-as 701
Seoul-1(config-router)#neighbor 211.21.2.1 description Internet Connection to ISP-A
Seoul-1(config-router)#neighbor 131.108.254.3 remote-as 25000
Seoul-1(config-router)#neighbor 131.108.254.3 description IBGP to SF-Core-1
Seoul-1(config-router)#neighbor 131.108.254.3 update-source loopback 0
Seoul-1(config-router)#^Z
```

When both routers are configured for BGP and the peers are established, the route for network 131.108.0.0 will be advertised to ISP A and ISP B by Seoul-1 and SF-Core-1, respectively. Using IOS EXEC commands described in the later section "Viewing Dynamic Routing Protocol Information," the network administrator can verify the establishment of the peers and the proper advertisement and receipt of network routes.

When IBGP peers exchange routing information learned from EBGP peers, it is important to note that the IBGP peer must have a route to the next-hop address for the route being learned from the EBGP peer. For example, if SF-Core-1 learns about the route 140.222.0.0/16 from ISP B, the next-hop address for that route will be 192.7.2.1. When the route is readvertised to the IBGP peer Seoul-1, the route cannot be installed in Seoul-1's BGP route table unless Seoul-1 has a route to the next-hop address of 192.7.2.1. If the route is not installed in Seoul-1's BGP table, it cannot be selected as the best route to be included in the primary route selection table, nor can it be evaluated against the same route that might be learned from ISP A. If the next-hop addresses are not part of the network address range for which your IGP provides routing information (for example, ISP assigned addressing), use the **redistribute** command, described in the next section, to advertise the directly connected or static routes for those addresses into your IGP routing process.

Managing Dynamic Routing Protocol Information

Network administrators often want to apply administrative policy to control the flow of network routing information both within and outside their networks. These policies include determining which routers participate in the routing process, whether subnet information is propagated between different major network address spaces, and what routes should be shared between routers. By implementing these policies, you can control network access traffic patterns and security. In this section, we examine five popular IOS commands that are used to manage dynamic routing protocols and to implement routing policy.

One of the most important attributes of managing dynamic routing protocols is the ability to permit and deny network routes from being propagated from one router to the network. This ability to filter routing information enables you to restrict one part of a network from being reached by another part of that network. In the case of BGP, restricting routes from being propagated and readvertised to peer routes prevents an autonomous system from inadvertently transiting packets between two or more ISPs.

The primary tool for filtering routing information is the IOS routing configuration subcommand **distribute-list**. The filtering capabilities of the **distribute-list** command are enabled through the use of standard IP access lists. Access lists are general tools for defining filtering criteria. When applied in conjunction with routing protocol subcommands, access lists can define which routes are permitted or denied. They are discussed in detail in the later section "Configuring IP Filtering via Access Lists." The **distribute-list** command applies an access list to the particular situation of controlling route propagation.

The **distribute-list** command takes several parameters, including the name or number of an IP access list, the keyword **in** or **out**, which controls the direction in which the filtering occurs, and an optional interface identifier. This identifier indicates that the filtering should occur only on routing updates for that specific interface. If this identifier is omitted, the distribute list applies to all routing updates that match the access list.

The following is an example of applying the **distribute-list** command on the SF-Core-1 router to prevent the reserved network address 10.0.0.0 from being learned by the BGP routing process and to permit every other address to be learned:

```
SF-Core-1#configure
Configuring from terminal, memory, or network [terminal]?
Enter configuration commands, one per line.  End with CNTL/Z.
```

```
SF-Core-1(config)#router bgp 25000
SF-Core-1(config-router)#distribute-list 1 in
SF-Core-1(config-router)#access-list 1 deny 10.0.0.0 0.0.0.0
SF-Core-1(config)#access-list 1 permit any
SF-Core-1(config)#^Z
```

NOTE   Because of the flooding nature of the LSA packets in link-state protocols such as OSPF and IS-IS, filtering of inbound routing information is not possible. Filtering of outbound routing information applies only to external routes.

When the **distribute-list** command is applied as a subcommand of a routing process, the filtering defined in the **distribute-list** applies to all sources of the routing updates. In many situations, it may be desirable to apply the filtering to only one source of routing information, such as a particular BGP peer. Filtering updates to and from particular BGP peers can be accomplished by applying the **distribute-list** to a particular BGP neighbor as an optional keyword of the BGP **neighbor** subcommand.

The following is the previous example rewritten to apply the **distribute-list** command on SF-Core-1 as an option to the **neighbor** subcommand so that only the EBGP peer is prevented from learning the reserved network address 10.0.0.0:

```
SF-Core-1(config)#router bgp 25000
SF-Core-1(config-router)#neighbor 192.7.2.1 distribute-list 1 in
SF-Core-1(config-router)#access-list 1 deny 10.0.0.0 0.0.0.0
SF-Core-1(config)#access-list 1 permit any
SF-Core-1(config)#^Z
```

Occasionally, you may want to have a router listen to routing updates on a specific interface, but to not advertise routing information to other routers on the interface. When this configuration is desired, an interface is said to be operating in passive mode. The IOS routing configuration subcommand **passive-interface** sets up passive mode. This command takes as a parameter the interface identifier on which outgoing routing updates are suppressed. The following is an example of configuring the ZIP San-Jose router with the **passive-interface** command to prevent routing updates from being sent on the router's Token Ring interface:

```
San-Jose#configure
Configuring from terminal, memory, or network [terminal]?
Enter configuration commands, one per line.  End with CNTL/Z.
San-Jose(config)#router eigrp 125000
San-Jose(config-router)#passive-interface tokenring 1/0
San-Jose(config-router)#^Z
```

You may want to configure a router with a list of specific neighbor routers with which it can exchange dynamic routing information. For example, to implement OSPF on non-broadcast media, specific neighbor routers must be specified for proper protocol operation. As another example, you can implement a more secure environment in which only specified neighbor routers are permitted to exchange routing information in a point-to-point fashion.

The IOS routing configuration subcommand **neighbor** is used to specify the IP address of a neighbor router with which to exchange routing information. When used with the **passive-interface** command, routing information is exchanged with only the specified neighbors through point-to-point (non-broadcast) exchanges. The **neighbor** command takes as a parameter an IP address for the neighbor router. The following is an example of configuring the ZIP Seoul-2 router to exchange point-to-point routing information with a UNIX server running RIP on the Ethernet segment. The **passive-interface** command is used to prevent RIP from being advertised on the serial interface.

```
Seoul-2#configure
Configuring from terminal, memory, or network [terminal]?
Enter configuration commands, one per line.  End with CNTL/Z.
Seoul-2(config)#router rip
Seoul-2(config-router)#passive-interface serial 0
Seoul-2(config-router)#passive-interface ethernet 0
Seoul-2(config-router)#neighbor 131.108.3.40
Seoul-2(config-router)#^Z
```

Occasionally, your Cisco IOS-based routers may need to communicate routing information with other devices that do not support the routing protocol selected for your network. For example, the ZIP network runs EIGRP. A UNIX platform cannot receive EIGRP routing updates because it has the capability to run only the RIP protocol. To accommodate such situations, the IOS software has the capability to pass routing information from one dynamic routing protocol to another. This process is called route redistribution.

The IOS routing configuration subcommand **redistribute** is used to enable route redistribution. This command takes as an argument the name of the routing process from which to redistribute routes. The keywords **static** or **connected** may also be specified in place of a routing process name. Using the **static** keyword allows manually configured static routes to be advertised into the routing process. The keyword **connected** allows the routes for directly connected interfaces not matching the address specified in the routing subcommand **network** to be advertised by the routing process. Because each dynamic routing protocol uses a different method to calculate its metric, automatic metric conversion may not be possible. The following is a list of the IOS-supported automatic metric conversions:

- RIP can automatically redistribute static routes. It assigns static routes a metric of 1 (directly connected).

- IGRP can automatically redistribute static routes and information from other IGRP-routed autonomous systems. IGRP assigns static routes a metric that identifies them as directly connected. IGRP does not change the metrics of routes derived from IGRP updates from other autonomous systems.

- Any protocol can redistribute other routing protocols if a default metric is in effect.

A default metric is defined with the IOS routing configuration subcommand **default-metric**. The command takes as an argument one or more routing protocol metric attributes, based on the particular routing protocol being configured. The following is an example of redistributing EIGRP into RIP on the ZIP Singapore router. Note that the **passive-interface** command is used to prevent RIP from being advertised on the serial interface and that the default metric is set to 3.

```
Singapore#configure
Configuring from terminal, memory, or network [terminal]?
Enter configuration commands, one per line.  End with CNTL/Z.
Singapore(config)#router rip
Singapore(config-router)#default-metric 3
Singapore(config-router)#redistribute eigrp 25000
Singapore(config-router)#passive-interface serial 0
Singapore(config-router)#^Z
```

TIP   Redistributing routing information from one protocol to another can be a tricky business. Mutual redistribution—in which routes are passed from one protocol to another, and vice versa—can cause routing loops because there are no sanity checks on the routes being redistributed. Mutual redistribution should be avoided, if possible. If mutual redistribution is absolutely required, the **passive-interface** and **distribute-list** commands should be used to restrict the advertisement of specific routes to specific routing protocols.

As discussed earlier, the IGP routing protocols that support VLSM automatically summarize all subnets to a single classful network route when passing routing information from one major network address to another. For example, subnets of the ZIP network 131.108.0.0 are not advertised into the 172.16.0.0 address space of another router running EIGRP. If there are subnets of the 131.108.0.0 address space that are connected beyond 172.16.0.0—a discontiguous network—it may be necessary to propagate subnet information from one part of the 131.108.0.0 network, through the 172.16.0.0 network, and then to the other portion of the 131.108.0.0 network. Clearly, route summarization is undesirable in this situation. The IOS routing configuration subcommand **no auto-summary** prevents automatic address summarization at classful network boundaries and allows propagation of subnet information.

The following is an example of deconfiguring autosummarization on the ZIP SF-Core-1 router:

```
SF-Core-1#configure
Configuring from terminal, memory, or network [terminal]?
Enter configuration commands, one per line.  End with CNTL/Z.
SF-Core-1(config)#router eigrp 25000
SF-Core-1(config-router)#no auto-summary
SF-Core-1(config-router)#^Z
```

Viewing Dynamic Routing Protocol Information

The operation and configuration of the dynamic routing protocols can be verified with a number of IOS EXEC commands. These commands fall into two categories, protocol-independent and protocol-specific. Let's look at the protocol-independent commands first.

As examined in the section "Configuring IP Routing Protocols," the IOS EXEC command **show ip route** can be used to determine whether routes are being learned via dynamic routing protocols and to determine the attributes of those routes.

Determining which routing protocols are running and the various attributes of those protocols is performed with the IOS EXEC command **show ip protocols**. This command takes an optional keyword parameter **summary**. The **summary** version of the command lists only the routing protocol name and the process-id, as applicable. The following is sample output from the **show ip protocols summary** command on the ZIP SF-Core-1 router:

```
SF-Core-1#show ip protocols summary
  Index  Process Name
  0      connected
  1      static
  2      eigrp 25000
  3      bgp 25000
```

The standard version of the **show ip protocols** command lists all the routing protocols being run and the numerous attributes of those protocols, including routing update sources, distribute filter lists applied, metric information, and which networks are being advertised. The following is an example of the output of the **show ip protocols** command on the ZIP SF-Core-1 router running EIGRP and BGP:

```
SF-Core-1#show ip protocols
Routing Protocol is "eigrp 25000"
  Outgoing update filter list for all interfaces is not set
  Incoming update filter list for all interfaces is not set
  Default networks flagged in outgoing updates
  Default networks accepted from incoming updates
  EIGRP metric weight K1=1, K2=0, K3=1, K4=0, K5=0
  EIGRP maximum hopcount 100
  EIGRP maximum metric variance 1
  Redistributing: connected, eigrp 1
  Automatic network summarization is not in effect
  Routing for Networks:
    131.108.0.0
  Routing Information Sources:
    Gateway          Distance      Last Update
    131.108.20.1          90       00:04:13
    131.108.20.2          90       00:04:13
    131.108.20.4          90       00:04:13
  Distance: internal 90 external 170

Routing Protocol is "bgp 25000"
  Sending updates every 60 seconds, next due in 0 seconds
  Outgoing update filter list for all interfaces is 2
  Incoming update filter list for all interfaces is 1
  IGP synchronization is disabled
  Automatic route summarization is enabled
  Neighbor(s):
    Address          FiltIn FiltOut DistIn DistOut Weight RouteMap
    192.7.2.1                                       150
  Routing for Networks:
    131.108.0.0
  Routing Information Sources:
    Gateway          Distance      Last Update
    (this router)        200       1w5d
    192.7.2.1             20       1w3d
  Distance: external 20 internal 200 local 200
```

Complex routing protocols such as EIGRP, OSPF, and BGP provide access to multiple attributes, tables, and databases of information regarding their operation, configuration, and topology. Tables 4-3, 4-4, and 4-5 show the common IOS EXEC commands used to view protocol information for EIGRP, OSPF, and BGP, respectively.

Table 4-3   *EIGRP IOS EXEC Commands*

IOS EXEC EIGRP Command	Function
show ip eigrp interfaces	Displays information about interfaces configured for IP EIGRP.
show ip eigrp neighbors	Displays the neighbors discovered by IP EIGRP.
show ip eigrp topology	Displays the IP EIGRP topology table.
show ip eigrp traffic	Displays the number of packets sent and received for the IP EIGRP process(es).

Table 4-4   *OSPF IOS EXEC Commands*

IOS EXEC OSPF Command	Function
show ip ospf	Displays general information about OSPF routing processes.
show ip ospf database	Displays multiple lists of information related to the OSPF database.
show ip ospf database router	Displays the router link information from the OSPF database.
show ip ospf database network	Displays the network link information from the OSPF database.
show ip ospf database external	Displays the external network link information from the OSPF database.
show ip ospf database database-summary	Displays summary information regarding the OSPF database.
show ip ospf border-routers	Displays the internal OSPF routing table entries to Area Border Routers (ABR) and Autonomous System Boundary Routers (ASBR).
show ip ospf interface	Displays interface-specific OSPF-related information.
show ip ospf neighbor	Displays OSPF neighbor information.

Table 4-5   *BGP IOS EXEC Commands*

IOS EXEC BGP Command	Function
show ip bgp cidr-only	Displays all BGP routes that contain subnet and supernet network masks.
show ip bgp filter-list *access-list-number*	Displays routes that are matched by the specified autonomous system path access list.
show ip bgp regexp *regular-expression*	Displays the routes that match the specified regular expression entered on the command line.
show ip bgp [network] [network-mask] [subnets]	Displays the contents of the BGP routing table.
show ip bgp neighbors	Displays detailed information on the TCP and BGP connections to individual neighbors.
show ip bgp neighbors [*address*] **routes**	Displays routes learned from a particular BGP neighbor.
show ip bgp neighbors [*address*] **advertised**	Displays routes advertised to a particular BGP neighbor.
show ip bgp neighbors [*address*] **paths**	Displays paths learned from a particular BGP neighbor.
show ip bgp paths	Displays all BGP paths in the BGP database.
show ip bgp summary	Displays the status of all BGP peer connections.

Configuring IP Filtering via Access Lists

Since the first time that multiple systems were connected to form a network, there has been a need to restrict access to some systems or portions of a network for security, privacy, and other reasons. By using the packet-filtering facilities of the Cisco IOS software, a network administrator can restrict access to certain systems, network segments, ranges of addresses, and services based on a variety of criteria. The capability to restrict access is increasingly important as a company's network begins to connect to other outside networks, such as partner companies and the Internet.

The packet-filtering capabilities of the IOS software IP access lists allow for restricting packet flow based on the following criteria:

- Source IP address
- Source and destination IP address
- IP protocol types, including TCP, UDP, and ICMP
- Source and destination TCP protocol services, such as sendmail and Telnet
- Source and destination UDP protocol services, such as bootp and NetBIOS datagram
- ICMP protocol services, such as ICMP echo and ICMP port unreachable

The preceding list is by no means exhaustive. The flexibility of the IP access list gives the network administrator broad discretion in what is filtered and how the filters are applied.

The key to understanding IP access lists in IOS software is that the packet filtering task is broken into two distinct steps. First, the filtering criteria is defined through the use of the **access-list** and **ip access-list** commands. Second, the filtering criteria is applied to the desired interfaces. We've already considered one method of applying access list filtering—in conjunction with the **distribute-list** command for filtering routing information. In the next sections, we focus on using access lists in conjunction with the **ip access-group** command. Let's first consider how to establish the filtering criteria.

Defining the Access List

The filtering criteria are defined in a list of permit and deny statements called an access list. Each line in the access list is evaluated in sequence against the IP addresses and other information in a data packet until a match occurs. As soon as a match occurs, the list is exited. This process makes access lists highly order-dependent.

When originally developed, the IOS software had just one command for creating access lists, the **access-list** command. By using this command and a number from a relevant range of numbers, the network administrator can specify the network protocol for which the list is created. For example, the number range 1 to 99 denotes a standard IP access list, and the range 900 to 999 denotes an IPX packet filter. (IPX access lists are discussed in Chapter 6, "IPX Basics.")

Citing the need for more flexibility and even greater numbers of access lists, the IOS software designers created versions of the **access-list** command for IP and IPX that allow for named access lists. That is, the new commands can use an arbitrary string of characters rather than just a number to identify the access list. The command for creating a named IP access list is **ip access-list**. (There is also an **ipx access-list** command for named IPX lists.)

Whether numbered or named, IP access lists fall into one of two categories, standard or extended. A standard IP access list evaluates only the source IP address of a packet, while an extended access list can evaluate the source and destination IP addresses, the IP protocol type, and the source and destination transport layer ports.

Use the IOS global configuration command **access-list** to establish a numbered access list. As noted earlier, the **access-list** command takes as a parameter a list number. Standard IP access lists are established by a number in the range from 1 to 99. Extended IP access lists are denoted by a number in the range from 100 to 199. Following the list number on each line of the access list is the keyword **permit** or **deny**, followed by the IP address, wildcard mask, protocol, and the protocol port number that is filtered. The following is an example of a numbered, standard IP access list on the ZIP SF-1 router that denies packets with a source IP address of 131.108.101.99 but permits all others on the 131.108.101.0/24 network:

```
SF-1#configure
Configuring from terminal, memory, or network [terminal]?
Enter configuration commands, one per line.  End with CNTL/Z.
SF-1(config)#access-list 1 deny 131.108.101.99
SF-1(config)#access-list 1 permit 131.108.101.0 0.0.0.255
SF-1(config)#^Z
```

As mentioned previously, the order of the lines in an access list determines how the filter operates. Reversing the order of the access list statements in the previous example would completely alter the functionality of the access list. The following is how the access list would look if we performed such a reversal:

```
SF-1#configure
Configuring from terminal, memory, or network [terminal]?
Enter configuration commands, one per line.  End with CNTL/Z.
SF-1(config)#access-list 1 permit 131.108.101.0 0.0.0.255
SF-1(config)#access-list 1 deny 131.108.101.99
SF-1(config)#^Z
```

Now, if a packet with IP address 131.108.101.99 is compared to this access list, it matches the first statement and then exits the list. The **deny** statement of the list is never evaluated for 131.108.101.99.

TIP

Access lists make use of a concept known as the *wildcard* or *don't care* mask. Although it looks similar to a network mask, the wildcard mask is different in that bit positions set to 1 match any value. A wildcard mask of 0.0.0.255 matches any number in the range from 0 to 255 that appears in the fourth octet of an IP address. A wildcard mask of 0.0.3.255 matches any IP address with a 0, 1, 2, or 3 in the third octet and any number in the fourth octet based on binary computation. Wildcard masks enable the network administrator to specify ranges of addresses that fall along bit boundaries of binary numbers.

The following is an example of a numbered extended IP access list on the ZIP SF-1 router that permits only packets from the TCP Simple Mail Transfer Protocol (SMTP) and the UDP domain name service (DNS) protocol to reach IP address 131.108.101.99. Note that the keyword **any** can replace the network address 0.0.0.0 with the wildcard mask 255.255.255.255:

```
SF-1#configure
Configuring from terminal, memory, or network [terminal]?
Enter configuration commands, one per line.  End with CNTL/Z.
SF-1(config)#access-list 100 permit tcp any host 131.108.101.99 eq smtp
SF-1(config)#access-list 100 permit udp any host 131.108.101.99 eq domain
SF-1(config)#access-list 100 deny ip any any log
SF-1(config)#^Z
```

TIP   All access lists have an implicit **deny** at the end of the list. This means that any packet failing to match the filtering criteria of one of the lines of the access list is denied. For better troubleshooting and administrative control of network security, we recommend that you put an explicit **deny** at the end of the access list with the optional keyword **log**. This action causes all packets that fail to match the list to have the violation logged to the console or, if syslogging is enabled, to the syslog server. (Logging is discussed in more detail in Chapter 7.) The optional keyword **log** may also be applied to any line of the access list for which the administrator wants to have logging information recorded.

Thus far, the examples we've considered have been of numbered access lists. As noted earlier, named access lists enable the administrator to use arbitrary character strings to reference the IP access lists. For example, you can name access lists in ways that are easy to remember and relevant to the filtering task at hand.

Named IP access lists are created with the **ip access-list** configuration command. The command takes as parameters the keyword **extended** or **standard** to denote the type of named access list being created and the actual name of the access list.

The **ip access-list** command causes the IOS software configuration to switch to the access list configuration submode. After the access list configuration is in submode, only the **permit** and **deny** statements, along with the network address and other filtering criteria, need to be supplied. The access list name need not be repeated for each line of the list. Let's review the preceding standard access list example, using a named access list instead of a numbered access list:

```
SF-1#configure
Configuring from terminal, memory, or network [terminal]?
Enter configuration commands, one per line.  End with CNTL/Z.
SF-1(config)#ip access-list  standard sorrycharlie
SF-1(config-std-nacl)#deny 131.108.101.99
SF-1(config-std-nacl)#permit 131.108.101.0 0.0.0.255
SF-1(config)#^Z
```

The following is the previous extended access list example, rewritten using named access lists:

```
SF-1#configure
Configuring from terminal, memory, or network [terminal]?
Enter configuration commands, one per line.  End with CNTL/Z.
SF-1(config)#ip access-list extended out-of-luck
SF-1(config-ext-nacl)#permit tcp any host 131.108.101.99 eq smtp
SF-1(config-ext-nacl)#permit udp any host 131.108.101.99 eq domain
SF-1(config-ext-nacl)#deny ip any any log
SF-1(config-ext-nacl)#^Z
```

Whether numbered or named, one of the challenges of managing access lists is recalling why certain hosts, networks, or services have been permitted or denied access. Over time, different network administrators may be responsible for maintaining the access lists on various devices throughout the network, and the reasons for certain access list entries may have been long forgotten.

In earlier versions of the IOS software, the only way to document information about access lists (or any configuration command) was to add comments to a copy of the startup configuration file that was stored on a server. Unfortunately, these comments are ignored when the configuration file is loaded into the router's memory, so there is no documentation actually in the NVRAM or running memory.

More recent versions of the IOS software have introduced the capability to add comments to both numbered and named access list commands. Adding comments to numbered access lists is achieved by using the keyword **remark** in place of the **permit** or **deny** keyword following the IOS global configuration command **access-list** and the list number. Remarks may be placed anywhere within the access list, and each can be up to 100 characters long. The following is an example of adding remarks to the numbered IP extended access list previously defined on the ZIP SF-1 router:

```
SF-1#configure
Configuring from terminal, memory, or network [terminal]?
Enter configuration commands, one per line.  End with CNTL/Z.
SF-1(config)#access-list 100 remark Allow smtp mail to John's machine per Jane
SF-1(config)#access-list 100 permit tcp any host 131.108.101.99 eq smtp
SF-1(config)#access-list 100 remark Allow DNS queries to John's machine per Jane
SF-1(config)#access-list 100 permit udp any host 131.108.101.99 eq domain
SF-1(config)#access-list 100 remark Nothing else gets through and gets logged
SF-1(config)#access-list 100 deny ip any any log
SF-1(config)#^Z
```

For adding comments to named access lists, the IP access list configuration submode command **remark** is used. Similar to the **permit** and **deny** statements used in this submode, the **remark** command is used after entering the access list configuration submode using the **ip access-list** command followed by the list name. As with numbered access list remarks, named access list remarks can appear anywhere within the list, and each can be up to 100 characters long. The following is an example of adding remarks to the named IP extended access list previously defined on the ZIP SF-1 router:

```
SF-1#configure
Configuring from terminal, memory, or network [terminal]?
Enter configuration commands, one per line.  End with CNTL/Z.
SF-1(config)#ip access-list extended out-of-luck
SF-1(config-ext-nacl)#remark Allow smtp mail to John's machine per Jane
SF-1(config-ext-nacl)#permit tcp any host 131.108.101.99 eq smtp
SF-1(config-ext-nacl)#remark Allow DNS queries to John's machine per Jane
SF-1(config-ext-nacl)#permit udp any host 131.108.101.99 eq domain
SF-1(config-ext-nacl)#remark Nothing else gets through and gets logged
SF-1(config-ext-nacl)#deny ip any any log
SF-1(config-ext-nacl)#^Z
```

Applying the Access List

After the filtering criteria of the access list is defined, it must be applied to one or more interfaces so that packets can be filtered. The access list may be applied in either an inbound or an outbound direction on the interface. When packets travel in the inbound direction, they come into the router from the interface. When they travel in the outbound direction, they leave the router and then go onto the interface. The access list is applied via the IOS interface configuration subcommand **ip access-group**. The command takes as a parameter the keyword **in** or **out**. If no parameter is provided, the **out** keyword is presumed. The following example applies the standard access list 1, defined previously, on the Fast Ethernet interface of the ZIP router SF-1. This configuration prevents packets originating from the address 131.108.101.99 from reaching destinations beyond the Fast Ethernet interface:

```
SF-1#configure
Configuring from terminal, memory, or network [terminal]?
Enter configuration commands, one per line.  End with CNTL/Z.
SF-1(config)#interface fastethernet 0
SF-1(config-if)#ip access-group 1 out
SF-1(config-if)#^Z
```

The following is an example of applying the previously defined access list, out-of-luck, on the Fast Ethernet interface of the ZIP SF-1 router. This configuration prevents packets originating from any address from exiting the router, with the exception of those packets traveling to the host 131.108.101.99 for SMTP and DNS services:

```
SF-1#configure
Configuring from terminal, memory, or network [terminal]?
Enter configuration commands, one per line.  End with CNTL/Z.
SF-1(config)#interface fastethernet 0
SF-1(config-if)#ip access-group out-of-luck out
SF-1(config-if)#^Z
```

After access lists are configured, they can be viewed and verified by using the IOS EXEC commands **show access-lists** and **show ip access-lists**. The former command shows all access lists defined on the router, while the latter shows only IP access lists defined on the router (whether numbered or named). Each command can take as a parameter a specific numbered or named access list and can display only the contents of that list. If no parameter is supplied, all lists are displayed. The following output of the **show access-lists** command for the ZIP SF-1 router shows that the previously defined access lists have been applied to the router:

```
SF-1#show access-lists
Standard IP access list 1
    deny 131.108.101.99  (50 matches)
    permit 131.108.101.0 0.0.0.255  (576 matches)
Standard IP access list sorrycharlie
    deny 131.108.101.99
    permit 131.108.101.0 0.0.0.255
Extended IP access list 100
    permit tcp any host 131.108.101.99 eq smtp
    permit udp any host 131.108.101.99 eq domain
    deny ip any any log
Extended IP access list out-of-luck
    permit tcp any host 131.108.101.99 eq smtp  (987 matches)
    permit udp any host 131.108.101.99 eq domain  (10987 matches)
    deny ip any any log  (453245 matches)
SF-1#
```

As seen in the output, the **show access-lists** and **show ip access-lists** commands count the number of times that each line of an access list has been matched and display the count in parentheses. This information can be useful in determining which lines of an access list are serving a useful purpose. It can also aid in troubleshooting, revealing possible access list misconfigurations. For example, if the counter for permitting UDP domain packets in the out-of-luck list does not increase and there are reports of domain name service outages from users, it is clear that domain packets are not passing the access list. Further evidence might be an increase in the counter for the last line of the out-of-luck list that is registering the number of packets that fail the access list.

The match counters on the commands **show access-lists** and **show ip access-lists** can be reset by the IOS EXEC command **clear ip access-list counters**. This command takes an optional parameter of an IP access list number or name for which to clear the match counters. If no parameter is specified, all match counters on all IP access lists are cleared.

The following is an example of clearing the match counters for the named IP access list out-of-luck on the ZIP SF-1 router:

```
SF-1#clear ip access-list counters out-of-luck
SF-1#
```

Determining where access lists are utilized is a bit tricky. When they are applied as packet filters with the **ip access-group** command, output from the **show ip interfaces** command indicates which access lists have been applied to which interfaces. When access lists are applied as route filters with the **distribute-list** command, output from the **show ip protocols** command indicates the inbound or outbound application of the filters to specific routing protocols. This discussion of commands for viewing and verifying access lists is by no means exhaustive, because access lists function as the enabler for many of the filtering features within the IOS software. Each specific application of access lists has corresponding verification commands.

The IP packet-filtering capabilities of the Cisco IOS software provide very powerful tools for limiting access to resources both inside and outside an entity's network. However, designing a firewall protection scheme is a complex and important task. Entire books are devoted to providing adequate security for the network. We recommend that you refer to such texts for more information on protecting your network resources (see the "References" section at the end of this chapter). Additionally, as of this writing, Cisco Systems maintains an excellent case study entitled *Increasing Security on IP Networks* on CCO at www.cisco.com/univercd/cc/td/doc/cisintwk/ics/cs003.htm.

Configuring Basic IP Dialup Services

Up to this point, we have been examining the IOS software's routing protocol and IP packet-switching capabilities. The IOS software also enables remote access in the routers and access servers. The remote access capability is available as both asynchronous dialup via external and integrated modem modules, and via ISDN. Remote access provides both remote users and remote routers with the capability to connect to IP network services when they are not connected directly to a network via a LAN or WAN interface.

Numerous IOS-based products support IP remote access services. These products offer many configuration options in both their hardware and IOS software feature configurations. As with other complex topics discussed in this chapter, entire books are devoted to the discussion of remote access services. We have chosen to present two of the common configurations for basic IP remote access that support dialup workstation users. Many of these commands and the configuration concepts are also applicable to the implementation of router-to-router remote access, which is known as dial-on-demand routing. For a discussion of the issues and the configuration of dial-on-demand routing, we recommend referring to the following Cisco Systems case studies. You can find *Dial-on-Demand Routing* and *Scaling Dial-on-Demand Routing* on CCO at www.cisco.com/univercd/cc/td/doc/cisintwk/ics/cs002.htm and www.cisco.com/univercd/cc/td/doc/cisintwk/ics/cs012.htm, respectively.

To ensure the reliability of the connection over a dialup service, such as a modem or ISDN, IP is transported on a link layer protocol over the dialup service. Several data link layer protocols are supported on dialup services, including PPP, HDLC, SLIP (Serial Line IP), and Frame Relay. At the time of this writing, PPP is the predominant choice as a data link layer protocol for dialup service.

Configuration of remote access services can be broken down into three major areas:

- Line or interface configuration
- Security configuration
- IP protocol configuration

Each of these is examined for both asynchronous and ISDN dialup scenarios on the ZIP network access servers located in Singapore. The asynchronous services are provided on a Cisco 2511 that supports 16 async lines. The ISDN services are provided on a Cisco 4500 with integrated ISDN BRI interfaces.

Configuring Asynchronous Dialup

Asychronous dialup (async for short) involves the use of analog modems to convert data into streams of information that can be carried over phone lines. These modems may be either integrated into the product, as with the Cisco AS5200 AccessServer and 3600 router, or attached externally, as with the 2511 AccessServer and the auxiliary port of most Cisco routers. Figure 4-9 shows a typical dialup scenario for a remote workstation user accessing a network via an access server with external modems.

Figure 4-9   *Remote Dialup Access to an Access Server Via Modems*

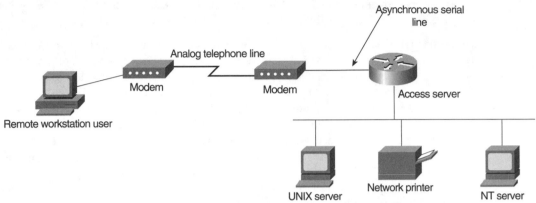

Regardless of whether there are physical async serial lines attached to the modems or virtual lines inside the integrated modem modules, the lines and modems must be configured properly to ensure proper communication. The speed of the line, the flow control method, the direction of the dialup, and the type of modem attached are some of the most important aspects that must be set up. Chapter 7 discusses the configuration of virtual terminal lines (vty) for the purposes of controlling remote access to the router via the IOS major configuration command line. We also use line commands to configure characteristics of the physical async lines (tty) used for connecting the modems.

To set the speed at which the access server communicates with the modems, use the IOS line configuration subcommand **speed**. The command takes as a parameter an integer that represents the speed as the number of bits per second to transmit and receive. The speed should be set to the highest speed supported by the data port on the modem (the highest speed supported on the access server is 115,200 bps).

To set the method used to control the flow of information from the access server to the modems, use the IOS line configuration subcommand **flowcontrol**. The command takes as a parameter the keyword **hardware** or **software**. These keywords represent the two types of flow control supported. With speeds of more than 9,600 bps, it is recommended that hardware flow control be used. The following is an example of configuring all 16 async lines on the ZIP Singapore access server to use hardware flow control at a speed of 115,200 bps. Note the use of the **line** major configuration command to reference async lines 1 through 16 that the subcommands are applied to:

```
Sing2511#configure
Configuring from terminal, memory, or network [terminal]?
Enter configuration commands, one per line.  End with CNTL/Z.
Sing2511(config)#line 1 16
Sing2511(config-line)#speed 115200
Sing2511(config-line)#flowcontrol hardware
Sing2511(config-line)#^Z
```

After the speed and flow control methods are selected, the access server must be supplied with information about the attached modem type and dialup direction information. Supplying information about the modem type eases the dialup configuration task by eliminating the need to configure the modem settings manually. Additionally, the access server can reset the modem settings after each call to ensure the proper operation of the dialup pool.

Dialup direction information instructs the access server how to react to the signals sent to it by the modem during call establishment. The IOS line configuration subcommand **modem** is used to configure both the attached modem type and the dialup direction. For configuring the modem type, use the **modem autoconfigure** command. This command takes as a parameter either the keyword **discovery** or the keyword **type**. The keyword **discovery** instructs the access server to try to determine the type of attached modem for selecting the modem settings. The keyword **type**, followed by one of the predefined or user-defined modem types, instructs the access server to select the modem settings of the named type.

The IOS software supports a number of popular modem types, including the U.S. Robotics Courier, the U.S. Robotics Sportster, and the Telebit T3000. If the type is not predefined, the user can establish additional types and the corresponding settings via the IOS configuration command **modemcap**. For establishing the dialup direction, the keyword parameter **dialin** or **inout** is used with the modem command. The following is an example of configuring the ZIP Singapore access server to use the modem settings associated with the U.S. Robotics Courier modem. The dialup direction is configured as **dialin**:

```
Sing2511#configure
Configuring from terminal, memory, or network [terminal]?
Enter configuration commands, one per line.  End with CNTL/Z.
Sing2511(config)#line 1 16
Sing2511(config-line)#modem autoconfigure type usr_courier
Sing2511(config-line)#modem dialin
Sing2511(config-line)#^Z
```

TIP

Even if the async lines are used only for dial-in, we recommend that you set the lines for inout operation during initial configuration and troubleshooting. This allows virtual terminal access via the Telnet protocol directly to the async line for manual modem configuration and verification. This virtual terminal access method, which is known as reverse Telnet, is described in more detail in the *Configuring Modems* tip on CCO at www.cisco.com/univercd/cc/td/doc/product/software/ios113ed/dsqcg/qcmodems.htm.

With the async line configuration complete, access server security is the next step in the configuration process. As discussed in the section "Basic Access Control" in Chapter 7, access security is broken into two steps. The first step is the authentication process, the process of identifying who is attempting access. The second step is authorizing the identified user to perform specific tasks or to give the user access to specific services. For the purposes of dialup IP, we introduce an authentication type and an authorization type that makes use of locally configured user information, which is not discussed in Chapter 7. These authentication and authorization commands make use of locally configured user information. Optionally, a security server such as a TACACS+ or a RADIUS server could be used in lieu of locally configured information, as discussed in Chapter 7.

For authenticating users who attempt to access IP services via PPP, AAA authentication type **ppp** is used. It is enabled via the IOS configuration command **aaa authentication ppp**. The command takes as parameters an authentication list name or the keyword **default** and one or more authentication methods, such as local or, in this case, TACACS+. After a PPP user is identified, that user must be authorized to use network services (of which PPP is one). Use of network services is authorized by the **aaa authorization network** command. This command takes as a parameter of one or more authorization types. The following is an example of configuring the ZIP Singapore access server to authenticate PPP users with locally configured user information and to authorize the use of network services for all users who pass authentication:

```
Sing2511#configure
Configuring from terminal, memory, or network [terminal]?
Enter configuration commands, one per line.  End with CNTL/Z.
Sing2511(config)#aaa authentication default ppp local
Sing2511(config)#aaa authorization network default if-authenticated
Sing2511(config)#^Z
```

Authentication information for the PPP users is being configured locally, so the actual usernames and passwords used for authentication must be configured. This information is configured via the IOS global configuration command **username**. The command takes as parameters the user ID to be used for authentication, the keyword **password**, and the password to be used for authenticating the user. Although the password is entered in readable clear text, it is converted to an encrypted string if password encryption is enabled, as discussed in Chapter 7. The following is an example of creating local usernames and passwords on the ZIP Singapore access server for two users, John and Jane:

```
Sing2511#configure
Configuring from terminal, memory, or network [terminal]?
Enter configuration commands, one per line.  End with CNTL/Z.
Sing2511(config)#username john password foo
Sing2511(config)#username jane password bar
Sing2511(config)#^Z
```

The final step in configuring IP async dialup services is providing the IP protocol information that is used to establish and maintain the dialup IP session. Rather than IP protocol information being entered as line subcommands, protocol information is associated with an interface type that represents the async line, just as with any other LAN or WAN media. This interface type is called an async interface, and each async line on the access server has a corresponding async interface. IP protocol information can be entered individually on each async interface on which dialup sessions may occur, or only once via a collective async interface called the group-async interface.

The group-async interface can be used to simplify configuration tasks when the same configuration commands would be applied repeatedly to multiple async interfaces. When the group-async interface is used, the IOS interface configuration subcommand **group-range** is used as well to identify which individual async interfaces should be included in the group structure. The following is an example of adding the **description** command to three async interfaces:

```
Sing2511#configure
Configuring from terminal, memory, or network [terminal]?
Enter configuration commands, one per line.  End with CNTL/Z.
Sing2511(config)#interface async 1
Sing2511(config-if)#description dialup pool on singapore 2511
Sing2511(config-if)#interface async 2
Sing2511(config-if)#description dialup pool on singapore 2511
Sing2511(config-if)#interface async 3
Sing2511(config-if)#description dialup pool on singapore 2511
Sing2511(config-if)#^Z
```

Here is the same configuration using a group-async interface:

```
Sing2511#configure
Configuring from terminal, memory, or network [terminal]?
Enter configuration commands, one per line.  End with CNTL/Z.
Sing2511(config)#interface group-async 1
Sing2511(config-if)#description dialup pool on singapore 2511
Sing2511(config-if)#group-range 1 3
Sing2511(config-if)#^Z
```

The IP protocol information that is assigned to the async interfaces falls into three categories:

- IP address configuration for the async interface
- IP address information to supply to the dialup users
- Information about how IP and PPP should operate on the async interface

We start by examining the PPP and IP operation commands. First, the async interface must be told to use PPP as the encapsulation method for services such as IP. The IOS interface configuration subcommand **encapsulation** is used to specify the encapsulation type. The command takes as a parameter a keyword (for example, **ppp** or **slip**) for the encapsulation type that is used on the interface.

After PPP is configured, the network administrator has the option of configuring the async line to operate as only a dialup network services port—that is, the user is allowed to use only the network services configured on the port, such as PPP or SLIP—or allowing the user to receive an EXEC prompt on dialup and to choose what service to run manually. The IOS interface configuration subcommand **async mode** is used to specify the desired operation. The command takes as a parameter the keyword **interactive** or **dedicated** to set the desired operation.

The level of expertise of the dial-in user and how the async interface is used usually determine which mode is chosen, interactive or dedicated. Configuring for dedicated operation precludes a network administrator from dialing up and being authorized to use the EXEC commands. Interactive mode can support both EXEC commands and network services. The drawback to interactive mode, however, is that inexperienced users may misconfigure their dialup software and be placed in an EXEC prompt unknowingly.

When the interactive mode is used, an additional set of line commands simplifies the dialup process for the user. These commands allow the access server to determine the type of connection being attempted without requiring the user to specify the service at an EXEC prompt. This process is called autoselection. It is enabled via the IOS line configuration subcommand **autoselect**. This command takes as a parameter a keyword that describes the link layer protocol to be autoselected or the time the autoselect is performed (normally at user authentication time). Using autoselection when async interactive mode is configured provides the simplest method for most users to access PPP and IP services on the access server.

The last PPP operations command required on the interface instructs PPP to perform authentication and authorization of dialup users before establishing PPP and IP network services. This ensures that only authorized users gain access to the network services available on the access server. This command also tells the access server which authentication protocol to use between the access server and the dialup client. Three protocols are possible—Challenge Handshake Authentication Protocol (CHAP), Microsoft Challenge Handshake Authentication Protocol (MS-CHAP), and Password Authentication Protocol (PAP).

The IOS interface configuration subcommand **ppp authentication** instructs the access server to perform the authentication process. The command takes as a parameter the keyword **chap**, **ms-chap**, or **pap** to specify the authentication protocol. A single protocol or combination of protocols may be specified in the same configuration command if dialup users are accessing with multiple authentication protocols. The command also takes an optional keyword, **callin**, which instructs the access server to perform the authentication challenge only on incoming dialup calls. The default is to challenge both incoming and outgoing calls. Some vendor implementations do not answer challenges if they receive an incoming call.

The commands described previously are the minimum required for configuring the operation of PPP for the dialup users. With the large number of Microsoft dialup users today, the network administrator might choose to add support for Microsoft Point-to-Point Compression (MPPC), described in RFC 2118, "Microsoft Point-to-Point Compression Protocol." Compression optimizes the transmission of information over a medium such as a dialup line, which allows more information to be transmitted than would typically be possible. On relatively slow dialup lines that operate at anywhere from 28,800 bps to 53,000 bps, compression can boost the rate at which information is transmitted by as much as 1.5 times.

Adding compression for the dialup users is accomplished via the IOS interface configuration subcommand **compress**. The **compress** command takes as a parameter the keyword **mppc**, **stac**, or **predictor** to indicate the type of compression that is to be negotiated when a dialup user is establishing a connection. The **stac** and **predictor** keywords denote using the STAC or Predictor compression algorithms. STAC is a common compression algorithm supported by many dialup clients, including Windows 95 systems, and it would be a good choice if you were supporting a large group of non-Microsoft or Windows 95 dialup users. Predictor is a much less common algorithm. Selecting Microsoft Point-to-Point Compression is accomplished via the **mppc** keyword. Given that Windows NT supports only MPPC, and Windows 95/98 supports both MPCC and STAC compression, selecting this compression algorithm provides the most flexibility for the network administrator supporting multiple Microsoft operating systems.

At this point, let's look at an example of configuring the PPP and IP operation commands on the ZIP Singapore access server. In this example, we configure all 16 of the async lines via the group-async interface method. We establish the interfaces as PPP-encapsulated interfaces and place them in interactive mode, allowing the async lines to perform auto selection of PPP during the login process. Additionally, we configure PPP to authenticate incoming dialup calls using the CHAP, MS-CHAP, or PAP authentication protocol and then allow Microsoft compression to be negotiated:

```
Sing2511#configure
Configuring from terminal, memory, or network [terminal]?
Enter configuration commands, one per line.  End with CNTL/Z.
Sing2511(config)#interface group-async 1
Sing2511(config-if)#group-range 1 16
Sing2511(config-if)#encapsulation ppp
Sing2511(config-if)#async mode interactive
Sing2511(config-if)#ppp authentication chap ms-chap pap callin
Sing2511(config-if)#compress mppc
Sing2511(config-if)#line 1 16
Sing2511(config-line)#autoselect ppp
Sing2511(config-line)#autoselect during-login
Sing2511(config-line)#^Z
```

With the operational mode of PPP defined, IP addressing on the async interfaces can now be performed. Normally, dialup IP users have only a single IP address associated with their workstations. Contrast this to a dialup router, which has an entire LAN segment attached and needs to perform routing with the central site for proper communications. Because each individual dialup user uses an IP address on a separate dialup connection and, therefore, a separate async interface, the actual IP address of the async interface is not important. In fact, each async interface can be treated as if it resides in the same IP address space as the attached LAN interface. These async interfaces can even be treated as if the dialup user's IP address is assigned from that address space. Looking at it from a different perspective, the dialup user is logically attached to the LAN segment via a long cable, the telephone line. No IP address is assigned to the telephone line in the same way that a LAN workstation is attached via a 10BaseT cable.

The workstation receives an IP address from the same IP network address space that is assigned to the access server's LAN interface. The access server has the responsibility to accept packets from the LAN on behalf of the dialup user. It directs those packets to the proper dialup telephone call. The access server achieves this by injecting a host route (a network route with a 32-bit network mask) into the routing table of the access server when a dialup connection is established and by answering ARP requests for the IP addresses that are assigned to dialup sessions.

The async interfaces themselves do not have IP addresses when using the preceding method, so the IOS interface configuration subcommand **ip unnumbered** can be used to enable IP processing on the async interfaces. This command was introduced in the section "Point-to-Point WAN Interface Addressing," earlier in this chapter. It is used in the same manner as described earlier—for specifying the LAN interface of the access server as the reference interface. The following is an example of making the async interfaces of the previously configured group-async interface unnumbered on the ZIP Singapore access server:

```
Sing2511#configure
Configuring from terminal, memory, or network [terminal]?
Enter configuration commands, one per line.  End with CNTL/Z.
Sing2511(config)#interface group-async 1
Sing2511(config-if)#ip unnumbered ethernet 0
Sing2511(config-if)#^Z
```

The last step in establishing IP dialup connectivity on the async interface is configuring what IP addresses are assigned to a dialup client at the time of the connection. The IOS interface configuration subcommand **peer default ip address** determines the method used to assign an IP address to the dialup client. By specifying a specific IP address as the parameter to the command, individual IP addresses can be assigned to each async interface. However, this requires that each async interface be manually configured with the IP address that will be assigned to dialup clients connecting on that interface.

A more flexible method is assigning IP addresses from one or more address pools that have been established on the access server with the command **parameter pool**. This method also gives users who have permanently assigned IP addresses the flexibility of dialing into any modem port, because the access server accepts the dialup client's suggested IP address if it falls into a predefined address pool. When the pool method is specified, it is accompanied by a specific address pool name.

The address pools themselves are defined using the IOS global configuration command **ip local pool**. This command takes as a parameter a pool name and the starting and ending IP addresses that form the pool. The IP addresses need to be from the same IP network as the access server's LAN interface. Of course, these addresses should not be assigned to any workstations that reside on the LAN segment. The following is an example of configuring the async interfaces of the previously defined group-async structure to assign IP addresses from a local pool called modem-users on the ZIP Singapore access server. Note that the pool is defined as having only 16 addresses because only 16 modems and async interfaces exist on the access server.

```
Sing2511#configure
Configuring from terminal, memory, or network [terminal]?
Enter configuration commands, one per line.  Fnd with CNTL/Z.
Sing2511(config)#interface group-async 1
Sing2511(config-if)#peer default ip address pool modem-users
```

```
Sing2511(config-if)#ip local pool modem-users 131.108.1.111 131.108.1.126
Sing2511(config-if)#^Z
```

Although address pools are the most flexible method for assigning IP addresses, no method exists for coordinating the assignment of addresses across multiple access servers. In this situation, it may be better to assign addresses from a central address authority server, such as a Dynamic Host Configuration Protocol (DHCP) server. To accommodate this method, the IOS software acts as a proxy DHCP client, requesting an IP address from the DHCP server on behalf of the dialup client. This configuration method is enabled by specifying the keyword parameter **dhcp** to the **peer default ip address** command. The access server must also be configured with the IP address of a DHCP server to query for address requests via the IOS global configuration command **ip dhcp-server**. The address pools defined on the DHCP server would contain addresses from the IP network address of the access server's LAN interface. The following is a configuration example of the ZIP Singapore access server configured to use DHCP to assign IP addresses to dialup clients:

```
Sing2511#configure
Configuring from terminal, memory, or network [terminal]?
Enter configuration commands, one per line.  End with CNTL/Z.
Sing2511(config)#interface group-async 1
Sing2511(config-if)#peer default ip address dhcp
Sing2511(config-if)#ip dhcp-server 131.108.21.70
Sing2511(config-if)#^Z
```

Many dialup client PPP implementations make use of a nonstandard method for obtaining DNS and NetBIOS/WINS nameserver IP addresses during the call establishment process. This method is described in the informational RFC 1877, "PPP Internet Protocol Control Protocol Extensions for Name Server Addresses." Although not a standard, this method has been widely implemented, most notably in the Microsoft dialup implementations. The access server can also support the methods described in RFC 1877 to supply both the DNS and NetBIOS/WINS nameserver addresses. Older implementations use the IOS global configuration command **async-bootp** to configure these options. When configuring the IP address(es) of DNS servers, the command takes as a parameter the keyword **dns-server**, followed by one or more IP addresses. When configuring the IP address(es) of NetBIOS/WINS servers, the command takes as a parameter the keyword **nbns-server**, followed by one or more IP addresses. The following is an example of configuring the ZIP Singapore access server to supply the IP addresses of DNS and NetBIOS/WINS nameservers according to the RFC 1877 method using the **async-bootp** command:

```
Sing2511#configure
Configuring from terminal, memory, or network [terminal]?
Enter configuration commands, one per line.  End with CNTL/Z.
Sing2511(config)#async-bootp dns-server 131.108.101.34 131.108.101.35
Sing2511(config)#async-bootp nbns-server 131.108.21.70
Sing2511(config)#^Z
```

Although supplying DNS and NetBIOS/WINS nameserver addresses has little to do with BOOTP, the **async-bootp** command was used to enable this feature in the IOS software by adding extensions to the existing SLIP BOOTP negotiation protocol commands. This method was chosen at the time in lieu of creating separate PPP commands and mechanisms to implement a nonstandard RFC.

The drawback to using the **async-bootp** command to supply DNS and NetBIOS/WINS server addresses is that the command is an IOS global configuration command. This results in the addresses configured via the command being supplied to all dialup users in the access server, regardless of the dialup interface to which they might be connected. This has proven to be an inflexible method for network administrators who want to support multiple types of dialup connections or different classes of users and who want to supply different server addresses for those connections or users. In newer versions of the IOS software, the IOS interface configuration subcommand **ppp ipcp** gives the network administrator more granular control of these options on a per-interface basis. When configuring the IP address(es) of DNS servers, the command takes as a parameter the keyword **dns**, followed by one or two IP addresses. When configuring the IP address(es) of NetBIOS/WINS servers, the command takes as a parameter the keyword **wins**, followed by one or two IP addresses. The following is an example of configuring the ZIP Singapore access server to supply the IP addresses of DNS and NetBIOS/WINS nameservers according to the RFC 1877 method using the **ppp ipcp** command:

```
Sing2511#configure
Configuring from terminal, memory, or network [terminal]?
Enter configuration commands, one per line.  End with CNTL/Z.
Sing2511(config)#interface group-async 1
Sing2511(config-if)#ppp ipcp dns 131.108.101.34 131.108.101.35
Sing2511(config-if)#ppp ipcp wins 131.108.21.70
Sing2511(config-if)#^Z
```

ISDN Dialup

Like asynchronous dialup, ISDN dialup involves the use of the public telephone network to enable remote workstation users to access services of a network when they are not directly connected via a LAN or WAN interface. ISDN differs from asynchronous dialup in that the calls are transmitted using synchronous digital signals. Data is converted into streams of digital information either by integrated ISDN interfaces on the router or through the use of external ISDN attachment devices called terminal adapters (TA), as discussed in Chapter 3. Remote workstation users also use either integrated ISDN PC boards or external TAs to connect to the ISDN service. Figure 4-10 shows a typical dialup scenario for a remote workstation user accessing a network via an access server with integrated ISDN Basic Rate Interfaces (BRI).

Figure 4-10 *Remote Dialup Access to an Access Server via ISDN*

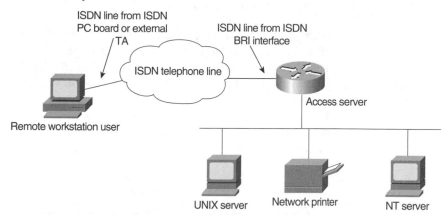

Many of the configuration tasks required to set up asynchronous IP dialup services are also required to establish ISDN IP dialup services. Unlike asynchronous configuration, however, no line commands are required because the router has a directly integrated ISDN interface or because the TA is attached directly to a synchronous serial interface. If the router has an integrated ISDN interface, any commands that control the interaction of the ISDN interface with the ISDN network are applied directly to the interface. Chapter 3 shows such an example of applying ISDN SPIDs to an ISDN BRI. If the router attaches to the ISDN network via an external TA, it is configured through its own methods for proper interaction with the ISDN network. This reduces the configuration of ISDN IP dialup services to two tasks, establishing security and defining IP information.

Like async interfaces, ISDN interfaces can be configured individually or as a group. When configured as a group, the configuration commands for the multiple ISDN interfaces are associated with an interface type called a dialer interface. Individual ISDN interfaces are still configured with their ISDN-specific commands, such as SPID information. However, PPP and IP operational and protocol commands are configured on the dialer interface. Each ISDN interface included in a dialer interface structure is configured with the command **dialer rotary-group**. This command takes as a parameter an integer representing the dialer interface to which an interface belongs. For example, interfaces in **dialer rotary-group 1** belong to interface dialer 1. The following is an example of configuring four BRI ISDN interfaces on the ZIP Singapore ISDN access server to belong to interface dialer 1:

```
SingISDN#configure
Configuring from terminal, memory, or network [terminal]?
Enter configuration commands, one per line.  End with CNTL/Z.
SingISDN(config)#interface bri 4
SingISDN(config-if)#dialer rotary-group 1
SingISDN(config-if)#interface bri 5
SingISDN(config-if)#dialer rotary-group 1
SingISDN(config-if)#interface bri 6
SingISDN(config-if)#dialer rotary-group 1
```

```
SingISDN(config-if)#interface bri 7
SingISDN(config-if)#dialer rotary-group 1
SingISDN(config-if)#^Z
```

We continue by reviewing the configuration of access server security for the dialup IP network services discussed in the preceding section. As with async dialup, PPP authentication and network authorization are performed with the IOS global configuration commands **aaa authentication ppp** and **aaa authorization network**, respectively. The IOS global configuration command **username** is used to define the remote usernames that access the network. The following is an example of configuring the ZIP Singapore ISDN access server for PPP authentication and authorization and defining username and password pairs for remote users Jim and Janet:

```
SingISDN#configure
Configuring from terminal, memory, or network [terminal]?
Enter configuration commands, one per line.  End with CNTL/Z.
SingISDN(config)#aaa authentication default ppp local
SingISDN(config)#aaa authorization network default if-authenticated
SingISDN(config)#username jim password dog
SingISDN(config)#username janet password house
SingISDN(config)#^Z
```

The IP protocol information assigned to ISDN interfaces falls into the same three categories as those of async interfaces:

- Information about how IP and PPP should operate on the ISDN interface
- IP address configuration for the ISDN interface
- IP address information to supply to the dialup users

We begin by recapping the PPP and IP operation commands previously discussed and introducing four new commands used with ISDN interfaces.

As seen with async IP, establishing PPP as the data link layer protocol for IP on ISDN interfaces is accomplished with the IOS interface configuration subcommand **encapsulation**. Enabling PPP authentication before beginning IP network services and specifying the authentication protocol is accomplished with the IOS interface configuration subcommand **ppp authentication**. Optionally, Microsoft compression can be added with the IOS interface configuration subcommand **compress mppc**. The following is an example of configuring the ZIP Singapore ISDN access server to use PPP on the ISDN dialer interface, instructing the access server to use authentication and authorization for network services, and enabling Microsoft compression on the dialer interface:

```
SingISDN#configure
Configuring from terminal, memory, or network [terminal]?
Enter configuration commands, one per line.  End with CNTL/Z.
SingISDN(config)#interface dialer 1
SingISDN(config-if)#encapsulation ppp
SingISDN(config-if)#ppp authentication chap ms-chap pap callin
SingISDN(config-if)#compress mppc
SingISDN(config-if)#^Z
```

ISDN is a channelized service—that is, it can support multiple connections over the same physical interface. This allows dialup ISDN clients to establish more than one connection at a time to an access server. This capability gives the dialup ISDN station access to twice the line capacity as using a single physical interface. Effective utilization of multiple channels is accomplished by multiplexing the data across the multiple connections using a software algorithm for PPP called multilink. Multilink PPP can be enabled via the IOS interface configuration subcommand **ppp multilink**.

To control when ISDN channels are made operational or shut down, a list of interesting packets is defined via the IOS global configuration command **dialer-list**. This command takes as parameters specific network protocols that should be considered interesting for the purposes of making (or keeping) a channel active. Additionally, access lists may be used to provide further granularity, down to specific IP addresses and transport protocol service types. The **dialer-list** rules are applied to an interface via the IOS interface configuration subcommand **dialer-group**, which specifies the list number as a parameter to the command. The following is an example of configuring the ZIP Singapore ISDN access server to support PPP multilink. The interesting packets list is defined by extended access list 102:

```
SingISDN#configure
Configuring from terminal, memory, or network [terminal]?
Enter configuration commands, one per line.  End with CNTL/Z.
SingISDN(config)#interface dialer 1
SingISDN(config-if)#ppp multilink
SingISDN(config-if)#dialer-group 1
SingISDN(config-if)#dialer-list 1 protocol ip list 102
SingISDN(config)#access-list 102 permit tcp any any eq telnet
SingISDN(config)#access-list 102 permit tcp any any eq www
SingISDN(config)#access-list 102 permit udp any any eq domain
SingISDN(config)#access-list 102 permit tcp any any eq ftp
SingISDN(config)#^Z
```

NOTE Finer control of the allocation of bandwidth through the use of multiple ISDN channels is defined in RFC 2125, "Bandwidth Allocation Control Protocol (BACP)." Bandwidth Allocation Protocol (BAP), which is a subset of BACP, provides a set of rules governing dynamic bandwidth allocation through call control—a standards method for adding and removing links from a multilink bundle. Access servers and dialup clients negotiate the rules under which dynamic bandwidth is added or removed during a session. BACP is a feature introduced in IOS software Release 11.3.

Assignment of IP addresses to the access server ISDN interfaces and remote dialup workstations works in the same manner as with async interfaces. The ISDN interfaces on the access server need not be assigned specific IP addresses when only ISDN dialup workstations are accessing those interfaces. The interface can be configured as unnumbered via the Cisco IOS interface configuration subcommand **ip unnumbered**. The remote dialup client IP addresses may be assigned using any of the three previously discussed methods using the **peer default ip address** subcommand. These methods include assigning an individual remote IP address associated with each ISDN interface, using a pool of IP addresses that will be assigned to the remote ISDN clients, or assigning IP addresses obtained from a DHCP server to the remote ISDN clients.

The following is an example of configuring the ZIP Singapore ISDN access server to assign IP addresses from an address pool called isdn-users for remote clients connecting on the ISDN interfaces:

```
SingISDN#configure
Configuring from terminal, memory, or network [terminal]?
Enter configuration commands, one per line.  End with CNTL/Z.
SingISDN(config)#interface dialer 1
SingISDN(config-if)#peer default ip address pool isdn-users
SingISDN(config-if)#ip local pool isdn-users 131.108.1.91 131.108.1.106
SingISDN(config-if)#^Z
```

DNS and NetBIOS/WINS nameserver IP addresses can also be supplied to ISDN dialup clients using the methods in RFC 1877. As with async interfaces, ISDN clients are supplied with those addresses by configuring the IOS global configuration commands **async-bootp dns-server** and **async-bootp nbns-server**, or the IOS interface configuration subcommands **ppp ipcp dns** and **ppp ipcp wins**. Using either method, the IP addresses are supplied as parameters of the commands. The following is an example of configuring the ZIP Singapore ISDN access server to supply DNS and NetBIOS/WINS IP addresses to ISDN dialup clients using the **async-bootp** commands:

```
SingISDN#configure
Configuring from terminal, memory, or network [terminal]?
Enter configuration commands, one per line.  End with CNTL/Z.
SingISDN(config)#async-bootp dns-server 131.108.101.34 131.108.101.35
SingISDN(config)#async-bootp nbns-server 131.108.21.70
SingISDN(config)#^Z
```

The following is an example of configuring the ZIP Singapore ISDN access server to supply DNS and NetBIOS/WINS IP addresses to ISDN dialup clients using the **ppp ipcp** commands:

```
SingISDN#configure
Configuring from terminal, memory, or network [terminal]?
Enter configuration commands, one per line.  End with CNTL/Z.
SingISDN(config)#interface dialer 1
SingISDN(config-if)#ppp ipcp dns 131.108.101.34 131.108.101.35
SingISDN(config-if)#ppp ipcp wins 131.108.21.70
SingISDN(config-if)#^Z
```

The configuration of ISDN and other dialup services described in this chapter is by no means exhaustive. We recommend that you review the documentation contained in the Cisco Systems manual sets, including case studies such as *Using ISDN Effectively in Multiprotocol Networks* (on CCO at www.cisco.com/univercd/cc/td/doc/cisintwk/ics/cs008.htm) to enhance your understanding of deploying dialup services.

Verifying IP Connectivity and Troubleshooting

At one point or another, every administrator must troubleshoot a user's complaint of not being able to reach some destination on the network. Lack of connectivity can be the result of network outages caused by WAN service failures, misconfiguration of routers and other devices in the network, access list controls (whether intentional or otherwise), and myriad other possibilities. Although there is no substitute for network test equipment, such as protocol analyzers, the router does provide several very useful tools for verifying IP connectivity and investigating potential problems. Let's examine a few of those tools.

As mentioned earlier, a router should have a specific route or some kind of default or summary route to every destination that an IP station might try to reach. One of the best tools for troubleshooting is the **show ip route** command, examined earlier in this chapter. When a station is having trouble reaching other stations—either within or outside the intranet—one of the first troubleshooting steps is to verify that the router closest to the user has a route to the destination IP address. If a specific route is not found, or if an expected default or summary route is not present, you probably need to investigate the dynamic routing protocols to determine why the route is not present. The reason could be obvious, such as a network segment failure (for example, a WAN service failure), or more subtle, such as a minor misconfiguration on another router in the network.

If you establish that a route to the desired destination exists, you should test to determine whether the router can reach the destination. UNIX users are familiar with the **ping** command, which is an acronym for the Packet Internet Groper. The **ping** command, which is implemented on the router, makes use of the IP Control Message Protocol (ICMP) to send echo requests to a destination IP address. The station receiving the ICMP echo request sends back an ICMP echo-response. In this way, a source station can determine whether a destination station is reachable and approximately how long the echo request and reply take to reach and return from the destination station. The following is an example of the IOS EXEC command **ping** being used on the ZIP SF-Core-1 to test the reachability of the San Jose router:

```
SF-Core-1#ping 131.108.100.1
Type escape sequence to abort.
Sending 5, 100-byte ICMP Echos to 131.108.100.1, timeout is 2 seconds:
!!!!!
Success rate is 100 percent (5/5), round-trip min/avg/max = 25/25/25 ms
SF-Core-1#
```

The router sends five ICMP echo requests and reports via the exclamation point (!) that all the replies are received. It also reports the number of echo request attempts and the number of echo replies received, and it calculates the percentage of successful **ping**s. Minimum, maximum, and average response times are also calculated.

NOTE   When a router **ping**s an IP address for the first time or again after a long period of time, the
router typically does not receive the first echo reply, resulting in four out of five **ping**
responses. This is because the router must wait for the ARP resolution of the IP address
before sending the echo request. Normally, the ARP reply does not arrive in time for the
first echo request to be sent and the reply to be received before the request times out.

Table 4-6 shows the different response characters that can be received as a result of a **ping**.

Table 4-6   *ping Command Response Characters*

Character	Description	Explanation
!	Each exclamation point indicates the receipt of a reply.	The echo reply was successfully received.
.	Each period indicates that the network server timed out while waiting for a reply.	The echo request likely made it to the destination, but the destination failed to respond or did not have a route back to the source of the request.
U	The destination is unreachable.	The destination IP address does not resolve to a MAC address or does not allow ICMP echo requests. The sending router has received an ICMP "destination unreachable" message.
N	The network is unreachable.	There is no route to the destination network for the target IP address. The sending router has received an ICMP "network unreachable" message.
P	The protocol is unreachable.	The destination IP address does not support the ICMP echo request. The sending router has received an ICMP "protocol unreachable" message.
Q	Source quench is requested.	The destination IP address is receiving more packets than it can buffer. The destination has sent the sending router an ICMP "source quench message" telling the sender to back off.
M	Fragmenting could not take place.	A packet has exceeded the maximum transmission unit of a network segment in the path to the destination, and the Do Not Fragment bit is set. The sending router has received an ICMP "could not fragment" message.

Table 4-6   *ping Command Response Characters (Continued)*

Character	Description	Explanation
A	The destination is administratively unreachable.	The packet to the destination address was discarded when it encountered a packet filter or firewall. The sending router has received an ICMP "administratively unreachable" message.
?	Packet is of unknown type.	The sending router has received an unknown response to the request.

The **ping** command has both a privileged and an unprivileged version. In user EXEC mode, the unprivileged version allows the user to only specify an IP address. The privileged version, available in enable EXEC mode, enables the user to modify parameters of the echo request, including the number of requests, the size of the packets sent, the timeout value, the source IP address of the request, the pattern of data in the echo request, and numerous other values. The following is an example of the privileged version of the **ping** command executed on the SF-Core-1 router. In this example, the source address has been specified as the IP address on the Fast Ethernet interface, the destination is the address 131.108.100.1 on the San-Jose router, and the packet size is 1500 bytes:

```
SF-Core-1#ping
Protocol [ip]:
Target IP address: 131.108.100.1
Repeat count [5]:
Datagram size [100]: 1500
Timeout in seconds [2]:
Extended commands [n]: y
Source address or interface: 131.108.20.3
Type of service [0]:
Set DF bit in IP header? [no]:
Validate reply data? [no]:
Data pattern [0xABCD]:
Loose, Strict, Record, Timestamp, Verbose[none]:
Sweep range of sizes [n]:
Type escape sequence to abort.
Sending 5, 1500-byte ICMP Echos to 131.108.100.1, timeout is 2 seconds:
!!!!!
Success rate is 100 percent (5/5), round-trip min/avg/max = 29/29/29 ms
SF-Core-1#
```

If you suspect that lack of connectivity is because of a missing route on a downstream router or an incorrect path that a packet is taking, the router has a command called **trace** that enables you to verify the path that a packet travels to reach a destination IP address. The **trace** function is similar to the UNIX traceroute utility. As with the **ping** command, the IOS EXEC command **trace** has both a privileged and an unprivileged version. The unprivileged version allows the user to only supply an IP destination address, while the privileged version enables the user to modify parameters, just as with the **ping** command.

The **trace** function makes use of the ICMP "TTL-Expired" (Time To Live) message to identify routers in the path to a destination IP address. The source router sends a UDP packet with a TTL of 1 toward the destination. The first router in the path receives the packet and decrements the TTL field by 1. As a result, the TTL expires (goes to 0), and the router does not forward the packet. Instead, this first router in the path sends an ICMP "TTL-Expired" message back to the source of the packet so that the source now knows the first router hop in the path.

The source router now sends another UDP packet, but it sets the TTL to 2. The first router in the path receives the packet, decrements the TTL to 1, and forwards the packet to the second router in the path. The second router receives the packet, decrements the TTL to 0, and does not forward the packet because the TTL has expired. The second router sends an ICMP "TTL-Expired" message back to the originating station, and now the source router knows the second router in the path. This process is repeated until the packet reaches the ultimate destination IP address. The packet is addressed to a high-number UDP port, usually above 33434, which the destination device does not support. Therefore, the destination IP address responds with an ICMP "Port Unreachable" message, which alerts the source router that the final destination has been reached.

The following is an example of the **trace** command on the ZIP SF-Core-1 router requesting the path to a station off of Seoul-1 router:

```
SF-Core-1#trace 131.108.3.5

Type escape sequence to abort.
Tracing the route to testy.zipnet.com (131.108.3.5)

  1 s0/0-SanJose-sj.zipnet.com (131.108.240.2) 25 msec 25 msec 25 msec
  2 s1-Seoul1-kr.zipnet.com (131.108.241.2) 176 msec * 176 msec
  3 testy.zipnet.com (131.108.3.5) 178 msec 178 msec 178 msec
SF-Core-1#
```

In the preceding example, time values are displayed after the name and IP addresses of the routers in the network path. These values are an approximation of the round-trip time from the source address to the router in the path. As many as three time values—one for each of the three packets (probes)—are displayed for each destination IP address. Some devices have limitations on the rate at which they can respond with ICMP messages. For such a device, fewer than three time values may appear. For each probe that the device does not respond to because of rate limitations, an asterisk is shown in place of the time value. You can see an example of this in the preceding output. The second-hop router was not capable of responding to the second probe, as indicated by the asterisk. Cisco IOS-based devices rate-limit ICMP responses to one per second.

In addition to rate-limiting ICMP messages, some routers in the path may not respond with an ICMP "TTL-Expired" message. Some may reuse the TTL of the incoming packet, which results in the expiration of the ICMP message's TTL before the message can return to the sender. And in some cases, packet filtering may prevent the ICMP response packets from reaching the source router. In all these cases, a line of asterisks is seen in an output line instead of address information. In the following **trace** output, the second router in the path has failed to respond to the **trace** queries:

```
SF-Core-1#trace 131.108.3.5

Type escape sequence to abort.
Tracing the route to testy.zipnet.com (131.108.3.5)

  1 s0/0-SanJose-sj.zipnet.com (131.108.240.2) 25 msec 25 msec 25 msec
  2 *    *    *
  3 testy.zipnet.com (131.108.3.5) 178 msec 178 msec 178 msec
SF-Core-1#
```

The privileged version of the **trace** command allows for adjusting the command's parameters, including whether IP addresses are reverse resolved to host names, the number of probes sent for each TTL step, a minimum and maximum TTL value, and so on. The following is a previous **trace** example repeated in privileged trace mode in which only the numeric responses are displayed:

```
SF-Core-1#trace
Protocol [ip]:
Target IP address: 131.108.3.5
Source address:
Numeric display [n]: y
Timeout in seconds [3]:
Probe count [3]:
Minimum Time to Live [1]:
Maximum Time to Live [30]:
Port Number [33434]:
Loose, Strict, Record, Timestamp, Verbose[none]:
Type escape sequence to abort.
Tracing the route to 131.108.3.5

  1 131.108.240.2 25 msec 25 msec 25 msec
  2 131.108.241.2 176 msec * 176 msec
  3 131.108.3.5 178 msec 178 msec 178 msec
SF-Core-1#
```

If a station that is reachable via a directly connected LAN interface is not responding, the reason may be that the router is not capable of resolving the IP address to the MAC address. To verify the MAC addresses that the router has been capable of resolving, use the Cisco IOS EXEC command **show ip arp**. This command takes as a parameter either a specific IP address, a specific interface, or a specific 48-bit MAC address. It displays only the ARP entries for that parameter. When no parameter is supplied, all IP ARP entries are displayed. The output of the command includes the IP-to-ARP mapping, the age of the entry in the table, and the interface that the ARP entry is associated with. (The router times out an ARP entry from the ARP table after four hours by default.) The following is an example of the **show ip arp** command on the ZIP SF-Core-1 router:

```
SF-Core-1#show ip arp
Protocol  Address        Age (min)  Hardware Addr   Type    Interface
Internet  131.108.20.         -      0000.0c07.b627  ARPA    FastEthernet0/0
Internet  131.108.20.2        4      0000.0c67.b62c  ARPA    FastEthernet0/0
Internet  131.108.20.4        2      0000.0cf1.a9c1  ARPA    FastEthernet0/0
Internet  131.108.20.1       12      0000.0cb8.02bc  ARPA    FastEthernet0/0
Internet  131.108.20.99       0      Incomplete      ARPA
SF-Core-1#
```

In the preceding example, the ARP table entry for 131.108.20.99 shows the word *incomplete* instead of an actual MAC hardware address, which indicates that the router sent an ARP request but that no reply was received to complete the ARP table entry. In this case, we can assume either that no station exists with this address or that the station is incapable of responding, perhaps because it is powered off.

Overall statistics about the operation of the IP protocol on the router can be obtained from the **show ip traffic** command. It includes counters for such information as the total number of packets received and sent by the router, the number of broadcasts received and sent, ICMP/UDP/TCP protocol statistics, and much more. These statistics can aid in determining whether the router has sent or received an ICMP echo, whether an IP address fails to resolve to a MAC address (known as an encapsulation failure), and where certain routing protocol packets are being received or sent. The counters in **show ip traffic** are cumulative, and they are reset only when the router is reloaded or power-cycled. The following is an example of the output of the **show ip traffic command** on the ZIP SF-Core-1 router:

```
SF-Core-1#show ip traffic
IP statistics:
  Rcvd:  4686565 total, 2623438 local destination
         0 format errors, 0 checksum errors, 77 bad hop count
         0 unknown protocol, 1 not a gateway
         0 security failures, 0 bad options, 0 with options
  Opts:  0 end, 0 nop, 0 basic security, 0 loose source route
         0 timestamp, 0 extended security, 0 record route
         0 stream ID, 0 strict source route, 0 alert, 0 other
  Frags: 0 reassembled, 0 timeouts, 0 couldn't reassemble
         0 fragmented, 0 couldn't fragment
  Bcast: 5981 received, 0 sent
  Mcast: 2482184 received, 3581861 sent
  Sent:  3893477 generated, 2062048 forwarded
         954 encapsulation failed, 208 no route
ICMP statistics:
  Rcvd: 0 format errors, 0 checksum errors, 5 redirects, 5070 unreachable
        3 echo, 16 echo reply, 0 mask requests, 0 mask replies, 0 quench
        0 parameter, 0 timestamp, 0 info request, 0 other
        0 irdp solicitations, 0 irdp advertisements
  Sent: 0 redirects, 18050 unreachable, 66 echo, 3 echo reply
        0 mask requests, 0 mask replies, 0 quench, 0 timestamp
        0 info reply, 7 time exceeded, 0 parameter problem
        0 irdp solicitations, 0 irdp advertisements
UDP statistics:
  Rcvd: 52836 total, 4 checksum errors, 18085 no port
  Sent: 50699 total, 5949 forwarded broadcasts
TCP statistics:
  Rcvd: 47895 total, 0 checksum errors, 1 no port
  Sent: 46883 total
Probe statistics:
  Rcvd: 0 address requests, 0 address replies
        0 proxy name requests, 0 where-is requests, 0 other
  Sent: 0 address requests, 0 address replies (0 proxy)
        0 proxy name replies, 0 where-is replies
EGP statistics:
  Rcvd: 0 total, 0 format errors, 0 checksum errors, 0 no listener
  Sent: 0 total
IGRP statistics:
  Rcvd: 0 total, 0 checksum errors
  Sent: 0 total
OSPF statistics:
  Rcvd: 0 total, 0 checksum errors
        0 hello, 0 database desc, 0 link state req
        0 link state updates, 0 link state acks
  Sent: 0 total
```

```
IP-IGRP2 statistics:
  Rcvd: 2105381 total
  Sent: 3140121 total
PIMv2 statistics: Sent/Received
  Total: 0/0, 0 checksum errors, 0 format errors
  Registers: 0/0, Register Stops: 0/0
IGMP statistics: Sent/Received
  Total: 0/0, Format errors: 0/0, Checksum errors: 0/0
  Host Queries: 0/0, Host Reports: 0/0, Host Leaves: 00
  DVMRP: 0/0, PIM: 0/0
ARP statistics:
  Rcvd: 8540 requests, 4 replies, 0 reverse, 0 other
  Sent: 89 requests, 9018 replies (0 proxy), 0 reverse
SF-Core-1#
```

The counters in the output of **show ip traffic** count both events that have occurred and types of packets that have been sent and received. If the encapsulation failed counter were increasing, it would indicate that the router did not receive ARP replies to its ARP requests for packets that were attempting to be switched to destination interfaces and that the packets were discarded. The ICMP echo count indicates how many pings the router is generating, and the echo reply count indicates the number of pings to which it is responding.

In addition to the troubleshooting and verification commands presented in this section, numerous IOS EXEC **debug** commands exist to aid in determining the operation of the IP on the router. These **debug** commands provide both general and detailed diagnostic output that can aid in troubleshooting problems and in verifying the operation of the router, routing protocols, and other functions. Some of the more common **debug** commands used for TCP/IP are summarized in Table 4-7.

Table 4-7   *Debug Commands for IP*

Command	Description
debug ip routing	Displays changes that occur in the routing table as the result of additions and deletions of routes.
debug ip packet	Displays the source and destination IP addresses of packets that traverse the router. This **debug** command can overload the router, so care must be taken when using it. It is recommended that an access list be used in conjunction with this command to limit the CPU load.
debug ip udp	Displays the UDP packets sent to the router.
debug ip icmp	Displays the ICMP messages sent to and generated by the router.
debug arp	Displays ARP requests generated by and replies sent to the router.

Debugging commands for the various dynamic routing protocols include **debug ip rip**, **debug ip eigrp**, **debug ip igrp**, **debug ip ospf**, and **debug ip bgp**. Each of these debugging commands has optional parameters that control what debugging information about the routing protocol is displayed to the user. Care should be exercised when using some versions of these commands, because they can be CPU-intensive. For a complete description of all debugging commands and sample output, refer to the Cisco Connection

Documentation CD-ROM or to the online version found at www.cisco.com/univercd/home/home.htm.

TIP

When using **debug** commands that are known to increase CPU load, do not execute them on the console port. Instead, disable console logging via the IOS global configuration command **no logging console**, and enable buffered logging via the IOS global configuration command **logging buffered**. Then execute the command from a virtual terminal session and view the output in that session. If the session becomes unresponsive, the console can be used to disable the debug because the console has higher priority than the virtual terminal session. The debug output can then be reviewed in the log buffer via the IOS EXEC command **show log**. If syslogging is enabled, the output can also be viewed in the log file on the syslog server.

Configuring Other IP Options

The IOS software found on Cisco routers and other devices has dozens of features to aid in the operation of the network and of the router itself. In this section, we examine four features commonly implemented on the router that enhance network operation and ease the use of the router itself.

Configuring Domain Name Services

In TCP/IP networks today, most people refer to servers, printers, workstations, and other IP devices by their names rather than by their IP addresses. Remembering IP addresses may be easy for the network administrator who is intimately familiar with the network, but for the average user, it is easier to remember the name of a system. To that end, servers that resolve names into IP addresses, called domain name service (DNS) servers, usually reside somewhere within an entity's intranet. Routers can make use of the DNS system to convert names into IP addresses and to help reduce the number of IP addresses that the network administrator must remember.

DNS normally comes enabled in the Cisco IOS software. However, if it has been disabled, it can be restored via the IOS global configuration command **ip domain-lookup**. After DNS is enabled, an IOS device should be configured with the domain name in which it resides and with the IP address of the DNS nameservers that it can use for name resolution. The domain name can be configured via the IOS global configuration command **ip domain-name**. The DNS nameserver(s) can be configured via the IOS global configuration command **ip name-server**. The **ip name-server** command takes one or more IP addresses of nameservers as parameters. If the IOS device resides within multiple DNS domains, the IOS global configuration command **ip domain-list** can be used to specify a list of domain names that should be postpended to unqualified names.

The following is an example of configuring DNS on the ZIP SF-Core-1 router. In this example, the domain name is zipnet.com and the nameserver IP addresses are 131.108.110.34 and 131.108.110.35:

```
SF-Core-1#configure
Configuring from terminal, memory, or network [terminal]?
Enter configuration commands, one per line.  End with CNTL/Z.
SF-Core-1(config)#ip domain-lookup
SF-Core-1(config)#ip domain-name zipnet.com
SF-Core-1(config)#ip domain-list zipnet.com
SF-Core-1(config)#ip domain-list zipnet.net
SF-Core-1(config)#ip name-server 131.108.110.34 131.108.110.35
SF-Core-1(config)#^Z
```

Verifying the setup of the DNS on the router can be accomplished via the IOS EXEC command **show host**. Additionally, the **show host** command displays a list of hosts that have had their names resolved to IP addresses and also displays the age of each entry. The following is an example of the output of the **show host** command from the ZIP SF-Core-1 router:

```
SF-Core-1#show host
Default domain is zipnet.com
Domain list: zipnet.com, zipnet.net
Name/address lookup uses domain service
Name servers are 131.108.110.34, 131.108.110.35

Host                       Flags       Age  Type  Address(es)
testy.zipnet.com           (temp, OK)  1    IP    131.108.3.5
s1-Seoul1-kr.zipnet.com    (temp, OK)  1    IP    131.108.241.2
s0/0-SanJose-sj.zipnet.com (temp, OK)  1    IP    131.108.240.2
SF-Core-1#
```

The host name-to-IP address mappings can also be configured statically on the router in situations in which DNS servers are not available, you prefer to create special names different from those in DNS, or you want to map individual terminal server ports to IP addresses. Static name-to-IP address mapping is configured with the IOS global configuration command **ip host**. The **ip host** command takes as parameters a host name, an optional Telnet protocol port, and one or more IP addresses to which the host name may resolve. The following is an example of statically mapping several different host names to IP addresses on the ZIP SF-Core-1 router:

```
SF-Core-1#configure
Configuring from terminal, memory, or network [terminal]?
Enter configuration commands, one per line.  End with CNTL/Z.
SF-Core-1(config)#ip host grouchy 131.108.3.5
SF-Core-1(config)#ip host grouchy-console 2001 131.108.3.50
SF-Core-1(config)#ip host farout 131.108.3.88 131.108.3.150
SF-Core-1(config)#^Z
```

The static host name-to-IP address mappings can also be verified via the **show host** command. The following is an example, again from the ZIP SF-Core-1 router, after the mappings of the static host names to IP addresses have been entered:

```
SF-Core-1#show host
Default domain is zipnet.com
Domain list: zipnet.com, zipnet.net
Name/address lookup uses domain service
```

```
Name servers are 131.108.110.34, 131.108.110.35

Host                         Flags         Age   Type    Address(es)
testy.zipnet.com             (temp, OK)    1     IP      131.108.3.5
s1-Seoul1-kr.zipnet.com      (temp, OK)    1     IP      131.108.241.2
s0/0-SanJose-sj.zipnet.com   (temp, OK)    1     IP      131.108.240.2
grouchy                      (perm, OK)    2     IP      131.108.3.5
grouchy-console              (perm, OK)    2     IP      131.108.3.50
farout                       (perm, OK)    2     IP      131.108.3.88   131.108.3.150
SF-Core-1#
```

The static entries in the host name table can be distinguished from those learned via DNS by the Flags field for the host name entry. A flag type of temp indicates that the name was learned dynamically via DNS and is aged out of the table after a period of time. A flag type of perm indicates that the name was statically configured and is never aged from the table.

Temporary entries in the IP host table can be cleared via the IOS EXEC command **clear host**. Individual host name mapping can be cleared by supplying a host name as the parameter to the command. All temporary host entries can be cleared by supplying an asterisk as the parameter. The following is an example of clearing the host name to IP mapping for the host name testy.zipnet.com on the ZIP SF-Core-1 router:

```
SF-Core-1#clear host testy.zipnet.com
SF-Core-1#
```

IP Broadcast Forwarding

One of the benefits that routers provide on a network is restricting IP and MAC broadcast packets to the local LAN segment. Most broadcasts are used for requesting information such as an unknown MAC address for an IP address (ARP) on a local segment, so isolating broadcasts to the local LAN segment presents no inherent problems and is highly beneficial to network performance.

In some situations, IP stations use UDP broadcasts to locate services that may not be on the local LAN segment. Applications that rely on NetBIOS over IP, for example, use UDP broadcasts to locate the particular type of service that the user needs. If that service resides on a LAN segment other than the one to which the user's station is attached, the router blocks the broadcast, making that service unavailable. Other services, such as DHCP and the Bootstrap Protocol (BOOTP), send UDP broadcasts to help IP stations determine their IP addresses during the boot process; the broadcasts are received by servers that assign addresses. If those servers reside off the local LAN segment, an IP station cannot receive a server-assigned IP address.

To compensate for the broadcast isolation features of the router, the IOS software has the capability to forward UDP broadcasts to a specific host or subnet. This feature, which is called IP broadcast forwarding, is enabled by using the IOS interface configuration subcommand **ip helper-address** and the IOS global configuration command **ip forward-protocol**. A common application of these commands is to forward DHCP address requests from a local LAN segment to the LAN segment where the DHCP server resides, as shown in Figure 4-11. Let's examine the use of the broadcast forwarding feature at the San Francisco ZIP site on the router SF-2.

Figure 4-11 *A DHCP Request Broadcast Is Forwarded by the Use of a Helper Address*

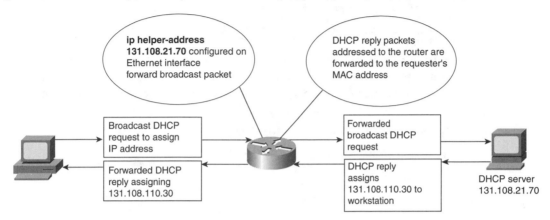

In the ZIP network in San Francisco, off of the SF-2 router, Microsoft Windows 95/98, NT, and Windows 2000 workstations use DHCP to obtain their IP addresses dynamically. Those workstations reside on the SF-2 routers Ethernet 0 and Ethernet 1 LAN segments. The DHCP server resides on the Fast Ethernet 0 LAN segment. Broadcasts from the Ethernet segments do not traverse the router, and thus the DHCP broadcasts do not reach the Fast Ethernet segment and the DHCP server. To enable the forwarding of broadcasts, the **ip helper-address** command can be applied to the Ethernet segments where the router receives the broadcasts. The **ip helper-address** command takes as a parameter an IP host address or an IP broadcast address. The address supplied is either the host address of the specific DHCP server or the broadcast address of the LAN segment where the DHCP server resides.

The following is an example of the **ip helper-address** command on the Ethernet 0 interface of the ZIP SF-2 router, which results in broadcasts being forwarded directly to the DHCP server at 131.108.21.70:

```
SF-2#configure
Configuring from terminal, memory, or network [terminal]?
Enter configuration commands, one per line.  End with CNTL/Z.
SF-2(config)#interface ethernet 0
SF-2(config-if)#ip helper-address 131.108.21.70
SF-2(config)#^Z
```

Instead of being forwarded directly to the DHCP server, the broadcast could be forwarded to the LAN segment where the DHCP server resides. This alternative is useful when more than one DHCP server could answer the request. The following is an example of using the

IP broadcast address of the LAN segment on which the DHCP server resides as the forwarding destination:

```
SF-2#configure
Configuring from terminal, memory, or network [terminal]?
Enter configuration commands, one per line.  End with CNTL/Z.
SF-2(config)#interface ethernet 1
SF-2(config-if)#ip helper-address 131.108.23.255
SF-2(config-if)#^Z
```

The **ip helper-address** is used to specify where the broadcasts should be forwarded. The **ip forward-protocol** command is used to control which UDP broadcasts get forwarded. By default, several types of UDP broadcasts get forwarded whenever the **ip helper-address** command is applied to an interface:

- Trivial File Transfer Protocol (TFTP) (port 69)
- Domain Naming System (port 53)
- Time service (port 37)
- NetBIOS Name Server (port 137)
- NetBIOS Datagram Server (port 138)
- Boot Protocol (BOOTP) client and server datagrams (ports 67 and 68)
- TACACS service (port 49)

If there is an application that broadcasts on a port other than the ones listed and its broadcasts need to be forwarded, the **ip forward-protocol** command is used to specify that the particular broadcast type should be included among those that are forwarded. With the addition of the keyword **no**, this command also can be used to restrict any of the default protocols from being forwarded. The **ip forward-protocol** command takes as parameters the type of forwarding to be performed (such as UDP) and the specific port number of the protocol to be forwarded. The following is an example of using the command to allow broadcasts on UDP port 1965 to be forwarded and to restrict the forwarding of NetBIOS Name Server and Datagram Server on the ZIP SF-2 router:

```
SF-2#configure
Configuring from terminal, memory, or network [terminal]?
Enter configuration commands, one per line.  End with CNTL/Z.
SF-2(config)#ip forward-protocol udp 1965
SF-2(config)#no ip forward-protocol udp 137
SF-2(config)#no ip forward-protocol udp 138
SF-2(config)#^Z
```

You can verify **ip helper-address** configurations with the **show ip interface** command, as discussed in previous sections.

Further Reference: Other Broadcast Applications

The broadcast forwarding technique discussed in this section is designed to meet the needs of a limited broadcast forwarding environment. It is well-suited to such tasks as forwarding

IP address requests via DHCP or BOOTP to a server or group of servers that reside at a central location on the network. Other applications exist for which more substantial broadcast forwarding may be required. These applications—for example, stock ticker data—typically use broadcasts to share information among a large group of workstation users over a large part of the network. Such applications are not well-suited to the helper address model. Instead, they require advanced techniques, such as UDP flooding and broadcast-to-multicast replication, to prevent the router's CPU from being overwhelmed by broadcast packet traffic and replication. Cisco Systems currently has a case study that discusses the implications of the helper address and flooding models. It can be found on CCO at www.cisco.com/univercd/cc/td/doc/cisintwk/ics/cs006.htm.

Dynamic Address Assignment with IOS DHCP Server

In the preceding section, we discussed forwarding DHCP address assignment requests as one of the applications for IP broadcast forwarding. When a router forwards these address assignment requests, it is said to be acting as a DHCP relay agent. The role of the DHCP relay agent is to receive local LAN broadcasts for address assignments and to forward them to a previously identified DHCP server. The DHCP server is typically a workstation or server such as a UNIX or Windows NT system running a DHCP server software package or service. Alternatively, an IOS-based router or access server may serve as the source for dynamic address assignments.

The IOS software DHCP server operates similarly to workstation-based DHCP servers, accepting address assignment requests/renewals and assigning the addresses from predefined groups of addresses called pools. The address pools may also be configured to supply additional information to the requesting client such as the IP address(es) of DNS server(s), the default router, and other useful information. The IOS DHCP server may accept broadcasts from locally attached LAN segments or from DHCP requests that have been forwarded by other DHCP relay agents within the network.

NOTE   In addition to the IOS software-based DHCP server, Cisco Systems makes a workstation-based DNS and DHCP server called *Cisco Network Registrar* that runs under such operating systems as Solaris, HP-UX, and Microsoft Windows operating systems. The decision of whether to use the IOS-based DHCP server or a workstation-based DHCP server involves many factors, including the size of your network, the number of nodes requiring dynamic addresses, the frequency of address requests and renewals, the need for redundancy, and cost. In general, the IOS-based DHCP server is most practical in small to medium-sized networks or for use in a decentralized model such as multiple remote offices. Workstation-based DHCP servers are more appropriate for large organizations with a need for redundancy and a highly centralized management scheme.

The IOS DHCP server will typically participate in two steps of the address assignment process, the DHCPOFFER and the DHCPACK. Figure 4-12 depicts the basic steps involved when a DHCP client requests an address from the DHCP server. The DHCP client sends a DHCPDISCOVER broadcast message to locate a DHCP Server. A DHCP server offers address assignment parameters to the client in a DHCPOFFER unicast response. The DHCP client then sends a formal DHCPREQUEST broadcast message for the offered address assignment back to the DHCP server. The DHCP server sends a DHCPACK unicast response indicating that the requested addresses have been assigned to the client. The four steps shown in Figure 4-12 depict the normal address negotiation process with no errors or conflicts. The complete address assignment process, including the handling of DHCPDECLINE messages, is described in RFC 2131, "Dynamic Host Configuration Protocol."

Figure 4-12   *DHCP Address Assignment by a DHCP Server*

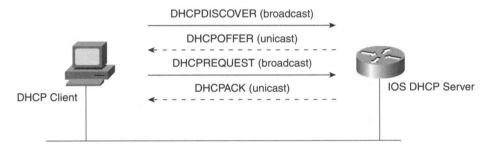

Enabling the IOS-based router or access server to perform as a DHCP server is accomplished with four major configuration steps:

- Identifying the location to log DHCP assignment information
- Creating a list of IP addresses to exclude from dynamic assignment
- Creating a pool of addresses to use for dynamic assignment
- Adding additional attributes to the address pools that will be supplied to requesting stations

We'll examine the configuration of the IOS DHCP server using the ZIP Kuala Lumpur router.

The first step to enabling the IOS DHCP server is configuring a location on the network to log and store the DHCP address assignments (also called bindings). This location is typically a workstation or server that supports TFTP, FTP, or the RCP file transfer protocol. Specifying this location allows the router or access server to be restarted without losing information about which addresses are allocated to which DHCP client systems. Additionally, it provides a location to log address assignment conflicts that may arise during the DHCP negotiation process. The IOS global configuration command **ip dhcp database** is used to specify the location. The command takes as a parameter a URL that specifies the server address and filename to use for the logging. The configuration command may be repeated multiple times to allow for storing the bindings on multiple servers. The following is an example of configuring the DHCP database location on the ZIP Kuala Lumpur router to log to a server with IP address 131.108.2.77 and a file called kl-dhcp-info using the TFTP protocol:

```
Kuala-Lumpur#configure
Configuring from terminal, memory, or network [terminal]?
Enter configuration commands, one per line.  End with CNTL/Z.
Kuala-Lumpur(config)#ip dhcp database tftp://131.108.2.77/kl-dhcp-info
Kuala-Lumpur(config)#^Z
```

During the address assignment process, the IOS DHCP server attempts to ensure that the IP address being offered is not in use. It does this by sending a series of **ping** packets to the address being offered before responding to the DHCP client. If the address is in use, it is logged as a conflict and is not offered until the network administrator resolves the conflict.

If no server is available for the logging of DHCP address bindings and the **ip dhcp database** command is not configured, the logging of DHCP conflicts must also be disabled. Disabling conflict logging is accomplished with the IOS global configuration command **no ip dhcp conflict logging**. In the ZIP network Kuala Lumpur location, a tftp server is available, but the following is an example of how DHCP conflict logging would be disabled if none were available:

```
Kuala-Lumpur#configure
Configuring from terminal, memory, or network [terminal]?
Enter configuration commands, one per line.  End with CNTL/Z.
Kuala-Lumpur(config)#no ip dhcp conflict logging
Kuala-Lumpur(config)#^Z
```

When a location is established for logging the bindings, a list of addresses that should be excluded as dynamically offered assignments is built. This list includes the address of the router(s) in a given address range, any statically assigned addresses, or an address that should be reserved and not offered to a DHCP client. The IOS global configuration command **ip dhcp excluded-address** is used to build these lists. The command takes as parameters either a single IP address to be excluded or a pair of addresses that represent the starting and ending addresses of an IP address range. The command may be repeated several times in the configuration to exclude multiple IP addresses that are not contiguous or that span multiple IP address assignment pools. The following is an example of excluding the IP address range 131.108.2.1 through 131.108.2.10 and the single IP address 131.108.2.57 on the ZIP Kuala Lumpur router:

```
Kuala-Lumpur#configure
Configuring from terminal, memory, or network [terminal]?
Enter configuration commands, one per line.  End with CNTL/Z.
Kuala-Lumpur(config)#ip dhcp excluded-address 131.108.2.1 131.108.2.10
Kuala-Lumpur(config)#ip dhcp excluded-address 131.108.2.57
Kuala-Lumpur(config)#^Z
```

The final step in enabling the IOS DHCP server is the definition of the IP address assignment pools that will be used to supply the dynamic addresses. At a minimum, the

DHCP address pool specifies the range of addresses that will be offered to DHCP clients requesting addresses (not including the excluded addresses). More than one pool may be defined on the IOS DHCP server if there are multiple LAN segments attached to the router or access server acting as a DHCP server, or if it serves addresses for multiple LAN segments elsewhere within the network. The IOS global configuration command **ip dhcp pool** establishes an address assignment pool. The command takes as a parameter either an arbitrary string to describe the pool or a numeric integer. Once defined, additional address pool commands are entered from the DHCP configuration subcommand mode, denoted by the **(config-dhcp)#** prompt. The following example configures a DHCP address pool called kl-users on the Kuala Lumpur router and places the network administrator in DHCP configuration subcommand mode to continue the address pool configuration:

```
Kuala-Lumpur#configure
Configuring from terminal, memory, or network [terminal]?
Enter configuration commands, one per line.  End with CNTL/Z.
Kuala-Lumpur(config)#ip dhcp pool kl-users
Kuala-Lumpur(config-dhcp)#^Z
```

The IOS DHCP configuration subcommand **network** is used to define the range of addresses that a given address pool will offer to DHCP clients. The **network** subcommand requires two parameters, an IP network address and a network mask or bit-count mask. The network address and mask specified for a given pool should correspond to the network address and mask on the LAN segment for which this pool will offer addresses. When the DHCP server will supply addresses for multiple LAN segments, separate DHCP pools should be defined, each with a **network** subcommand with the appropriate address and mask, for that LAN segment. The following is an example of establishing the DHCP address pool kl-users again on the Kuala Lumpur router, using the **network** subcommand to specify the range of addresses to be assigned to DHCP clients (note the use of the /25 bit-count mask in lieu of the 255.255.255.128 network mask):

```
Kuala-Lumpur#configure
Configuring from terminal, memory, or network [terminal]?
Enter configuration commands, one per line.  End with CNTL/Z.
Kuala-Lumpur(config)#ip dhcp pool kl-users
Kuala-Lumpur(config-dhcp)#network 131.108.2.0 /25
Kuala-Lumpur(config-dhcp)#^Z
```

In this example, specifying network 131.108.2.0 with a /25 bit-count mask means that addresses in the range of 131.108.2.1 to 131.108.2.127 will be offered to DHCP clients (not including the previously excluded addresses). When viewing the running or startup configuration file, the /25 bit-count mask will be converted to a network mask of 255.255.255.128.

Additional DHCP configuration subcommands enable the network administrator to configure the IOS DHCP server to supply supplementary information to the DHCP client using the address negotiation process. The additional information is typically the address(es) of the client's default router on the LAN segment, addresses of the DNS servers, addresses of the NetBIOS/WINS servers, and other information that would otherwise have to be configured manually on each client either by the user or by the network administrator. The following is the list of the most commonly configured DHCP configuration subcommands:

- **domain-name** subcommand—Specifies the DNS domain name to which this client will belong.

- **dns-server** subcommand—Specifies one or more IP addresses of DNS servers that the client can query to resolve names to IP addresses.

- **netbios-name-server** subcommand—Specifies one or more IP addresses of NetBIOS/WINS servers that NetBIOS clients (typically Microsoft workstations) can query to locate resources on the network.

- **netbios-node-type** subcommand—Specifies the operating mode of the NetBIOS client on the network.

- **default-router** subcommand—Specifies one or more IP addresses of a default router to which clients can forward packets for unknown destinations.

- **lease** subcommand—Specifies how long a DHCP assigned address (a lease) is valid before requiring renewal.

The **dns-server**, **netbios-name-server**, and **default-router** subcommands each take as parameters from one to eight IP addresses that the client may contact for each of those functions. The **domain-name** subcommand takes as a parameter an arbitrary string that represents the name of the DNS domain for the client. The **lease** subcommand takes as parameters up to three integers to specify the number of days, hours, and minutes that an assigned address is valid. The keyword **infinite** may also be used to specify that a lease is valid for an unlimited period of time. The **netbios-node-type** subcommand takes as a parameter the character values of b, p, m, or h, which represent a NetBIOS broadcast node, peer-to-peer node, a mixed node, or a hybrid node, respectively, to denote the operating mode of the client. If you are unfamiliar with these operating modes, selecting the hybrid mode is recommended.

The following is an example of configuring the Kuala Lumpur router with additional DHCP configuration subcommands to supply to DHCP clients with information about servers in the ZIP network:

```
Kuala-Lumpur#configure
Configuring from terminal, memory, or network [terminal]?
Enter configuration commands, one per line.  End with CNTL/Z.
Kuala-Lumpur(config)#ip dhcp pool kl-users
Kuala-Lumpur(config-dhcp)#dns-server 131.108.101.34 131.108.101.35
Kuala-Lumpur(config-dhcp)#domain-name zipnet.com
Kuala-Lumpur(config-dhcp)#netbios-name-server 131.108.21.70
Kuala-Lumpur(config-dhcp)#netbios-node-type h
Kuala-Lumpur(config-dhcp)#default-router 131.108.2.1
Kuala-Lumpur(config-dhcp)#lease 0 1
Kuala-Lumpur(config-dhcp)#^Z
```

As mentioned previously, multiple DHCP address pools may be configured on the same IOS DHCP server. The collection of DHCP address pools on that server is referred to as the DHCP database. The DHCP database is arranged in a hierarchical or tree structure so that one address pool may be a subnetwork of the network address of a different DHCP address pool. This hierarchical structure allows for properties to be inherited by the address pool, which is a subnetwork of the other. Properties that are common to multiple pools should be defined at the highest network or subnetwork level that is appropriate for the DHCP server or network being configured. Properties defined at a higher level can be overridden at a lower subnetwork level. Let's take a look at this on the ZIP Kuala Lumpur router.

In the previous example, an address pool called kl-users was defined for a network of 131.108.2.0/25. In the example, additional properties were specifically defined for DNS servers, the default router, and so on. If in the future a second address pool were created for the network address 131.108.2.128/25, the additional properties would again need to be specifically defined in a new address pool because it is not a subnetwork of the previously defined pool. Thus, the configuration on the Kuala Lumpur router for this new address pool would be as follows:

```
Kuala-Lumpur#configure
Configuring from terminal, memory, or network [terminal]?
Enter configuration commands, one per line.  End with CNTL/Z.
Kuala-Lumpur(config)#ip dhcp excluded-address 131.108.2.129 131.108.2.135
Kuala-Lumpur(config)#ip dhcp pool kl-users-2
Kuala-Lumpur(config-dhcp)#network 131.108.2.128/25
Kuala-Lumpur(config-dhcp)#dns-server 131.108.101.34 131.108.101.35
Kuala-Lumpur(config-dhcp)#domain-name zipnet.com
Kuala-Lumpur(config-dhcp)#netbios-name-server 131.108.21.70
Kuala-Lumpur(config-dhcp)#netbios-node-type h
Kuala-Lumpur(config-dhcp)#default-router 131.108.2.129
Kuala-Lumpur(config-dhcp)#lease 0 1
Kuala-Lumpur(config-dhcp)#^Z
```

In the configuration of the kl-users-2 address pool, there are a number of subcommands whose parameters are the same as the parameters of the kl-users pool, making the properties assigned to the clients identical for those subcommands.

To avoid the subcommand repetition in both kl-users and kl-users-2, those address pools can be reconfigured to be subnetworks of another network address pool. When this is completed, only the subcommands that define properties that are unique to that address pool will be needed. For the ZIP Kuala Lumpur router, an address pool will be defined for the network address 131.108.2.0/24, and the properties that will be inherited by the subnetwork address pools will be defined. The rewritten kl-users and kl-users-2 address pool will be reduced from seven subcommands to only two subcommands.

Here is an example of the rewritten DHCP address pools on the Kuala Lumpur router in which the kl-users and kl-users-2 address pools will inherit properties from an address pool called kl-common:

```
Kuala-Lumpur#configure
Configuring from terminal, memory, or network [terminal]?
Enter configuration commands, one per line.  End with CNTL/Z.
Kuala-Lumpur(config)#ip dhcp pool kl-common
Kuala-Lumpur(config-dhcp)#network 131.108.2.0/24
Kuala-Lumpur(config-dhcp)#dns-server 131.108.101.34 131.108.101.35
Kuala-Lumpur(config-dhcp)#domain-name zipnet.com
Kuala-Lumpur(config-dhcp)#netbios-name-server 131.108.21.70
```

```
Kuala-Lumpur(config-dhcp)#netbios-node-type h
Kuala-Lumpur(config-dhcp)#lease 0 1
Kuala-Lumpur(config-dhcp)#ip dhcp pool kl-users
Kuala-Lumpur(config-dhcp)#network 131.108.2.0/25
Kuala-Lumpur(config-dhcp)#default-router 131.108.2.1
Kuala-Lumpur(config-dhcp)#ip dhcp pool kl-users-2
Kuala-Lumpur(config-dhcp)#network 131.108.2.128/25
Kuala-Lumpur(config-dhcp)#default-router 131.108.2.129
Kuala-Lumpur(config-dhcp)#^Z
```

In this example, because 131.108.2.0/25 and 131.108.2.128/25 are subnetworks of 131.108.2.0/24, the corresponding address pools will inherit the common properties from the higher-level network address pool. Only the **default-router** subcommand is used to define the specific IP address that is appropriate for each subnetwork address pool.

When the address pools and their properties are defined and the IOS DHCP server has begun assigning IP addresses, the operation of the DHCP server can be verified using several different IOS EXEC commands. Verifying that the IOS DHCP server is logging binding and conflict information to the configured workstation or server is accomplished via the IOS EXEC command **show ip dhcp database**. The command takes as a parameter the URL to display information about a specific database logging location. If none is supplied, information about all locations is displayed. The following is an example of the **show ip dhcp database** command on the ZIP Kuala Lumpur router:

```
Kuala-Lumpur>show ip dhcp database
URL        : tftp://131.108.2.77/kl-dhcp-info
Read       : Never
Written    : Jun 30 2000 12:01 AM
Status     : Last Write Successful.
Delay      : 300 seconds
Timeout    : 300 seconds
Failures : 0
Successes: 72
Kuala-Lumpur>
```

The output of **show ip dhcp database** indicates the location to which binding information is being written, the date and time of the last read or write to the binding database, the status of the last read or write, and the number of successes and failures in attempting to write to the bindings database.

Specific address assignment information can be viewed using the IOS EXEC command **show ip dhcp binding**. When an IP address is supplied as an optional parameter to the command, only the binding information for that address is shown; otherwise, all binding information is displayed. The following is an example of the **show ip dhcp binding** command on the ZIP Kuala Lumpur router, which displays the currently allocated address assignments, the associated MAC address of the DHCP client, and the lease expiration time:

```
Kuala-Lumpur>show ip dhcp binding
IP address      Hardware address      Lease expiration       Type
131.108.2.89    00a0.9802.32de        Jul  01 2000 12:00 AM  Automatic
131.108.2.156   00a0.9478.43ae        Jul  01 2000  1:00 AM  Automatic
Kuala-Lumpur>
```

Information for address conflicts that occurred when the IOS DHCP server was attempting to assign an address to a DHCP client can be viewed with the **show ip dhcp conflict** command. When an IP address is supplied as an optional parameter to the command, only the conflict information for that address is shown (if any); otherwise, all conflict information is displayed. The following is an example of the **show ip dhcp conflict** command on the ZIP Kuala Lumpur router, which indicates the IP address in conflict, the detection time, and the method of detection:

```
Kuala-Lumpur>show ip dhcp conflict
IP address       Detection Method    Detection time
131.108.2.126    Ping                Jul 02 2000 12:28 AM
131.108.2.254    Gratuitous ARP      Jul 02 2000 01:12 AM
Kuala-Lumpur>
```

The Detection Method column indicates what method was used by the IOS DHCP server to determine that the address was in conflict. The **ping** detection method indicates that before address assignment, the IOS DHCP server attempted to **ping** the address and received a successful response. The Gratuitous ARP detection method indicates that before address assignment, the IOS DHCP server detected a current and valid ARP entry for the address in its ARP table. Either of these detection methods indicates that the address is likely in use (perhaps because of an unauthorized use or because someone forgot to add to the excluded addresses list).

Verifying that the IOS DHCP server is receiving and responding to DHCP requests can be accomplished with the IOS EXEC command **show ip dhcp server statistics**. The command provides useful information such as the number of configured address pools, the amount of memory being consumed by the DHCP bindings database, and counters that indicate the number of different types of DHCP messages that have been both sent and received. The following is an example of the **show ip dhcp server statistics** command on the ZIP Kuala Lumpur router:

```
Kuala-Lumpur>show ip dhcp server statistics
Memory usage         40392
Address pools        3
Database agents      1
Automatic bindings   48
Manual bindings      0
Expired bindings     7
Malformed messages   0

Message              Received
BOOTREQUEST          22
DHCPDISCOVER         175
DHCPREQUEST          168
DHCPDECLINE          0
DHCPRELEASE          0
DHCPINFORM           0

Message              Sent
BOOTREPLY            17
DHCPOFFER            166
DHCPACK              155
DHCPNAK              3
Kuala-Lumpur>
```

IP Redundancy with the Hot Standby Router Protocol

Many network administrators worry about having single points of failure in the network. They want to provide both redundant paths and redundant equipment in key locations of the network to prevent any single device from causing vital network resources to become unavailable. Routers (and some servers) handle multiple IP paths very well by exchanging dynamic routing information about the various paths through the network, selecting the best path(s) at any given time, and rerouting when there are path changes because of equipment or circuit failure.

However, many workstation, server, and printer implementations are not capable of exchanging dynamic routing information. These devices typically are configured with a single default gateway IP address that serves as their conduit to the rest of the network. If the router that is the default gateway fails, the device is limited to communicating only on the local IP network segment and is effectively cut off from the rest of the network. Even if a redundant router exists that could serve as a default gateway, there is no dynamic method for the workstations to use to switch to a new default gateway IP address, and manual reconfiguration is often beyond the user's technical ability.

To assist network administrators with this troublesome situation, Cisco Systems developed the Hot Standby Router Protocol (HSRP). HSRP was designed for the LAN segment, where multiple routers are present and where there are devices that use only a static default gateway IP address.

The concept of HSRP is quite simple. The administrator creates a virtual default gateway address and assigns it to the redundant routers that participate in HSRP on the given LAN segment. The IP devices are configured to use the virtual gateway address as the default gateway. The routers manage this virtual gateway address, communicating among themselves to determine which router is responsible for forwarding traffic sent to the virtual IP address. At regular intervals, they exchange information to determine which routers are still present and capable of forwarding traffic. If the primary or lead router of a group of HSRP routers fails, a standby router in the same group begins to forward traffic for the HSRP group. Because the routers decide among themselves which one forwards traffic for the virtual address, and because the workstations on a segment are aware of only the virtual IP address as their default gateway, a failure of the primary forwarding router is barely detectable by the workstation users and requires no intervention on the part of the user or the network administrator.

HSRP is very flexible. The network administrator can control all behavior of the routers in an HSRP group—including which router is the primary forwarding router, which router (or routers) is the standby router, whether the standby router retains the forwarding role when the primary is again available, and the capability of another interface on the router to force traffic onto the standby router.

Let's examine the configuration of HSRP on the ZIP routers located in Seoul, Korea. In Seoul, two routers, Seoul-1 and Seoul-2, are attached to the same logical IP network,

131.108.3.0. The presence of two or more routers that can act as default gateways on the LAN segment is the first part of the criteria for configuring HSRP. The other part of the criteria is having IP devices on the network that can support only a single IP address as the default gateway. In this case, printers, servers, and PC workstations fit the criteria.

The basic configuration of HSRP requires only the IOS interface configuration subcommand **standby ip**. This command takes as a parameter the IP address that is used as the virtual default gateway IP address. The command is applied to all routers on the same logical IP network that participate in the same HSRP group. The following is an example of configuring HSRP on the ZIP routers Seoul-1 and Seoul-2 with a standby virtual IP address of 131.108.3.3:

```
Seoul-1#configure
Configuring from terminal, memory, or network [terminal]?
Enter configuration commands, one per line.  End with CNTL/Z.
Seoul-1(config)#interface ethernet 0
Seoul-1(config-if)#standby ip 131.108.3.3
Seoul-1(config-if)#^Z

Seoul-2#configure
Configuring from terminal, memory, or network [terminal]?
Enter configuration commands, one per line.  End with CNTL/Z.
Seoul-2(config)#interface ethernet 0
Seoul-2(config-if)#standby ip 131.108.3.3
Seoul-2(config-if)#^Z
```

After the HSRP standby address is configured, the routers negotiate which one will be the primary forwarding router and which will be the standby. Additionally, both routers enter the IP address and the MAC address for the virtual IP address in the ARP table. The primary forwarding router begins forwarding traffic sent to the standby virtual IP address as well as answering **ping**s and accepting virtual terminal sessions to that address. Note that the MAC address for the virtual IP address on Ethernet, Fast Ethernet, Gigabit Ethernet, and FDDI interfaces is of the form 0000.0c07.acXX, where XX is an HSRP group identifier. The MAC address of the virtual IP address on the Token Ring is a functional address of the form 1000.xxxx.xxxx. The following is an example of the **show ip arp** 131.108.3.3 command on the ZIP Seoul-1 router, which is configured with HSRP:

```
Seoul-1#show ip arp 131.108.3.3
  Protocol   Address      Age (min)   Hardware Addr    Type   Interface
  Internet   131.108.3.3      -       0000.0c07.ac00   ARPA   Ethernet0
  Seoul-1#
```

TIP   Some devices on Token Ring do not accept the MAC address of an IP device as a group functional address. In this case, use the IOS interface configuration subcommand **standby use-bia** to force the HSRP virtual IP address to use the hardware burned-in address of the interface, which limits the number of HSRP groups on the interface to one.

As mentioned previously, the network administrator has several configuration options that control the behavior of HSRP. To control which router is the primary forwarding router, use the IOS interface configuration subcommand **standby priority**. The command takes as a parameter a value between 0 and 255. The router in an HSRP group with the highest priority becomes the forwarding router. In this example, we configure the ZIP Seoul-1 router with an HSRP priority of 100 and the Seoul-2 router with a priority of 95, causing Seoul-1 to become the active forwarding router:

```
Seoul-1#configure
Configuring from terminal, memory, or network [terminal]?
Enter configuration commands, one per line.  End with CNTL/Z.
Seoul-1(config)#interface ethernet 0
Seoul-1(config-if)#standby priority 100
Seoul-1(config-if)#^Z

Seoul-2#configure
Configuring from terminal, memory, or network [terminal]?
Enter configuration commands, one per line.  End with CNTL/Z.
Seoul-2(config)#interface ethernet 0
Seoul-2(config-if)#standby priority 95
Seoul-2(config-if)#^Z
```

If the standby router is required to become the active router, it automatically assumes that role. You can control whether the former primary router resumes its active forwarding role when it is available again. The IOS interface configuration subcommand **standby preempt** causes the router to resume the active forwarding role from a router with a lower priority. In the case of our ZIP Seoul example, Seoul-2 has a lower priority than Seoul-1. If Seoul-1 fails, Seoul-2 assumes the active forwarding role. Without the **standby preempt** command on Seoul-1, Seoul-2 retains the active forwarding role. The following example of the **standby preempt** command causes the ZIP Seoul-1 router to resume the active forwarding role upon restoration because it has the higher HSRP priority:

```
Seoul-1#configure
Configuring from terminal, memory, or network [terminal]?
Enter configuration commands, one per line.  End with CNTL/Z.
Seoul-1(config)#interface ethernet 0
Seoul-1(config-if)#standby preempt
Seoul-1(config-if)#^Z
```

In some situations, the operational status of an interface directly affects which router you want to be the active forwarding router. This is particularly true when each of the routers in an HSRP group has a different path to other parts of the network. In the case of the ZIP network, Seoul-1 has a connection to San Jose, which in turn has connectivity to San Francisco. The Seoul-2 router has direct connectivity to San Francisco and then on to San Jose. If the WAN connection on Seoul-1 is degraded or fails, packets sent to Seoul-1, the active forwarding router, cannot reach San Francisco or San Jose. Eventually, the dynamic routing protocols result in the Seoul-1 router sending packets to Seoul-2 for forwarding over its functional WAN, but reconvergence may take several minutes and disrupt the normal flow of network traffic. However, if Seoul-2 could assume the active forwarding role, it could immediately forward packets to San Francisco and San Jose via its functional WAN connection.

The IOS software provides an HSRP feature so that Seoul-1 can be made to adjust the HSRP priority of the HSRP group on Ethernet 0 in such a way that Seoul-2 becomes the active forwarding router. This functionality, which is called interface tracking, is enabled with the IOS interface configuration subcommand **standby track**. This command takes as a parameter the interface to be tracked and, optionally, the amount to decrement from the HSRP priority for the configured interface. If no priority decrement value is specified, the router deducts the standard amount of ten from the HSRP priority.

The following is an example of configuring the **standby track** command on the ZIP Seoul-1 router so that if the WAN interface Serial 1 becomes unoperational, Seoul-2 becomes the active forwarding router:

```
Seoul-1#configure
Configuring from terminal, memory, or network [terminal]?
Enter configuration commands, one per line.  End with CNTL/Z.
Seoul-1(config)#interface ethernet 0
Seoul-1(config-if)#standby track serial 1
Seoul-1(config-if)#^Z
```

You can verify the operation of HSRP with the IOS EXEC command **show standby**. The command takes as an optional parameter the specific interface for which to display HSRP information. Without the optional interface parameter, HSRP information is displayed for all interfaces. The following is an example of the output of the **show standby** command on the ZIP Seoul-1 and Seoul-2 routers:

```
Seoul-1#show standby
Ethernet0 - Group 0
  Local state is Active, priority 100, may preempt
  Hellotime 3 holdtime 10
  Next hello sent in 00:00:01.880
  Hot standby IP address is 131.108.3.3 configured
  Active router is local
  Standby router is 131.108.3.2 expires in 00:00:07
 Tracking interface states for 1 interface, 1 up:
    Up   Serial0
Seoul-1#

Seoul-2#show standby
Ethernet0 - Group 0
  Local state is Standby, priority 95, may preempt
  Hellotime 3 holdtime 10
  Next hello sent in 00:00:01.380
  Hot standby IP address is 131.108.3.3 configured
  Active router is 131.108.3.1 expires in 00:00:06
  Standby router is local
Seoul-2#
```

The **show standby** command displays HSRP information, which includes the forwarding state, the HSRP priority, and the interfaces being tracked for the router being queried. It also displays information about the configured standby IP address and the IP address(es) of possible standby routers within each HSRP group.

One of the drawbacks of the original HSRP was that it did not allow the network administrator to load-share the traffic across both the routers in the standby group. Basically, the standby router would just sit idle unless the active forwarding router failed.

To address this concern, the capability to support multiple HSRP groups on the same interface was added to the IOS software. On the same interface, you can create multiple HSRP groups—each with a different virtual IP address—to back up one another. For example, on the ZIP routers Seoul-1 and Seoul-2, the first HSRP group has a virtual IP address of 131.108.3.3, and Seoul-1 has been designated the primary forwarding router by virtue of its higher HSRP priority. A second HSRP group can be configured for which the virtual IP address is 131.108.3.4, but Seoul-2 is designated as the primary forwarding router by means of setting its HSRP priority higher than Seoul-1 in the second HSRP group. Seoul-1 would then be the active forwarding router, and Seoul-2 would be the standby router for the first HSRP group, while Seoul-2 would be the active forwarding router and Seoul-1 would be the standby router for the second HSRP group.

With two HSRP groups and two virtual IP addresses defined, the network administrator can configure the default gateway on some of the hosts with one of the HSRP virtual addresses and some of the hosts with the other. Although it does not achieve exactly equal load balancing, this configuration shares the load between the two routers instead of substantially overloading one while the other is completely unused.

Multiple HSRP groups are created by specifying an optional group number in all the standby commands. For example, **standby 1 ip address 131.108.3.3** and **standby 1 priority 100** specify that these HSRP commands apply to standby group 1. The commands **standby 2 ip address 131.108.3.4** and **standby 2 priority 100** specify that these HSRP commands apply to standby group 2.

Summary

In this chapter, we have examined the basic configuration of some of the most common elements of the TCP/IP network protocol with the example ZIP network. As with all features of the Cisco IOS software, there are hundreds of additional subfeatures and knobs that the network administrator can configure to enhance the operation of the network and the router. Through investigating the various documentation resources and experimenting in the lab, the network administrator can begin to more thoroughly understand and appreciate the power of the IOS software to create a robust and powerful networking environment. The following are the key concepts of this chapter:

- IP addresses are decimal representations of 32-bit binary numbers. IP addresses are grouped as network address blocks and are categorized into particular network classes. Network administrators can subdivide network address space among multiple LAN and WAN segments via subnetting.

- Configuring IP addresses involves assigning IP addresses to interfaces of the router. IP addresses are assigned out of either public or private network address space. Public addresses are provided by either an ISP or a regional address registry. Configuring IP addresses on WAN interfaces requires additional commands to manually map data-link addresses to IP addresses.

- IP routing configuration enables the router to perform the IP switching function. Static routes can be used to build the table of destination network addresses, which is called a routing table. Summary and default routes provide reachability information while minimizing the amount of information that must be maintained in the routing table. Classless routing allows routers to send packets destined to network addresses that do not fall on traditional classful network boundaries.

- Dynamic IP routing protocols enable routers to exchange reachability information about the networks that are locally attached to them. Dynamic routing protocols are grouped into two major categories, Interior Gateway Protocols and Exterior Gateway Protocols. The two major types of Interior Gateway Protocols are distance vector and link-state protocols. The IOS software provides tools to control the propagation of network routing information and the interaction of routers exchanging dynamic routing information.

- IP access lists provide the capability to filter the flow of packets in an IP network for security and privacy purposes. Access lists are enabled in two steps—defining the filtering criteria and then applying it. Access lists serve as the tool to enable other types of filtering, such as dynamic routing information.

- Basic IP dialup services permit remote users to access the network via modem and ISDN dialup as if they were attached via a LAN medium.

- IP connectivity can be verified with commands such as **show ip route** and **ping**. The diagnostic capabilities of the **trace** and **debug** commands enable the network administrator to detect misconfigurations and troubles within his router and network.

- IP features such as domain name service ease the support burden on the network administrator. Broadcast forwarding permits broadcast-based services, such as DHCP, to work in a routed network. IOS DHCP Server provides a router- or access server-based dynamic address assignment service for small and medium-sized networks. Hot Standby Router Protocol provides fault tolerance and redundancy for IP stations that cannot support dynamic routing protocols.

Table 4-8   *Summary of EXEC Commands for IP*

Command	Description
clear host	Removes temporary entries from the IP host table.
clear ip access-list counters	Clears the count of the number of times that each line of an IP access list has been matched.
clear ip route	Clears the entire routing table or, if specified, a particular route.
ping ip-address	Tests the indicated IP address to determine whether it is reachable and responsive.
show {frame-relay | atm | x25 | dialer} map	Shows mappings of IP addresses to data-link addresses on the specified WAN media type.

Table 4-8   *Summary of EXEC Commands for IP (Continued)*

Command	Description
show access-lists	Shows all access lists defined on the router.
show host	Verifies the DNS configuration on a router and displays a list of hosts that have had their names resolved to IP addresses.
show interface *interface*	Provides general information about an interface, including the IP address and network mask.
show ip access-lists	Shows all IP access lists defined on the router.
show ip arp	Displays all IP addresses that the router has been capable of resolving to MAC addresses.
show ip dhcp binding	Displays information about the IOS DHCP server address assignments.
show ip dhcp conflict	Displays information about IP address conflicts detected by the IOS DHCP server during the allocation process.
show ip dhcp database	Displays information about the location and status of the database used by the IOS DHCP server for logging DHCP bindings and conflicts.
show ip dhcp server statistics	Displays status information and counters relating to the operation of the IOS DHCP server.
show ip interface brief	Shows a brief summary of IP address information and interface statuses for all available interfaces on the device.
show ip interface *interface*	Shows all the parameters associated with the IP configuration of an interface.
show ip masks *network-address*	Lists the network masks that have been applied to the designated network and the number of routes that use each mask.
show ip protocols	Shows which routing protocols are running and various attributes of those protocols. When used with the keyword **summary**, it shows only protocol names and process-id numbers.
show ip route	Outputs the IP routing table of the router.
show ip route connected	Shows the routes associated with the operational, directly connected interfaces of the router.
show ip route *ip-address*	Shows routing information for the specified route.
show ip route static	Shows the routes that are derived from manually configured network route commands.
show ip traffic	Outputs overall statistics about the operation of the IP on the router.

continues

Table 4-8 *Summary of EXEC Commands for IP (Continued)*

Command	Description
show standby	Displays information on the operation of HSRP.
Terminal ip netmask-format {**decimal**	**bit-count**	**hexidecimal**}	Specifies the display format of network masks to be used during the existing virtual terminal or console session.
trace *ip-address*	Displays each step of the network path that a packet travels to reach the indicated IP address.

Table 4-9 *Summary of Configuration Commands for IP*

Command	Description
aaa authentication ppp *list method*	Specifies that PPP should be authenticated via the listed AAA method.
aaa authorization network *method*	Specifies that network services should be authenticated via the listed AAA method.
access-list	Creates a numbered access list and its associated filtering criteria.
arp-server	Identifies the ATM ARP server that can resolve IP addresses to ATM NSAP addresses.
async-bootp dns-server *ip-address*	Specifies the IP address(es) of a DNS server supplied to dialup clients during call establishment on a global basis.
async-bootp nbns-server *ip-address*	Specifies the IP address(es) of a NetBIOS/WINS nameserver supplied to dialup clients during call establishment on a global basis.
async mode {**interactive**	**dedicated**}	Specifies the user interaction method on an async interface for dialup users.
autoselect during-login	Specifies that the autoselection process should be performed during the authentication process.
autoselect ppp	Specifies that autodetection of PPP should be performed on an async line that is configured in interactive mode.
compress	Specifies that a compression algorithm should attempt to be negotiated during PPP dialup negotiation.
default-metric	Assigns default routing metric values to be used during route redistribution between dynamic routing protocols.
default-router *address*	Defines one or more default router IP addresses that are supplied to DHCP clients by the IOS DHCP server.
dialer-group *integer*	Specifies the dialer group to which an interface belongs and specifies which dialer list is used to define interesting traffic.

Table 4-9   *Summary of Configuration Commands for IP (Continued)*

Command	Description
dialer-list *list-number* **protocol** *type method*	Defines a dialer list that specifies which network protocols and which methods are used to define traffic as interesting for dialup sessions.
dialer map ip	Maps an IP address to the system name and the phone number for ISDN calls.
dialer rotary-group *integer*	Assigns an ISDN interface to the dialer interface group structure.
distribute-list	Applies an access list to the task of filtering the receipt and advertisement of network routes.
dns-server *address*	Defines one or more DNS server IP addresses that are supplied to DHCP clients by the IOS DHCP server.
domain-name *domain*	Defines a DNS domain name that is supplied to DHCP clients by the IOS DHCP server.
flowcontrol {**hardware** | **software**}	Specifies the flow control method on an async line.
frame-relay map ip	Maps an IP address to a Frame Relay DLCI.
group-range *start end*	Specifies which async interfaces are included in the group-async interface structure.
ip access-group *list* {**in** | **out**}	Applies the indicated access list to the task of filtering incoming or outgoing packets on an interface.
ip access-list {**extended** | **standard**} *name*	Creates a named IP access list and its associated filtering criteria.
ip address *ip-address network-mask*	Assigns an IP address and network mask to LAN and WAN interfaces.
ip classless	Enables the router to operate in classless mode, in which destination IP addresses match supernet and CIDR block routes.
ip default-information originate	Causes OSPF to generate the default route from the autonomous system boundary router into the rest of the OSPF domain.
ip default-network *network-address*	Configures the specified network address as a summary or default network.
{**no**} **ip dhcp conflict logging**	Enables or disables the logging of address conflict information by the IOS DHCP server.
ip dhcp database *url*	Defines the location and method for logging the IOS DHCP server bindings and conflict information.

continues

Table 4-9   *Summary of Configuration Commands for IP (Continued)*

Command	Description
ip dhcp excluded-address	Specifies one or more IP addresses that should be excluded from DHCP offers to DHCP clients by the IOS DHCP server.
ip dhcp pool *name*	Creates a DHCP address pool that can be configured with additional DHCP configuration subcommands.
ip dhcp-server *ip-address*	Specifies the IP address of a DHCP server that can dynamically assign IP addresses to dialup clients.
ip domain-list *name*	Establishes a list of domain names to append to unqualified host names.
ip domain-lookup	Enables DNS.
ip domain-name *name*	Configures the primary domain name to append to unqualified host names.
ip forward-protocol udp type	Controls which type of UDP broadcasts get forwarded.
ip helper-address *ip-address*	Forwards UDP broadcasts to the specified IP address.
ip host	Configures static mapping of a host name to the IP address(es).
ip local pool {default | pool-name} *start-ip-address end-ip-address*	Creates an IP address pool for dynamically assigning IP addresses to dialup clients.
ip name-server *ip-address*	Configures DNS nameserver(s).
ip netmask-format {decimal | bit-count | hexidecimal}	Configures the display format of network masks to be used during virtual terminal or console sessions.
ip ospf network {broadcast | non-broadcast | point-to-multipoint}	Configures the network type—broadcast, non-broadcast, or point-to-multipoint—that OSPF believes is connected to the interface.
ip rip {send | receive} version	Specifies which RIP version to send and receive on a specific interface.
ip route 0.0.0.0 0.0.0.0 *destination-ip-address*	Configures a default route of 0.0.0.0.
ip route *network-address network-mask destination-ip-address*	Configures a static route.
ip route *network-address network-mask ip-subnet-address*	Configures a summary route, taking as parameters the summary route, the network mask, and the nonconnected subnet.
ip routing	Enables IP routing on the router.
ip subnet-zero	Allows the first subnet in a network address range (subnet zero) to be assigned to an interface.

Table 4-9   *Summary of Configuration Commands for IP (Continued)*

Command	Description
ip unnumbered *interface*	Configures an unnumbered IP point-to-point WAN interface.
map-group	Assigns a named map group to an interface for use in mapping IP addresses to ATM data link addresses on an interface.
map-list	Creates a named map list to configure the mapping of IP addresses to PVCs or SVCs in ATM addressing.
modem autoconfigure {**discover** | *type modemtype*}	Specifies that a modem attached to an async line should be automatically configured by discovery or by using the settings of the named modem type.
modem {**dialin** | **inout**}	Specifies the allowed direction of async calls.
neighbor *ip-address*	Specifies the IP address of a neighbor router with which to exchange dynamic routing information.
neighbor *ip-address* **description**	Allows for comments to be added to the BGP **neighbor** command.
neighbor *ip-address* **distribute-list**	Allows for route filtering on a per-BGP peer basis.
neighbor *ip-address* **remote-as** *asn*	Configures the neighbor router with the indicated address in the indicated autonomous system as a BGP peer.
neighbor *ip-address* **update-source** *interface*	Specifies that the source IP address for establishing the BGP peer session should be derived from the named interface.
netbios-name-server *address*	Defines one or more NetBIOS/WINS server IP addresses to supply to DHCP clients by the IOS DHCP server.
netbios-node-type *type*	Defines the NetBIOS behavior mode that is supplied to DHCP clients by the IOS DHCP server.
network *network-address*	Specifies that connected interfaces matching the indicated network address should be included in routing advertisements.
network *network-address* **area** *area#*	Specifies that connected interfaces matching the indicated address should be included in OSPF routing advertisements and that the interfaces should be assigned to the specified area.
network *network-number* [*mask* | *prefix-length*]	Specifies the range of IP addresses that will be offered to DHCP clients for a given DHCP address pool by the IOS DHCP server.
no auto-summary	Prevents automatic address summarization at classful network boundaries and allows for the propagation of subnet information.
no inverse-arp	Disables the dynamic IP-address-to-DLCI mapping function of Frame Relay.

continues

Table 4-9   *Summary of Configuration Commands for IP (Continued)*

Command	Description
passive-interface *interface*	Configures the router to listen to but not to advertise routing information on the indicated interface.
peer default ip address {**pool** | **dhcp** | *ip-address*}	Specifies the method used to assign an IP address to a dialup client workstation.
ppp authentication *method*	Specifies that PPP authentication should be performed before allowing network services to begin. The named authentication protocol is used between the access server and the dialup client.
ppp ipcp {**dns** | **wins**}	Specifies the IP address(es) of DNS or NetBIOS/WINS servers to be supplied to dialup clients during PPP session establishment on a per-interface basis.
ppp multilink	Specifies that software-based channel multiplexing should be enabled on an interface.
redistribute protocol	Enables route redistribution from the indicated protocol.
router {**rip** | **igrp** | **ospf** | **eigrp** | **bgp**}	Enables the router to run the specified dynamic routing protocol.
speed *bits-per-second*	Specifies the transmission speed on an async line.
standby ip *ip-address*	Configures the indicated IP address as the virtual IP address for an HSRP group.
standby preempt	Causes a higher-priority HSRP router to resume active forwarding when it becomes available again.
standby priority *priority*	Assigns a priority value to an HSRP router to control the selection of the primary forwarding router.
standby track *interface*	Enables the dynamic adjustment of the HSRP priority of an HSRP router based on the operational status of the specified interface.
standby use-bia	Forces the HSRP virtual IP address to be associated with the hardware burned-in MAC address of an interface.
{**no**} **synchronization**	Enables or disables the requirement for routes to be learned via the IGP routing process before advertising to EBGP neighbors.
username *name* **password** *word*	Defines a local username/password pair to use for authenticating dialup users.
version *rip-version*	Specifies which version of RIP is used on a RIP-enabled router.
x25 map ip	Maps an IP address to an X.121 address.

References

The following references further explore the subjects in this chapter:

Bellovin, S.M., and W. R. Cheswick. *Firewalls and Internet Security: Repelling the Wily Hacker.* Reading, Massachusetts: Addison-Wesley, 1994.

Comer, D. E. *Internetworking with TCP/IP.* Volume 1, Fourth Edition. Englewood Cliffs, New Jersey: Prentice Hall, 2000.

Halabi B., and D. McPherson. *Internet Routing Architectures*, Second Edition. Indianapolis, Indiana: Cisco Press, 2000.

Zwicky, E. D., et al. *Building Internet Firewalls*, Second Edition. Sebastopol, California: O'Reilly & Associates, 2000.

AppleTalk Addressing and Address Structure—Fundamentals of the address and network structure of the AppleTalk protocol.

Configuring AppleTalk Addresses—Overview of the AppleTalk addressing scheme, plus address configuration examples for different LAN and WAN interface types.

AppleTalk Routing Configuration—Basics of AppleTalk routing configuration using static routes and verifying AppleTalk routing.

Configuring AppleTalk Routing Protocols—Characteristics of the AppleTalk RTMP and EIGRP dynamic routing protocols, and basic configuration examples.

Configuring AppleTalk Filtering via Access Lists—Controlling network access and security through the use of the **access-list** and **appletalk access-group** commands.

Configuring Basic AppleTalk Dialup Services—Options for configuring the IOS to provide remote access to dialup AppleTalk users.

Verifying AppleTalk Connectivity and Troubleshooting—Identifying connectivity problems through the use of the **show**, **ping**, and **debug** commands.

CHAPTER 5

AppleTalk Basics

AppleTalk is one of the earliest implementations of client-server computing. It was created during the mid-1980s by Apple Computer for end users of the Macintosh product family to share resources, primarily printers and files located on servers.

While it gained a loyal following among its end users for its ease of use, AppleTalk simultaneously developed a somewhat negative reputation among network engineers and designers as a nonscalable protocol that was difficult to maintain in large corporate environments. While enhancements have eased some of the criticisms from the network community, the strongest advocates of AppleTalk remain its end users. Ironically, some of the features of AppleTalk that led designers to criticize it for excessive network utilization, such as dynamic address negotiation, have since been implemented on other widely deployed protocols, notably IP in the form of Dynamic Host Configuration Protocol (DHCP).

Figure 5-1 shows the various protocols within the AppleTalk suite of networking protocols. We do not cover all these protocols, but we instead focus on several at the network and transport layers—namely, AppleTalk Address Resolution Protocol (AARP), Datagram Delivery Protocol (DDP), Routing Table Maintenance Protocol (RTMP), Name Binding Protocol (NBP), and AppleTalk Echo Protocol (AEP). Additionally, we explore Zone Information Protocol (ZIP) in the section "Configuring AppleTalk Filtering via Access Lists." The other networking protocols in Figure 5-1, which you might be familiar with, are provided as a frame of reference.

Figure 5-1   *AppleTalk Protocols Suite*

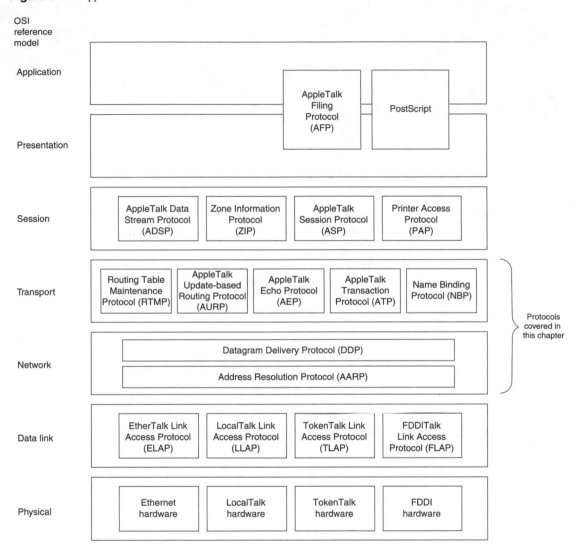

AppleTalk Addressing and Address Structure

While TCP/IP—which is examined in Chapter 4, "TCP/IP Basics"—is described as an open protocol, AppleTalk is a proprietary protocol controlled by Apple Computers. AppleTalk has a unique network address structure and a unique naming methodology for network services.

This section explores the AppleTalk network address structure that all clients (also called workstations) and servers must have to communicate within an AppleTalk internetwork.

The AppleTalk network address is a 24-bit address consisting of two distinct components—namely, a 16-bit network portion and an 8-bit node address. The network portion identifies a LAN or WAN segment, while the node address identifies a workstation or server. The two components are usually written together as *network.node* using decimal notation. For example, the address 52.6 identifies workstation or server 6 in network 52. Unlike TCP/IP, which has multiple levels of address hierarchy and summarization, AppleTalk is limited to these two levels. The DDP coordinates address administration within the AppleTalk network in addition to providing connectionless delivery of AppleTalk packets.

Network addresses for LAN and WAN segments are determined by the network administrator in the same way that TCP/IP subnets are assigned by the administrator to identify a network segment. AppleTalk identifies two different types of network addressing methods for LAN and WAN segments, AppleTalk Phases 1 and 2. In AppleTalk Phase 1, network segments are identified by a single network number.

In AppleTalk Phase 2, network segments are identified by a cable-range that corresponds to one or more logical network numbers. A cable-range is either one network number or a contiguous sequence of several network numbers specified by a starting and ending network number in the format *start-end*. For example, the cable-range 100–100 identifies a logical network that has the single network number 100, while the cable-range 50–64 identifies a logical network that spans 15 network numbers, from 50 through 64.

Each device in an AppleTalk network needs a node number with which to communicate with other devices. Unlike network protocols that require the network administrator to assign node or host addresses, an AppleTalk device determines its node address dynamically. As with the network portion of the address, AppleTalk Phases 1 and 2 have different requirements that control the selection of the node address during the negotiation process.

AppleTalk Phase 1 network segments may have up to 254 node addresses—127 are reserved for workstations, and 127 are reserved for servers. Each workstation or server in the Phase 1 network segment must have a unique node number. In AppleTalk Phase 1, a logical network segment could support only 127 AppleTalk hosts. This proved to be a scalability issue that was solved in AppleTalk Phase 2.

AppleTalk Phase 2 network segments have two classifications for node addresses, which are called extended and nonextended. On a nonextended Phase 2 network segment, 253 node numbers can be associated with a single network address on the segment. Each server or workstation is assigned a unique node address in the range 1–253. Extended Phase 2 network segments also allow for the assignment of node addresses in the range 1–253. However, because multiple network numbers may exist on the segment (via the cable-range), each workstation or server is assigned a unique combination network.node address. The difference between extended and nonextended addresses might seem a bit subtle. In a nutshell, an extended network can support multiple network numbers, and a nonextended network can support only a single network address.

NOTE

Phase 2 nonextended network segments are usually either LocalTalk networks or WAN segments. LocalTalk is Apple's first implementation of networking at the data link and physical layers that uses the telephone cable as the physical transport and carrier sense multiple access collision detect (CSMA/CD) at the data link layer. LocalTalk and AppleTalk Phase 1 were developed for workgroup applications. AppleTalk Phase 2 resulted from the need to enhance the scalability of the AppleTalk protocol to support deployment on an enterprise-wide scale. Because many of the same characteristics are shared between AppleTalk Phase 1 and nonextended Phase 2 network segments, you can think of a Phase 1 network segment as simply a nonextended Phase 2 network segment.

Cisco routers have never supported LocalTalk, although WAN segments may be addressed in AppleTalk Phase 1 style. We recommend, however, that Phase 2 addressing be used exclusively when configuring Cisco devices for the sake of consistency, clarity, and flexibility.

As mentioned previously, the node address is negotiated dynamically at the time an AppleTalk device boots or is reset. AARP is responsible for negotiating node addresses for devices on a network segment. Dynamic address assignment is accomplished using a very simple algorithm. Any time an AppleTalk device is rebooted and attempts to attach to the network, it checks to see whether a network address has been previously assigned to it. If so, the device sends out an AARP packet to verify that the address is still valid and has not been claimed by another node on the network segment. If available, the address is uscd, and the node begins normal network operations. If the address has been claimed, the node sends out a series of additional AARP packets proposing a new node address until a valid address is found. Figure 5-2 depicts the address negotiation process.

Figure 5-2   *AppleTalk Node Address Selection Process*

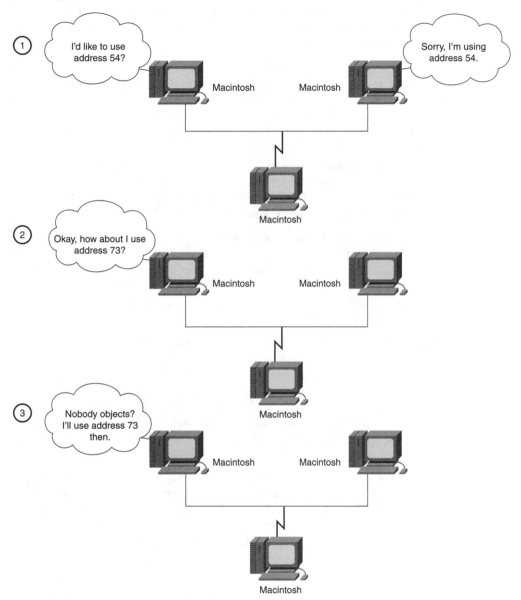

To enhance the user's interaction with the AppleTalk network, Apple decided that users should be shielded from knowing the specifics of network and node addressing. Rather than knowing that workstation 5 in network 10 wants to communicate with server 8 in network

20, the user needs to know only device names. Apple created a naming scheme that allows for the logical grouping of workstations and for the assignment of individual names to individual workstations and servers. The term used for a logical collection of workstations or servers is a *zone*.

Zones can be defined for any logical characteristic of an organization, such as its distinct operations, departments, and geographical locations. For example, a company might create a Marketing Zone, a Sales Zone, and an Engineering Zone, all of which might cross multiple geographies. Alternatively, a company might have a New York City Zone that encompasses all the organizational functions for the identified geographical area. The selection and assignment of zone names is completely at the discretion of the network administrator. To accommodate logical grouping across multiple physical LAN or WAN segments, the administrator can apply the same zone to multiple networks. Additionally, a network segment can be assigned multiple zone names to accommodate the different logical groups that can have network resources attached to that segment.

In contrast to zone names, which are determined by the network administrator, the names for individual workstations and servers are determined by the user or administrator of that device. An individual may name a workstation John's Mac or Godzilla, while a server administrator may name a server after its function, such as Finance or Publications. These names, along with the zone in which they reside, are registered with the network shortly after device startup by the NBP.

NBP associates AppleTalk names and device attributes with addresses. It orchestrates the name-binding process, including name registration, name confirmation, name deletion, and name lookup. When names are registered in NBP, the earlier example of workstation 10.5 wanting to communicate with server 20.8 might be expressed as follows: John's Mac in the New York Zone wants to communicate with server Finance in the Accounting Zone. As you can see, NBP enables users to refer to network resources by names, much like the domain name service (DNS) of TCP/IP.

NOTE   Cisco IOS devices use the name assigned with the global command **hostname** to register with NBP. A Cisco router registers itself with NBP as type ciscoRouter. NBP associations can be viewed by using the IOS EXEC command **show appletalk nbp**, which is examined later in the section "Verifying AppleTalk Connectivity and Troubleshooting."

While zone name assignment is not part of the network address, it is an integral part of the proper operation of an AppleTalk network. Proper configuration of AppleTalk on routers requires that zones be assigned in addition to network numbers or cable-ranges.

Table 5-1 summarizes the differences between the various network and node numbering requirements.

Table 5-1   *AppleTalk Phase 1 and Phase 2 Capabilities*

Capability	AppleTalk Phase 1	AppleTalk Phase 2
Networks, nodes, and zones		
Number of logical networks (cable segments)	1	65279
Maximum number of devices	254[*]	253[**]
Maximum number of end nodes	127	No limit on end nodes; 253 total node limit
Maximum number of servers	127	No limit on servers; 253 total node limit
Number of zones in which a network can exist	1	1 (nonextended); 255 (extended)
Media-level encapsulation		
Nonextended network	Does not apply	Yes
Extended network	Does not apply	Yes
Cable addressing	Does not apply; uses network numbers	Single network number (nonextended); cable range of 1 or more (extended)

[*] Node numbers 1 and 255 are reserved

[**] Node numbers 0, 254, and 255 are reserved

Configuring AppleTalk Addresses

In this section, we examine the configuration of AppleTalk addresses on LAN and WAN interfaces. Before you assign addresses, you should develop a sensible, overall addressing scheme for your network. A few rules govern the addressing. The following are tips to help guide you:

- Single network numbers should appear on only one LAN or WAN segment.

- Cable-ranges should appear on only one LAN or WAN segment, and no cable-range or portion of a cable-range should be duplicated on different network segments.

- A cable-range of one network number should be assigned to WAN interfaces.

- As a guideline, you should add one network number to a cable-range for each 50 nodes on a network segment.

- Use of a logical network addressing scheme can help simplify troubleshooting in the future.

The last recommendation may seem a bit obvious, but let's explore it a bit further by looking at the address assignments for the San Francisco location in the ZIP network. Table 5-2 shows the assignment of AppleTalk network addresses for the ZIP San Francisco location.

Table 5-2   *ZIP San Francisco AppleTalk Network Assignments*

Cable-Range	Geography	Floor	Resource
1–10	San Francisco	Independent	FDDI ring and server backbone
11–100	San Francisco	1st floor	User workstations
101–200	San Francisco	2nd floor	User workstations
201–900	San Francisco	Reserved for future growth	Reserved for future growth
901–901	SF-San Jose	—	WAN link
902–902	SF-Seoul	—	WAN link
903–1000	SF-outbound	Reserved for future growth	Unassigned WAN

In the ZIP network, ranges of network addresses have been reserved for certain locations. In this case, all San Francisco network addressing is in the range 1–1000. When troubleshooting network problems, the ZIP network administrators can quickly identify an AppleTalk device as being located in San Francisco based on its network address. Similarly, the range 1–1000 has been split into smaller parts. The range 1–10 has been reserved for the server backbone, and the range 11–900 has been reserved for building floors where user workstations and printers reside. Lastly, the range 901–1000 has been reserved for the addressing of WAN links.

As you can see, this logical approach to network address assignment facilitates quick recognition of the function and location of devices in this AppleTalk network.

LAN Interface Configuration

All Cisco routers that are routing AppleTalk have a unique AppleTalk network.node address on each of their attached LAN segments. This network.node address is determined dynamically based on either the Phase 1 network number or the Phase 2 cable-range assigned to the interface. Assigning unique addresses to each interface enables the router to know which networks are connected to each interface and where packets for those networks should be sent.

As with TCP/IP, each of the five LAN types described in Chapter 3, "The Basics of Device Interfaces," (Ethernet/IEEE 802.3, Fast Ethernet, Gigabit Ethernet, Token Ring/IEEE 802.5, and FDDI) support the concept of dynamically mapping the MAC address found on the LAN adapter to the AppleTalk address assigned to the interface. This address resolution process is supported by AARP, which also plays a role in dynamic node address assignment. When an AppleTalk workstation needs to contact another AppleTalk workstation on the same logical network and doesn't know that station's data-link address, it sends a broadcast requesting that a data-link address be supplied for the desired AppleTalk address. Each station in that logical network examines the request; if a station's MAC address matches the requested AppleTalk address, it responds with its MAC address.

Like Address Resolution Protocol (ARP) in TCP/IP, AARP eliminates the need to know which MAC addresses reside on a station's logical network to communicate with other workstations or servers. Many of the WAN protocols do not support a dynamic mapping of data link to AppleTalk addresses, so WAN configuration requires additional AppleTalk address configuration to communicate with other stations across the WAN interface.

NOTE   AppleTalk works well with each of the LAN interfaces described in Chapter 3. Although the link-layer protocol for AppleTalk is the same on each of the LAN implementations— namely, IEEE 802.2 SNAP LLC—Apple refers to its implementations of AppleTalk on each of the media by different names. Apple refers to AppleTalk over Ethernet as EtherTalk, AppleTalk over Token Ring as TokenTalk, and AppleTalk over FDDI as FDDITalk.

Apple has also named each of the link-layer protocols that support AppleTalk over these media. These protocols include EtherTalk Link Access Protocol (ELAP), TokenTalk Link Access Protocol (TLAP), and FDDITalk Link Access Protocol (FLAP). The primary difference among these link-layer types is in their SNAP encapsulation. On Ethernet, Token Ring, and FDDI interfaces, the SNAP encapsulation consists, respectively, of a standard IEEE 802.3, a standard IEEE 802.5 or an FDDI header, and the IEEE 802.2 SNAP LLC header. Naming the link-layer protocols simply makes it easier to discuss the AppleTalk implementation on those media and to reference the drivers that the Apple operating systems need to support AppleTalk on those media.

Assigning AppleTalk Phase 1 network numbers on both LAN and WAN interfaces is accomplished with the Cisco IOS interface subcommand **appletalk address**. This command takes as a parameter the AppleTalk network and node number in the format *network.node*. The network number supplied must agree with other operational routers already present on the LAN or WAN segment being configured. The node number supplied is a suggested node number. It may change in the dynamic negotiation process described earlier. Although the ZIP network has chosen to implement Phase 2 addressing exclusively, the following is an example of configuring the SF-1 router with an AppleTalk Phase 1 address on its unused interface ethernet 1:

```
SF-1#configure
Configuring from terminal, memory, or network [terminal]?
Enter configuration commands, one per line.  End with CTRL+Z.
SF-1(config)#interface ethernet 1
SF-1(config-if)#appletalk address 201.1
SF-1(config-if)#^Z
```

Assigning AppleTalk Phase 2 cable-ranges on both LAN and WAN interfaces is accomplished with the Cisco IOS interface subcommand **appletalk cable-range**. This command takes as a parameter a number range of the format *start-end* that indicates the starting and ending network address numbers to be included in the cable-range. The cable-range supplied must agree with other operational routers already present on the LAN or WAN segment being configured. The command takes as an optional parameter the initial network.node address to be used during dynamic address negotiation. In the following example, we configure the SF-2 router with an AppleTalk Phase 2 cable-range on each of its three LAN interfaces:

```
SF-2#configure
Configuring from terminal, memory, or network [terminal]?
Enter configuration commands, one per line.  End with CTRL+Z.
SF-2(config)#interface ethernet 0
SF-2(config-if)#appletalk cable-range 151-200
SF-2(config-if)#interface ethernet 1
SF-2(config-if)#appletalk cable-range 101-150
SF-2(config-if)#interface fddi 0
SF-2(config-if)#appletalk cable-range 1-10
SF-2(config-if)#^Z
```

After configuring addresses, configuring zone names on the interfaces is the next step in successfully establishing AppleTalk addressing. Zone names on LAN and WAN interfaces are configured using the Cisco IOS interface subcommand **appletalk zone**. The command takes as a parameter a character string, which is the zone name. The zone name may include alpha, numeric, and special characters. Additionally, characters from the Macintosh special character set may be included. Simply type a colon, followed by the hexadecimal value from the special character set. Zone names are case-sensitive.

Multiple zone names can be specified by entering the **appletalk zone** command multiple times for a given interface. The first zone name specified is considered the primary zone name for that interface. The interface zone configurations must match exactly—in name and in number of zones—the zones already configured on the same network segment's operating AppleTalk routers. In the following example, we configure each of the SF-2 router interfaces with a unique zone name:

```
SF-2#configure
Configuring from terminal, memory, or network [terminal]?
Enter configuration commands, one per line.  End with CTRL+Z.
SF-2(config)#interface ethernet 0
SF-2(config-if)#appletalk zone Marketing
SF-2(config-if)#interface ethernet 1
SF-2(config-if)#appletalk zone Sales
SF-2(config-if)#interface fddi 0
SF-2(config-if)#appletalk zone SF Zone
SF-2(config-if)#^Z
```

AppleTalk and Cisco IOS software support the concept of dynamically configuring the network address and zone name(s) for LAN interfaces based on information available from operational routers already present on the network segment. Dynamic configuration is accomplished by placing the interface in discovery mode. Discovery mode is useful when a router is already present on the network segment and has had its network address and zone name(s) manually established via configuration commands (whether these commands are for Cisco IOS routers or other router types). New routers added to that network segment simply acquire their configuration from the established AppleTalk router.

Discovery mode also allows for easy reconfiguration of all routers on a network segment because only the manually configured router—the *seed router*—requires manual reconfiguration. The other routers in discovery mode on that network segment relearn their configuration from the reconfigured seed router.

For discovery mode to work properly, at least one seed router must be present on the network segment. If all routers on the network segment are placed in discovery mode, no router can establish its AppleTalk configuration and begin passing AppleTalk traffic.

Configuring AppleTalk discovery mode on LAN interfaces is accomplished using the Cisco IOS interface subcommand **appletalk discovery**. This command is typically used in lieu of the **appletalk address** or **appletalk cable-range** commands. Alternatively, discovery mode can be established by specifying the network.node address 0.0 as a parameter to the **appletalk address** or **appletalk cable-range** command. Regardless of the command used to implement discovery mode, the **appletalk zone** command is not used. Although discovery mode is not implemented on the ZIP network, the following is an example of configuring AppleTalk on the San Jose router's **tokenring 0/0** interface:

```
San-Jose#configure
Configuring from terminal, memory, or network [terminal]?
Enter configuration commands, one per line.  End with CTRL+Z.
San-Jose(config)#interface tokenring 0/0
San-Jose(config-if)#appletalk discovery
San-Jose(config-if)#^Z
```

WAN Interface Configuration

WAN addressing in AppleTalk is similar to LAN addressing in that it is configured using the **appletalk address** or **appletalk cable-range** interface configuration subcommand in conjunction with the **appletalk zone** command. AppleTalk discovery mode is not supported on any WAN interface. In this section, we explore assigning AppleTalk network numbers to point-to-point and multipoint WAN interfaces. Note that WAN interfaces require specific encapsulation methods (such as X.25 or Frame Relay) to operate and that AppleTalk uses these encapsulation methods on the WAN media. All WAN interfaces require unique AppleTalk node addresses, but the specific interfaces on the same WAN share a common cable-range and zone name.

Point-to-Point WAN Interface Addressing

As noted in Chapter 4 during the discussion of IP, a point-to-point WAN interface is one that connects exactly two devices. For two routers to route AppleTalk over a point-to-point WAN interface, they both must be configured with the same AppleTalk network number or cable-range on the connected interfaces. Like on a LAN interface, each device on a WAN interface has a dynamically determined unique AppleTalk node number.

Configuring AppleTalk network numbers on the point-to-point WAN interfaces is accomplished with the Cisco IOS interface subcommand **appletalk address** for Phase 1 addresses or the Cisco IOS interface subcommand **appletalk cable-range** for Phase 2 addresses. Each separate point-to-point WAN connection (or point-to-point subinterface) should be assigned a separate AppleTalk network number or cable range. AppleTalk zone names can also be assigned to the point-to-point WAN interfaces using the Cisco IOS interface subcommand **appletalk zone**. In the following example, we configure the Seoul-1 router with AppleTalk cable ranges and zone names on each of its point-to-point interfaces (two Frame Relay subinterfaces and one High-Level Data Link COntrol [HDLC] interface):

```
Seoul-1#configure
Configuring from terminal, memory, or network [terminal]?
Enter configuration commands, one per line.  End with CTRL+Z.
Seoul-1(config)#interface serial 0.16 point-to-point
Seoul-1(config-if)#appletalk cable-range 2901-2901
Seoul-1(config-if)#appletalk zone WAN Zone
Seoul-1(config-if)#interface serial 0.17 point-to-point
Seoul-1(config-if)#appletalk cable-range 2902-2902
Seoul-1(config-if)#appletalk zone WAN Zone
Seoul-1(config-if)#interface serial 1
Seoul-1(config-if)#appletalk cable-range 1901-1901
Seoul-1(config-if)#appletalk zone WAN Zone
Seoul-1(config-if)#^Z
```

Multipoint WAN Interface Addressing

The general issues involved with configuring network protocol addresses on multipoint WAN interfaces were discussed in Chapter 4 with reference to IP. Like IP, AppleTalk can be used with many different multipoint WAN interfaces, including Frame Relay, X.25, ISDN, and ATM. You can configure each of these multipoint WAN interfaces to route AppleTalk by using the IOS interface subcommand **appletalk address** or **appletalk cable-range**, as discussed in previous sections. As with the previous interface types, the IOS interface subcommand **appletalk zone** is required for proper operation of AppleTalk on multipoint WAN interfaces.

AppleTalk also requires the specific data link layer address to be mapped to a specific AppleTalk network.node address. This mapping is configured differently for each WAN protocol. The commands used to perform these mappings require a specific network.node address. It is recommended that network.node addresses be supplied as parameters to the **appletalk address** or **appletalk cable-range** commands to ensure that the network administrator knows which node addresses are assigned to which routers on the multipoint WAN cloud.

For Frame Relay multipoint interfaces, the router needs to map data-link connection identifier (DLCI) numbers on a multipoint Frame Relay interface to an AppleTalk network.node number. Frame Relay Inverse ARP can map the DLCI number to an AppleTalk network and node number dynamically. Alternatively, you can use the interface configuration subcommand **frame-relay map appletalk** to statically map the Frame Relay DLCI address associated to an AppleTalk network and a node number that are reachable through the multipoint WAN interface.

Addressing multipoint X.25 WAN interfaces is similar to addressing Frame Relay interfaces in that both use static map interface configuration subcommands. X.25 interfaces must have their AppleTalk network.node addresses mapped to the X.121 addresses used to set up the virtual circuits between systems. Each virtual circuit is identified by the X.121 address used to set up the connection. Use the interface configuration subcommand **x25 map appletalk** to establish the static mapping between the AppleTalk address and the X.121 address on a multipoint WAN interface.

Addressing multipoint ISDN interfaces also requires static map commands. With AppleTalk, unlike IP, ISDN mapping commands are required for any device that wants to communicate with another device over an ISDN connection. The IOS interface configuration subcommand **dialer map appletalk** is used to provide the mapping between AppleTalk network.node addresses and the system names and phone numbers used to set up calls over ISDN.

The mapping between ATM data-link virtual path identifier/virtual channel identifier (VPI/VCI) addresses and the AppleTalk network.node number on the multipoint ATM interface depends on the types of ATM protocols and virtual circuits used. For AppleTalk, you can use logical link control/SNAP (LLC/SNAP) encapsulation over ATM with both permanent virtual circuits (PVCs) and switched virtual circuits (SVCs). With PVCs, a permanent virtual circuit is established through the ATM network, and packets are identified as being destined for an AppleTalk address at the other end of the specific virtual circuit. With SVCs, AppleTalk packets are identified as being destined for a specific, statically defined ATM link layer address. The ATM switch establishes the virtual circuit on demand when the router requests a connection to the ATM address for a specific AppleTalk network.node address.

LLC/SNAP encapsulation with PVCs makes use of the IOS interface configuration subcommand **map-group** and the IOS global configuration command **map-list** to map AppleTalk network.node addresses to specific PVCs. LLC/SNAP encapsulation with SVCs makes use of the IOS interface configuration subcommand **map-group** and the IOS global configuration command **map-list** to map AppleTalk network.node addresses to the network service access point (NSAP) addresses used to identify the remote devices on the ATM network.

Verifying AppleTalk Address Configuration

Verifying the AppleTalk addresses and other AppleTalk attributes that have been assigned to your interfaces can be accomplished via the EXEC command **show appletalk interface**. This command provides a complete look at the parameters associated with the AppleTalk configuration of all interfaces. If a specific interface is supplied as a parameter to the command, only the information about that interface is displayed. Following is the output of the **show appletalk interface ethernet 0** command executed on the ZIP network's SF-2 router:

```
SF-2#show appletalk interface ethernet 0
Ethernet0 is up, line protocol is up
  AppleTalk cable range is 151-200
  AppleTalk address is 198.72, Valid
  AppleTalk zone is "Marketing"
  AppleTalk address gleaning is disabled
  AppleTalk route cache is enabled
```

In the first line of the output, you can see the administrative and operational status of the interface. During the validation of the AppleTalk configuration of this interface with other operational routers on the network segment, status information is displayed above and on this line. The second line shows the AppleTalk cable-range network address. The third line shows the network.node address and indicates whether the address conflicts with any other address on this interface. The fourth line shows the zone name to which this interface belongs. Additional lines may be present in the output of this command if additional AppleTalk features, such as packet filters, are applied. An example of this situation comes up in the section "Configuring AppleTalk Filtering via Access Lists," later in this chapter.

The IOS EXEC **show appletalk interface** command has an optional form that enables you to see a brief summary of AppleTalk address information and the statuses of all available interfaces on the device. This summarized version is obtained using the **show appletalk interface brief** command.

Following is the output of the **show appletalk interface brief** command executed on the ZIP SF-2 router:

```
SF-2#show appletalk interface brief
Interface    Address     Config        Status/Line Protocol  Atalk Protocol
Ethernet0    198.72      Extended         up                 up
Ethernet1    120.45      Extended         up                 up
Fddi0        7.12        Extended         up                 up
Loopback1    unassigned  not config'd     up                 n/a
```

In addition to verifying the AppleTalk configuration on the interface itself, you can view both the static and the dynamic mappings of the AppleTalk network.node addresses to data-link addresses on the various WAN multipoint media. To do so, use the IOS EXEC commands **show frame-relay map**, **show atm map**, and **show dialer maps**, as demonstrated in previous chapters.

AppleTalk Routing Configuration

The assignment of AppleTalk network numbers and zone names to IOS devices and interfaces is necessary but not sufficient for AppleTalk devices to communicate with each other. To pass data back and forth, the workstations and servers on the AppleTalk network also must know which paths to take to reach one another. AppleTalk routers build and refer to tables of network numbers, which are known as routing tables. The AppleTalk routing tables operate much like IP routing tables, providing network path information that allows the router to deliver data directly to the end destination or to the next router in the path to the end destination. To determine where AppleTalk networks are located, and to share that information with one another, routers employ routing algorithms, also known as routing protocols.

Within AppleTalk, routing protocols can be either static or dynamic in nature. In static protocols, you manually configure the AppleTalk routing table with the network path information. Dynamic routing protocols rely on the routers themselves to advertise information about the different AppleTalk networks to which they are attached. AppleTalk uses two different dynamic routing protocols, which are examined in the section "Configuring AppleTalk Routing Protocols," later in this chapter.

Configuring AppleTalk Routing Commands

Before the router can be configured with AppleTalk protocol information and can begin passing AppleTalk traffic, AppleTalk routing must be enabled. Cisco IOS devices do not automatically enable AppleTalk routing, as they do with TCP/IP.

To enable AppleTalk routing, the IOS global configuration command **appletalk routing** is used. In the following example, we enable AppleTalk routing on the ZIP router SF-2:

```
SF-2#configure
Configuring from terminal, memory, or network [terminal]?
Enter configuration commands, one per line.  End with CTRL+Z.
SF-2(config)#appletalk routing
SF-2(config)#^Z
```

After AppleTalk routing is enabled, the router builds the routing table used for switching packets. By default, when an AppleTalk address or cable-range is configured on a LAN or WAN interface and that interface is placed in an operational state, the AppleTalk network information for the interface is placed in the routing table. All operational interfaces connected to the router are placed in the routing table. If only one router is in your network, it contains information about all of its connected AppleTalk networks. Only when two or more routers exist in the network are dynamic routing table entries created. These dynamic routing table entries are created using Routing Table Maintenance Protocol (RTMP), which we discuss later in this chapter.

You can use the IOS EXEC command **show appletalk route** to view the AppleTalk routing table. When the command is entered with no parameters, the entire AppleTalk routing table is displayed. The following example shows the SF-2 router on the ZIP network, with only the connected operational interfaces and no additional routing table entries:

```
SF-2#show appletalk route
Codes: R - RTMP derived, E - EIGRP derived, C - connected, A - AURP
       S - static  P - proxy
3 routes in internet

The first zone listed for each entry is its default (primary) zone.

C Net 1-10 directly connected, Fddi0, zone SF Zone
C Net 101-150 directly connected, Ethernet1, zone Sales
C Net 151-200 directly connected, Ethernet0, zone Marketing
```

The **show appletalk route** command provides useful data to the network administrator. It is the key tool used to determine what path an AppleTalk packet follows through the network. The output of this command is similar to the **show ip route** command that displays the IP routing table, as discussed in Chapter 4.

The first section of output is the legend for the first column of the table. It tells you from where a route was derived. Each of the last three lines in this AppleTalk routing table shows a single route to a set of AppleTalk networks specified as cable-ranges, how the routes were derived, the zones to which the networks belong, and the interface associated with the routes. The "C" in the first column indicates that all the routes are known from operational connected AppleTalk networks. We further explore the **show appletalk route** command in the section "Verifying AppleTalk Routing Configuration," later in this chapter.

Configuring Static Routing

In the discussion of IP routing in Chapter 4, we introduced various reasons for using static IP routes, including unstable network links and dialup network connections. The same reasons can be applied to the use of static AppleTalk routes. You can use the global configuration command **appletalk static** to configure static AppleTalk routes in the AppleTalk routing table. In the following example, the ZIP SF-2 router is configured with a static route that directs AppleTalk packets destined to network 40000-40000 to a node 5.10, which is found on the FDDI. In this example, the zone name SF Zone is associated with the cable-range 40000–40000 by the **appletalk static** command:

```
SF-2#configure
Configuring from terminal, memory, or network [terminal]?
Enter configuration commands, one per line.  End with CTRL+Z.
SF-2(config)#appletalk static cable-range 40000-40000 to 5.10 zone SF Zone
SF-2(config)#^Z
```

Using the **show appletalk route** command, we can verify the entry of the static route in the SF-2 router's routing table:

```
SF-2#show appletalk route
Codes: R - RTMP derived, E - EIGRP derived, C - connected, A - AURP
       S - static  P - proxy
4 routes in internet
```

The first zone listed for each entry is its default (primary) zone.

```
C Net 1-10 directly connected, Fddi0, zone SF Zone
C Net 101-150 directly connected, Ethernet1, zone Sales
C Net 151-200 directly connected, Ethernet0, zone Marketing
S Net 40000-40000 [1/G] via 5.10, 315 sec, Fddi0, zone SF Zone
```

AppleTalk static routes also can be viewed with the IOS EXEC command **show apple static**:

```
SF-2#show apple static

                AppleTalk    Static    Entries:
                --------------------------------

     Network    NextIR    Zone                Status

   40000- 40000  5.10     SF Zone              A
```

Verifying AppleTalk Routing Configuration

As examined earlier, AppleTalk routing configuration can be verified using the IOS EXEC command **show appletalk route**. In this section, we explore additional commands that aid in verifying and managing AppleTalk routing table configuration.

The **show appletalk route** command is the tool used to view the state of the AppleTalk routing table. Whether static routes are configured or dynamic routing protocols are running, this command shows whether the routes that have been configured or that are expected to be learned are actually present on the router. We explore dynamic AppleTalk routing protocols in the next section of this chapter. Following is an excerpt from the output of the **show appletalk route** command on the ZIP SF-2 router:

```
SF-2#show appletalk route
Codes: R - RTMP derived, E - EIGRP derived, C - connected, A - AURP
       S - static  P - proxy
5 routes in internet

The first zone listed for each entry is its default (primary) zone.

C Net 1-10 directly connected, Fddi0, zone SF Zone
C Net 101-150 directly connected, Ethernet1, zone Sales
C Net 151-200 directly connected, Ethernet0, zone Marketing
R Net 11-100 [1/G] via 2.12, 10 sec, Fddi0, zone Operations
S Net 40000-40000 [1/G] via 5.10, 315 sec, Fddi0, zone SF Zone
```

In the preceding output, we see routes to the directly connected AppleTalk networks on the SF-2 router and a dynamically learned route to AppleTalk network 11-100, which is learned from the SF-1 router by using the AppleTalk dynamic routing protocol RTMP. The output also provides the following information:

- The next-hop AppleTalk router network.node address and the output interface for the displayed routes (or just the output interface in the case of directly connected routes).

- If the route is dynamically learned, the length of time (in seconds) the route has been in the table, or the length of time since the last update, depending on the particular routing protocol.

- The routing protocol metric (the number to the left of the slash inside the brackets) and the state of the route for all but directly connected routes. The route state is the letter to the right of the slash inside the brackets. The value G, S, or B is used to indicate that the route is good (that is, active and available), suspect, or bad, respectively.

  Route states are maintained by a separate process, which checks every 20 seconds for particular routes that have not been updated. For each 20-second period that passes without an update about a route, its status changes from G to S and then from S to B. After 1 minute with no updates, the route is flushed. Every time a useful update is received, the status of the route is reset to G. Updates are useful if they advertise a route that is as good as or better than the one currently in the table.

As with the **show ip route** command, you can view a specific route using the **show appletalk route** command by specifying a network number as a parameter. You can also clear AppleTalk routes from the routing table using the privileged EXEC command **clear appletalk route**. When troubleshooting AppleTalk routing problems, you can use this command to manually clear a route and then use **show appletalk route** to verify from where the router originally learns that route.

AppleTalk zone name configuration can be verified using the IOS EXEC command **show appletalk zone**. When no zone name is supplied as a parameter to the command, all zone names are displayed. The following is an excerpt from the output of **show appletalk zone** from the ZIP SF-2 router:

```
SF-2#show appletalk zone
Name                           Network(s)
SF Zone                        1-10 40000-40000
Sales                          101-150
Marketing                      151-200
Operations                     11-100
Total of 4 zones
```

When two or more AppleTalk routers are present on a network, they exchange dynamic routing information. The IOS EXEC command **show appletalk neighbors** can be used to verify that AppleTalk routing is enabled and to verify the existence of other AppleTalk routers on the network. The following example is an excerpt from the output of the **show appletalk neighbors** command on the SF-2 router. It shows that the SF-2 router has learned about its AppleTalk neighbor router SF-1 and that SF-1 is running the dynamic routing protocol RTMP:

```
SF-2#show appletalk neighbors
AppleTalk neighbors:
  2.12      SF-1.Fddi0        Fddi0, uptime 33:27, 2 secs
                              Neighbor is reachable as a RTMP peer
```

Configuring AppleTalk Routing Protocols

As indicated in the discussion of dynamic routing protocols for TCP/IP in Chapter 4, many factors affect the decision of which routing protocol to implement on your network. These factors—network topology, scalability, ease of implementation, and convergence speed— are just as important in your decision of what dynamic routing protocol to use for AppleTalk as they are for IP.

The Cisco IOS offers two dynamic AppleTalk routing protocols: Routing Table Maintenance Protocol (RTMP) and AppleTalk EIGRP. Unlike TCP/IP, AppleTalk has a default dynamic routing protocol, RTMP, that operates without manual configuration by the network administrator. AppleTalk EIGRP can be implemented on a network's IOS devices on a segment-by-segment basis. However, because only Cisco IOS devices support EIGRP, network segments with non-IOS AppleTalk routers or the segments with a mixture of both continue to require RTMP for AppleTalk to operate properly.

The sample ZIP network uses both RTMP and EIGRP. EIGRP is implemented to reduce the bandwidth consumption on WAN links, which is caused by RTMP. If your AppleTalk network is sufficiently small in size and has sufficient WAN bandwidth, RTMP alone likely will suffice, eliminating the need to configure the additional commands required to implement EIGRP.

In the following sections, we examine RTMP and EIGRP routing configuration.

Configuring AppleTalk RTMP

RTMP is the default AppleTalk dynamic routing protocol; it is similar in function to IP Routing Information Protocol (IP RIP). AppleTalk RTMP is a distance vector routing protocol that establishes and maintains AppleTalk routing tables between AppleTalk routers. We examined the properties of distance vector routing protocols and IP RIP in Chapter 4. AppleTalk RTMP is an interior gateway protocol (IGP). AppleTalk does not use exterior gateway protocol (EGP) routing protocols because AppleTalk runs on intranets, not over the public Internet. AppleTalk RTMP is enabled on all AppleTalk interfaces by default when you use the global configuration command **appletalk routing**.

As the first dynamic routing protocol for AppleTalk networks, RTMP lacks some of the advanced features of newer dynamic routing protocols, primarily in the areas of scalability and reduced bandwidth consumption. One of the primary failings of RTMP is the extremely "chatty" nature of the routing protocol—it sends routing updates every 10 seconds. As we will see in the next section, more recently developed dynamic routing protocols solve some of these issues.

AppleTalk RTMP uses a hop count metric similar to IP RIP. The hop count is the measure of the number of router hops a packet must traverse to go from the packet source to the destination. AppleTalk RTMP supports a maximum hop count of 30. Any route farther than 30 hops is marked as inaccessible. In the output of **show appletalk route** from the SF-2 router, we can see that the route to AppleTalk network 11-100 has a metric of 1 hop, shown as [1/G] in the AppleTalk routing table:

```
SF-2#show appletalk route
Codes: R - RTMP derived, E - EIGRP derived, C - connected, A - AURP
       S - static  P - proxy
5 routes in internet

The first zone listed for each entry is its default (primary) zone.

C Net 1-10 directly connected, Fddi0, zone SF Zone
C Net 101-150 directly connected, Ethernet1, zone Sales
C Net 151-200 directly connected, Ethernet0, zone Marketing
R Net 11-100 [1/G] via 2.12, 10 sec, Fddi0, zone Operations
S Net 40000-40000 [1/G] via 5.10, 315 sec, Fddi0, zone SF Zone
```

By default, only one route to an AppleTalk network is kept in the routing table at any given time. This behavior is different than in IP routing, in which the router automatically retains multiple equal-cost paths. To enable the router to place equal-cost paths in its AppleTalk routing table, use the global configuration command **appletalk maximum-paths**. For example, the command **appletalk maximum-paths 2** allows the router to learn about two equal-cost paths for a given AppleTalk network destination. The number of equal-cost paths you enable on your router depends on your AppleTalk network topology. When multiple equal-cost paths are retained, the router load shares on a per-packet basis over all parallel equal-cost paths for an AppleTalk network destination.

Configuring AppleTalk EIGRP

AppleTalk EIGRP is an enhanced version of Cisco's original Interior Gateway Routing Protocol (IGRP) adapted for use in AppleTalk networks. AppleTalk EIGRP uses the same transport mechanism, DUAL update algorithm, and neighbor discovery process as used by EIGRP for IP, discussed in Chapter 4. EIGRP for AppleTalk offers features found in link state protocols, such as partial incremental updates and decreased convergence time. EIGRP sends routing updates only when changes occur in the network topology, so it uses less bandwidth than RTMP, which sends frequent complete routing table updates. Implementing EIGRP, on WAN links, particularly on those of limited bandwidth, can result in better network performance for the traffic traversing those links.

Configuring the AppleTalk EIGRP routing process consists of two steps: enabling the router to run EIGRP, and identifying which interfaces are included in the EIGRP routing process.

To enable EIGRP for AppleTalk, use the IOS global configuration command **appletalk routing eigrp**. This command takes as a parameter a process identifier, which is often the autonomous system number used in configuring IP EIGRP or IP BGP. In the following example, we enable AppleTalk EIGRP on the Singapore router using autonomous system number 25000:

```
Singapore#configure
Configuring from terminal, memory, or network [terminal]?
Enter configuration commands, one per line.  End with CTRL+Z.
Singapore(config)#appletalk routing eigrp 25000
Singapore(config)#^Z
```

After AppleTalk EIGRP is enabled, you must identify which interfaces of the router should be included in EIGRP routing updates. The IOS interface configuration subcommand **appletalk protocol** is used to instruct the router which AppleTalk dynamic routing protocol to use on the particular interface. The command takes as a parameter the keyword **eigrp** or **rtmp**. Within the ZIP network, we have enabled AppleTalk EIGRP on all WAN interfaces. The following is an example of configuring EIGRP as the routing protocol on the WAN interface of the ZIP Singapore router:

```
Singapore#configure
Configuring from terminal, memory, or network [terminal]?
Enter configuration commands, one per line.  End with CTRL+Z.
Singapore(config)#interface serial 0.100
Singapore(config-if)#appletalk protocol eigrp
Singapore(config-if)#^Z
```

Because RTMP is configured by default on all AppleTalk interfaces, both EIGRP and RTMP routing updates are sent on interfaces on which EIGRP is enabled. This can be verified using the **show apple interface** command, as seen on the ZIP Singapore router:

```
Singapore#show appletalk interface serial 0.100
Serial0.100 is up, line protocol is up
  AppleTalk cable range is 2902-2902
  AppleTalk address is 2902.2, Valid
  AppleTalk zone is "WAN Zone"
  Routing protocols enabled: RTMP & EIGRP
  AppleTalk address gleaning is not supported by hardware
  AppleTalk route cache is not initialized
```

Note that after AppleTalk EIGRP has been enabled on the router, automatic redistribution of routing information between AppleTalk EIGRP and RTMP is performed. This process ensures that routes learned by either dynamic routing protocol are mutually exchanged so that EIGRP and RTMP routers are aware of all network addresses available. The IOS global configuration command **appletalk route-redistribution** is automatically inserted into the configuration of the router configured for AppleTalk EIGRP to invoke the redistribution. Intentionally disabling the automatic redistribution can cause EIGRP routers to be unaware of RTMP-derived routes and vice versa, potentially making some network resources unavailable to some users.

On interfaces in which only Cisco IOS AppleTalk routers are present, RTMP routing can be disabled to eliminate the redundant advertisement of routing updates. It is important not to disable RTMP on any interface in which there are AppleTalk workstations, servers, printers, or non-IOS-based AppleTalk routers. Disabling RTMP on interfaces with those devices prevents them from accessing AppleTalk network services. In the ZIP network, we have disabled RTMP on all WAN interfaces in which only Cisco IOS AppleTalk routers are present. To disable RTMP, use the IOS interface configuration subcommand **no appletalk**

protocol rtmp. The following is an example of disabling RTMP on the WAN interface of the ZIP Singapore router:

```
Singapore#configure
Configuring from terminal, memory, or network [terminal]?
Enter configuration commands, one per line.  End with CTRL+Z.
Singapore(config)#interface serial 0.100
Singapore(config-if)#no appletalk protocol rtmp
Singapore(config-if)#^Z
```

As just noted, RTMP cannot be completely disabled on AppleTalk interfaces where other AppleTalk end stations and non-IOS AppleTalk routers reside. However, if only AppleTalk end stations are attached to the network segment (which is known as a stub network), the advertisement of complete RTMP routing updates can be suppressed in favor of a modified short routing update. The short form of the routing update is sufficient to allow AppleTalk servers, workstations, and printers to continue to operate, and it does not have the added network overhead of sending complete routing table updates via RTMP.

The IOS interface configuration subcommand **appletalk rtmp-stub** configures the router to send only the stub update on the interface on which the command is configured. Although we have chosen not to implement this feature on the ZIP network, the following is an example of configuring the command if we chose to implement it on the Singapore router's Ethernet interface:

```
Singapore#configure
Configuring from terminal, memory, or network [terminal]?
Enter configuration commands, one per line.  End with CTRL+Z.
Singapore(config)#interface ethernet
Singapore(config-if)#appletalk rtmp-stub
Singapore(config-if)#^Z
```

The operation of both AppleTalk EIGRP and RTMP can be verified with the previously examined **show appletalk route** command. To further assist you in verifying AppleTalk EIGRP configuration and operation, additional IOS EXEC commands can be used, as indicated in Table 5-3.

Table 5-3 *AppleTalk EIGRP IOS EXEC Commands*

IOS EXEC EIGRP Command	Function
show appletalk eigrp interfaces	Displays information about interfaces configured for AppleTalk EIGRP.
show appletalk eigrp neighbors	Displays the AppleTalk EIGRP-discovered neighbors.
show appletalk eigrp topology	Displays the AppleTalk EIGRP topology table.
show appletalk eigrp traffic	Displays the number of packets sent and received for AppleTalk EIGRP process(es).

Configuring AppleTalk Filtering via Access Lists

The packet-filtering facilities for AppleTalk in the Cisco IOS software enable a network administrator to restrict access to certain AppleTalk resources—including individual servers, printers, network segments, ranges of addresses, and entire zones—based on a variety of criteria. Like access list configuration for TCP/IP, the packet-filtering process consists of defining the filtering criteria and then applying the criteria to specific AppleTalk interfaces.

Defining Access Lists

AppleTalk access lists are slightly more complicated than TCP/IP access lists, in part because of the logical zones that can span multiple interfaces and AppleTalk network numbers. Furthermore, AppleTalk makes extensive use of device names—as registered in NBP—for workstation and server access to network resources. As examined earlier, the network.node addresses associated with those network resources may change over time based on the dynamic negotiation of a device's node address.

As a result of these conditions, we advise against using the AppleTalk filtering capabilities that allow filtering based on network addresses. Attempting to restrict access to resources in a particular zone by restricting access to a particular network or cable-range can be extremely tricky when that zone spans multiple interfaces and multiple geographies. Furthermore, an access list based on a network or node address may no longer work if that resource's address dynamically changes at some point in the future. Misconfigurations can result in allowing access where none is desired or unintentionally blocking access to those who need it.

Instead of filtering based on AppleTalk network addresses, we recommend filtering based on AppleTalk service names—as registered in NBP—and on the basis of zone name requests and propagation. Because these concepts are tightly coupled with AppleTalk operation, it is logical to control access based on these criteria. We examine both NBP and zone name filtering in the remaining portion of this section.

All AppleTalk filtering criteria are implemented via the IOS global configuration command **access-list** using the lists numbered in the range 600–699. Unlike IP and Internetwork Packet Exchange (IPX) access lists, the order of the AppleTalk access list commands is not important. However, two important criteria should be observed in the design of AppleTalk access lists.

First, access list entries should not overlap one another. An example of an overlap is permitting a particular network with a **permit network** command and then denying the same network with a **deny network** command. If you do enter entries that overlap, the last one you enter overwrites and removes the previous one from the access list. In this case, the **permit network** statement is removed from the access list when you type the **deny network** statement.

Second, AppleTalk logical filtering criteria and AppleTalk network filtering are implemented with the same access list, and both are evaluated simultaneously. Therefore, each access list must always have a method for handling packets or routing updates that do not satisfy any of the access control statements in the access list. To explicitly specify how you want these packets or routing updates to be handled, you must use one of the following commands, depending on your circumstances:

- The **access-list other-access** global configuration command, when defining access conditions for networks and cable ranges

- The **access-list additional-zones** global configuration command, when defining access conditions for zones

- The **access-list other-nbps** global configuration command, when defining access conditions for named network resources using NBP packets

These commands can be placed anywhere in the access list. The Cisco IOS software automatically places an **access-list deny other-access** command at the end of the access list. It also places **access-list deny additional-zones** and **access-list deny other-nbps** commands at the end of the access list when zones and NBP access conditions are denied, respectively. If you do not explicitly specify how to handle packets or routing updates that do not satisfy any of the access control statements, the packets or routing updates are automatically denied and, in the case of data packets, discarded.

To implement filtering based on network resource names, as they are registered with NBP, use the **nbp** keyword parameter of the numbered AppleTalk access list. Additional keywords enable you to filter based on object types, object names, the zone in which an object resides, or the type of NBP function. In the following example, we define an NBP filter on the San Jose router to prevent access to all servers in San Jose except a designated public server within the engineering department. The defined access list allows access to a named resource (in this case, the server Engineering Public), an object type (an AppleTalk file server or AFPServer), and the zone within which the object resides (San Jose Zone). The **deny other-nbps** option prevents access to all other named resources:

```
San-Jose#configure
Configuring from terminal, memory, or network [terminal]?
Enter configuration commands, one per line.  End with CTRL+Z.
San-Jose(config)#access-list 601 permit nbp 1 object Engineering Public
San-Jose(config)#access-list 601 permit nbp 1 type AFPServer
San-Jose(config)#access-list 601 permit nbp 1 zone San Jose Zone
San-Jose(config)#access-list 601 deny other-nbps
San-Jose(config)#^Z
```

Zone name filtering allows for filtering both zone name requests and zone name propagation. We examine how each is applied in the next section. Both types of zone name filtering lists are implemented with the **zone** keyword parameter to the numbered AppleTalk access list. In the following example, we define a zone name filter on the

Singapore router that denies access to the Operations Zone while permitting access to all others via the **additional-zones** keyword:

```
Singapore#configure
Configuring from terminal, memory, or network [terminal]?
Enter configuration commands, one per line.  End with CTRL+Z.
Singapore(config)#access-list 605 deny zone Operations
Singapore(config)#access-list 605 permit additional-zones
Singapore(config)#^Z
```

Applying Access Lists

After the filtering criteria of an AppleTalk access list is defined, you must apply it to one or more interfaces so that packets can be filtered. Some applications of the access list can be applied in either an inbound or outbound direction on the interface. For the inbound direction, packets are coming into the router from the interface. For the outbound direction, packets are leaving the router and traveling onto the interface.

When AppleTalk access lists are defined as NBP filters, they are applied via the IOS interface configuration subcommand **appletalk access-group**. This command takes as a parameter the keyword **in** or **out**, with the default being **out** if no keyword is supplied. The following example applies the previously defined AppleTalk access list 601 on the San Jose router to the WAN interfaces, thereby allowing access to only the engineering public server from other parts of the ZIP network:

```
San-Jose#configure
Configuring from terminal, memory, or network [terminal]?
Enter configuration commands, one per line.  End with CTRL+Z.
San-Jose(config)#interface serial 0/0
San-Jose(config-if)#appletalk access-group 601
San-Jose(config-if)#interface serial 1/0
San-Jose(config-if)#appletalk access-group 601
San-Jose(config-if)#^Z
```

To understand how AppleTalk access lists defined for zone name filtering are applied to zone name requests and propagation, a quick explanation of zone name management is required.

Zone names are mapped to network numbers on routers by the Zone Information Protocol (ZIP). When a router receives a new network advertisement in its routing table, ZIP enters the network into the Zone Information Table (ZIT) and sends out ZIP request broadcasts requesting information on which zones are mapped to the new network address. In this way, ZIP can build a complete list of all the zones that correspond to the network addresses learned via RTMP or EIGRP.

Workstation users are the primary beneficiaries of ZIP information. When an Apple Macintosh user opens the Chooser, ZIP zone list request packets are broadcast onto the local network segment. Any AppleTalk router on the local network segment can reply with a list of the available zones.

NOTE   Do not confuse our discussion of the Zone Information Protocol (ZIP) with our sample
network for the Zoom Integrated Products (ZIP) company.

With the role of ZIP in mind, we can examine the two applications of AppleTalk zone name
filters. To filter the propagation of zone names from one router to another, the IOS interface
configuration subcommand **appletalk zip-reply-filter** is used. This filter works by causing
the router to reply to ZIP requests for network-to-zone-name mappings with only the zone
names permitted in the access list. Consequently, the **appletalk zip-reply-filter** applies
only to reply packets that are outbound from the interface on which it is configured. In the
following example, we configure the Singapore router with the previously defined
AppleTalk access list 605 on its Ethernet interface to prevent any unknown routers from
learning about the Operations Zone:

```
Singapore#configure
Configuring from terminal, memory, or network [terminal]?
Enter configuration commands, one per line.  End with CTRL+Z.
Singapore(config)#interface ethernet 0
Singapore(config-if)#appletalk zip-reply-filter 605
Singapore(config-if)#^Z
```

To prevent users from learning about certain zones, use the IOS interface configuration
subcommand **appletalk getzonelist-filter**. The filter works by causing the router to reply
to ZIP requests for zone lists with only the zone names permitted by the access list. As with
the **appletalk zip-reply-filter**, the only reply packets that are filtered are the ones outbound
from the interface on which the **getzonelist-filter** is configured. In the following example,
we configure the Singapore router with the previously defined AppleTalk access list 605 on
its Ethernet interface to prevent any end user workstations from learning about the
Operations Zone when viewing resources in their Choosers:

```
Singapore#configure
Configuring from terminal, memory, or network [terminal]?
Enter configuration commands, one per line.  End with CTRL+Z.
Singapore(config)#interface ethernet 0
Singapore(config-if)#appletalk getzonelist-filter 605
Singapore(config-if)#^Z
```

TIP   As stated previously, when multiple routers are on a network segment, any one of them may
respond to ZIP GetZoneList requests. Given this fact, it is important that zone name filtering
be applied to all routers on the same network segment identically. Failure to filter identically
causes users to be supplied with different zone lists, depending on which device responds to
the request. Also, inconsistent filtering can cause the zones to appear and then disappear on
the user's workstation every few seconds. Given the potential for inconsistencies, you should
normally apply zone name filters only when all routers are IOS-based, unless the non-IOS
routers have similar filtering capabilities.

You can view the behavior of access lists and verify that they have been configured properly by using the IOS EXEC commands **show access-lists** and **show appletalk access-lists**. The former command shows all access lists defined on the router, while the latter shows only AppleTalk access lists defined on the router. Each command can take as a parameter an access list number and can display only the contents of that list. If no parameter is supplied, all lists are displayed. Following is the output of the **show appletalk access-lists** command on the Singapore router for the earlier access list example:

```
Singapore#show appletalk access-lists
AppleTalk access list 605:
  deny zone Operations
  permit additional-zones
```

The IOS EXEC command **show appletalk interface** shows where AppleTalk access lists are applied on an interface and for what filtering application. The last two lines of the following output on the Singapore router indicate that AppleTalk access list 605 has been applied as both a **zip-reply-filter** and a **getzonelist-filter**:

```
Singapore#show appletalk interface ethernet 0
Ethernet0 is up, line protocol is up
  AppleTalk cable range is 4001-4010
  AppleTalk address is 4008.30, Valid
  AppleTalk zone is "Manufacturing"
  AppleTalk address gleaning is disabled
  AppleTalk route cache is enabled
  AppleTalk GetZoneList filter is 605
  AppleTalk Zip Reply filter is 605
```

Configuring Basic AppleTalk Dialup Services

Throughout this chapter, we have been looking at the routing capabilities for AppleTalk in the Cisco IOS. The Cisco IOS also allows remote access from AppleTalk clients, similar to the functionality covered in the previous chapter for dialup IP. AppleTalk remote access provides users with the capability to use AppleTalk network services, although they are not physically connected to a dedicated LAN segment on the network.

Within the IOS, the remote access capability for AppleTalk is available over asynchronous dialup lines and ISDN. In this chapter, we have chosen to discuss the specific AppleTalk commands commonly used for asynchronous dialup clients accessing network services via the AppleTalk Remote Access Protocol (ARAP) and the AppleTalk Control Protocol (ATCP) of the Point-to-Point Protocol (PPP). AppleTalk access over ISDN is commonly used in dial-on-demand routing between routers, a topic beyond the scope of this book.

As we saw in Chapter 4 during the configuration of IP dialup services, remote access consists of setting up the asynchronous line configuration, enabling the AAA services for users, and configuring the protocol-specific options. For AppleTalk, asynchronous line configuration is nearly identical to that shown for IP in Chapter 4.

Only ARAP requires additional asynchronous line configuration commands. AppleTalk clients using ARAP require the configuration of additional AAA services, while users of the PPP data-link protocol use the configuration of AAA services, as previously discussed for IP and in further discussions in Chapter 7, "Basic Administrative and Management Issues." Both ARAP and AppleTalk PPP dialup users require that protocol-specific configuration commands be applied to the group-async interface of the access server.

We first give an example of the additional configuration commands required to support ARAP dialup clients. Three async line commands are required to implement ARAP dialup services. These commands enable the ARA protocol, specify the ARAP authentication method, and determine how ARAP is invoked during the dialup session.

The IOS line configuration subcommand **arap enable**, the first of these three commands, allows the ARA protocol to operate on the dialup lines. The IOS line configuration subcommand **arap authentication default** instructs the access server to use the default ARAP authentication method configured via the AAA service. Lastly, the IOS line configuration subcommand **autoselect arap** configures the access server to automatically recognize that a dialup user is attempting to connect with the ARA protocol. The following is an example of adding the ARAP line configuration subcommands to the Singapore access server Sing2511, which was previously configured for dialup IP services:

```
Sing2511#configure
Configuring from terminal, memory, or network [terminal]?
Enter configuration commands, one per line.  End with CTRL+Z.
Sing2511(config#line 1 16
Sing2511(config-line)#arap enable
Sing2511(config-line)#arap authentication default
Sing2511(config-line)#autoselect arap
Sing2511(config-line)#^Z
```

Additional AAA authentication commands are required to verify the identity of dialup users accessing via the ARA protocol. The IOS global configuration command **aaa authentication arap** is used to specify the criteria by which ARAP users are identified. The command takes as parameters a method name and a list of authentication methods. As with PPP, ARAP can be authenticated using a local username or an authentication server, such as Terminal Access Controller Access Control System (TACACS+). Control of guest logins can also be specified with the keyword **auth-guest**, which specifies that guest ARAP login is allowed only if a user has previously been authenticated to the IOS EXEC during the dialup session.

ARAP dialup users must also be supplied an AppleTalk network and zone number, to which they are assigned during their dialup session. The IOS global configuration command **arap network** is used to specify the ARAP network number and zone name.

In the following example, the Singapore access server named Sing2511 is configured with authentication and AppleTalk protocol information to allow ARAP dialup users to access the AppleTalk network. ARAP users are authenticated to the local username database configured on this access server and are assigned to the AppleTalk network 2500 in the Mac-dialup Zone:

```
Sing2511#configure
Configuring from terminal, memory, or network [terminal]?
Enter configuration commands, one per line.  End with CTRL+Z.
Sing2511(config#aaa authentication arap default auth-guest local
```

```
Sing2511(config)#arap network 2500 Mac-dialup
Sing2511(config)#^Z
```

Allowing dialup users access to AppleTalk services with ATCP and PPP requires only two protocol commands in addition to the PPP and line configuration commands configured previously for IP dialup services in Chapter 4. As with ARAP, AppleTalk PPP clients must have an AppleTalk network and zone name to which they can be assigned. Although the ARAP network number and zone name may be the same, a separate IOS command is used to create the dialup PPP network number and zone name.

After the PPP dialup network number and zone name are established, AppleTalk PPP client services are enabled on the group-async interface. The IOS global configuration command **appletalk virtual-net** is used to establish the PPP network number and zone name by supplying those items as parameters to the command. The IOS interface configuration subcommand **appletalk client-mode** enables PPP dialup services on the interface to which it is applied. When client mode is enabled, AppleTalk routing is disabled on the interface, and routing updates are not sent. The following is an example of configuring the Singapore access server named Sing2511 to support AppleTalk PPP dialup clients that are assigned to AppleTalk network 2501 and Zone Mac-dialup:

```
Sing2511#configure
Configuring from terminal, memory, or network [terminal]?
Enter configuration commands, one per line.  End with CTRL+Z.
Sing2511(config)#apple virtual-net 2501 Mac-dialup
Sing2511(config)#interface group-async 1
Sing2511(config-if)#appletalk client-mode
Sing2511(config-if)#^Z
```

Verifying AppleTalk Connectivity and Troubleshooting

The IOS software offers numerous tools to aid the network administrator in tracking down AppleTalk connectivity problems, network configuration errors, and dynamic routing protocol problems. In this section, we examine IOS EXEC **show** commands, **debug** commands, and diagnostic commands that facilitate identifying network issues.

As previously examined, the IOS EXEC command **show appletalk interface** is a useful tool for identifying network number and zone name misconfigurations, as well as tracking the progress of the AppleTalk interface initialization. The second line of output from this command tracks the status of the initialization and also informs you of any misconfigurations. The following is an example of a misconfiguration caused by missing zone name information on ethernet 0 of the ZIP SF-2 router:

```
SF-2#show appletalk interface ethernet 0
Ethernet0 is up, line protocol is up
  AppleTalk node down, Port configuration error
  AppleTalk cable range is 151-200
  AppleTalk address is 198.72, Invalid
  AppleTalk zone is not set.
  AppleTalk address gleaning is disabled
  AppleTalk route cache is enabled
```

The IOS EXEC command **show appletalk nbp** is useful in determining the network number associated with a particular named resource. The command displays the network.node address associated with a name that is registered with NBP. The network administrator can verify whether the named resource has the expected network.node number, or vice versa. The following is an excerpt from the output of the **show appletalk nbp** command on the ZIP SF-1 router, which shows its interface registrations with NBP:

```
SF-1#show appletalk nbp
  Net   Adr   Skt   Name              Type          Zone
   2    12    254   SF-1.Fddi0        ciscoRouter   SF Zone
   22    7    254   SF-1.Ethernet0    ciscoRouter   Operations
```

In troubleshooting connectivity problems, it is useful to determine whether a station that should be reachable via a directly connected LAN interface is responding. To verify that the router has been capable of resolving the AppleTalk network address to a MAC address, use the IOS EXEC command **show appletalk arp**. This command can take as a parameter a specific AppleTalk network.node address. When no parameter is supplied, all AppleTalk ARP entries are displayed. The output of this command includes the AppleTalk address-to-MAC mapping, the age of the entry in the table, and the interface with which the ARP entry is associated. (The router times an ARP entry out of the ARP table after four hours.) Following is an example of the **show appletalk arp** command on the ZIP SF-1 router:

```
SF-1#show appletalk arp
Address   Age (min)   Type      Hardware Addr        Encap   Interface
2.12          -       Hardware  0000.0c0c.34d1.0000  SNAP    Fddi0
9.159         -       Hardware  0000.0c0c.23d1.0000  SNAP    Ethernet1
5.20          -       Dynamic   0000.030c.11c4.0000  SNAP    Fddi0
```

Like TCP/IP, AppleTalk implements an echo request/response protocol called AppleTalk Echo Protocol (AEP). The AEP allows an AppleTalk station to send an echo request to a destination station. When the station receives the request, it sends an echo reply to the originating station. This simple protocol allows network administrators to test the reachability of AppleTalk servers, printers, and other devices. AEP is implemented in the IOS software as the **ping appletalk** command. In addition to providing basic reachability information, the **ping appletalk** command informs you of approximately how long the echo request and reply take to reach and return from the destination station. In the following example, the IOS EXEC command **ping appletalk** sends five 100-byte AEP requests to the given AppleTalk address, as seen on the SF-1 router:

```
SF-1#ping appletalk 5.20

Type escape sequence to abort.
Sending 5, 100-byte AppleTalk Echos to 5.20, timeout is 2 seconds:
!!!!!
Success rate is 100 percent (5/5), round-trip min/avg/max = 1/2/4 ms
```

The router sends five AEP echo requests and reports via the exclamation point (!) that all the replies are received. It also reports the number of echo request attempts and the number of echo replies received. The router then calculates the percentage of successful pings. Minimum, maximum, and average response times are also calculated.

Table 5-4 shows the different response characters that can be received as a result of an AppleTalk ping.

Table 5-4   *Ping Command Response Characters*

Character	Meaning
!	Each exclamation point indicates the receipt of a reply (echo) from the target address.
.	Each period indicates that the network server timed out while waiting for a reply from the target address.
B	The echo received from the target address was bad or malformed.
C	An echo with a bad DDP checksum was received.
E	Transmission of an echo packet to the target address failed to find a MAC address.
R	Transmission of the echo packet to the target address failed because it lacked a route to the target address.

The **ping appletalk** command, like its IP counterpart, has both a privileged and a nonprivileged version. In the user EXEC mode, the nonprivileged version allows the user only to specify an AppleTalk address. The privileged version, available in the enable EXEC mode, allows the user to modify parameters of the echo request, including the number of requests, the size of the packets sent, the timeout value, and numerous other values. Following is an example of the privileged version of the **ping appletalk** command executed on the SF-1 router; the request packet size has been increased to 500 bytes:

```
SF-1#ping appletalk
Target AppleTalk address: 5.20
Repeat count [5]:
Datagram size [100]: 500
Timeout in seconds [2]:
Verbose [n]:
Sweep range of sizes [n]:
Type escape sequence to abort.
Sending 5, 500-byte AppleTalk Echos to 5.20, timeout is 2 seconds:
!!!!!
Success rate is 100 percent (5/5), round-trip min/avg/max = 1/4/6 ms
```

Overall information about the performance and operation of AppleTalk on the Cisco router can be obtained using two different IOS EXEC commands. The **show appletalk traffic** command includes counters for such information as the total number of packets received and sent by the router, the number of broadcasts received and sent, RTMP and EIGRP statistics, and whether the router has sent or received AppleTalk Echoes. The counters in **show appletalk traffic** are cumulative, and they can be reset with the IOS privileged EXEC command **clear appletalk traffic** or by reloading or power cycling the router. The following is an example of the output from the **show appletalk traffic** command on the ZIP Singapore router:

```
Singapore#show appletalk traffic
AppleTalk statistics:
  Rcvd:  90 total, 0 checksum errors, 0 bad hop count
         45 local destination, 0 access denied, 0 fast access denied
         0 for MacIP, 0 bad MacIP, 0 no client
         0 port disabled, 0 no listener
         0 ignored, 0 martians
  Bcast: 0 received, 18766 sent
  Sent:  18766 generated, 0 forwarded, 0 fast forwarded, 45 loopback
         0 forwarded from MacIP, 0 MacIP failures
         25 encapsulation failed, 0 no route, 0 no source
  DDP:   135 long, 0 short, 0 macip, 0 bad size
  NBP:   30 received, 0 invalid, 0 proxies
         0 replies sent, 55 forwards, 25 lookups, 0 failures
  RTMP:  0 received, 0 requests, 0 invalid, 0 ignored
         17624 sent, 0 replies
  ATP:   0 received
  ZIP:   0 received, 20 sent, 0 netinfo
  Echo:  40 received, 0 discarded, 0 illegal
         20 generated, 20 replies sent
  Responder:  0 received, 0 illegal, 0 unknown
         0 replies sent, 0 failures
  AARP:  0 requests, 0 replies, 0 probes
         0 martians, 0 bad encapsulation, 0 unknown
         153 sent, 0 failures, 0 delays, 25 drops
  Lost: 0 no buffers
  Unknown: 0 packets
  Discarded: 0 wrong encapsulation, 0 bad SNAP discriminator
  AURP: 0 Open Requests, 0 Router Downs
        0 Routing Information sent, 0 Routing Information received
        0 Zone Information sent, 0 Zone Information received
        0 Get Zone Nets sent, 0 Get Zone Nets received
        0 Get Domain Zone List sent, 0 Get Domain Zone List received
        0 bad sequence
  EIGRP: 0 received, 0 hellos, 0 updates, 0 replies, 0 queries
         1097 sent,   0 hellos, 0 updates, 0 replies, 0 queries
```

The second IOS EXEC command to provide general information about AppleTalk operation is the **show appletalk globals** command. This command provides information about various configuration option settings for the dynamic routing protocols, the number of network routes and zones with the AppleTalk network, and how packets with errors will be handled when they arrive at the router. This command is useful for verifying that the desired configuration options are configured and are operating as expected on your routers. The following example shows the output of the **show appletalk globals** command on the ZIP SF-1 router:

```
SF-1#show appletalk globals
AppleTalk global information:
  Internet is incompatible with older, AT Phase1, routers.
  There are 16 routes in the internet.
  There are 11 zones defined.
  Logging of significant AppleTalk events is disabled.
  ZIP resends queries every 10 seconds.
  RTMP updates are sent every 10 seconds.
  RTMP entries are considered BAD after 20 seconds.
  RTMP entries are discarded after 60 seconds.
  AARP probe retransmit count: 10, interval: 200 msec.
```

```
AARP request retransmit count: 5, interval: 1000 msec.
DDP datagrams will be checksummed.
RTMP datagrams will be strictly checked.
RTMP routes may not be propagated without zones.
Routes will be distributed between routing protocols.
Routing between local devices on an interface will not be performed.
IPTalk uses the udp base port of 768 (Default).
EIGRP router id is: 2500
EIGRP maximum active time is 3 minutes
Alternate node address format will not be displayed.
Access control of any networks of a zone hides the zone.
```

In addition to the troubleshooting and verification commands presented in this section, numerous privileged IOS EXEC **debug** commands exist to aid in determining the operation of the AppleTalk protocol on the router. These **debug** commands provide both general and detailed diagnostic output that can aid in troubleshooting and in verifying the operation of the router, routing protocols, and other functions. For example, the output from the **debug appletalk errors** command can help isolate network address and zone name misconfigurations on router interfaces. Some of the more common **debug** commands used for AppleTalk are summarized in Table 5-5.

Table 5-5   *Debug Commands for AppleTalk*

Command	Description
debug appletalk arp	Displays AARP requests generated and replies sent to the router and AARP ager activity.
debug appletalk eigrp-packet	Displays the contents of AppleTalk EIGRP packets sent and received by the router.
debug appletalk eigrp-update	Displays the update activity of the AppleTalk EIGRP on the router.
debug appletalk errors	Displays information about errors that occur with the AppleTalk protocol.
debug appletalk events	Displays significant AppleTalk events that occur on the router.
debug appletalk nbp	Displays the activities of the NBP on the router.
debug appletalk packet	Displays the source and destination AppleTalk addresses of packets that are routed by the router. As with the **debug ip** packet, this **debug** command can overload the router, so care must be taken when using it. It is suggested that packet debugging be limited to a particular interface.
debug appletalk routing	Displays changes that occur in the routing table as the result of the addition and deletion of routes for EIGRP and RTMP.

continues

Table 5-5   *Debug Commands for AppleTalk (Continued)*

Command	Description
debug appletalk rtmp	Displays changes that occur in the routing table as the result of the addition and deletion of routes for RTMP routes only.
debug appletalk zip	Displays the activities of the Zone Information Protocol on the router.

Summary

In this chapter, we have examined the basic configuration required to implement AppleTalk with the sample ZIP network. While these basic commands and features can get your AppleTalk network up and running, many other advanced features can enhance your network's operation and scalability. The texts and Web resources cited in the "Reference" section serve as excellent tutorials on understanding, implementing, and troubleshooting those features. Following are the key concepts of this chapter:

- AppleTalk Phase 1 addressing uses a single network number to identify a network segment. Phase 2 addressing uses either a single network number or a contiguous sequence of numbers of the form *start-end* to identify one or more networks.

- A nonextended Phase 2 address can support only a single network address, while an extended Phase 2 address can support multiple network numbers.

- Node numbers are assigned dynamically by AARP.

- LAN network numbers and zones can be configured manually or through the use of a seed router and discovery mode.

- The dynamic routing protocols offered by the Cisco IOS for use with AppleTalk are RTMP and EIGRP. RTMP is configured by default when AppleTalk routing is enabled with the **appletalk routing** command. EIGRP is useful in reducing bandwidth consumption on LAN links.

- Due to the flexible and dynamic nature of AppleTalk addresses, using them as a basis for filtering in access lists is not recommended. Instead, filter on the basis of service names as registered in NBP and on the basis of zone name requests and propagation.

- Access list commands are not order-dependent in AppleTalk, as they are in IP and IPX. When there are conflicting or overlapping commands, the earlier one in the list is disregarded, and the later one is implemented.

- Each access list must specify a method for handling packets and routing updates that do not satisfy any of the access control statements in the access list. Otherwise, those packets and routing updates are automatically denied or discarded.

- A variety of **show**, **debug**, and **ping** commands are available for verifying configurations and for troubleshooting your AppleTalk network. In addition to those summarized in Table 5-6, see Tables 5-3 and 5-5 for a review of pertinent commands.

Table 5-6   *Summary of EXEC Commands for AppleTalk*

Command	Definition
clear appletalk route	Clears the entire routing table or, if specified, a particular route.
clear appletalk traffic	Clears the counters in **show appletalk traffic**.
ping appletalk *network.node*	Tests to determine whether the indicated AppleTalk address is reachable and responsive.
show appletalk access-lists	Shows all AppleTalk access lists defined on the router or, if specified, the contents of a particular list.
show appletalk globals	Provides general information about AppleTalk configuration and operation.
show appletalk interface brief	Shows a brief summary of AppleTalk address information and interface status for all available interfaces on the device.
show appletalk interface *interface*	Shows all the parameters associated with the AppleTalk configuration of an interface.
show appletalk nbp	Shows the network number associated with a particular named resource.
show appletalk neighbors	Provides a list of AppleTalk neighbors learned via dynamic routing.
show appletalk route *network-address*	Shows the routing table in its entirety or, if specified, a particular route.
show appletalk static	Shows static routes that have been configured.
show appletalk traffic	Outputs overall statistics about the operation of the AppleTalk protocol on the router.
show appletalk zone	Displays a list of all AppleTalk zones known to this router.

Table 5-7   *Summary of Configuration Commands for AppleTalk*

Command	Definition
aaa authentication arap *list method*	Specifies that ARAP should be authenticated via the listed AAA method.
access-list	Creates a numbered access list and its associated filtering criteria.
access-list *number* [**permit** | **deny**] **additional-zones**	Permits or denies packets and routing updates, on the basis of zones, that do not satisfy any other access control statements in the access list.
access-list *number* [**permit** | **deny**] **other-access**	Permits or denies packets and routing updates, on the basis of network numbers or cable ranges, that do not satisfy any other access control statements in the access list.
access-list *number* [**permit** | **deny**] **other-nbps**	Permits or denies packets and routing updates that do not satisfy any other access control statements based on NBP.
appletalk access-group *number*	Applies the indicated access list to the task of filtering incoming or outgoing packets on an interface.
appletalk address *network.node*	Assigns a Phase I network number to a LAN or WAN interface.
appletalk cable-range *start-end*	Assigns a Phase II cable-range to a LAN or WAN interface.
appletalk client-mode	Enables AppleTalk PPP dialup services on the asynchronous interface to which it is applied.
appletalk discovery	Implements the dynamic configuration of a network address and zone name(s) by discovery.
appletalk getzonelist-filter *number*	Applies the indicated access list to the task of filtering outgoing ZIP GetZoneList replies sent to workstations and servers.
appletalk maximum-paths *number*	Configures the router to permit the specified number of equal-cost paths in its AppleTalk routing table.
appletalk protocol [**eigrp** | **rtmp**]	Specifies which routing protocol (EIGRP or RTMP) to use on a particular interface in AppleTalk networks where EIGRP is enabled.
appletalk route-redistribution	Invokes route redistribution between EIGRP and RTMP.
appletalk routing	Enables AppleTalk routing on a router.
appletalk routing eigrp *autonomous-system*	Enables EIGRP for AppleTalk on a router.

Table 5-7   *Summary of Configuration Commands for AppleTalk (Continued)*

Command	Definition
appletalk rtmp-stub	Configures the router to send only stub updates on the interface to which it is applied.
appletalk static	Configures a static AppleTalk route.
appletalk virtual-net	Establishes the PPP network number and zone name for dialup users.
appletalk zip-reply-filter *number*	Applies the indicated access list to the task of filtering outgoing ZIP zone name replies sent to other routers.
appletalk zone *name*	Configures a zone name on an interface.
arap authentication default	Specifies that ARAP authentication should be performed prior to allowing network services to begin. The default authentication protocol is used between the access server and the dialup client.
arap enable	Allows ARAP to operate on asynchronous lines.
arap network	Specifies the ARAP network number and zone name for dialup users.
autoselect arap	Specifies that autodetection of ARAP should be performed on an async line configured in interactive mode.
dialer map appletalk	Maps an AppleTalk network.node address to the system name and phone number for ISDN calls.
frame-relay map appletalk	Statically maps an AppleTalk network.node address to a Frame Relay DLCI.
map-group	Assigns a named map group to an interface for use in mapping AppleTalk addresses to ATM data-link addresses on an interface.
map-list	Creates a named map list to configure the mapping of AppleTalk addresses to PVCs or SVCs in ATM addressing.
x25 map appletalk	Statically maps an AppleTalk network.node address to an X.121 address.

References

Cisco Systems. *Troubleshooting Internetworking Systems: AppleTalk Connectivity*. (This guide covers troubleshooting for numerous protocols and network technologies. It is available directly from Cisco as well as online at the following address: www.cisco.com/univercd/cc/td/doc/cisintwk/tis_doc/76523.htm.)

Sidhu, G., R. Andrews, and A. Oppenheimer. *Inside AppleTalk*, 2nd Edition. Reading, Massachusetts: Addison-Wesley, 1990.

Vandersluis, K. and A. Eissa. *Troubleshooting Macintosh Networks: A Comprehensive Guide to Troubleshooting and Debugging Macintosh Networks*. Indianapolis, Indiana: IDG Books Worldwide, 1993.

IPX Addressing and Address Structure—Fundamentals of the address and network structure of the IPX protocol.

Configuring IPX Addresses—Overview of the IPX addressing scheme, plus address configuration examples for different LAN and WAN interface types.

IPX Routing Configuration—Basics of IPX routing configuration using static routes and verifying IPX routing.

Configuring IPX Routing Protocols—Characteristics of the IPX RIP and NLSP dynamic routing protocols and basic configuration examples.

Configuring IPX Filtering via Access Lists—Controlling network access and security through the use of the **access-list** and **ipx access-group** commands.

Configuring Basic IPX Dialup Services—Setting up IPX client asynchronous dialup connectivity.

Verifying IPX Connectivity and Troubleshooting—Identifying connectivity problems through the use of **show**, **ping**, and **debug** commands.

Configuring IPX Type 20 Packet Forwarding—Options for configuring the IOS to forward IPX type 20 packets.

CHAPTER 6

IPX Basics

In the late 1970s, Xerox created a network protocol called Xerox Network Systems (XNS) that was widely implemented by most major LAN vendors, including Novell, Inc. Novell made some changes to the protocol in the early 1980s, renamed it Internet Packet Exchange protocol (IPX), and incorporated it as part of NetWare. The NetWare transport layer protocol, the Streams Packet Exchange (SPX), was also derived from the XNS protocol suite. Novell NetWare operates over the IPX/SPX protocol suite as well as on the TCP/IP protocol suite.

NetWare is a suite of protocols for sharing resources—primarily print and file services— among workstations through a client/server implementation. Novell describes NetWare as a network operating system (NOS) because it gives end users access to resources that are available via the LAN or WAN. NetWare, a dominant corporate NOS, is widely deployed in many internetworks.

Figure 6-1 shows the multiple protocols commonly used in the NetWare protocol suite. We do not cover each of these protocols in this chapter. Instead, we concentrate on explaining the protocols on the network and transport layers—namely, IPX, IPX Routing Information Protocol (RIP), NetWare Link State Protocol (NLSP), Service Advertisement Protocol (SAP), and SPX. The protocols shown in Figure 6-1 reference other internetwork technologies with which you may be familiar.

NOTE

Not all revisions of the Cisco IOS support IPX. You must make sure that the IOS version you are running on your router supports the *Desktop Protocols Suite*.

Figure 6-1   *The IPX Protocols Suite*

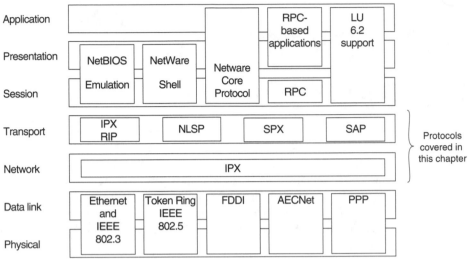

IPX Addressing and Address Structure

IPX is a network layer protocol with its own proprietary addressing structure. This section introduces the IPX address structure that each IPX client (sometimes called a *workstation* in NetWare documentation) or server must have to communicate with other IPX devices on an internetwork.

An IPX address has two components, a 32-bit *network* component that applies to a given LAN or WAN segment, and a 48-bit *node* component that uniquely identifies a client or a server. Most nodes determine this unique number by reading the 48-bit data link layer (Layer 2) address on their LAN interface. As we will see, it is not a requirement of IPX to have the data link layer address of the device match the node component, but by convention, these two numbers often do match.

These two components, expressed together as *network.node*, are written using hexadecimal format. The two-layer hierarchy of the IPX address structure makes this addressing scheme scalable for internetworks, yet not as scalable as the multiple hierarchies of the IP addressing structure.

The network administrator assigns the network number for an IPX network segment in the same way that he selects IP subnets for given LAN and WAN segments. All IPX clients, IPX servers, and Cisco routers on the same LAN or WAN segment must have the same network number.

NetWare servers have internal IPX network numbers that differ from the IPX network numbers for any LAN or WAN interface. The internal IPX network number is used as the source network number for NetWare services on the server. We'll discuss service advertisement later in this chapter when we discuss SAP. A Cisco router can be configured with an internal IPX network number using the global configuration command **ipx internal-network**. We discuss this internal network number further in the section "Configuring NLSP."

Each IPX server or client needs to have a unique node number on a LAN or WAN segment. Typically, IPX clients derive this unique number by reading the 48-bit data-link address on their LAN interface and then using that number as their unique network layer node address. Although the LAN interface data-link address is the same as the IPX node address, you should not conclude that a client uses these two addresses in the same manner. The data link layer address is used for data link layer encapsulation, such as with Ethernet or Token Ring. The IPX node address is the second portion of the IPX network layer network.node address for a given client. An IPX client on network 10 with a data-link address of 0802.044d.d88f on its Ethernet interface would be known on the IPX network as 10.0802.044d.d88f by reading the 48-bit data link layer address on its LAN interface.

Using the data link layer address to determine a unique 48-bit IPX node address is not required by the IPX protocol. You can have a node address that does not match a data link layer address, as long as the node address is unique on a given IPX network. For example, we have seen that an IOS device can have multiple LAN interfaces. When IPX routing is enabled, the IOS device chooses the data link layer address on the first LAN interface in the device as the unique node address for all IPX network segments. Now imagine that the data link layer address on Ethernet 0 of a router is 0000.0c11.12ab. If Ethernet 0 is the first LAN interface in this router, and if the router is connected to IPX network 10 and IPX network 20, the router is seen as 10.0000.0c11.12ab on IPX network 10 and 20.0000.0c11.12ab on IPX network 20.

The IOS global configuration command **ipx routing** enables IPX routing in an IOS device (and enables IPX RIP, which we will discuss later in this chapter). The device automatically chooses an IPX node number based on the first LAN interface when this global configuration command is configured. In the following example, we enable IPX routing on the SF-2 router on the ZIP network:

```
SF-2#configure
Configuring from terminal, memory, or network [terminal]?
Enter configuration commands, one per line.  End with CTRL+Z.
SF-2(config)#ipx routing
SF-2(config)#^Z
```

NOTE   If your router does not have a LAN interface, you must configure a unique IPX node address as an optional parameter to the **ipx routing** command. The node address must have 12 decimal digits and must be a unique node number for the IPX networks connected to the router.

The use of the data link layer address to determine the IPX node address simplifies the job of the network administrator, because IPX clients do not need manual configuration. Also, this mapping of data link layer address to network layer address can eliminate the need for a separate protocol to map between the addresses on these two layers, such as ARP. This is discussed in Chapter 4, "TCP/IP Basics."

Configuring IPX Addresses

This section discusses how to configure IPX addresses on LAN and WAN interfaces for Cisco routers. We also discuss the configuration of the four IPX LAN interface encapsulations used in an IPX environment.

LAN Interface Configuration

All Cisco routers that are routing IPX have a unique IPX network.node address on each of the attached LAN segments. This address enables the router to know which networks are connected to each interface and where packets for those networks should be sent.

Assigning IPX network addresses to both LAN and WAN interfaces is accomplished with the Cisco IOS interface subcommand **ipx network**. The IPX node address is set via the **ipx routing** global configuration command, as we mentioned earlier in this chapter. In the following example, we configure the SF-2 router with IPX addresses on each of its three LAN interfaces:

```
SF-2#configure
Configuring from terminal, memory, or network [terminal]?
Enter configuration commands, one per line.  End with CTRL+Z.
SF-2(config)#interface ethernet 0
SF-2(config-if)#ipx network 200
SF-2(config-if)#interface ethernet 1
SF-2(config-if)#ipx network 150
SF-2(config-if)#interface fddi 0
SF-2(config-if)#ipx network 10
SF-2(config-if)#^Z
```

IPX LAN Interface Encapsulations

As seen in Figure 6-1, IPX operates over a variety of data-link protocols. Originally, IPX was developed over Ethernet. Then, as new data-link protocols were invented—such as IEEE 802.3, IEEE 802.5, and FDDI—IPX was enhanced to support encapsulations for these data-link protocols. As a result, different versions of NetWare support different data-link protocols and their associated encapsulation methods. IPX uses a single data link layer protocol for most newer LAN technologies but has four different encapsulation methods for Ethernet LAN segments.

LAN encapsulations are known by different names to IPX and the Cisco IOS. Table 6-1 maps IPX frame type names to Cisco IOS encapsulation syntax.

Table 6-1   *IPX Encapsulation Terminology and Cisco IOS Encapsulation Syntax*

IPX Frame Type	Cisco IOS Encapsulation Name
Ethernet_802.2	sap
Ethernet_802.3	novell-ether
Ethernet_II	arpa
Ethernet_Snap	snap
Token-Ring	sap
Token-Ring_Snap	snap
Fddi_Snap	snap
Fddi_802.2	sap
Fddi_Raw	novell-fddi

NOTE   The default Cisco IOS encapsulation type for all Ethernet interfaces on Cisco routers is novell-ether. Cisco Token Ring interfaces default to sap encapsulation, while Cisco FDDI interfaces default to snap encapsulation.

The Cisco IOS encapsulation name sap is the default encapsulation used by NetWare Version 4.0. On Ethernet interfaces, this frame type uses a standard IEEE 802.3 header, followed by an IEEE 802.2 logical link control (LLC) header, also known as the service access point (SAP). The IEEE 802.2 LLC header provides a means for the data link layer to determine the network layer protocol in a data link protocol frame. On Token Ring interfaces, the sap encapsulation, which is the default encapsulation, consists of a standard IEEE 802.5 header, followed by an IEEE 802.2 LLC header. Similarly, on FDDI interfaces, this frame type consists of a standard FDDI header, followed by an IEEE 802.2 LLC header.

NOTE   Do not confuse the IEEE 802.2 LLC SAP (service access point) encapsulation method with the NetWare SAP (Service Advertising Protocol). We discuss NetWare SAP later in this chapter.

The Cisco IOS novell-ether encapsulation, which is the same as Novell's Ethernet_802.3 encapsulation, operates only on Ethernet interfaces. The novell-ether frame type consists of a standard IEEE 802.3 header, followed by the IPX header with the checksum field set to the hexadecimal value of FFFF. The novell-ether default encapsulation is used by NetWare Version 3.11 and by the IOS on Cisco routers.

For Ethernet interfaces that need to handle TCP/IP and IPX traffic, you should use the Novell Ethernet_II encapsulation (called arpa in the Cisco IOS). This encapsulation simply uses an Ethernet header, which is followed by an IPX header.

The Cisco IOS encapsulation snap on Ethernet uses a standard IEEE 802.3 header, followed by an IEEE 802.2 SNAP LLC header. Subnetwork Access Protocol (SNAP) is a standard method of encapsulating network layer datagrams in IEEE protocols. On Token Ring and FDDI interfaces, the SNAP frame type consists of a standard IEEE 802.5 or FDDI header, followed by an IEEE 802.2 SNAP LLC header.

On FDDI interfaces, the Cisco IOS novell-fddi encapsulation matches Novell's Fddi_Raw encapsulation. This frame type consists of a standard FDDI header, followed by the IPX header with the checksum field set to the hexadecimal value of FFFF.

To summarize this discussion, four encapsulations are possible on Ethernet interfaces (sap, arpa, novell-ether, and snap), three are possible on FDDI (sap, snap, and novell-fddi), and two are possible on Token Ring (sap and snap). Figure 6-2 shows the four Ethernet encapsulation schemes.

Figure 6-2   *Encapsulation Formats for IPX Data Link Layer Protocols*

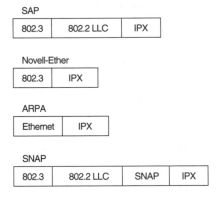

NOTE   Although multiple IPX data-link encapsulations exist, the NetWare release (such as NetWare 3.11 or NetWare 4.0) running on your network often determines which encapsulation method is needed. All devices must be running the same IPX encapsulation for NetWare clients, NetWare servers, and Cisco routers to communicate properly on a given IPX LAN segment.

Configuring Encapsulations

To configure the encapsulation method on a LAN interface, use the **ipx network** command with the **encapsulation** option. In the following example, we configure the snap encapsulation on Ethernet 0 of the ZIP network's SF-2 router:

```
SF-2#configure
Configuring from terminal, memory, or network [terminal]?
Enter configuration commands, one per line.  End with CTRL+Z.
SF-2(config)#interface ethernet 0
SF-2(config-if)#ipx network 200 encapsulation snap
SF-2(config-if)#^Z
```

In some situations, you may need to run several NetWare data link layer encapsulations on the same LAN interface at the same time. For example, you may need to transition some IPX clients from NetWare 3.11 to NetWare 4.0, each of which uses a different data link layer encapsulation method. Normally, different client and server encapsulation methods would prevent the clients from communicating with servers using a different version of NetWare. However, by using two different encapsulations on one IPX LAN segment, the Cisco router permits communication between clients and servers running different versions of NetWare.

When running multiple encapsulation methods, you must assign unique network numbers for each data-link encapsulation method on a router interface. One of the networks becomes the primary IPX network, and the other becomes the secondary IPX network. Both are assigned to the same physical interface. Use the **secondary** option with the **ipx network** command to assign secondary networks on a LAN interface that is running different encapsulation methods. We assign the arpa encapsulation to Ethernet 0 of the ZIP network's SF-2 router in the following example:

```
SF-2#configure
Configuring from terminal, memory, or network [terminal]?
Enter configuration commands, one per line.  End with CTRL+Z.
SF-2(config)#interface ethernet 0
SF-2(config-if)#ipx network 201 encapsulation arpa secondary
SF-2(config-if)#^Z
```

WAN Interface Configuration

WAN addressing in IPX, which is similar to LAN addressing, is configured using the **ipx network** interface configuration subcommand. In this section, we explore assigning IPX network numbers to point-to-point and multipoint WAN interfaces. Recall from Chapter 3, "The Basics of Device Interfaces," that specific encapsulation methods (such as X.25 or Frame Relay) usually have to be explicitly configured to operate on a WAN interface. Such is the case for the WAN encapsulation methods used by IPX.

Point-to-Point WAN Interface Addressing

As seen in the discussion about IP in Chapter 4, a point-to-point WAN interface connects exactly two devices. For two routers to route IPX over a point-to-point WAN interface, they must both be configured with the same IPX network number on the connected interfaces. As on a LAN interface, each device must have a unique IPX node number on a WAN interface.

You can configure the IPX network number on point-to-point WAN interfaces using the **ipx network** interface configuration subcommand. Following is an example of assigning an IPX network number to the point-to-point WAN interfaces (two Frame Relay subinterfaces and one HDLC interface) on the Seoul-1 router:

```
Seoul-1#configure
Configuring from terminal, memory, or network [terminal]?
Enter configuration commands, one per line.  End with CTRL+Z.
Seoul-1(config)#interface serial 0.16 point-to-point
Seoul-1(config-if)#ipx network 2901
Seoul-1(config-if)#interface serial 0.17 point-to-point
Seoul-1(config-if)#ipx network 2902
Seoul-1(config-if)#interface serial 1
Seoul-1(config-if)#ipx network 1901
Seoul-1(config-if)#^Z
```

Multipoint WAN Interface Addressing

Multipoint WAN interface addressing issues were covered in Chapter 4 with reference to IP. Like IP, IPX can be used with many different multipoint WAN interfaces, including Frame Relay, X.25, ISDN, and ATM. You can configure each of these multipoint WAN interfaces to route IPX using the **ipx network** interface configuration subcommand. The mapping from the specific data link layer address to the IPX network number is configured differently for each WAN protocol.

When you are using Frame Relay multipoint interfaces, the router needs to map DLCI numbers on a multipoint Frame Relay interface to an IPX network.node number. Frame Relay Inverse ARP can dynamically map the DLCI number to an IPX network and node number. Alternatively, you can use the interface configuration subcommand **frame-relay map ipx** to statically map the Frame Relay DLCI address to an IPX network.node number that is reachable through the multipoint WAN interface.

Addressing multipoint X.25 WAN interfaces is similar to addressing Frame Relay interfaces in that both use static map interface configuration subcommands. X.25 interfaces must have their IPX addresses mapped to the X.121 addresses used to set up the virtual circuits between systems. Each virtual circuit is identified by the X.121 address used to set up the connection. Use the interface configuration subcommand **x25 map ipx** to establish the static mapping between the IPX address and the X.121 address on a multipoint WAN interface.

Addressing multipoint ISDN interfaces also requires static map commands. In ISDN, however, the mapping commands are required only when a device wants to establish a call to another device. The IOS interface configuration subcommand **dialer map ipx** is used to map IPX addresses to system names and phone numbers that are used to set up calls over ISDN.

The mapping between ATM data-link VPI/VCI addresses and the IPX network number on the multipoint ATM interface depends on the type of ATM protocols and virtual circuits used. For IPX, you can use LLC/SNAP encapsulation over ATM with both PVCs and SVCs. With PVCs, a permanent virtual circuit is established through the ATM network, and packets are identified as being destined for an IPX address at the other end of the specific virtual circuit. With SVCs, IPX packets are identified as being destined for a specific, statically defined ATM link layer address. When the router requests a connection to the ATM address for a specific IPX address, the ATM switch establishes the virtual circuit on demand.

LLC/SNAP encapsulation with PVCs makes use of the IOS interface configuration subcommand **map-group** and the IOS global configuration command **map-list** to map IPX addresses to specific PVCs. LLC/SNAP encapsulation with SVCs makes use of the IOS interface configuration subcommand **map-group** and the IOS global configuration command **map-list** to map IPX addresses to the network service access point (NSAP) addresses used to identify the remote devices on the ATM network.

Verifying IPX Address Configuration

Verifying the IPX addresses and other IPX attributes assigned to your interfaces can be accomplished via the EXEC command **show ipx interface**. This command provides a complete look at all the parameters associated with the IPX configuration of all interfaces. If a specific interface is supplied as a parameter to the command, only the information about that interface is displayed. Following is the output of the **show ipx interface ethernet 0** command executed on the ZIP network's SF-2 router:

```
SF-2#show ipx interface ethernet 0
Ethernet0 is up, line protocol is up
  IPX address is 200.0000.0c0c.11bb, NOVELL-ETHER [up]
  Delay of this IPX network, in ticks is 1 throughput 0 link delay 0
  IPXWAN processing not enabled on this interface.
  IPX SAP update interval is 60 seconds
  IPX type 20 propagation packet forwarding is disabled
  Incoming access list is not set
  Outgoing access list is not set
  IPX helper access list is not set
  SAP GNS processing enabled, delay 0 ms, output filter list is 1010
  SAP Input filter list is not set
  SAP Output filter list is not set
  SAP Router filter list is not set
  Input filter list is not set
  Output filter list is not set
  Router filter list is not set
  Netbios Input host access list is not set
```

```
Netbios Input bytes access list is not set
Netbios Output host access list is not set
Netbios Output bytes access list is not set
Updates each 60 seconds, aging multiples RIP: 3 SAP: 3
SAP interpacket delay is 55 ms, maximum size is 480 bytes
RIP interpacket delay is 55 ms, maximum size is 432 bytes
IPX accounting is disabled
IPX fast switching is configured (enabled)
RIP packets received 6, RIP packets sent 1861
SAP packets received 330, SAP packets sent 4
```

In the first line of the output, you can see the administrative and operational status of the interface. The second line shows the IPX network.node address and IPX encapsulation. The output also shows the status of many different IPX filters and access lists, some of which we discuss later in this chapter.

The IOS EXEC **show ipx interface** command has an option that enables you to see a brief summary of IPX address information and the interface statuses for all available interfaces on the device. This summarized version is obtained using the **show ipx interface brief** command. Following is the output of the **show ipx interface brief** command executed on the ZIP SF-2 router:

```
SF-2#show ipx interface brief
Interface   IPX Network  Encapsulation   Status    IPX State
Ethernet0   200          NOVELL-ETHER    up        [up]
Ethernet1   150          NOVELL-ETHER    up        [up]
Fddi0       0            SNAP            up        [up]
Loopback1   unassigned   not config'd    up        n/a
```

From the preceding output, you can see the IPX network number assigned to each interface, the Novell encapsulation, and the operational status of each interface.

In addition to verifying the IPX configuration on the interface itself, you can view both the static and the dynamic mappings of IPX addresses to data-link addresses on the various WAN multipoint media. To do so, use the IOS EXEC commands **show frame-relay map**, **show atm map**, **show x25 map**, and **show dialer maps**.

IPX Routing Configuration

The assignment of IPX network.node addresses to IOS devices and interfaces is necessary to route IPX. Another vital component is IPX routing. Routers must be routing IPX and have routes to IPX networks in an internetwork to enable full communication, just as in IP networks. To determine where IPX networks exist, routers use a routing table created by routing algorithms, which are also known as routing protocols.

Within IPX, routing protocols can be either static or dynamic in nature. In static protocols, you manually configure the IPX routing table with the network path information. Dynamic routing protocols rely on the routers themselves to advertise information about the different IPX networks to which they are attached. IPX uses three different dynamic routing protocols, which are examined in the section "Configuring IPX Routing Protocols" later in this chapter.

Configuring IPX Routing Commands

As mentioned earlier in this chapter, you enable IPX routing with the global configuration command **ipx routing**. After IPX routing is enabled, the router builds the routing table used for routing. By default, when an IPX address is configured on a LAN or WAN interface and that interface is placed in an operational state, the IPX network address for that interface is placed in the routing table. All operational interfaces connected to the router are placed in the routing table. If only a single router is in your network, it has information about all of its connected IPX networks, and there is no need to configure static or dynamic routing. Only when two or more routers exist in the network are static or dynamic routing table entries needed.

You can use the IOS EXEC command **show ipx route** to view the IPX routing table. When entered with no parameters, the entire IPX routing table is displayed. The following example shows the SF-2 router on the ZIP network with only the connected operational interfaces and no additional routing table entries:

```
SF-2#show ipx route
Codes: C - Connected primary network,    c - Connected secondary network
       S - Static, F - Floating static, L - Local (internal), W - IPXWAN
       R - RIP, E - EIGRP, N - NLSP, X - External, A - Aggregate
       s - seconds, u - uses, U - Per-user static

3 Total IPX routes. Up to 1 parallel paths and 16 hops allowed.

No default route known.

C          10 (NOVELL-FDDI),  Fd0
C         150 (NOVELL-ETHER), Et1
C         200 (NOVELL-ETHER), Et0
```

The **show ipx route** command provides useful data to the network administrator and is the key tool used to determine what path an IPX packet will follow through the network. The output of this command is similar to the **show ip route** command that displays the IP routing table, as discussed in Chapter 4.

The first section of output is the legend for the first column of the table. It tells you from where a route was derived. Each of the last three lines in this IPX routing table shows a single route to an IPX network, how the route was derived, the IPX LAN encapsulation method, and the interface associated with the route. The "C" in the first column indicates that all these routes are known from operational connected primary IPX networks. We explore the **show ipx route** command in the section after the next one, "Verifying IPX Routing Configuration."

Configuring Static Routing

In Chapter 4, we discussed various reasons for using static IP routes. The same reasons can be applied to static IPX routes. You can use the global configuration command **ipx route** to configure static IPX routes in the IPX routing table.

Verifying IPX Routing Configuration

As noted earlier, the command for verifying IPX routing configuration is the IOS EXEC command **show ipx route**. In this section, we explore other commands that aid in verifying and managing IPX routing table configuration.

The **show ipx route** command is the tool used to view the state of the IPX routing table. Whether or not static routes are configured or dynamic routing protocols are running, this command shows whether the routes that have been configured or that are expected to be learned are actually present on the router. We explore dynamic IPX routing protocols in the next section. Following is an excerpt from the output of the **show ipx route** command on the ZIP SF-2 router:

```
SF-2#show ipx route

Codes:    C - Connected primary network, c - Connected secondary network
          S - Static, F - Floating static, L - Local (internal), W - IPXWAN
          R - RIP, E - EIGRP, N - NLSP, X - External, A - Aggregate
          s - seconds, u - uses

4 Total IPX routes. Up to 1 parallel paths and 16 hops allowed.

No default route known.

C          10  (NOVELL-FDDI),   Fd0
C         150  (NOVELL-ETHER),  Et1
C         200  (NOVELL-ETHER),  Et0
R 100 [02/01] via 100.0000.1c2c.23bb, 19s, Fd0
```

In the preceding output, we see routes to the directly connected IPX networks on the SF-2 router and a route to IPX network 100 that is dynamically learned, using IPX RIP, from the SF-1 router.

You can view a specific route with the **show ipx route** command by specifying a network number, just as you can when using the **show ip route** command. You can clear IPX routes from the routing table using the privileged EXEC command **clear ipx route**. In debugging IPX routing, you can use this command to manually clear a route and then use **show ipx route** to verify where the router learns that route.

Configuring IPX Routing Protocols

In Chapter 4, we discussed the following issues, which you need to consider when choosing a dynamic routing protocol:

- Network topology
- Address and route summarization
- Convergence speed
- Route selection criteria
- Scalability

- Ease of implementation

- Security

In the Cisco IOS, there are multiple dynamic IPX routing protocols. When choosing the optimal protocol for your network, you need to consider the preceding criteria.

Before delving into the individual dynamic routing protocols, however, we must consider SAP. SAP is a dynamic service protocol that is tightly coupled with dynamic IPX routing protocols. After explaining SAP, we discuss the IPX dynamic routing protocols IPX RIP, NLSP, and IPX EIGRP.

SAP

Service Advertisement Protocol (SAP) is a Novell proprietary protocol that advertises NetWare services on an IPX network. A service is a resource that IPX clients may want to use, such as a file service or print service. All services have a service type, which is denoted by a hexadecimal number. Some service types are defined by Novell, while others are proprietary to vendors that make services for NetWare. For example, SAP type 4 is the standard service type for NetWare file service, and SAP type 7 is the standard service type for printers.

By default, NetWare servers broadcast SAP packets every 60 seconds to advertise known services. Each NetWare server learns of SAP services in much the same way that it learns dynamic routing protocol information, and it builds a table of that information, called a SAP table.

Cisco routers enable SAP by default for all interfaces configured for IPX. A router builds a SAP table from SAP information learned from NetWare servers and other routers. To view the SAP table on a Cisco router, use the IOS EXEC command **show ipx servers**. The following example shows the output from **show ipx servers** on the ZIP network's SF-1 router:

```
SF-1#show ipx servers
Codes: S - Static, P - Periodic, E - EIGRP, N - NLSP, H - Holddown, + = detail
2 Total IPX Servers
Table ordering is based on routing and server info
Type Name              Net  Address        Port    Route   Hops    Itf
P    4 SF-MAIN         100.0001.0002.0006:0451   2/01    1       Et0
P    4 SF-ENG          100.0809.0001.0002:0451   2/01    1       Et0
```

This output shows that the SF-1 router has learned of two IPX servers, each offering a file service (shown as the number 4 in the first part of the server name). For each IPX service, you can see the IPX address of the server offering the service, the IPX route metric for the service, and the interface where the router heard the service. Both of the services in this example are identified as periodic, which means that they were learned by SAP (which advertises services on a regular periodic interval). We explore other methods to learn about IPX services in the sections "Configuring NLSP" and "Configuring IPX EIGRP" later in this chapter.

Just as you can have static IPX routes, you also can have static SAP table entries. You can define static SAP table entries using the global configuration command **ipx sap**. Static SAP table entries may be useful in some network environments, such as those that utilize dialup or dial backup.

After a server or router has a SAP table, it can respond to NetWare clients that ask for services. NetWare clients send IPX Get Nearest Server (GNS) messages to look for a server that can provide the services they need. NetWare servers that know about the service can respond to the client, giving it the specific IPX address where the service resides. A Cisco router can also respond to clients with the IPX address of a service if the service is in the router's SAP table. If a Cisco router hears a GNS message on a LAN segment where the service is known to exist, the router does not answer the GNS message.

NOTE   The nearest server is defined as one that provides the service and has the shortest route in the SAP table. If multiple servers match this criteria, a Cisco router responds with the server most recently heard. This could result in multiple NetWare clients receiving GNS responses for the same server. This is not an optimal situation if the IPX network has multiple servers providing the same service for load balancing of client requests.

Use the **ipx gns-round-robin** global configuration command to tell the router to rotate in round-robin fashion through a set of eligible servers when it responds to GNS requests. See the following section for information on filtering GNS responses sent by a router on specific interfaces.

SAP Filters

The Cisco IOS permits a network administrator to filter on the basis of which SAP services a device sends from and receives into its SAP table. SAP filters are commonly used on an internetwork to limit the amount of SAP traffic sent and received by a router.

Many IPX networks use SAP filters to reduce the number of SAP messages sent over WAN interfaces, thereby reducing traffic load. Filtering received SAP advertisements can reduce the number of IPX services a router has in RAM and can provide limited network security. The limited network security is accomplished by not allowing the IOS device to provide SAP table entries for services that want to remain somewhat hidden on an IPX network. For more information on filtering IPX packets, see the section "Configuring IPX Filtering via Access Lists" later in this chapter.

You can use the global configuration command **access-list** to make SAP filters based on IPX addresses or the SAP service type. SAP filters use **access-list** numbers 1000 through 1099. Like IP and AppleTalk access lists, these access lists allow for the use of *wildcard* or *don't care* masks. This capability enables a single IOS global configuration access list command to represent multiple IPX addresses.

In the following example on ZIP's San-Jose router, we make a SAP filter to permit only SAP services advertised by the single NetWare server 10.0000.0000.a0b0:

```
San-Jose#configure
Configuring from terminal, memory, or network [terminal]?
Enter configuration commands, one per line.  End with CTRL+Z.
San-Jose(config)#access-list 1000 permit 10.0000.0000.a0b0
San-Jose(config)#access-list 1000 deny -1
San-Jose(config)#^Z
```

NOTE   When building SAP filters (and IPX access lists for packet filters, as discussed later in this chapter), the IPX network number −1 denotes all IPX networks. Thus, in the preceding example, the second line of access list 1000 denies all SAPs. Like access lists in IP, a final deny line is implicit in IPX access lists. The explicit configuration is shown here only to illustrate the use of the −1 IPX network number.

After configuring a SAP filter, you must apply it to a given interface on the IOS device. You can filter on SAP messages received or sent by the device on an interface basis using the **ipx input-sap-filter** and **ipx output-sap-filter** interface configuration subcommands. We apply a SAP filter using access list 1000 to all output SAP advertisements on interface Serial 0 of the San-Jose router:

```
San-Jose#configure
Configuring from terminal, memory, or network [terminal]?
Enter configuration commands, one per line.  End with CTRL+Z.
San-Jose(config)#interface serial 0
San-Jose(config-if)#ipx output-sap-filter 1000
San-Jose(config-if)#^Z
```

As another example, you may want to build a SAP filter that permits, from all servers, only file and print services to be advertised over a WAN interface. In the following example, we build a SAP filter to allow only file service (SAP type 4) and print service (SAP type 7) from all servers. We apply this filter to the SAP output advertisements on interface Serial 0 of the San-Jose router on the ZIP network:

```
San-Jose#configure
Configuring from terminal, memory, or network [terminal]?
Enter configuration commands, one per line.  End with CTRL+Z.
San-Jose(config)#access-list 1005 permit -1 4
San-Jose(config)#access-list 1005 permit -1 7
San-Jose(config)#interface serial 0
San-Jose(config-if)#ipx output-sap-filter 1005
San-Jose(config-if)#^Z
```

Another type of SAP filter permits or denies NetWare services based on the IPX address of a router. One application of this type of SAP filter is to hide all services originating from a given router. The IOS interface configuration command **ipx router-sap-filter** applies a router SAP filter to a given interface. In the following example, we apply a router SAP filter to interface FDDI 0/0 of the ZIP network's SF-Core-1 router to hide all NetWare services from an engineering server:

```
SF-Core-1#configure
Configuring from terminal, memory, or network [terminal]?
Enter configuration commands, one per line.  End with CTRL+Z.
SF-Core-1(config)#access-list 1001 permit aa.0207.0104.0874
SF-Core-1(config)#interface fddi 0/0
SF-Core-1(config-if)#ipx router-sap-filter 1001
SF-Core-1(config-if)#^Z
```

The Cisco IOS enables you to filter, on a per-interface basis, which SAP table services are eligible as responses to GNS queries sent by NetWare clients. Using a GNS filter on the output of an interface is useful in preventing clients from ever identifying specific servers as the nearest server or in forcing all GNS queries to be handled by a specific server. In the following example on the SF-Core-1 router, we specify an IPX access list to permit a single NetWare server to be used as an answer to GNS queries. We apply this access list as an output GNS filter to the FDDI 0/0 interface of the SF-Core-1 router by using the IOS interface configuration subcommand **ipx output-gns-filter**:

```
SF-Core-1#configure
Configuring from terminal, memory, or network [terminal]?
Enter configuration commands, one per line.  End with CTRL+Z.
SF-Core-1(config)#access-list 1010 permit aa.0207.0104.0874
SF-Core-1(config)#interface fddi 0/0
SF-Core-1(config-if)#ipx output-gns-filter 1010
SF-Core-1(config-if)#^Z
```

Configuring IPX RIP

IPX RIP is a NetWare dynamic routing protocol similar in function to IP RIP. IPX RIP is a distance vector routing protocol that establishes and maintains IPX routing tables between IPX routers and NetWare servers. We discussed IP RIP and the properties of distance vector routing protocols in Chapter 4. IPX RIP is an interior gateway protocol (IGP). There is no exterior gateway protocol (EGP) routing protocol in IPX because NetWare runs on intranets, not over the public Internet. IPX RIP is enabled on all IPX interfaces by default when you use the global configuration command **ipx routing**.

IPX RIP was the first dynamic routing protocol for IPX networks, so it lacks some advanced features of newer dynamic routing protocols in terms of address and route summarization, convergence speed, route selection criteria, and scalability. As you will see later in this section, NLSP and EIGRP—more modern dynamic routing protocols for IPX—solve some of these issues.

While IP RIP uses hop count as its routing metric, IPX RIP uses a different metric, known as *clock ticks,* to make routing decisions. A clock tick represents one-eighth of a second. The clock tick metric for a destination is measured by examining the bandwidth on the interface used to reach that destination. In the output of **show ipx route** from the SF-2 router, the route to IPX network 100 has a metric of two clock ticks and one hop, shown as [02/01] in the IPX routing table:

```
SF-2#show ipx route

Codes:    C - Connected primary network, c - Connected secondary network
S - Static, F - Floating static, L - Local (internal), W - IPXWAN
R - RIP, E - EIGRP, N - NLSP, X - External, A - Aggregate
s - seconds, u - uses

4 Total IPX routes. Up to 1 parallel paths and 16 hops allowed.

No default route known.

C          10  (NOVELL-FDDI),   Fd0
C         150  (NOVELL-ETHER),  Et1
C         200  (NOVELL-ETHER),  Et0
R 100 [02/01] via 100.0000.1c2c.23bb, 19s, Fd0
```

If the number of clock ticks to reach a destination is equal for multiple routes in the IPX RIP routing table, the router uses the shortest number of router hops to break the tie. IPX RIP has a default maximum hop count of 16, just like IP RIP. Like all routed protocols in the IOS, the router load-shares the traffic to the destination through all available equal-cost paths if the routing table has equal-cost paths (if both clock ticks and router hops tie).

NOTE

By default, a router using the Cisco IOS does not learn about multiple IPX parallel equal-cost paths to a given destination. The router learns a single path to a destination and discards information about alternative parallel equal-cost paths, as indicated by the **show ipx route** phrase "Up to 1 parallel paths and 16 hops allowed." This default behavior is based on the implementation of some NetWare clients and services that cannot handle IPX packets arriving out of order—which can happen when load sharing occurs over parallel equal-cost paths.

To enable a router to place equal-cost paths in its IPX routing table, use the global configuration command **ipx maximum-paths**. For example, the command **ipx maximum-paths 2** allows the router to learn about two equal-cost paths for a given destination. The number of equal-cost paths you enable on your router depends on your IPX network topology.

The default behavior of a Cisco router is to load-share on a per-packet basis over all parallel equal-cost paths for a destination IPX address. For performance reasons, you may want all packets for each unique destination IPX address to take the same path even if multiple equal-cost paths exist. To enable this feature, use the IOS global configuration command **ipx per-host-load-share**.

Configuring NLSP

NLSP is a link state interior gateway protocol for IPX networks. NLSP, which is based on the OSI Intermediate System-to-Intermediate System (IS-IS) protocol, has features similar to those of other link state protocols, such as OSPF. Like other link state protocols, NLSP supports hierarchical addressing and fast convergence.

NLSP has the capability to use hierarchical routing techniques to aggregate and summarize IPX network numbers. Route aggregation and summarization are useful in large IPX networks for the same reasons they are useful in large IP networks.

The first level in NLSP routing is an *area*. An NLSP area is a logical group of IPX network addresses; it is conceptually similar to an OSPF area, which is a collection of IP networks and subnets. NLSP *Level 1 routing* occurs within an area. NLSP communication between areas is called *Level 2 routing*. You can group all areas with NLSP routers communicating with Level 2 routing into a hierarchical collection called a *routing domain*. NLSP communication between routing domains is *Level 3 routing*. Figure 6-3 shows an NLSP internetwork.

Figure 6-3 *The Hierarchical Structure of an NLSP IPX Network*

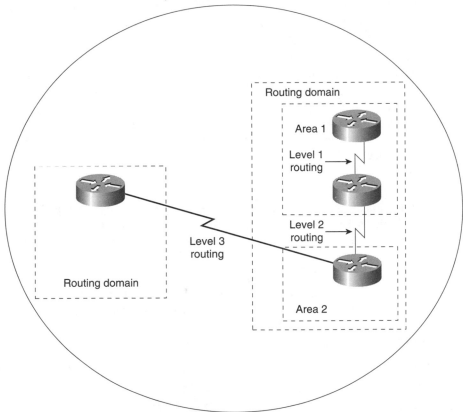

An NLSP IPX Internetwork

NLSP requires an internal IPX network number to be configured on a Cisco router. You can do so by using the IOS global configuration command **ipx internal-network**, as noted earlier in this chapter in the "IPX Addressing and Address Structure" section.

To enable NLSP, use the IOS global configuration command **ipx router nlsp**. This configuration command requires that a *tag* parameter be used to specify the NLSP process in the IOS. To define a set of network numbers as part of the current NLSP area, use the **area-address** IOS global configuration command. The **area-address** command takes two options, an IPX network address and a mask. The mask indicates how much of the area number identifies the area and how much of that number identifies individual networks in the area. Although we do not use NLSP in the ZIP network, the following example shows the enabling of NLSP on the Singapore router. The following use of the **area-address** command describes an area of 16 networks in the range of 4000 through 400F:

```
Singapore#configure
Configuring from terminal, memory, or network [terminal]?
Enter configuration commands, one per line.  End with CTRL+Z.
Singapore(config)#ipx router nlsp 1
Singapore(config-ipx-router)#area-address 4000 FFF0
Singapore(config-ipx-router)#^Z
```

NLSP needs to be enabled on a per-interface basis using the IOS interface subcommand **ipx nlsp enable**. This configuration command specifies the NLSP process tag to use when sending routing information on a given interface. We enable NLSP process 1 on the Singapore router's interface Ethernet 0 in the following example:

```
Singapore#configure
Configuring from terminal, memory, or network [terminal]?
Enter configuration commands, one per line.  End with CTRL+Z.
Singapore(config)#interface ethernet 0
Singapore(config-if)#ipx nlsp 1 enable
Singapore(config-if)#^Z
```

Configuring IPX EIGRP

You can use EIGRP as an IPX dynamic routing protocol. As seen in earlier chapters, EIGRP has features found in both distance vector (updates only sent to neighbors) and link state protocols (partial incremental updates and decreased convergence time). To enable EIGRP for IPX, use the major configuration command **ipx router eigrp**. This command requires an autonomous system number to identify the EIGRP process. Throughout a single IPX administrative domain, the EIGRP autonomous system number must be the same for all routers communicating with IPX EIGRP.

The subcommand **network** associates an IPX network number with EIGRP, instructing EIGRP to pass routing information about that IPX network number. In the following example, we enable EIGRP for IPX on the Singapore router using autonomous system number 25000. We tell EIGRP to pass routing information about IPX networks 4010 and 2902:

```
Singapore#configure
Configuring from terminal, memory, or network [terminal]?
Enter configuration commands, one per line.  End with CTRL+Z.
```

```
Singapore(config)#ipx router eigrp 25000
Singapore(config)#network 4010
Singapore(config-ipx-router)#network 2902
Singapore(config-ipx-router)#^Z
```

TIP   You can enable EIGRP for all IPX networks on a router using the **ipx router eigrp** subcommand **network all**.

When using IPX EIGRP, you can make the IOS send SAP messages periodically or only when a change occurs in the SAP table. EIGRP sends periodic SAP messages by default on LAN interfaces, allowing SAP advertisements to reach IPX servers and clients. Periodic SAP messages are also sent by default on any interface that does not have any EIGRP routers, because the interface can connect to IPX servers and clients.

If an interface has only EIGRP routers, you can configure EIGRP to send SAP messages only when a change occurs in the SAP table. This feature can help reduce the traffic on WAN interfaces that interconnect IOS devices by eliminating periodic SAP messages that consume bandwidth. If an EIGRP router is present on a WAN interface, the default behavior of the IOS is to send SAP updates only when the SAP table changes.

To send SAP messages only when a change occurs in the SAP table, use the IOS interface configuration subcommand **ipx sap-incremental-eigrp**. This command requires as a parameter the autonomous system number for EIGRP. The output from the IOS EXEC command **show ipx servers** tells you whether an IPX service was learned from a periodic SAP update or from EIGRP.

Configuring IPX Filtering via Access Lists

The IPX packet filtering facilities of the Cisco IOS software enable a network administrator to restrict access to certain systems, network segments, ranges of addresses, and services based on a variety of criteria. Like SAP filtering, IPX filtering is accomplished with access lists. SAP filters apply access lists to SAP messages sent or received. IPX packet filtering uses access lists to permit or deny routed IPX traffic on an interface basis.

Defining Access Lists

Standard IPX access lists, which are numbered 800 through 899, allow for restricting packet flow based on source IPX addresses and destination IPX addresses. A range of addresses can be specified using *wildcards* or *don't care* masks.

Extended IPX access lists, numbered 900 to 999, enable the same filtering capabilities as standard IPX access lists. Furthermore, they allow for filtering on the basis of NetWare protocols (such as RIP, SAP, and SPX) and IPX socket numbers. IPX sockets are used to identify upper-layer NetWare application services. You can log access list activity with the parameter keyword **log**. We explore logging in more detail in Chapter 7, "Basic Administrative and Management Issues."

In the following example on the ZIP SF-2 router, we configure a standard IPX access list to permit packets from source IPX network 10 to reach destination IPX network 200:

```
SF-2#configure
Configuring from terminal, memory, or network [terminal]?
Enter configuration commands, one per line.  End with CTRL+Z.
SF-2(config)#access-list 800 permit 10 200
SF-2(config)#^Z
```

Just as with IP access lists, you can assign names to IPX access lists. The protocol's provision for named IPX access lists means that you can specify an arbitrary string of characters rather than a number to identify the access list. The command for creating a named IPX access list is the IOS global configuration command **ipx access-list**. You can create standard, extended, or SAP filters using IPX named access lists. In the following example, we name the preceding IPX numbered access list pass-marketing on the ZIP network's SF-2 router:

```
SF-2#configure
Configuring from terminal, memory, or network [terminal]?
Enter configuration commands, one per line.  End with CTRL+Z.
SF-2(config)#ipx access-list standard pass-marketing
SF-2(config-ipx-std-nacl)#permit 10 200
SF-2(config-ipx-std-nacl)#^Z
```

Applying Access Lists

After the filtering criteria of an IPX access list is defined, you must apply it to one or more interfaces so that packets can be filtered. The access list can be applied in either an inbound or an outbound direction on the interface. For the inbound direction, packets are coming into the router from the interface. For the outbound direction, packets are traveling from the router onto the interface. The access list is applied via the IOS interface configuration subcommand **ipx access-group**. The command takes as a parameter the keyword **in** or **out**, with the default being **out** if no keyword is supplied. The following example applies the standard access list 800, defined in the previous section, on the FDDI 0 interface of the ZIP SF-1 router:

```
SF-1#configure
Configuring from terminal, memory, or network [terminal]?
Enter configuration commands, one per line.  End with CTRL+Z.
SF-1(config)#interface fddi 0
SF-1(config-if)#ipx access-group 800 out
SF-1(config-if)#^Z
```

You can view the behavior of access lists and verify that they have been configured properly by using the IOS EXEC commands **show access-lists** and **show ipx access-lists**. The former command shows all access lists defined on the router, while the latter shows only

IPX access lists defined on the router. Each command can take as a parameter an access list number and display only the contents of that list. If no parameter is supplied, all lists are displayed. Following is the output of the **show ipx access-lists** command on the ZIP SF-1 router for the previous access list examples:

```
SF-1#show ipx access-lists
IPX standard access list 800
    permit 10 200
IPX standard access list pass-marketing
    permit 10 200
```

The IOS EXEC command **show ipx interface** shows whether IPX access lists are set on an interface. In the eighth line of the following output on the SF-1 router, you can see IPX standard access list 800 applied to outgoing IPX packets:

```
SF-2#show ipx interface fddi 0
Fddi0 is up, line protocol is up
  IPX address is 10.0000.0c0c.11bb, SNAP [up]
  Delay of this IPX network, in ticks is 1 throughput 0 link delay 0
  IPXWAN processing not enabled on this interface.
  IPX SAP update interval is 60 seconds
  IPX type 20 propagation packet forwarding is disabled
  Incoming access list is not set
  Outgoing access list is 800
  IPX helper access list is not set
  SAP GNS processing enabled, delay 0 ms, output filter list is not set
  SAP Input filter list is not set
  SAP Output filter list is not set
  SAP Router filter list is not set
  Input filter list is not set
  Output filter list is not set
  Router filter list is not set
  Netbios Input host access list is not set
  Netbios Input bytes access list is not set
  Netbios Output host access list is not set
  Netbios Output bytes access list is not set
  Updates each 60 seconds, aging multiples RIP: 3 SAP: 3
  SAP interpacket delay is 55 ms, maximum size is 480 bytes
  RIP interpacket delay is 55 ms, maximum size is 432 bytes
  IPX accounting is disabled
  IPX fast switching is configured (enabled)
  RIP packets received 54353, RIP packets sent 214343
  SAP packets received 94554422, SAP packets sent 93492324
```

Configuring Basic IPX Dialup Services

Throughout this chapter, we have been looking at the IPX routing capabilities in the Cisco IOS. The Cisco IOS also allows remote access from IPX clients, much like the functionality we have seen in previous chapters with dialup IP and AppleTalk. IPX remote access provides users with the ability to use NetWare services even though they are not physically connected to a dedicated LAN segment on the network.

Within the IOS, the remote access capability is available over asynchronous dialup lines and ISDN. In this chapter, we have chosen to discuss the specific IPX commands commonly used for asynchronous dialup IPX clients. IPX access over ISDN is commonly used in dial-on-demand routing between routers, a topic beyond the scope of this book.

As we have seen in the previous two chapters, establishing remote access consists of setting up the asynchronous line configuration, enabling the AAA services for users, and configuring the protocol-specific options. IPX asynchronous line configuration is the same as for IP, as discussed in Chapter 4. IPX clients use the PPP data link protocol, making the configuration of AAA services for IPX the same as for previously discussed network protocols. This subject is discussed further in Chapter 7.

The first step in adding IPX-specific asynchronous dialup options in an access server is to assign an IPX address to the interface Loopback 0 using the IOS interface configuration subcommand **ipx network** (discussed earlier in this chapter). This address becomes the IPX network number used by IPX dialup clients. We then use the IOS interface subcommand **ipx ppp-client loopback** to assign the Novell IPX network number of Loopback 0 to the group asynchronous interface. We configure the Sing2511 access server on the ZIP network as follows:

```
Sing2511#configure
Configuring from terminal, memory, or network [terminal]?
Enter configuration commands, one per line.  End with CTRL+Z.
Sing2511(config)#interface loopback 0
Sing2511(config-if)#ipx network 2500
Sing2511(config-if)#interface group-async1
Sing2511(config-if)#ipx ppp-client loopback 0
Sing2511(config-if)#^Z
```

Dialup IPX clients do not need to hear IPX RIP or SAP information. To avoid sending the normal periodic updates every 60 seconds on asynchronous interfaces, we can use the IOS interface configuration subcommand **ipx update interval**. This subcommand requires a parameter of **sap** or **rip** and a value in seconds for how often to send the appropriate updates on the interface. In the following example, we configure the Sing2511 access server to send IPX RIP and SAP updates every 10 hours (36,000 seconds). We set the **ipx update interval** to this high value with the assumption that an IPX dialup client does not stay connected for 10 hours:

```
Sing2511#configure
Configuring from terminal, memory, or network [terminal]?
Enter configuration commands, one per line.  End with CTRL+Z.
Sing2511(config)#interface group-async1
Sing2511(config-if)#ipx update interval sap 36000
Sing2511(config-if)#ipx update interval rip 36000
Sing2511(config-if)#^Z
```

Verifying IPX Connectivity and Troubleshooting

IPX ping is a useful tool in helping to identify IPX connectivity issues. Two different types of pings are available in IPX. The first, a Cisco Echo, is Cisco proprietary; only IOS devices answer these Echo packets. The second, a Novell Standard Echo, is supported by IOS devices and NetWare servers running version 1.0 or later of the NLSP specification.

From an IOS device in EXEC nonprivileged mode, you can send Cisco Echoes using the IOS EXEC command **ping ipx**. The IOS EXEC command **ping ipx** sends five 100-byte IPX Cisco Echoes to a given IPX address, as shown in the following example on the SF-Core-1 router:

```
SF-Core-1#ping ipx 10.0000.0c0c.23ce

Type escape sequence to abort.
Sending 5, 100-byte IPX cisco Echoes to 10.0000.0c0c.23ce, timeout is 2 seconds:
!!!!!
Success rate is 100 percent (5/5), round-trip min/avg/max = 1/1/4 ms
```

In the preceding example, you can see five IPX Cisco Echoes sent and five replies from the target address. Table 6-2 shows the meaning of the characters displayed by the router for each IPX ping sent.

Table 6-2   *IPX Ping Command Response Characters*

!	An exclamation point denotes the receipt of a reply from the target address.
.	A period indicates that the network server timed out while waiting for a reply from the target address.
U	An IPX destination unreachable error was received.
C	An IPX congestion experienced packet was received.
I	A user manually interrupted the test.
?	An unknown IPX packet type was received.
&	The IPX packet lifetime was exceeded.

In privileged mode, the IOS EXEC command **ping** can be used to send either Cisco Echoes or Novell Standard Echoes. The privileged mode **ping** command also enables you to specify multiple characteristics of the echoes sent, such as the number of echoes to repeat, the size of the echoes, and the timeout period to wait for an echo. In the next example, we send an IPX ping from the ZIP router SF-Core-1 using the privileged mode **ping** command:

```
SF-Core-1#ping

Protocol [ip]:ipx
Target IPX address:10.0000.0c0c.23ce
Repeat count [5]:
Datagram size [100]:
Timeout in seconds [2]:
Verbose [n]:
Novell Standard Echo [n]:
Type escape sequence to abort.
Sending 5 100-byte IPX echoes to 10.0000.0c0c.23ce, timeout is 2 seconds.
!!!!!
Success rate is 100 percent (5/5)
```

You can obtain overall statistics about the operation of the IPX protocol on a Cisco router with the **show ipx traffic** command. It includes counters for such information as the total number of packets received and sent by the router; the number of broadcasts received and sent; SAP, IPX RIP, EIGRP, and NLSP statistics; and whether the router has sent or received IPX Echoes. The cumulative counters in **show ipx traffic** are reset only when the router is reloaded or power-cycled. Following is an example of the output of the **show ipx traffic** command on the ZIP SF-Core-1 router:

```
SF-Core-1#show ipx traffic
System Traffic for 0.0000.0000.0001 System-Name: zipnet
Rcvd:    603143 total, 94947 format errors, 0 checksum errors, 0 bad hop count,
         0 packets pitched, 401 local destination, 0 multicast
Bcast:   406 received, 6352 sent
Sent:    6355 generated, 0 forwarded
         0 encapsulation failed, 19 no route
SAP:     368 SAP requests, 0 SAP replies, 2 servers
         0 SAP Nearest Name requests, 0 replies
         0 SAP General Name requests, 0 replies
         27 SAP advertisements received, 138 sent
         20 SAP flash updates sent, 0 SAP format errors
RIP:     6 RIP requests, 0 RIP replies, 5 routes
         5629 RIP advertisements received, 6139 sent
         0 RIP flash updates sent, 0 RIP format errors
Echo:    Rcvd 0 requests, 0 replies
         Sent 0 requests, 0 replies
         0 unknown: 0 no socket, 0 filtered, 0 no helper
         0 SAPs throttled, freed NDB len 0
Watchdog:
         0 packets received, 0 replies spoofed
Queue lengths:
         IPX input: 0, SAP 0, RIP 0, GNS 0
         SAP throttling length: 0/(no limit), 0 nets pending lost route reply
         Delayed process creation: 0
EIGRP:   Total received 0, sent 0
         Updates received 0, sent 0
         Queries received 0, sent 0
         Replies received 0, sent 0
         SAPs received 0, sent 0
NLSP:    Level-1 Hellos received 0, sent 0
```

In addition to the troubleshooting and verification commands presented in this section, numerous privileged IOS EXEC **debug** commands exist to aid in determining the operation of the IPX protocol on the router. These **debug** commands provide both general and detailed diagnostic output that can aid in troubleshooting and in verifying the operation of the router, routing protocols, and other functions. Some of the more common **debug** commands used for IPX are summarized in Table 6-3.

Table 6-3   *debug Commands for IPX*

Command	Description
debug ipx eigrp	Displays contents of IPX EIGRP packets sent and received by the router.
debug ipx nlsp	Displays the activities of the NLSP protocol running on the router.
debug ipx packet	Displays the source and destination IPX addresses of packets that are routed by the router.
debug ipx routing	Displays changes that occur in the IPX routing table as the result of route additions and deletions.
debug ipx sap	Displays information about SAP advertisements sent and received by the router.

As mentioned in earlier chapters, some **debug** commands can adversely affect router performance. Care should be taken when using these privileged EXEC commands.

Configuring IPX Type 20 Packet Forwarding

Many applications in the NetWare environment use the Network Basic Input/Output System (NetBIOS) request services from IPX servers. These services include session establishment and termination and information transfer.

On a NetWare client, a NetBIOS application using IPX broadcasts type 20 propagation packets to all IPX networks to get information about named nodes on the network. NetBIOS uses named nodes for resources on the network. To communicate with these resources, NetWare clients need to map these named nodes to IPX addresses.

NetBIOS uses an IPX mechanism to map named nodes to IPX address. As you have seen throughout this book, Cisco routers block all network layer broadcast packets by default, including IPX type 20 propagation packets. If a router does not forward any type 20 propagation packets, and a NetWare client with an application using NetBIOS needs to traverse the router to obtain information about a named node on the network, the NetWare client is not capable of communicating with the server.

The IOS interface subcommand **ipx type-20-propagation** instructs the router to accept and forward type 20 propagation packets to other IPX interfaces that also have this subcommand configured. The IOS attempts to forward the IPX type 20 propagation packets in an intelligent manner—such as by not putting the packets on interfaces that route to the original source interface.

Instead of forwarding IPX type 20 propagation packets to multiple network segments, you can forward these packets to a specific IPX network address, thereby potentially reducing the number of broadcast packets sent throughout your IPX network. The IOS global configuration command **ipx type-20-helpered** enables the forwarding of IPX type 20 packets to a specific IPX address. The IOS interface subcommand **ipx helper-address** specifies the IPX address to forward type 20 packets to. The **ipx type-20-helpered** and the **ipx type-20-propagation** commands are mutually exclusive. The IOS must either forward type 20 propagation packets to other similarly configured interfaces or forward type 20 packets to an IPX address.

In the following configuration on the ZIP network, we forward all IPX type 20 packets on the Singapore router, via interface Ethernet 0, to a specific IPX server in San Francisco at IPX address aa.0005.0112.0474:

```
Singapore#configure
Configuring from terminal, memory, or network [terminal]?
Enter configuration commands, one per line.  End with CTRL+Z.
Singapore(config)#ipx type-20-helpered
Singapore(config)#interface ethernet 0
Singapore(config-it)#ipx helper-address aa.0005.0112.0474
Singapore(config-if)#^Z
```

Summary

We have covered the basics of the IPX protocol suite, the core commands for bringing up an IPX network, and some of the additional commands often implemented on large IPX networks. By no means will this chapter make you an expert in IPX networks, but it will get you up and running. Following are the central concepts of the chapter:

- An IPX address takes the form *network.node*, in which *network* is a 32-bit number designating a LAN or WAN segment and *node* is a 48-bit number designating a client or server. The network portion is assigned by the network administrator. The node portion is often the same as the 48-bit data link layer address for the device.

- For NetWare clients, NetWare servers, and Cisco routers to communicate properly on an IPX LAN segment, they must be running the same IPX encapsulation. Although in some situations you can choose from among multiple encapsulation methods, most often the version of NetWare dictates which one must be used.

- Like IP routing, IPX routing can be configured manually or via dynamic routing protocols. RIP, NLSP, and EIGRP are dynamic routing protocols for IPX. IPX RIP is enabled on all IPX interfaces by default when you use the global configuration command **ipx routing**.

- SAP is a dynamic services protocol that advertises what services are available on an IPX network. It is configured by default on all IPX-configured interfaces. SAP filters can be used to limit the amount of SAP traffic sent and received by a router.

- To enable NetBIOS broadcasts to be received and sent by a Cisco router, you must use the **ipx type-20-propagation** or **ipx type-20-helpered** command.

- A variety of **show**, **debug**, and **ping** commands are available for verifying configurations and for troubleshooting your IPX network. In addition to those summarized in the Table 6-4, see Table 6-5 for a review of pertinent commands.

Table 6-4   *Summary of EXEC Commands for Configuring IPX*

Command	Description
clear ipx route	Clears the entire IPX routing table or, if specified, a particular route.
ping *network.node*	Tests the indicated IPX address to determine whether it is reachable and responsive.
ping ipx *network.node*	In privileged mode, used to send either Cisco Echoes or Novell Standard Echoes to the indicated IPX address to determine whether it is reachable and responsive.
show ipx access-lists	Shows all IPX access lists defined on the router.
show ipx interface brief	Shows a brief summary of IPX network information and interface statuses for all available interfaces on the device.
show ipx interface *interface*	Shows all the parameters associated with the IPX configuration of an interface.

continues

Table 6-4 *Summary of EXEC Commands for Configuring IPX (Continued)*

Command	Description
show ipx route	Outputs the IPX routing table of the router.
show ipx route *network.node*	Shows IPX routing information for the specified route.
show ipx servers	Shows a list of all the currently known IPX servers.
show ipx traffic	Outputs overall statistics about the operation of IPX on the router.

Table 6-5 *Summary of Configuration Commands for IPX Networks*

Command	Description
access-list	Creates a numbered access list and its associated filtering criteria.
area-address *address mask*	Defines the area address prefix and mask for NLSP.
dialer map ipx	Statically maps an IPX address to system names and phone numbers for ISDN calls.
frame-relay map ipx	Maps an IPX address to a Frame Relay DLCI.
ipx access-group *list* **[in | out]**	Applies the indicated access list to the task of filtering incoming or outgoing packets on an interface.
ipx access-list {extended | sap | standard} *name*	Assigns a named IPX access and its associated filtering criteria.
ipx gns-round-robin	Stipulates a round-robin selection method for choosing among multiple eligible servers when the router responds to GNS requests.
ipx input-sap-filter *list*	Interface subcommand that instructs the router to filter inbound SAP packets based on specific access list criteria.
ipx internal-network *network*	Defines an internal network number on the router for NLSP.
ipx maximum paths *number*	Configures the router to permit the specified number of equal-cost paths in its IPX routing table.
ipx network *network* **[encapsulation | secondary]**	Defines the IPX network for that interface. Optionally, defines the encapsulation method (for example, **snap** and **arpa**) used on that interface and whether or not the network is primary or secondary on the interface.
ipx output-gns-filter *list*	Interface subcommand that instructs the router to filter outbound GNS packets from routers based on specific access list criteria.
ipx output-sap-filter *list*	Interface subcommand that instructs the router to filter outbound SAP packets based on specific access list criteria.
ipx ppp-client loopback	Interface subcommand that assigns the IPX number of a loopback interface for use by IPX PPP clients.

Table 6-5   *Summary of Configuration Commands for IPX Networks (Continued)*

ipx route	Configures a static IPX route.
ipx router eigrp *autonomous-system*	Enables EIGRP as a routing process for IPX.
ipx router nlsp *tag*	Enables the specified NLSP process as a routing process for IPX.
ipx router-sap-filter	Applies a filter to all SAP advertisements based on specific access list criteria.
ipx routing	Enables IPX routing on the router.
ipx sap	Defines static SAP table entries.
ipx sap-incremental-eigrp	Configures a router to send SAP messages only when a change occurs in the SAP table.
ipx update interval {rip | sap} *seconds*	Interface subcommand that changes the IPX RIP or SAP interval to the number of seconds specified.
map group	Assigns a named map group to an interface for use in mapping IPX addresses to ATM data-link addresses on an interface.
map list	Creates a named map list to configure the mapping of IPX addresses to PVCs or SVCs in ATM addressing.
network *network*	Associates an IPX network number with EIGRP.
x25 map ipx	Statically maps an IPX address to an X.121 address.

References

The following references explore the subjects in this chapter further:

Currid, C. and A. Currid. *Novell's Introduction to Networking.* Foster City, California: IDG Books Worldwide, 1997.

Heywood, D. *Novell's Guide to TCP/IP and Intranetware.* Foster City, California: IDG Books Worldwide, 1997.

Siyan, K.S. et al. *Novell Intranetware Professional Reference.* Indianapolis, Indiana: New Riders Publishing, 1997.

Basic Access Control—The basics of configuring device access control using the RADIUS and TACACS+ protocols in the Cisco IOS.

Basic Attack Prevention—The basics of setting up the features in the IOS to prevent some basic Internet Denial-of-Service (DoS) attacks.

Basic Network Management—A brief overview of the Simple Network Management Protocol (SNMP) and its configuration in the Cisco IOS.

Basic Time Control—Setting up the Network Time Protocol and the system clock on Cisco devices.

CHAPTER 7

Basic Administrative and Management Issues

This chapter explains the Cisco IOS management basics that are essential for creating reliable, redundant, and efficient data networks. These basics include controlling access to a Cisco device, logging system activity, preventing attacks, configuring network management protocols, and synchronizing the time and date of Cisco IOS devices.

Basic Access Control

The Cisco IOS offers a series of mechanisms and protocols that help control the accessibility of devices. These basic access control mechanisms can help you restrict who is accessing your network devices and what they are doing on each device. This important task is needed to ensure the security of your network and to create an audit trail of any changes on the network.

Connecting to a Virtual Terminal Using Telnet and SSH

Common methods of accessing a device running the IOS are via the console port (as discussed in Chapter 2, "The Basics of Device Configuration") or via virtual terminal lines (vty). Virtual terminal lines are software that enables you to connect to the router via a data network. An IOS device also supports five simultaneous sessions through virtual terminal lines.

Using a Telnet client or using a Secure Shell (SSH) client are the two most common methods for connecting to a virtual terminal line. A Telnet client uses a standard protocol defined in RFC 854 to provide an unsecure connection to server software running on a virtual terminal line. By default, all IOS devices have a Telnet server enabled on all virtual terminal lines; we discuss securing these lines in the following section, "Enabling the SSA Server."

SSH is a protocol that provides a secure and encrypted connection between an SSH client and server running on a virtual terminal line with functionality that is similar to a Telnet connection. In contrast to the Telnet server, an SSH server is not enabled by default on the virtual terminal lines. Enabling the SSH server is discussed in the next section.

Your system administrator should be able to help use the Telnet client or SSH client on your local system. Also, from an EXEC prompt, an IOS device can be a Telnet client or an SSH client using the **telnet** or **ssh** commands.

NOTE   Currently, two versions of SSH are available: SSH Version 1 and SSH Version 2. At this time, the Cisco IOS supports only SSH Version 1.

SSH clients and servers can provide user authentication using a public key cryptographic system invented by Rivest, Shamir, and Adelman (RSA). RSA user authentication available in SSH clients is not supported in the SSH server for Cisco IOS. The Cisco IOS authenticates users using a user ID and password combination only. The SSH server in the IOS does use RSA to generate the key pair that is used for setting up an encrypted session to the client, as shown in the next section.

SSH secures the connection between the SSH client and server using the DES (56-bit) or Triple DES (168-bit) encryption algorithm. Not all IOS versions support DES or Triple DES, though, and you should use the **show version** command to see if the version of IOS that you are running supports these encryption algorithms.

NOTE   Some encryption algorithms (including 56-bit data encryption, among others) are subject to United States government export controls. Using these algorithms—and the version of the IOS that supports them—outside the United States requires an export license.

Enabling the SSH Server

To enable the SSH server and allow SSH clients to connect to virtual terminal lines, your IOS device must have a properly configured host name and domain name. You configure these parameters with the global configuration commands **hostname** and **ip domain-name**, discussed previously.

To configure the SSH server, you must generate an RSA key pair used to encrypt the session between the client and server. On the IOS device, you generate the RSA key pair using the global configuration command **crypto key generate rsa**. When you generate an RSA key pair for the IOS device, you automatically enable the SSH server on the virtual terminal lines. To delete an RSA key, you use the **crypto key zeroize rsa** global configuration command, which automatically disables the SSH server.

The global configuration command **crypto key generate rsa** will not appear in the output of **show running-config** or **show startup-config**.

The global configuration command **ip ssh** enables the SSH server on all virtual terminal lines:

```
SF-1#configure
Configuring from terminal, memory, or network [terminal]?
Enter configuration commands, one per line. End with CNTL/Z.
SF-1(config)#crypto key generate rsa
SF-1(config)#ip ssh
SF-1(config)#^Z
```

Verifying SSH Configuration

You can view the public RSA key used by SSH using the EXEC command **show crypto key mypubkey rsa**:

```
SF-1>show crypto key mypubkey rsa
% Key pair was generated at: 19:01:46 EDT Aug 7 2000
Key name: SF-1.zipnet.com
 Usage: General Purpose Key
 Key Data:
  305C300D 06092A86 4886F70D 01010105 00034B00 30480241 00C6F6D1 CCBF8B9A
  6D3E451F C362DD75 866F084B 04F43C95 0B68BA44 0B8D5B8C 35264CFA 04B8B532
  0FF6473C 4768C46F CD820DAF B7CA8C75 4977CF6E 7ED1ACE3 FF020301 0001
% Key pair was generated at: 23:14:52 EDT Aug 29 2000
Key name: SF-1.zipnet.com.server
 Usage: Encryption Key
 Key Data:
  307C300D 06092A86 4886F70D 01010105 00036B00 30680261 00C5D98C E628790E
  17B0BA2B C31C9521 8543AE24 F19E0988 BF2901DC 11D723EF 3512DD29 C28DBC53
  8112755C 307AC527 14B955F0 A0DD29AD AE53BA00 4D84657B 4C605E8E 6EBDDB6E
  4FB98167 8616F964 E067604A F852A27D 1F9B7AFF 3EC73F5C 75020301 0001
```

Furthermore, you can view the active SSH sessions on your IOS device using the **show ip ssh** command:

```
SF-1#sh ip ssh
Connection      Version     Encryption     State    Username
    0             1.5          3DES           6      admin
```

Securing the Console Port and Virtual Terminals

At the level of individual IOS devices, you can set up a password for access via the console port using the IOS major command **line console 0** and the IOS subcommand **password**. For the virtual terminal lines, you can add passwords using the major command **line vty 0 4** and the **password** subcommand.

Using the **line** subcommand **access-class**, you can specify a list of IP addresses that are capable of connecting to or being reached from terminal lines on an IOS device. You can specify whether an access class is used for inbound or outbound sessions by using the **in** or **out** keyword. This subcommand uses an IP access list to qualify IP addresses before any incoming or outgoing sessions are started. You can use the **access-class** subcommand as a way to permit only the network administrator's workstations to reach the virtual terminal lines on your IOS devices, which is an additional method of securing access to the devices.

In the following example, the SF-1 router is configured with the console and virtual terminal password Zipmein:

```
SF-1#configure
Configuring from terminal, memory, or network [terminal]?
Enter configuration commands, one per line. End with CNTL/Z.
SF-1(config)#line console 0
SF-1(config)#password Zipmein
SF-1(config)#line vty 0 4
SF-1(config)#password Zipmein
SF-1(config)#^Z
```

The console and virtual terminal passwords are kept in clear text in the running and startup configurations. If you want to encrypt all passwords displayed by any EXEC command (such as **show running-config** or **show startup-config**), you can use the global configuration command **service password-encryption**. As a result of this command, decrypted versions of the passwords are no longer visible via any EXEC command. Cisco has documented password recovery procedures for each device type, in case you forget your passwords.

An alternative to configuring passwords on a device-by-device basis for access control is to use an access control protocol on the network. These access control protocols perform three functions: authentication, authorization, and accounting, which are known collectively as AAA. *Authentication* is the process of identifying and verifying a user. Within the Cisco IOS, several methods can be used to authenticate a user, including a combination of a username and password, or the passing of a unique key. *Authorization* determines what a user can do after being authenticated, such as gaining access to and performing tasks on certain network devices or access hosts. *Accounting* is the method of recording what a user is doing or has done.

AAA requires two components: a client that functions on a Cisco IOS device, and related access control server software, which typically runs on a network workstation. The Remote Authentication Dial-In User Service (RADIUS) and Terminal Access Controller Access Control System (TACACS+) are two protocols commonly used to provide communication between the AAA client on a Cisco device and access control server software.

Consider a user who uses the Telnet application to connect to a router on which no access control protocol is configured. The user is immediately prompted for the virtual terminal line password, as follows:

```
% telnet singapore
Trying...

Password:
```

If the user enters the correct password, he or she is granted access to the EXEC mode of the router. This user is not subject to an authentication and authorization process and is free to perform any task (including entering privileged mode, if the password is known). Furthermore, the user who performs this action is not logged. Clearly, such an open policy is unacceptable in almost all networks. One exception may be in a laboratory or test environment in which unaccounted access to a device by many users does not affect network security, configuration, or performance.

If a Cisco IOS device is set up to use an access control protocol, the device prompts the user for a username and password:

```
% telnet singapore
Trying...

Username: allan
Password:
```

Using an access control protocol, the Cisco IOS device performs the following tasks:

1   The access control client in the device prompts for the username and password when it receives the inbound Telnet connection request.

2   The access control client queries the user and sends the username and password combination in the authentication request message to the access control server.

3   The access control server authenticates the username and password combination. The combination passes or fails authentication, and the appropriate message is returned to the client. The server may give the client information about its authorization. The server accounts for the transaction.

4   The access control client permits or denies the username and password combination. If permitted, the user gains access to the system and is authorized to perform the actions specified in the authorization information passed by the server.

This sequence of communication between the access control client and the server is shown in Figure 7-1.

Figure 7-1   *As an AAA Client, the Cisco IOS Device Exchanges Information with the AAA Server to Perform Access Control*

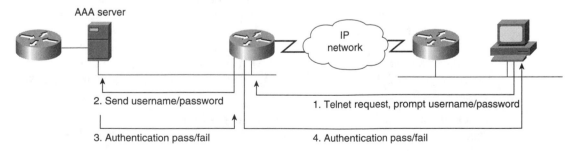

Enabling AAA

To enable all AAA services in the Cisco IOS, you need to use the global configuration command **aaa new-model**.

You can then enable the AAA client for specific authentication, authorization, and accounting configuration using the following global configuration commands: **aaa authentication, aaa authorization,** and **aaa accounting**. Each of the AAA commands is configured using method lists. A method list is a configured list that describes the AAA methods to be attempted, in an ordered sequence, to authenticate a user, authorize an activity, or account for an action. For example, with method lists, you can specify multiple authentication mechanisms in an attempt to authenticate a user in case the initial method fails. An IOS device attempts to use the first method listed to authenticate users; if that method fails to respond, the device tries the next authentication method listed in the method list. This continues until there is successful communication with a listed authentication method, or until all methods defined are used. Method lists for authorization and accounting work in a similar fashion to those described previously for authentication.

NOTE

An IOS device attempts to use the next method in a method list only if the device cannot communicate with the previous method. For example, if any authentication method responds but fails to authenticate the user, the next authentication method is not used.

Two common AAA protocols are RADIUS and TACACS+, which are described later in this section. With the **aaa authentication**, **aaa authorization**, and **aaa accounting** global configuration commands, you can specify the method to use as RADIUS using the **group radius** method and as TACACS+ using the **group tacacs+** method.

The **aaa authentication** command specifies authentication protocols in an ordered method list, which the device can attempt to use to verify access. The **aaa authorization** command enables you to specify whether authorization is done on EXEC commands or at the start of EXEC or network sessions (such as PPP sessions). It also enables you to specify the protocol to use to perform these tasks. The **aaa accounting** command enables you to specify when accounting messages are sent to the AAA server, such as at the beginning or end of each user session and after each command. This command also specifies the type of accounting that the AAA client performs. You can account for IOS system activity, network-related services (such as PPP and ARAP), and EXEC sessions. You can use both TACACS+ and RADIUS to send accounting information from an AAA client to an AAA server.

In the following example, AAA processes are configured for the Singapore router. AAA authentication is enabled for login sessions by using the **aaa authentication login** global configuration command. The first authentication protocol in the method list is TACACS+.

If the TACACS+ agent is incapable of contacting the server to perform authentication, the device performs authentication via a second method—namely, by using the **enable secret** or **enable password** global configuration command. This method list is seen in the **aaa authentication login** command as the option **group tacacs+**, followed by the option **enable**.

TIP   We recommend that you do not rely solely on an AAA protocol for authentication of your login sessions on your IOS devices. Having a second authentication method for login sessions ensures that you can always gain access to your device if an AAA server is unavailable.

In configuring the **aaa accounting** and the **aaa authorization** commands, we apply the same logic as we did with the **aaa authentication** commands. You can specify different authorization methods for EXEC sessions and network sessions (such as PPP) using the **exec** and **network** options to the **aaa authorization** global configuration command. The **if-authenticated** method keyword tells the AAA client to grant authorization if authentication has passed for the session.

Finally, all EXEC sessions are accounted for when they have stopped using the TACACS+ protocol using the **aaa accounting** global configuration command.

```
Singapore#configure
Configuring from terminal, memory, or network [terminal]?
Enter configuration commands, one per line. End with CNTL/Z.
Singapore(config)#aaa new-model
Singapore(config)#aaa authentication login default group tacacs+ enable
Singapore(config)#aaa authorization exec group tacacs+ if-authenticated
Singapore(config)#aaa authorization network group radius if-authenticated
Singapore(config)#aaa accounting exec stop-only group tacacs+
Singapore(config)#^Z
```

In this example, the **group tacacs+** option instructs the IOS device to contact the TACACS+ servers defined by the global configuration command **tacacs-server host**, as discussed later in the section "TACACS+." You can optionally define your own groups of AAA servers with a user-defined name with an AAA server group using the global configuration command **aaa server group** and the subcommand **server**. A user-defined AAA server group is useful when you have a group of users who rely on one AAA server and another group of users who rely on another AAA server. These two groups may or may not be using the same AAA protocol (such as RADIUS). Before the invention of AAA server groups, only a single set of AAA servers could be used for each method for all users. A common example of using AAA server groups is authenticating dialup users using one RADIUS server and authenticating network administrators on another RADIUS server.

In the following sections, you can see how to specify the RADIUS and TACACS+ servers to the AAA client.

RADIUS

The RADIUS protocol was originally published by Livingston Enterprises, Inc., as a standard protocol that exchanges AAA information between a RADIUS client and server. RADIUS is an open protocol; a variety of network devices have a RADIUS client. A RADIUS server is a workstation running RADIUS server software from a vendor or organization such as Livingston, Merit, or Microsoft. You can specify the IP address of the RADIUS server with which the IOS client communicates by using the **radius-server host** global configuration command.

When performing authentication, the RADIUS protocol encrypts the passwords sent between the client and the server. You need to configure a secret string for this password encryption on both your RADIUS server and in the Cisco IOS. To configure this string in the Cisco IOS client, use the **radius-server key** global configuration command.

The San Jose router is configured on the ZIP network with a RADIUS server and encryption key, as follows:

```
San Jose#configure
Configuring from terminal, memory, or network [terminal]?
Enter configuration commands, one per line. End with CNTL/Z.
San Jose(config)#radius-server host 131.108.110.33
San Jose(config)#radius-server key Radius4Me
San Jose(config)#^Z
```

TACACS+

TACACS+ is an AAA protocol that is conceptually similar to RADIUS. TACACS+ is the third revision of the TACACS protocol. The second revision is called Extended TACACS, or XTACACS. TACACS+ is a Cisco proprietary protocol, and all IOS devices have a native TACACS+ client.

TACACS+ server software is available from a variety of sources, including Cisco (in the CiscoSecure product) and other vendors, on many workstation hardware platforms. You can specify the IP address of the TACACS+ server with which the IOS client communicates by using the **tacacs-server host** global configuration command.

The TACACS+ protocol encrypts all communication sent between the client and the server. You must configure a secret string for this communication encryption on both your TACACS+ server and in the Cisco IOS. To configure the string in the Cisco IOS client, use the **tacacs-server key** global configuration command.

The SF-Core-1 router is configured on the ZIP network with a TACACS+ server and encryption key, as follows:

```
SF-Core-1#configure
Configuring from terminal, memory, or network [terminal]?
Enter configuration commands, one per line. End with CNTL/Z.
SF-Core-1(config)#tacacs-server host 131.108.110.33
SF-Core-1(config)#tacacs-server key ZIPSecure
SF-Core-1(config)#^Z
```

RADIUS and TACACS+ Compared

The differences between RADIUS and TACACS+ are numerous, but their functionality is essentially the same. RADIUS, which is a standard, uses the UDP transport layer. TACACS+, which is proprietary, uses the TCP transport layer. RADIUS works well in IP-only environments, while TACACS+ is useful in multiprotocol environments. RADIUS currently supports more attributes in the protocol and allows the client and server to pass more information than TACACS+. RADIUS encrypts only the password sent between the client and server, while TACACS+ encrypts all communication.

Many vendors that support one protocol or the other vehemently argue the merits of the AAA protocol that they support. Cisco supports both protocols. If your network is largely heterogeneous, RADIUS is perhaps the right AAA protocol to use because many vendors currently support it. If your network mainly uses Cisco devices, TACACS+ is most likely the correct solution.

Basic Attack Prevention

The TCP intercept and unicast reverse path forwarding features of the IOS enable you to configure some basic security against two types of denial-of-service attacks: TCP SYN flooding and source IP address forgery.

A denial-of-service (DoS) attack is one in which a hacker overwhelms a network resource with traffic intended not to harm data, but to utilize enough resources on the network resource so that it cannot perform its intended function. For example, a TCP SYN (synchronization) flood attack occurs when a hacker floods a server with a large number of TCP SYN requests (used to initiate a TCP connection) from an invalid source IP address. Each of these requests has an unreachable source IP address that means that the connections cannot be established. The large number of open connections that are not established overwhelms the server and can cause it to deny service to valid requests, denying users from connecting to the server and performing their desired tasks.

TCP Intercept

The TCP intercept feature helps prevent SYN flooding by intercepting and validating TCP connection requests as they pass through a router. You can have the TCP intercept feature intercept incoming TCP SYN messages or watch TCP connections as the router forwards them.

In intercept mode, the router actively intercepts each incoming TCP SYN and answers for the actual destination server with a TCP ACK and a SYN. This is the first step in a standard TCP connection establishment process called a *three-way handshake*. The router then waits for a TCP ACK of the second TCP SYN from the source. When that ACK is received, the router has set up a valid TCP connection with the source and has completed the three-way handshake. Next, the router sends the original TCP SYN to the actual destination server and performs a second three-way handshake. The router then joins the two TCP connections transparently, forwarding packets between the two TCP connections throughout the life of the connection.

In intercept mode, the TCP intercept feature helps to prevent the TCP SYN DoS attack because packets from an unreachable host will never reach the destination server. You can configure the router to intercept requests based on an IP extended access list, allowing you to specify which requests the router should intercept.

As an alternative to intercepting each TCP connection, you can have the TCP intercept feature watch connection requests as they are forwarded by the router. If a TCP connection fails to initiate in a configurable interval, the IOS software will then intercept and terminate the connection attempt.

You configure the TCP intercept feature using the IOS global configuration command **ip tcp intercept mode**. The global configuration command **ip tcp intercept list** assigns an IP extended access list for specifying which requests the router should intercept. The **ip tcp intercept watch-timeout** command specifies the number of seconds that the router should allow before resetting a TCP connection that has not completed a valid three-way handshake with the destination server. By default, a router will reset a TCP connection if a three-way handshake does not complete in 30 seconds. In the following example, the SF-Core-1 router is configured to watch all TCP connections from network 131.108.0.0 and to reset connections that are not established after 15 seconds:

```
SF-Core-1#configure
Configuring from terminal, memory, or network [terminal]?
Enter configuration commands, one per line. End with CNTL/Z.
SF-Core-1(config)#access-list 120 permit ip any 131.108.0.0 0.0.255.255
SF-Core-1(config)#ip tcp intercept mode watch
SF-Core-1(config)#ip tcp intercept list 120
SF-Core-1(config)#ip tcp intercept watch-timeout 15
SF-Core-1(config)#^Z
```

The EXEC command **show tcp intercept connections** displays all incomplete and established TCP connections. The **show tcp intercept statistics** EXEC command shows you statistics about the behavior of the TCP intercept feature.

Unicast Reverse Path Forwarding

The unicast reverse path forwarding (RPF) feature can help prevent the source IP address forgery (sometimes called IP spoofing) DoS attack. The source IP address forgery attack uses malformed source IP addresses or a rapidly changing source IP to attack a network. If your network is being attacked by a malformed source IP address or a set of rapidly changing source IP addresses, it could be impossible to configure an IP access list to stop the attack.

NOTE	The unicast RPF feature is available on your IOS device only if you are using Cisco Express Forwarding (CEF). CEF is an advanced mechanism used to forward packets and to build IP routing tables. At this time, CEF operates only on certain high-end IOS devices.

The unicast RPF feature helps to solve this by automatically discarding IP packets that do not have a verifiable source IP address. The router verifies a source IP addresses by looking at all packets received on an interface to make sure that the source address and source router interface appear in the IP routing table and match the interface on which the packet was received. The received route and the route backward as seen in the routing table to the source IP address must be symmetrical. A route is symmetrical if a packet arrives at a router interface on one of the best return paths to the source of the packet, not limited to the exact source router interface, allowing you to use routing techniques such as equal-cost load balancing.

If there is no reverse path route on the same source interface or return path from which the packet was received, it might mean that the source address was modified or forged, and the packet is discarded. Verifying that the source IP address is reachable via the reverse path on which the packet will be forwarded helps prevent source IP address forgery.

The unicast RPF feature can be used in any network configuration in which there is a single path of connectivity from the network. When you have a single path of connectivity, even with multiple load-shared paths, the network routing is nearly always symmetrical. This configuration often occurs at the upstream network exit point to the Internet. You should not use the unicast RPF feature on your internal network when multiple diverse routes exist to IP destinations.

The configuration of the unicast RPF feature is done via a single interface subcommand, **ip verify unicast reverse-path**. In a common environment, you would apply this command only on the upstream interface (or interfaces in a load-sharing environment) on your router that connects to the Internet.

Cisco IOS devices have the capability to log messages about system activity. These log messages can be useful in tracking system activity, errors, and notifications. Logging uses eight levels of notification messages, as summarized in Table 7-1.

Table 7-1   *Cisco IOS Logging Messages*

Level	Description
Level 0—Emergencies	The system has become unusable.
Level 1—Alerts	Immediate action is needed to restore system stability.
Level 2—Critical	Critical conditions have occurred that may require attention.
Level 3—Errors	Error conditions have occurred that may help track problems.

continues

Table 7-1   *Cisco IOS Logging Messages (Continued)*

Level	Description
Level 4—Warnings	Warning conditions have occurred that are not severe.
Level 5—Notifications	Normal but significant conditions bear notification.
Level 6—Informational	These informational messages do not require action.
Level 7—Debugging	These are debugging messages for system troubleshooting only.

In the IOS, you set the minimum level of logging messages (in terms of severity) that you want logged. You do so by identifying the level by name in the configuration command. Emergencies (Level 0) is the severest level, while debugging (Level 7) is the least severe level. All messages at the level that you identify and at more severe levels are sent to one of four locations:

- A syslog server, configured using the **logging trap** command
- An internal device buffer, configured using the **logging buffered** command
- The console port of a device, configured using the **logging console** command
- The terminal lines of a device, configured using the **logging monitor** command

The preceding **logging** commands are global configuration commands that enable you to specify the level of messages sent to each logging location. A syslog server is an excellent logging location because the system normally saves messages to a disk. Also, because syslog is a general purpose utility that many different programs utilize, you can have one central source for logging messages from different devices.

The internal device buffer is a useful logging facility if you do not have a syslog server or if you want each device to keep a separate log of events. The internal device buffer has a default size of 4096 bytes. You can alter the size by using the **logging buffered** command. For example, you can specify a larger buffer size, such as **logging buffered 8192**, which specifies an internal device buffer of 8192 bytes. While useful for some situations, the internal device buffer is in the RAM of the device, so it is lost with each device reload.

Logging messages to the console or terminal lines of a device (including virtual terminal sessions) is useful for immediate notification of critical events. The four different logging locations are not mutually exclusive, and you can use multiple logging facilities at the same time.

NOTE	You must use the EXEC command **terminal monitor** to see logging messages on a terminal line or virtual terminal session. This command can be performed in privileged mode.

You can configure messages to the syslog server via the **logging trap** command. To enable syslog logging in the IOS, you must use the global configuration command **logging** to specify the IP address of the logging host.

As mentioned previously, it is possible to log messages to more than one of the locations. For example, you may want all Level 7 and more severe level messages to be sent to the syslog server. You may want emergency messages to be sent to the device console as well because of their critical nature. In the following example, the Seoul-1 router is configured on the ZIP network for logging in the manner just described:

```
Seoul-1#configure
Configuring from terminal, memory, or network [terminal]?
Enter configuration commands, one per line. End with CNTL/Z.
Seoul-1(config)#logging 131.108.110.33
Seoul-1(config)#logging trap debugging
Seoul-1(config)#logging console emergencies
Seoul-1(config)#^Z
```

NOTE   The syslog utility logs system messages to a text file on UNIX and other types of workstations. To log IOS device messages to a syslog server, you must configure your syslog process. You need to be a superuser on a UNIX workstation to enable the syslog facility local7, the facility used by all IOS devices. As superuser (root access), you should add the following line to the /etc/syslog.conf file:

```
local7.debug              /var/adm/router.log
```

Next, restart the syslog daemon on the UNIX workstation, which is typically done with the following command:

```
% kill -HUP 'cat /etc/syslog.pid'
```
If all works well, you are now ready for your IOS devices to log to this UNIX workstation.

If an IOS device is configured to log to an internal buffer, the log results can be viewed with the EXEC command **show logging**. Assuming that the Seoul-1 router is configured to log to a buffer as well as to syslog and console, the **show logging** output is as follows:

```
Seoul-1>show logging
Syslog logging: enabled (0 messages dropped, 0 flushes, 0 overruns)
    Console logging: level debugging, 2 messages logged
    Monitor logging: level debugging, 2 messages logged
    Trap logging: level debugging, 2 message lines logged
        Logging to 131.108.110.33, 2 message lines logged
    Buffer logging: level debugging, 2 messages logged

Log Buffer (4096 bytes):
Mar 17 17:45:56: %LINK-3-UPDOWN: Interface Serial0, changed state to down
Mar 17 18:23:10: %LINK-3-UPDOWN: Interface Serial0, changed state to up
```

The preceding output shows that syslog logging is enabled. It also shows the number of messages logged to the device console, to the terminal lines of the device (monitor logging), and to a syslog logging host also show the number of messages buffered. The last two lines of the output display the log buffer, with two logging messages showing link-state change messages (Level 6 messages).

Note the timestamp information in the output. The section "Basic Time Control," later in this chapter, discusses how to configure the router to maintain this information.

TIP We recommend that you enable logging at the debug level to at least one logging location. This enables you to ensure that all error messages the IOS device sends are recorded. Most network managers tend to set **logging trap debug** to enable syslog to log all IOS device messages.

Basic Network Management

Network management is the process of managing faults, controlling configurations, monitoring performance, ensuring security, and accounting for activity on a data network. Each of these tasks is necessary to have complete control of a data network environment, which is an essential component of an organization. The ISO Network Management Forum has defined network management as the sum of all activities required to perform fault, configuration, performance, security, and accounting management for a data network.

Network management platforms are software systems designed to perform the activities of network management. Some examples of network management platforms are Hewlett-Packard OpenView, Cabletron Spectrum, Sun Solstice Enterprise Manager, IBM NetView/AIX, and CiscoWorks2000. Network management platforms provide the software architecture for network management applications that perform a wide variety of tasks. They cannot be grouped into a single category. Some present a network map and check on the status of all network devices, providing a fault management function. Some performance management tools plot network link utilization and send warnings if errors occur on a LAN interface. Still others look for network security issues and send warnings via e-mail or alphanumeric pagers.

Network management applications communicate with software on network devices called agents. The manager-to-agent communication enables the manager to gather a standard set of information, which is defined in a management information base (MIB). Each piece of information that exists in a MIB is called an object. A MIB contains objects useful to managers for accomplishing the tasks of network management. Figure 7-2 shows the relationship between a manager and an agent.

Figure 7-2   *In a Network Management Protocol, the Manager Requests and Sets Information in the MIB, and the Agent Sends Trap Messages, Which Contain Information About Device Events to the Manager*

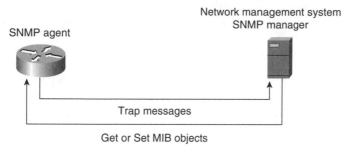

The two types of MIBs are standard and proprietary. Standard MIBs, such as MIB-II (RFC 1213), provide basic objects applicable to nearly all devices on a data network. For example, MIB-II contains system information about a device, such as its uptime and name, interface-specific traffic and error counters, and IP protocol information. Technology-specific MIBs, which are standard, are for protocols such as Frame Relay (RFC 1285) or Token Ring (RFC 1315). They contain objects relating to a specific technology on a network device. Vendor-specific MIBs, which are proprietary, define objects specific to a single vendor's network devices.

Network management applications gather MIB information from devices and change the behavior of those network devices through the use of a network management protocol. The Simple Network Management Protocol (SNMP), defined in RFC 1157, is a standard network management protocol and is the most widely used. SNMP uses UDP at the transport layer and IP at the network layer. Proprietary network management protocols exist as well, and some vendors have implemented them in their network devices.

Communication between an SNMP agent and a manager occurs with five packet types:

- Get-Request
- Get-Next-Request
- Set-Request
- Get-Response
- Trap

A Get-Request is a message from the manager to an agent requesting a set of specific MIB objects, such as a device's name, location, number of physical interfaces, and so on. A Get-Next-Request is a message from the manager to an agent requesting the next piece of tabular data, as referenced from a specific point in the MIB. This message type is useful in MIB table traversal and in the retrieval of a table such as the IP routing table. A Set-Request is a message requesting the agent to change the value of a specific MIB object, such as changing the status of an interface on a device. An agent responds to each Get-Request, Get-Next-Request, or Set-Request by sending a Get-Response to the manager that contains the requested values of the MIB objects or shows the value of a MIB object that has been changed. A Trap message is an unsolicited message from the agent to the manager about an event.

Each SNMP agent is set up with a verification string called a *community string*. The community string is included in each request from the manager to get or set MIB information. The agent verifies it before responding. A community string is weak authentication encoded in ASCII. It should not be relied upon as a sole way of securing SNMP access to an agent. (See the tip that appears later in this section for suggestions on improving security.)

The Cisco IOS global configuration command **snmp-server community** configures the agent with the community string. An option of this command enables you to stipulate that the community string is applicable to read-only or read-write messages to the agent. Get-Request and Get-Next-Request messages are read-only; Set-Request messages are read-write. The keywords used to stipulate read-only and read-write are **RO** and **RW**, respectively. The default read-only community string for many network management applications is **public**, and the default read-write is often **private**. A final option of this global command is to specify an IP standard access list of hosts permitted to query the agent using the valid community strings.

In the following example, the Singapore router is configured for the RO community string **Zipnet** and the RW community string **ZIPprivate**. IP **access-list 2** also is defined to permit the network manager at IP address 131.108.20.45 to use either community string. The access list number is the last optional parameter on both **snmp-server community** commands in the following example:

```
Singapore#configure
Configuring from terminal, memory, or network [terminal]?
Enter configuration commands, one per line. End with CNTL/Z.
Singapore(config)#access-list 2 permit 131.108.20.45
Singapore(config)#snmp-server community Zipnet RO 2
Singapore(config)#snmp-server community ZIPprivate RW 2
Singapore(config)#^Z
```

NOTE   To augment the security of the SNMP agent on your IOS device, we suggest that you set up different community strings for RO and RW access. Furthermore, we recommend that you limit the hosts that can query your IOS devices via SNMP by using the **access-list** option to the **snmp-server community** command.

You must configure your Cisco IOS device to send SNMP Trap messages. The six standard SNMP Trap messages that all agents send are defined in RFC 1157:

- coldStart
- warmStart
- linkUp
- linkDown
- authenticationFailure
- egpNeighborLoss

A coldStart signifies that the agent has just been started. The warmStart Trap indicates that the agent software itself has just been reset. In practice, most agents send only coldStart Traps because the agent typically restarts when the device on which the agent is running is powered on. The linkUp and linkDown Traps alert a manager about the change of status for a link on the device. An authenticationFailure indicates that a manager has sent the agent an SNMP request with an incorrect community string. Finally, the egpNeighborLoss Trap tells the manager that an External Gateway Protocol (EGP) neighbor has become unreachable. This last Trap is rarely used because EGP has been superseded by BGP4.

The preceding six Trap messages are the standard SNMP Traps, but they are not the only ones that an agent can send. Many MIBs define protocol-specific Traps, such as Traps specific to ISDN, Frame Relay, or BGP4. At the time of this writing, the IOS supports the Traps for a variety of protocols and IOS functions, including BGP, Frame Relay, ISDN, X.25, environmental monitor, and IOS configuration changes.

The Cisco IOS can be set up to send SNMP Traps to any number of managers. You must use the **snmp-server host** command to specify the IP address and community string of the manager to which Traps should be sent. In the following example, the Singapore router is configured on the ZIP network to send SNMP Traps to the manager at IP address 131.108.20.45 using the community string **Zipnet**. The optional parameters of the **snmp-server host** command also are to specify that we want the agent to send SNMP, Frame Relay, and IOS configuration change Traps.

```
Singapore#configure
Configuring from terminal, memory, or network [terminal]?
Enter configuration commands, one per line. End with CNTL/Z.
Singapore(config)#snmp-server host 131.108.20.45 Zipnet snmp frame-relay config
Singapore(config)#^Z
```

TIP

We suggest that you configure your SNMP agent to send Traps about all the technologies that are active in the device. SNMP Trap messages typically do not consume much bandwidth, and they can provide useful information for diagnosing network problems.

You can manually configure the SNMP agent in the IOS with the physical location and contact person for the device. Network management applications then can retrieve this information. You must use the global configuration commands **snmp-server location** and **snmp-server contact** to set up this information. Each of these commands enables you to enter a text string of 255 characters to describe the location or contact. In the next example, the Singapore router is configured with contact and location information:

```
Singapore#configure
Configuring from terminal, memory, or network [terminal]?
Enter configuration commands, one per line. End with CNTL/Z.
Singapore(config)#snmp-server location 1 Raffles Place, Singapore
Singapore(config)#snmp-server contact Allan Leinwand, allan@telegis.net
Singapore(config)#^Z
```

The EXEC command **show snmp** demonstrates the SNMP statistics for a given device. This command is useful in helping you monitor the SNMP activity on the device. Following is the output of **show snmp** from the Singapore router:

```
Singapore>show snmp
Chassis: 25014624
Contact: Allan Leinwand, allan@digisle.net
Location: 45 Raffles Place, Singapore
4620211 SNMP packets input
    0 Bad SNMP version errors
    0 Unknown community name
    0 Illegal operation for community name supplied
    0 Encoding errors
    23493606 Number of requested variables
    0 Number of altered variables
    576553 Get-request PDUs
    4043613 Get-next PDUs
    0 Set-request PDUs
4623230 SNMP packets output
    0 Too big errors (Maximum packet size 1500)
    1757 No such name errors
    0 Bad values errors
    0 General errors
    4620166 Get-response PDUs
    3064 SNMP trap PDUs

SNMP logging: enabled
    Logging to 131.108.20.45, 0/10, 3064 sent, 0 dropped.
```

In the preceding output, you can see statistics relative to SNMP. The first line of output shows the system board serial number available via the Cisco proprietary MIB. The second and third lines show the text strings for the contact and the location of the device, as configured using the **snmp-server contact** and **snmp-server location** global configuration commands. Statistics on the total number of SNMP packets that are input, the total number of SNMP packets that are input with the wrong community string, and the total number of SNMP objects requested by managers (referred to as variables) are available in the beginning of the output. You can also see a breakdown of the SNMP packet types received.

The second section of the output shows the total number of SNMP packets that are output, various standard SNMP protocol errors sent, and the total number of response and Trap messages sent. The last two lines of the output show whether the agent is set up to send Traps (called SNMP logging), the IP addresses of each manager receiving Traps, and the number of Traps sent to each specific manager.

Basic Time Control

The Cisco IOS allows a device to track the current time and date using a system clock. The system clock starts when the device powers on and can distribute the time to a variety of internal systems, such as recording the time and date for configuration changes, displaying the time of buffered log messages, and sending the time and date in SNMP messages. On Cisco 7000 routers only, the system clock time is set in hardware. On other models, the system clock is set by default to midnight on March 1, 1993.

After it is set, the system clock determines whether the date and time are from a reliable source. If the time source is reliable, it is redistributed to other processes in the IOS; otherwise, the time is available only for display purposes. The following sections discuss how to ensure that the time source you set, such as an atomic clock source, is a reliable source.

You can view the time and date of the system clock using the EXEC command **show clock**:

```
SF-1>show clock
06:56:50.314 PST Fri Mar 30 2001
```

Cisco 7000 series routers contain a calendar that tracks the date and time across system restarts and power outages. On a system restart, the calendar is always initially used to set the system clock. Then another protocol may alter or update the clock. In a network in which no other authoritative time source exists, the calendar can be used as an authoritative time source and can be passed to other processes (such as the Network Time Protocol, NTP, which is discussed in a later section). You can see the current setting of the calendar system by using the **show calendar** EXEC command:

```
SF-1>show calendar
06:57:26 PST Fri Mar 30 2001
```

The system clock keeps track of time internally based on Coordinated Universal Time (UTC), also referred to as Greenwich Mean Time (GMT). The IOS enables you to configure a device with the local time zone and, if relevant, with daylight saving time (referred to as **summer-time** in the syntax of the IOS) so that the device displays the correct time throughout the year.

NOTE   If you want your IOS device to indicate the current date and time in debugging and log messages, use the global configuration command **service timestamps**. You can display the time since the IOS device restarted, the date and time using GMT or the local time zone, and the time to the accuracy of milliseconds. We recommend that you use the configuration commands **service timestamps log datetime localtime** and **service timestamps debug datetime localtime**. The command **service timestamps log datetime localtime** adds the date and time to log messages; **service timestamps debug datetime localtime** adds the date and time to debug messages.

Several sources can be used to set the system clock. Three of the most commonly used sources are as follows:

* Manually
* NTP
* SNTP

These are discussed in greater detail in the next sections.

Manual Time and Date Configuration

If your IOS device is isolated and cannot use an outside authoritative time source, you can set the time and date of the device manually. These settings are valid until the device resets or is reloaded. You should use these manual time control services only when another authoritative time source is unavailable.

To manually set the time zone for your IOS device, use the **clock timezone** global configuration command. This command takes as options the time zone on which the device is located and the number of hours of difference between that time zone and UTC. For example, for Pacific Standard Time (PST), which is eight hours behind UTC, you enter the following global command: **clock timezone PST -8**.

If the time zone on which the IOS device resides uses daylight saving time, you need to use the global configuration command **clock summer-time recurring**. This configuration command takes as an argument the name of the summertime time zone, such as Pacific Daylight Time (PDT). The system clock is set using the global configuration command clock set. In the following example, we set the time zone of the SF-1 router to be PST, enable summertime with the time zone PDT, and set the clock to March 17, 2001, at 14:25:

```
SF-1#configure
Configuring from terminal, memory, or network [terminal]?
Enter configuration commands, one per line. End with CNTL/Z.
SF-1(config)#clock timezone PST -8
SF-1(config)#clock summer-time PDT recurring
SF-1(config)#clock set 14:25 17 3 2001
SF-1(config)#^Z
```

To set the calendar on Cisco 7000 series routers manually, use the global configuration command **calendar set**. For this calendar to be a valid source of time and date for other IOS functions, use the **clock calendar-valid** global configuration.

Network Time Protocol

The Network Time Protocol (NTP), documented in RFC 1305, is a protocol that synchronizes the times of devices operating over an IP data network. The Cisco IOS contains an NTP process that allows a device to send and receive NTP packets. Many vendors have similar NTP processes on their devices and hosts, making NTP the preferred mechanism to synchronize time across your entire network.

NTP distributes a time setting that it gets from an authoritative time source throughout a network. As noted previously, you can set your IOS device manually to be this time source, but preferably your time source will be an atomic clock attached to a time server. You do not need your own atomic clock to use NTP. You can synchronize your time with another source that has heard from an atomic clock.

Like many telephony network clocks, NTP measures the distance between the device on which it is running and an authoritative time source in increments called *stratum*. A clock that is a *stratum 1* time source is directly attached to an atomic clock, a *stratum 2* source is synchronized with a *stratum 1* source, and so forth. You cannot connect your IOS device directly to a *stratum 1* time source. The NTP process in the Cisco IOS automatically synchronizes with the time source that has the lowest stratum. The Cisco NTP process does not synchronize with a time source that is not synchronized with another time source at the same stratum or less. If NTP encounters a time source that has a vastly different time than others in the network, it does not synchronize to this source, even if it is the lowest stratum source.

One device running NTP communicates with another NTP device by making an *association*. Associations are configured in the Cisco IOS using either the **ntp server** or the **ntp peer** global configuration command. A *server association* means that the IOS device establishes an association with the configured device, not the reverse. In a *peer association* the devices establish an association with each other. The most common type of association is a server association, in which one authoritative time source is a server for multiple NTP processes on a variety of devices. Figure 7-3 shows a server association between NTP clients and a Cisco IOS device.

Figure 7-3 *These NTP Clients Have a Server Association with a Cisco IOS Device That Is Synchronized with a Public Internet Authoritative Time Source*

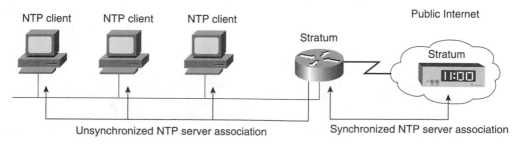

TIP

We recommend that you locate an authoritative time source on the public Internet to serve your network. These sources can be located using search tools on the Web and are updated regularly (search for the keyword NTP). A common practice is to have multiple authoritative time sources from multiple locations where your network may connect to the public Internet. For example, if your network has a public Internet connection in Europe and one in the United States, choose an authoritative time source on each continent and let NTP synchronize with the best time source available.

On Cisco 7000 series routers, you can synchronize periodically from NTP to the calendar system. Use the global configuration command **ntp update-calendar** to perform this task.

On a LAN, you can send and receive NTP messages using broadcast messages, eliminating the need to configure and make an association with every NTP device on the LAN. Use the interface configuration subcommand **ntp broadcast client** to listen to NTP broadcast messages on an interface. To broadcast NTP messages to a given LAN segment, use the interface subcommand **ntp broadcast**. A common configuration is to set up your IOS devices on a server association with a public Internet authoritative time source and then to broadcast NTP messages on all LAN interfaces on which other NTP devices reside. In the following example, we configure the NTP process on the SF-1 router to use two public Internet authoritative time sources in Northern California, to update the calendar system periodically based on using NTP date and time, and to broadcast NTP messages on interface (Ethernet 0):

```
SF-1#configure
Configuring from terminal, memory, or network [terminal]?
Enter configuration commands, one per line. End with CNTL/Z.
SF-1(config)#ntp server 192.216.191.10
SF-1(config)#ntp server 129.189.134.11
SF-1(config)#ntp update-calendar
SF-1(config)#interface (Ethernet 0)
SF-1(config)#ntp broadcast
SF-1(config)#^Z
```

You can see the NTP associations on an IOS device by using the EXEC command **show ntp associations**. The first character of each output line tells the status of a particular association, in terms of whether it is synchronized (the last line of the output is a key to the first-column characters). The output also shows the address of each configured association, the stratum level of the time source, and the master server. Following is an example:

```
SF-1>show ntp assoc
    address       ref clock   st   when   poll  reach   delay   offset   disp
*~192.216.191.10  .GPS.        1    127    512   377    285.5    7.57    32.8
+~129.189.134.11  .PPS.        1    207    512   377    147.2   -22.19   18.4
* master (synced), # master (unsynced), + selected, - candidate, ~ configured
```

You can view NTP status using the EXEC command **show ntp status**. In the following output, you can see that NTP is synchronized, is at stratum Level 2, and is referencing the authoritative time source at IP address 192.216.191.10:

```
SF-1>show ntp status
Clock is synchronized, stratum 2, reference is 192.216.191.10
nominal freq is 250.0000 Hz, actual freq is 250.0003 Hz, precision is 2**24
reference time is B853B821.9813EB8D (06:58:10 PST Fri Mar 30 2001)
clock offset is -7.3067 msec, root delay is 285.46 msec
root dispersion is 41.95 msec, peer dispersion is 32.82 msec
```

If you want to disable NTP, you can do so on a specific interface using the interface sub-command **ntp disable**. You can limit the type of NTP association that an IOS device can have using the global configuration command **ntp access-group**. This command requires you to specify the type of association permitted to a specific set of IP addresses given in an IP access list. You can permit the device to establish a peer association or a server association. You can also permit it to allow time requests from systems only or to permit NTP messages only. In the following example, server associations are permitted from all systems on the 131.108.0.0 network on the SF-1 router:

```
SF-1#configure
Configuring from terminal, memory, or network [terminal]?
Enter configuration commands, one per line. End with CNTL/Z.
SF-1(config)#access-list 50 permit 131.108.0.0 0.0.255.255
SF-1(config)#ntp access-group serve 50
SF-1(config)#^Z
```

Simple Network Time Protocol

Cisco 1003, 1004, and 1005 routers run only the Simple Network Time Protocol (SNTP), which is documented in RFC 2030. SNTP is a simplified version of NTP that can receive the time from only NTP servers. SNTP cannot be an authoritative time source for other devices. This limited functionality was deemed appropriate by Cisco because these Cisco 1000 series routers are small devices with a fixed number of interfaces and relatively low performance. SNTP provides time information that is accurate to within approximately 100 milliseconds to the device for use by the IOS.

You can configure SNTP to request and accept packets from configured servers using the global configuration command **sntp server**. You can have the SNTP process on the router listen to NTP broadcasts by using the global configuration command **sntp broadcast client**. If you set up both a specific server and the capability of the router to receive broadcast information, the device prefers the highest-strata server, or the configured server if strata from multiple sources are equal. You can view statistics about SNTP using the EXEC command **show sntp**.

Summary

The administrative and management tools discussed in this chapter, which are summarized in the following list, are the final pieces of basic IOS configuration that are necessary to configure the ZIP network. In the next chapter, you can see complete configurations for all Cisco IOS devices on the network.

- Access control of network devices through authentication, authorization, and accounting procedures (AAA) generally is advised. Two access control protocols commonly used with the Cisco IOS are RADIUS and TACACS+.

- Cisco IOS devices have the capability to log messages about system activity. Messages are classed into eight levels of severity, and you can stipulate the minimum level of severity of the message to be logged, as well as the location to which the logged messages are sent.

- Network management applications can collect information about and change the behavior of network devices. SNMP is the standard network management protocol.

- For optimal use of SNMP, use different community strings for RO and RW access, and use an access list to limit the number of hosts that can query your IOS devices via SNMP. Also, configure your SNMP agent to send Traps about all technologies that are active in the device.

- The system clock for a Cisco IOS device can be set manually, by the NTP, or by the SNTP.

Table 7-2   *Summary of Configuration Commands for Administration and Management*

Command	Description
aaa accounting	Enables accounting on a specific client.
aaa authentication	Enables authentication on a specific client.
aaa authorization	Enables authorization on a specific client.
aaa new-model	Enables all AAA services in the Cisco IOS.
aaa server-group	Defines the AAA server group.
access-class *access-list* **in**	Line subcommand. Specifies an access list for inbound terminal line access.
access-class *access-list* **out**	Line subcommand. Specifies an access list for outbound terminal line access.
calendar set	Manually sets the date on the system clock.
clock calendar-valid	Makes the calendar date and time together a valid source of time for other IOS functions.
clock set	Manually sets the time on the system clock.
clock summer-time recurring	Sets the daylight saving time zone.
clock timezone	Manually sets the time zone for the IOS device.
crypto key generate rsa	Generates the RSA key pair used for the encryption of the session between an SSH server and client. Enables the SSH server on all virtual terminal lines.

Table 7-2   *Summary of Configuration Commands for Administration and Management (Continued)*

Command	Description
crypto key zeroize rsa	Removes the RSA key pair used for the encryption of the session between an SSH server and client. Disables the SSH server on all virtual terminal lines.
ip ssh	Enables the SSH server.
ip tcp intercept list *access-list*	Specifies an IP extended access list that defines the TCP connections relevant to the TCP intercept feature.
ip tcp intercept mode {intercept | watch}	Sets the TCP intercept mode to intercept or watch connections.
ip tcp intercept watch-timeout *seconds*	Specifies the number of seconds before resetting a TCP session that is watched and not established.
ip verify unicast reverse-path	An interface subcommand for enabling unicast RPF.
line console 0	A major command for configuration of console line parameters.
line vty *start end*	A major command for configuration of virtual terminal lines numbered from start to end.
logging buffered *size*	Specifies the size, in bytes, of the internal device buffer.
logging *location level*	Specifies the logging of messages at and more severe than the indicated level to the specified location.
ntp access-group	Limits the type of NTP associations an IOS device can have to the types defined in an IP access list.
ntp broadcast	Configures an interface to broadcast NTP messages to a given LAN segment.
ntp broadcast client	Configures an interface to listen to NTP broadcasts.
ntp peer	Configures a peer association between two NTP-configured devices.
ntp server	Configures a server association between an IOS device and an NTP-configured device.
ntp update-calendar	Periodically synchronizes the calendar of a 7000-series router to the NTP calendar.
password *password*	Specifies the line subcommand password.
radius-server host	Specifies the RADIUS server with which an IOS client communicates.
radius-server key	Configures a secret string for communication encryption between a RADIUS server and the Cisco IOS.

continues

Table 7-2   *Summary of Configuration Commands for Administration and Management (Continued)*

Command	Description
server	AAA server subcommand. Defines IP addresses of servers in the AAA server group.
service password-encryption	Configures the IOS device to encrypt all passwords in EXEC command output.
service timestamps *type*	Configures the IOS device to add timestamps to log and debug messages.
snmp-server community	Configures a community string for security purposes on an SNMP agent.
snmp-server contact	Configures a text string to give as the contact of the IOS device.
snmp-server host	Specifies the IP address and community string of the manager to which Traps should be sent.
snmp-server location	Configures a text string to give as the location of the IOS device.
sntp broadcast client	Configures the SNTP process on a router to listen to NTP broadcasts.
sntp server	Configures SNTP to request and accept packets from configured servers.
tacacs-server host	Configures the TACACS+ server with which an IOS client communicates.
tacacs-server key	Configures a secret string for communication encryption between a TACACS+ server and the Cisco IOS.

Table 7-3   *Summary of EXEC Commands for Administration and Management*

Command	Description
show clock	Displays the current date and time as known by the system clock.
show calendar	Displays the current date and time as known by the system calendar on Cisco 7000 series routers.
show crypto key mypubkey rsa	Displays the RSA public key used by SSH for encryption.
show ip ssh	Displays the current SSH sessions on the device.
show logging	Describes the current logging status of the device.

Table 7-3   *Summary of EXEC Commands for Administration and Management (Continued)*

Command	Description
show ntp associations	Displays the current NTP associations and their current states.
show ntp status	Displays the current status of NTP on the IOS device.
show snmp	Shows SNMP statistics for the SNMP agent on the IOS device.
show sntp	Displays the status of SNTP on the IOS device.
show tcp intercept connections	Displays the current incomplete and established TCP sessions.
show tcp intercept statistics	Displays statistics for the TCP intercept feature.

References

The following references explore the subjects in this chapter further:

Carasik, Anne. *UNIX SSH: Using Secure Shell.* New York: McGraw-Hill Companies, Inc., 1999.

Case, J.D., M. Fedor, M.L. Schoffstall, and C. Davin. RFC 1157, "Simple Network Management Protocol (SNMP)." May 1990.

Ferguson, P., and D. Senie. RFC 2827, "Network Ingress Filtering: Defeating Denial of Service Attacks Which Employ IP Source Address Spoofing." May 2000.

Finseth, C. RFC 1492, "An Access Control Protocol, Sometimes Called TACACS." July 1993.

Leinwand, Allan, and Karen Fang-Conroy. *Network Management: A Practical Perspective*, Second Edition. Reading, Massachusetts: Addison-Wesley Publishing, 1996.

McCloghrie, K., and M. Rose. RFC 1213, "Management Information Base for Network Management Information of TCP/IP-based Internets: MIBII." March 1991.

Mills, D. RFC 1305, "Network Time Protocol (Version 3) Specification, Implementation, and Analysis." March 1992.

Mills, D. RFC 2030, "Simple Network Time Protocol (SNTP) Version 4 for IPv4, IPv6, and OSI." October 1996.

Postel, J., and J. Reynolds. RFC 854, "The Telnet Specification." May 1983.

Rigney, C. RFC 2866, "RADIUS Accounting." June 2000.

Rigney, C., S. Willens, A. Rubens, and W. Simpson. RFC 2865, "Remote Authentication Dial-In User Service (RADIUS)." June 2000.

CHAPTER 8

Comprehensive IOS Configuration for the ZIP Network

This chapter shows the complete IOS configuration commands for all routers and access servers on the ZIP network. The EXEC command **show running-confg** is used to display the current configuration commands on an IOS device.

When reviewing these configuration commands, note the following:

- The ZIP network is running IOS software version 12.1. Some IOS configuration commands may not operate as described in earlier versions.

- Some of the devices have unused interfaces because the number of interfaces required for ZIP network connectivity is less than the number of interfaces available as configured by Cisco.

- The IOS configuration commands do not appear in an IOS device in the order in which you enter them into the device.

- An IOS device separates some major configuration command segments with the exclamation point (!) character. All characters following an exclamation point on a given line in a configuration file are not interpreted by an IOS device.

- All routers in the ZIP network are using EIGRP routing for IP, AppleTalk, and IPX.

- The ZIP network devices use a combination of TACACS+ and RADIUS for authentication, authorization, and accounting.

The Kuala-Lumpur Router

The Kuala-Lumpur device on the ZIP network is a Cisco 2501 router. The configuration of this router features the following:

- An Ethernet interface to the local Kuala Lumpur LAN segment

- A Frame Relay point-to-point interface connecting Kuala Lumpur to the Seoul-1 router

- An IOS DHCP server that assigns IP addresses to DHCP clients on the local Kuala Lumpur LAN segment

The complete configuration for the Kuala-Lumpur router follows:

```
version 12.1
service timestamps debug datetime localtime
service timestamps log datetime localtime
service password-encryption
!
hostname Kuala-Lumpur
!
aaa new-model
aaa authentication login default group tacacs+ enable
aaa authorization exec group tacacs+ if-authenticated
aaa authorization network group radius if-authenticated
aaa accounting exec stop-only group tacacs+
enable secret 5 $2$5toY$IJQPTVD4.aEDLwZ8nPrvX.
!
ip domain-list zipnet.com
ip domain-list zipnet.net
ip domain-name zipnet.com
ip name-server 131.108.110.34
ip name-server 131.108.110.35
ip dhcp database tftp://131.108.2.77/kl-dhcp-info
ip dhcp excluded-address 131.108.2.1 131.108.2.10
ip dhcp excluded-address 131.108.2.57
ip dhcp excluded-address 131.108.2.129 131.108.2.135
!
ip dhcp pool kl-common
    network 131.108.2.0/24
    dns-server 131.108.101.34 131.108.101.35
    domain-name zipnet.com
    netbios-name-server 131.108.21.70
    netbios-node-type h
    lease 0 1
!
ip dhcp pool kl-users
    network 131.108.2.0/25
    default-router 131.108.2.1
!
ip dhcp pool kl-users-2
    network 131.108.2.128/25
    default-router 131.108.2.129
!
appletalk routing eigrp 25000
appletalk route-redistribution
ipx routing 0000.0b1c.2c3e
!
clock timezone MST +8
!
interface Loopback1
 description Kuala-Lumpur router loopback
 ip address 131.108.254.9 255.255.255.255
!
interface Ethernet0
 description Kuala-Lumpur LAN Segment
 ip address 131.108.2.1 255.255.255.128

 ntp broadcast
 appletalk cable-range 3001-3010
 appletalk zone Asia Manufacturing
 ipx network 3010
!
interface Serial0
 description IETF frame relay PVCs on circuit M234563KL
 no ip address
```

```
 encapsulation frame-relay ietf
 bandwidth 128
 frame-relay lmi-type ansi
!
interface Serial0.100 point-to-point
 description FR PVC 100 to Seoul-1
 ip address 131.108.242.2 255.255.255.252
 bandwidth 128
 frame-relay interface-dlci 100
 appletalk cable-range 2901-2901
 appletalk zone WAN Zone
 appletalk protocol eigrp
 no appletalk protocol rtmp
 ipx network 2901
!
interface Serial1
 no ip address
 shutdown
!
router eigrp 25000
 network 131.108.0.0
 no auto-summary
!
ip classless
logging trap debugging
logging console emergencies
logging 131.108.110.33
access-list 1 permit 131.108.0.0   0.0.255.255
access-list 2 permit host 131.108.20.45
!
ipx router eigrp 25000
 network 2901
 network 3010
!
tacacs-server host 131.108.110.33
tacacs-server key ZIPSecure
radius-server host 131.108.110.33
radius-server key Radius4Me
snmp-server community Zipnet RO 2
snmp-server community ZIPprivate RW 2
snmp-server host 131.108.20.45 Zipnet snmp frame-relay config
snmp-server location 1 KLCC Towers, Kuala Lumpur, Malaysia
snmp-server contact Allan Leinwand, allan@telegis.net
!
line con 0
 password 7 095B59
line aux 0
line vty 0 4
 password 7 095B59
 access-class 1 in
!
ntp update-calendar
ntp server 192.216.191.10
ntp server 129.189.134.11
!
end
```

The SF-1 Router

The SF-1 device on the ZIP network is a Cisco 4700 router. The configuration of this router features the following:

- A Fast Ethernet LAN interface to the local San Francisco backbone segment
- An Ethernet connecting to a local San Francisco LAN segment
- An IPX Get-Nearest-Server output filter on the local San Francisco LAN segment

The complete configuration for the SF-1 router follows:

```
version 12.1
service timestamps debug datetime localtime
service timestamps log datetime localtime
service password-encryption
!
hostname SF-1
!
aaa new-model
aaa authentication login default group tacacs+ enable
aaa authorization exec group tacacs+ if-authenticated
aaa authorization network group radius if-authenticated
aaa accounting exec stop-only group tacacs+
enable secret 5 $2$5toY$IJQPTVD4.aEDLwZ8nPrvX.
!
ip domain-list zipnet.com
ip domain-list zipnet.net
ip domain-name zipnet.com
ip name-server 131.108.110.34
ip name-server 131.108.110.35
appletalk routing eigrp 25000
appletalk route-redistribution
ipx routing 0000.1c2c.23bb
!
clock timezone PST -8
clock summer-time PDT recurring
!
interface Loopback1
 description SF-1 router loopback
 ip address 131.108.254.1 255.255.255.255
!
interface FastEthernet0
 description San Francisco FastEthernet backbone LAN
 ip address 131.108.20.1 255.255.252.0
 appletalk cable-range 1-10
 appletalk zone SF Zone
 ipx network 1010
 full-duplex
!
interface Ethernet0
 description SF-1 LAN Segment
 ip address 131.108.101.1 255.255.255.0
 ip helper-address 131.108.21.70
 media-type 10BaseT
 ntp broadcast
 appletalk cable-range 11-100
 appletalk zone Operations
 ipx network 100
 ipx output-gns-filter 1010
!
interface Ethernet1
```

```
 no ip address
 shutdown
!
router eigrp 25000
 network 131.108.0.0
 no auto-summary
!
ip classless
logging 131.108.110.33
logging trap debugging
logging console emergencies
access-list 1 permit 131.108.0.0 0.0.255.255
access-list 2 permit host 131.108.20.45
access-list 1010 permit aa.0207.0104.0874
access-list 1010 deny -1
!
ipx router eigrp 25000
 network 100
 network 1010
!
tacacs-server host 131.108.110.33
tacacs-server key ZIPSecure
radius-server host 131.108.110.33
radius-server key Radius4Me
snmp-server community Zipnet RO 2
snmp-server community ZIPprivate RW 2
snmp-server host 131.108.20.45 Zipnet snmp frame-relay config
snmp-server location 22 Cable Car Drive, San Francisco, CA, USA
snmp-server contact Allan Leinwand, allan@telegis.net
!
line con 0
 password 7 095B59
line aux 0
line vty 0 4
 password 7 095B59
 access-class 1 in
!
ntp update-calendar
ntp server 192.216.191.10
ntp server 129.189.134.11
!
end
```

The SF-2 Router

The SF-2 device on the ZIP Network is a Cisco 4700 router. The configuration of this router features the following:

- A Fast Ethernet LAN interface to the local San Francisco backbone segment
- Two Ethernets connecting to two local San Francisco LAN segments
- An IPX Get-Nearest-Server output filter on one of the local San Francisco LAN segments

The complete configuration for the SF-2 router follows:

```
version 12.1
service timestamps debug datetime localtime
service timestamps log datetime localtime
```

```
service password-encryption
!
hostname SF-2
!
aaa new-model
aaa authentication login default group tacacs+ enable
aaa authorization exec group tacacs+ if-authenticated
aaa authorization network group radius if-authenticated
aaa accounting exec stop-only group tacacs+
enable secret 5 $2$5toY$IJQPTVD4.aEDLwZ8nPrvX.
!
ip domain-list zipnet.com
ip domain-list zipnet.net
ip domain-name zipnet.com
ip name-server 131.108.110.34
ip name-server 131.108.110.35
appletalk routing eigrp 25000
appletalk route-redistribution
ipx routing 0000.0c0c.11bb
!
clock timezone PST -8
clock summer-time PDT recurring
!
interface Loopback1
 description SF-2 router loopback
 ip address 131.108.254.2 255.255.255.255
!
interface FastEthernet0

 description San Francisco FastEthernet backbone LAN
 ip address 131.108.20.2 255.255.252.0
 appletalk cable-range 1-10
 appletalk zone SF Zone
 ipx network 10
!
interface Ethernet0
 description SF-2 LAN Segment 1
 ip address 131.108.110.1 255.255.255.0
 ip helper-address 131.108.21.70
 media-type 10BaseT
 ntp broadcast
 appletalk cable-range 151-200
 appletalk zone Marketing
 ipx network 200
 ipx output-gns-filter 1010
!
interface Ethernet1
 description SF-2 LAN Segment 2
 ip address 131.108.120.1 255.255.255.0
 ip helper-address 131.108.21.70
 media-type 10BaseT
 ntp broadcast
 appletalk cable-range 101-150
 appletalk zone Sales
 ipx network 150
!
router eigrp 25000
 network 131.108.0.0
 no auto-summary
!
ip classless
logging 131.108.110.33
logging trap debugging
logging console emergencies
```

```
access-list 1 permit 131.108.0.0  0.0.255.255
access-list 2 permit host 131.108.20.45
access-list 1010 permit aa.0207.0104.0874
access-list 1010 deny -1
!
ipx router eigrp 25000
 network 10
 network 150
 network 200
!
tacacs-server host 131.108.110.33
tacacs-server key ZIPSecure
radius-server host 131.108.110.33
radius-server key Radius4Me
snmp-server community Zipnet RO 2
snmp-server community ZIPprivate RW 2
snmp-server host 131.108.20.45 Zipnet snmp frame-relay config
snmp-server location 22 Cable Car Drive, San Francisco, CA, USA
snmp-server contact Allan Leinwand, allan@telegis.net
!
line con 0
 password 7 095B59
line aux 0
line vty 0 4
 password 7 095B59
 access-class 1 in
!
ntp update-calendar
ntp server 192.216.191.10
ntp server 129.189.134.11
!
end
```

The SF-Core-1 Router

The SF-Core-1 device on the ZIP network is a Cisco 7505 router. The configuration of this router features the following:

- A Fast Ethernet LAN interface to the local San Francisco backbone segment.

- An HDLC serial link to the San Jose router.

- An HDLC serial link to the ZIP network ISP.

- An HSRP group between SF-Core-1 and SF-Core-2.

- EBGP routing between the ZIP network and ISP-B, a local provider. The routes advertised and received by BGP are controlled using distribute lists.

- Redistribution of static routes used for default routing into the EIGRP routing process.

- An extended IP access list used for filtering traffic from the public Internet and the ZIP network.

- An IPX router SAP filter on the FastEthernet segment.

The complete configuration for the SF-Core-1 router follows:

```
Version 12.1
Service timestamps debug datetime localtime
```

```
Service timestamps log datetime localtime
Service password-encryption
!
hostname SF-Core-1
!
aaa new-model
aaa authentication login default group tacacs+ enable
aaa authorization exec group tacacs+ if-authenticated
aaa authorization network group radius if-authenticated
aaa accounting exec stop-only group tacacs+
enable secret 5 $2$5toY$IJQPTVD4.aEDLwZ8nPrvX.
!
ip tcp intercept mode watch
ip tcp intercept list 120
ip tcp intercept watch-timeout 15
ip domain-list zipnet.com
ip domain-list zipnet.net
ip domain-name zipnet.com
ip name-server 131.108.110.34
ip name-server 131.108.110.35
appletalk routing eigrp 25000
appletalk route-redistribution
ipx routing 0000.0e0d.1eb0
!
clock timezone PST -8
clock summer-time PDT recurring!
interface Loopback1
 description SF-Core-1 router loopback
 ip address 131.108.254.3 255.255.255.255
!
interface FastEthernet0/0
 description San Francisco FastEthernet backbone LAN
 ip address 131.108.20.3 255.255.252.0
 appletalk cable-range 1-10
 appletalk zone SF Zone
 ipx network 10
 standby ip 131.108.20.5
 standby preempt
 ipx router-sap-filter 1001
!
interface Serial1/0
 description HDLC leased line on circuit 456WS34209 to San-Jose
 ip address 131.108.240.1 255.255.255.252
 appletalk cable-range 901-901
 appletalk zone WAN Zone
 appletalk protocol eigrp
 no appletalk protocol rtmp
 ipx network 901
!
interface Serial1/1
 description HDLC leased line on circuit 789WS34256 to ISP-B
 ip address 192.7.2.2 255.255.255.252
 ip access-group 101 in
!
interface Serial1/2
 no ip address
 shutdown
!
interface Serial1/3
 no ip address
 shutdown
!
router eigrp 25000
```

```
    redistribute static
    redistribute bgp 25000  network 131.108.0.0
    distribute-list 1300 out
    no auto-summary
  !
  router bgp 25000
   no synchronization
   network 131.108.0.0
   neighbor 192.7.2.1 remote-as 1
   neighbor 192.7.2.1 description Internet Connection to ISP-B
   neighbor 192.7.2.1 distribute-list ISP-routes in
   neighbor 192.7.2.1 distribute-list ZIP-routes out
   neighbor 131.108.254.6  remote-as 25000
   neighbor 131.108.254.6  description IBGP to Seoul-1
   neighbor 131.108.254.6  update-source Loopback 0
  !
  ip classless
  ip default-network 131.119.0.0
  ip default-network 140.222.0.0

  ip route 131.108.232.0 255.255.255.0 FastEthernet0/0
  ip route 131.108.0.0 255.255.0.0 Null0
  logging 131.108.110.33
  logging trap debugging
  logging console emergencies
  ip access-list standard ZIP-routes
   permit 131.108.0.0
  ip access-list standard ISP-routes
  deny   host 0.0.0.0 deny 127.0.0.0 0.255.255.255
  deny 10.0.0.0 0.255.255.255
  deny 172.16.0.0 0.15.255.255
  deny 192.168.0.0 0.0.255.255
  deny 192.0.2.0 0.0.0.255
  deny 128.0.0.0 0.0.255.255
  deny 191.255.0.0 0.0.255.
  deny 192.0.0.0 0.0.0.255
  deny 223.255.255.0 0.0.0.255
  deny 224.0.0.0 31.255.255.255
   permit any
  access-list 1 permit 131.108.0.0 0.0.255.255
  access-list 2 permit host 131.108.20.45
  access-list 101 remark Permits NTP, DNS, WWW, and SMTP
  access-list 101 deny tcp host 192.7.2.2 host 192.7.2.2 log
  access-list 101 deny ip 131.108.0.0 0.0.255.255 any log
  access-list 101 deny ip 10.0.0.0 0.255.255.255 any
  access-list 101 deny ip 172.16.0.0 0.15.255.255 any
  access-list 101 deny ip 192.168.0.0 0.0.255.255 any
  access-list 101 deny ip 127.0.0.0 0.255.255.255 any
  access-list 101 permit ip host 192.7.2.1 192.7.2.2
  access-list 101 deny ip any host 192.7.2.2
  access-list 101 permit udp any 131.108.101.99 eq domain
  access-list 101 permit udp host 15.255.160.64 host 131.108.254.3 eq ntp
  access-list 101 permit udp host 128.4.1.1 host 131.108.254.3 eq ntp
  access-list 101 permit udp host 16.1.0.4 host 131.108.254.3 eq ntp
  access-list 101 permit udp host 204.123.2.5 host 131.108.254.3 eq ntp
  access-list 101 permit tcp host 192.52.71.4 host 131.108.101.34 eq domain
  access-list 101 permit tcp host 192.52.71.4 host 131.108.101.35 eq domain
  access-list 101 permit tcp any host 131.108.101.34 eq smtp
  access-list 101 permit tcp any host 131.108.101.35 eq smtp
  access-list 101 permit tcp any host 131.108.101.100 eq www
  access-list 101 permit tcp any host 131.108.101.100 eq ftp
  access-list 101 permit tcp any host 131.108.101.100 eq ftp-data
  access-list 101 permit tcp any gt 1023 host 131.108.101.100 gt 1023
  access-list 101 permit icmp any any echo-reply
```

```
access-list 101 permit icmp any any time-exceeded
access-list 101 permit icmp any any port-unreachable
access-list 101 permit tcp any any established
access-list 101 permit tcp any any eq 22
access-list 101 deny   tcp any any eq ident
access-list 101 deny   ip any any log
access-list 120 permit ip any 131.108.0.0 0.0.255.255
access-list 1001 permit aa.0005.0112.0474
access-list 1001 deny -1
access-list 1300 permit 131.108.0.0 0.0.255.255
access-list 1300 permit 131.119.0.0
access-list 1300 permit140.222.0.0
!
ipx router eigrp 25000
 network 10
 network 901
!
tacacs-server host 131.108.110.33
tacacs-server key ZIPSecure
radius-server host 131.108.110.33
radius-server key Radius4Me
snmp-server community Zipnet RO 2
snmp-server community ZIPprivate RW 2
snmp-server host 131.108.20.45 Zipnet snmp frame-relay config
snmp-server location 22 Cable Car Drive, San Francisco, CA, USA
snmp-server contact Allan Leinwand, allan@telegis.net
!
line con 0
 password 7 095B59
line aux 0
line vty 0 4
 password 7 095B59
 access-class 1 in
!
ntp update-calendar
ntp server 192.216.191.10
ntp server 129.189.134.11
!
end
```

The SF-Core-2 Router

The SF-Core-2 device on the ZIP network is a Cisco 7505 router. The configuration of this router features the following:

- A Fast Ethernet LAN interface to the local San Francisco backbone segment
- An HDLC serial link to the Seoul-2 router
- An HSRP group between SF-Core-1 and SF-Core-2
- Redistribution of static routes used for default routing into the EIGRP routing process
- An IPX router SAP filter on the FastEthernet segment

The complete configuration for the SF-Core-2 router follows:

```
version 12.1
service timestamps debug datetime localtime
service timestamps log datetime localtime
service password-encryption
!
```

```
hostname SF-Core-2
!
aaa new-model
aaa authentication login default group tacacs+ enable
aaa authorization exec group tacacs+ if-authenticated
aaa authorization network group radius if-authenticated
aaa accounting exec stop-only group tacacs+
enable secret 5 $2$5toY$IJQPTVD4.aEDLwZ8nPrvX.
!
ip domain-list zipnet.com
ip domain-list zipnet.net
ip domain-name zipnet.com
ip name-server 131.108.110.34
ip name-server 131.108.110.35
appletalk routing eigrp 25000
appletalk route-redistribution
ipx routing 0000.cc0c.010b
!
clock timezone PST -8
clock summer-time PDT recurring
!
interface Loopback1
 description SF-Core-2 router loopback
 ip address 131.108.254.4 255.255.255.255
!
interface FastEthernet0/0
description San Francisco FastEthernet backbone LAN
 ip address 131.108.20.4 255.255.252.0
 appletalk cable-range 1-10
 appletalk zone SF Zone
 ipx network 10
 standby ip 131.108.20.5
 standby preempt
 ipx router-sap-filter 1001
!
interface Serial1/0
 description HDLC leased line on circuit WSZ02980189 to Seoul-2
 ip address 131.108.240.5 255.255.255.252
 appletalk cable-range 902-902
 appletalk zone WAN Zone
 appletalk protocol eigrp
 no appletalk protocol rtmp
 ipx network 902
!
interface Serial1/1
 no ip address
 shutdown
!
interface Serial1/2
 no ip address
 shutdown
!
interface Serial1/3
 no ip address
 shutdown
!
router eigrp 25000
 redistribute static
 network 131.108.0.0
 no auto-summary
!
ip classless
ip route 131.108.0.0 255.255.0.0 Null0
logging 131.108.110.33
```

```
logging trap debugging
logging console emergencies
access-list 1 permit 131.108.0.0 0.0.255.255
access-list 2 permit host 131.108.20.45
access-list 1001 permit aa.0005.0112.0474
access-list 1001 deny -1
!
ipx router eigrp 25000
 network 10
 network 902
!
tacacs-server host 131.108.110.33
tacacs-server key ZIPSecure
radius-server host 131.108.110.33
radius-server key Radius4Me
snmp-server community Zipnet RO 2
snmp-server community ZIPprivate RW 2
snmp-server host 131.108.20.45 Zipnet snmp frame-relay config
snmp-server location 22 Cable Car Drive, San Francisco, CA, USA
snmp-server contact Allan Leinwand, allan@telegis.net
!
line con 0
 password 7 095B59
line aux 0
line vty 0 4
 password 7 095B59
 access-class 1 in
!
ntp update-calendar
ntp server 192.216.191.10
ntp server 129.189.134.11
!
end
```

The San-Jose Router

The San-Jose device on the ZIP network is a Cisco 3640 router. The configuration of this router features the following:

- A 16-MB Token Ring interface to the local San Jose LAN segment

- An HDLC serial link to the SF-Core-1 router

- An HDLC serial link to the Seoul-1 router

- An AppleTalk access list used to permit traffic to the public portion of the engineering zone

- An IPX output SAP filter on the serial links to advertise access to a public IPX server in engineering

The complete configuration for the San-Jose router follows:

```
version 12.1
service timestamps debug datetime localtime
service timestamps log datetime localtime
service password-encryption
!
hostname San-Jose
!
aaa new-model
```

```
aaa authentication login default group tacacs+ enable
aaa authorization exec group tacacs+ if-authenticated
aaa authorization network group radius if-authenticated
aaa accounting exec stop-only group tacacs+
enable secret 5 $2$5toY$IJQPTVD4.aEDLwZ8nPrvX.
!
ip domain-list zipnet.com
ip domain-list zipnet.net
ip domain-name zipnet.com
ip name-server 131.108.110.34
ip name-server 131.108.110.35
appletalk routing eigrp 25000
appletalk route-redistribution
ipx routing 0000.c10e.100d
!
clock timezone PST -8
clock summer-time PDT recurring
!
interface Loopback1
 description San-Jose router loopback
 ip address 131.108.254.4 255.255.255.255
!
interface TokenRing0/0
 no ip address
 shutdown
!
interface Serial0/0
 description HDLC leased line on circuit BCS20198ASL to SF-Core-1
 ip address 131.108.240.2 255.255.255.252
 appletalk cable-range 901-901
 appletalk zone WAN Zone
 appletalk protocol eigrp
 no appletalk protocol rtmp
 ipx network 901
 ipx output-sap-filter 1000
 appletalk access-group 601
!
interface Serial0/1
 no ip address
 shutdown
!
interface TokenRing1/0
 description San Jose LAN Segment
 ip address 131.108.100.1 255.255.255.128
 ip helper-address 131.108.21.70
 ring-speed 16
 early-token-release
 ntp broadcast
 appletalk cable-range 1001-1010
 appletalk zone Engineering
 ipx network 1010
!
interface Serial1/0
 description HDLC leased line on circuit BCS1014343-9901 to Seoul-1
 ip address 131.108.241.2 255.255.255.252
 appletalk cable-range 1901-1901
 appletalk zone WAN Zone
 appletalk protocol eigrp
 no appletalk protocol rtmp
 ipx network 1901
 ipx output-sap-filter 1000
 appletalk access-group 601
!
interface Serial1/1
```

```
  no ip address
  shutdown
!
router eigrp 25000
network 131.108.0.0
no auto-summary
!
ip classless
logging 131.108.110.33
logging trap debugging
logging console emergencies
access-list 1 permit 131.108.0.0  0.0.255.255
access-list 2 permit host 131.108.20.45
access-list 601 permit nbp 1 object Engineering Public
access-list 601 permit nbp 1 type AFPServer
access-list 601 permit nbp 1 zone San Jose Zone
access-list 601 deny other-nbps
access-list 1000 permit 10.0000.0000.a0b0
access-list 1000 deny -1
!
ipx router eigrp 25000
 network 901
 network 1010
 network 1901
!
tacacs-server host 131.108.110.33
tacacs-server key ZIPSecure
radius-server host 131.108.110.33
radius-server key Radius4Me
snmp-server community Zipnet RO 2
snmp-server community ZIPprivate RW 2
snmp-server host 131.108.20.45 Zipnet snmp frame-relay config
snmp-server location 20 Market Street, San Jose, CA, USA
snmp-server contact Allan Leinwand, allan@telegis.net
!
line con 0
 password 7 095B59
line aux 0
line vty 0 4
 password 7 095B59
 access-class 1 in
!
ntp update-calendar
ntp server 192.216.191.10
ntp server 129.189.134.11
!
end
```

The Seoul-1 Router

The Seoul-1 device on the ZIP network is a Cisco 4700 router. The configuration of this router features the following:

- An Ethernet interface to the local Seoul LAN segment with redundant HSRP groups
- Two point-to-point Frame Relay interfaces to the Singapore router, and the other to the Kuala-Lumpur router

The complete configuration for the Seoul-1 router follows:

```
version 12.1
service timestamps debug datetime localtime
```

```
service timestamps log datetime localtime
service password-encryption
!
hostname Seoul-1
!
aaa new-model
aaa authentication login default group tacacs+ enable
aaa authorization exec group tacacs+ if-authenticated
aaa authorization network group radius if-authenticated
aaa accounting exec stop-only group tacacs+
enable secret 5 $2$5toY$IJQPTVD4.aEDLwZ8nPrvX.
!
ip tcp intercept mode watch
ip tcp intercept list 120
ip tcp intercept watch-timeout 15
ip domain-list zipnet.com
ip domain-list zipnet.net
ip domain-name zipnet.com
ip name-server 131.108.110.34
ip name-server 131.108.110.35
appletalk routing eigrp 25000
appletalk route-redistribution
ipx routing 0000.0011.bceb
!
clock timezone KST +9
!
interface Loopback1
 description Seoul-1 router loopback
 ip address 131.108.254.6 255.255.255.255
!
interface Ethernet0
 description Seoul LAN Segment
 ip address 131.108.3.1 255.255.255.128
 ip helper-address 131.108.21.70
 no ip redirects
 media-type 10BaseT
 ntp broadcast
 appletalk cable-range 2001-2010
 appletalk zone Asia Distribution
 ipx network 2010
 standby 1 ip 131.108.3.3
 standby 1 priority 100
 standby 1 track Serial1
 standby 1 preempt
 standby 2 ip 131.108.3.4
 standby 2 priority 95
 standby 2 preempt
!
interface Serial0
 description IETF frame relay PVCs on circuit S123789y
 no ip address
 encapsulation frame-relay ietf
 bandwidth 256
 frame-relay lmi-type ansi
!
interface Serial0.16 point-to-point
 description FR PVC 16 to Kuala-Lumpur
 ip address 131.108.242.1 255.255.255.252
 bandwidth 128
 frame-relay interface-dlci 16
 appletalk cable-range 2901-2901
 appletalk zone WAN Zone
 appletalk protocol eigrp
 no appletalk protocol rtmp
```

```
 ipx network 2901
!
interface Serial0.17 point-to-point
 description FR PVC 17 to Singapore
 ip address 131.108.242.5 255.255.255.252
 bandwidth 128
 frame-relay interface-dlci 17
 appletalk cable-range 2902-2902
 appletalk zone WAN Zone
 appletalk protocol eigrp
 no appletalk protocol rtmp
 ipx network 2902
!
interface Serial1
 description HDLC leased line on circuit MC23-01-KL889 to San Jose
 ip address 131.108.241.2 255.255.255.252
 appletalk cable-range 1901-1901
 appletalk zone WAN Zone
 appletalk protocol eigrp
 no appletalk protocol rtmp
 ipx network 1901
!
interface Serial2
 description HDLC leased line on circuit ZW2390-1-H to ISP-A
 ip address 211.21.2.2 255.255.255.252
 ip access-group 101 in
!
interface Serial3
 no ip address
 shutdown
!
router eigrp 25000
 redistribute bgp 25000 network 131.108.0.0
 distribute-list 1300 out
 no auto-summary
!
router bgp 25000
 no synchronization
 network 131.108.0.0
 neighbor 211.21.2.1 remote-as 701
 neighbor 211.21.2.1 description Internet Connection to ISP-A
 neighbor 211.21.2.1 distribute-list ISP-routes in
 neighbor 211.21.2.1 distribute-list ZIP-routes out
 neighbor 131.108.254.3 remote-as 25000
 neighbor 131.108.254.3 description IBGP to SF-Core-1
 neighbor 131.108.254.3 update-source Loopback 0
!
ip classless
logging 131.108.110.33
logging trap debugging
logging console emergencies
ip access-list standard ZIP-routes
 permit 131.108.0.0
ip access-list standard ISP-routes
 deny host 0.0.0.0
 deny 127.0.0.0 0.255.255.255
 deny 10.0.0.0 0.255.255.255
 deny 172.16.0.0 0.15.255.255
 deny 192.168.0.0 0.0.255.255
 deny 192.0.2.0 0.0.0.255
 deny 128.0.0.0 0.0.255.255
 deny 191.255.0.0 0.0.255.
 deny 192.0.0.0 0.0.0.255
 deny 223.255.255.0 0.0.0.255
```

```
 deny 224.0.0.0 31.255.255.255
 permit any
access-list 1 permit 131.108.0.0  0.0.255.255
access-list 2 permit host 131.108.20.45
access-list 101 remark Permits NTP, DNS, WWW, and SMTP
access-list 101 deny tcp host 192.7.2.2 host 192.7.2.2 log
access-list 101 deny ip 131.108.0.0 0.0.255.255 any log
access-list 101 deny ip 10.0.0.0 0.255.255.255 any
access-list 101 deny ip 172.16.0.0 0.15.255.255 any
access-list 101 deny ip 192.168.0.0 0.0.255.255 any
access-list 101 deny ip 127.0.0.0 0.255.255.255 any
access-list 101 permit ip host 192.7.2.1 host 192.7.2.2
access-list 101 deny ip any host 192.7.2.2
access-list 101 permit udp any 131.108.101.99 eq domain
access-list 101 permit udp host 15.255.160.64 host 131.108.254.3 eq ntp
access-list 101 permit udp host 128.4.1.1 host 131.108.254.3 eq ntp
access-list 101 permit udp host 16.1.0.4 host 131.108.254.3 eq ntp
access-list 101 permit udp host 204.123.2.5 host 131.108.254.3 eq ntp
access-list 101 permit tcp host 192.52.71.4 host 131.108.101.34 eq domain
access-list 101 permit tcp host 192.52.71.4 host 131.108.101.35 eq domain
access-list 101 permit tcp any host 131.108.101.34 eq smtp
access-list 101 permit tcp any host 131.108.101.35 eq smtp
access-list 101 permit tcp any host 131.108.101.100 eq www
access-list 101 permit tcp any host 131.108.101.100 eq ftp
access-list 101 permit tcp any host 131.108.101.100 eq ftp-data
access-list 101 permit tcp any gt 1023 host 131.108.101.100 gt 1023
access-list 101 permit icmp any any echo-reply
access-list 101 permit icmp any any time-exceeded
access-list 101 permit icmp any any port-unreachable
access-list 101 permit tcp any any established
access-list 101 permit tcp any any eq 22
access-list 101 deny tcp any any eq ident
access-list 101 deny ip any any log access-list 120 permit ip any 131.108.0.0
0.0.255.255
access-list 1300 permit 131.108.0.0 0.0.255.255
access-list 1300 permit 131.119.0.0
access-list 1300 permit 140.222.0.0
!
ipx router eigrp 25000
 network 1901
 network 2010
 network 2901
!
tacacs-server host 131.108.110.33
tacacs-server key ZIPSecure
radius-server host 131.108.110.33
radius-server key Radius4Me
snmp-server community Zipnet RO 2
snmp-server community ZIPprivate RW 2
snmp-server host 131.108.20.45 Zipnet snmp frame-relay config
snmp-server location 251 Second Street, Seoul, Korea
snmp-server contact Allan Leinwand, allan@telegis.net
!
line con 0
 password 7 095B59
line aux 0
line vty 0 4
 password 7 095B59
 access-class 1 in
!
ntp update-calendar
ntp server 192.216.191.10
ntp server 129.189.134.11
!
end
```

The Seoul-2 Router

The Seoul-2 device on the ZIP network is a Cisco 4700 router. The configuration of this router features the following:

- An Ethernet interface to the local Seoul LAN segment, with redundant HSRP groups

- An HDLC serial link to the SF-Core-2 router

The complete configuration for the Seoul-2 router follows:

```
version 12.1
service timestamps debug datetime localtime
service timestamps log datetime localtime
service password-encryption
!
hostname Seoul-2
!
aaa new-model
aaa authentication login default group tacacs+ enable
aaa authorization exec group tacacs+ if-authenticated
aaa authorization network group radius if-authenticated
aaa accounting exec stop-only group tacacs+
enable secret 5 $2$5toY$IJQPTVD4.aEDLwZ8nPrvX.
!
ip domain-list zipnet.com
ip domain-list zipnet.net
ip domain-name zipnet.com
ip name-server 131.108.110.34
ip name-server 131.108.110.35
appletalk routing eigrp 25000
appletalk route-redistribution
ipx routing 0000.dcec.e1b0
!
clock timezone KST +9
!
interface Loopback1
 description Seoul-2 router loopback
 ip address 131.108.254.7 255.255.255.255
!
interface Ethernet0
 description Seoul LAN Segment
 ip address 131.108.3.2 255.255.255.128
 ip helper-address 131.108.21.70
 no ip redirects
 media-type 10BaseT
 ntp broadcast
 appletalk cable-range 2001-2010
 appletalk zone Asia Distribution
 ipx network 2010
 standby 1 priority 95
 standby 1 preempt
 standby 1 ip 131.108.3.3
 standby 2 priority 100
 standby 2 track Serial0
 standby 2 preempt
 standby 2 ip 131.108.3.4
!
interface Serial0
 description HDLC leased line on circuit ZW983800-03 to SF-Core-2
 ip address 131.108.240.6 255.255.255.252
 appletalk cable-range 902-902
 appletalk zone WAN Zone
```

```
 appletalk protocol eigrp
 no appletalk protocol rtmp
 ipx network 902
!
interface Serial1
 no ip address
 shutdown
!
router eigrp 25000
 network 131.108.0.0
 no auto-summary
!
ip classless
logging 131.108.110.33
logging trap debugging
logging console emergencies
access-list 1 permit 131.108.0.0  0.0.255.255
access-list 2 permit host 131.108.20.45
!
ipx router eigrp 25000
 network 902
 network 2010
!
tacacs-server host 131.108.110.33
tacacs-server key ZIPSecure
radius-server host 131.108.110.33
radius-server key Radius4Me
snmp-server community Zipnet RO 2
snmp-server community ZIPprivate RW 2
snmp-server host 131.108.20.45 Zipnet snmp frame-relay config
snmp-server location 251 Second Street, Seoul, Korea
snmp-server contact Allan Leinwand, allan@telegis.net
!
line con 0
 password 7 095B59
line aux 0
line vty 0 4
 password 7 095B59
 access-class 1 in
!
ntp update-calendar
ntp server 192.216.191.10
ntp server 129.189.134.11
!
end
```

The Singapore Router

The Singapore device on the ZIP network is a Cisco 2501 router. The configuration of this router features the following:

- An Ethernet interface to the local Singapore LAN segment
- A point-to-point Frame Relay interface to the Seoul-1 router
- The use of RIP and the redistribution of EIGRP information into RIP on the local Singapore LAN segment

The complete configuration for the Singapore router follows:

```
version 12.1
service timestamps debug datetime localtime
service timestamps log datetime localtime
service password-encryption
!
hostname Singapore
!
aaa new-model
aaa authentication login default group tacacs+ enable
aaa authorization exec group tacacs+ if-authenticated
aaa authorization network group radius if-authenticated
aaa accounting exec stop-only group tacacs+
enable secret 5 $2$5toY$IJQPTVD4.aEDLwZ8nPrvX.
!
ip domain-list zipnet.com
ip domain-list zipnet.net
ip domain-name zipnet.com
ip name-server 131.108.110.34
ip name-server 131.108.110.35
appletalk routing eigrp 25000
appletalk route-redistribution
ipx routing 0000.ceec.eebb
!
clock timezone SST +8
!
interface Loopback1
 description Singapore router loopback
 ip address 131.108.254.8 255.255.255.255
!
interface Ethernet0
 description Singapore LAN Segment
 ip address 131.108.1.1 255.255.255.128
 ip helper-address 131.108.21.70
 ntp broadcast
 appletalk cable-range 4001-4010
 appletalk zone Asia Manufacturing
 ipx network 4010
!
interface Serial0
 description IETF frame relay PVCs on Circuit Z-234987-12-MS-01
 no ip address
 encapsulation frame-relay ietf
 bandwidth 128
 frame-relay lmi-type ansi
!
interface Serial0.100 point-to-point
 description FR PVC 100 to Seoul-1
 ip address 131.108.242.6 255.255.255.252
 bandwidth 128
 frame-relay interface-dlci 100
 appletalk cable-range 2902-2902
 appletalk zone WAN Zone
 appletalk protocol eigrp
 no appletalk protocol rtmp
 ipx network 2902
!
interface Serial1
 no ip address
 shutdown
!
router eigrp 25000
 network 131.108.0.0
```

```
    no auto-summary
   !
   router rip
    redistribute eigrp 25000
    passive-interface Serial0.100
    network 131.108.0.0
    default-metric 3
   !
   ip classless
   logging trap debugging
   logging console emergencies
   logging 131.108.110.33
   access-list 1 permit 131.108.0.0 0.0.255.255
   access-list 2 permit host 131.108.20.45
   !
   ipx router eigrp 25000
    network 4010
    network 2902
   !
   tacacs-server host 131.108.110.33
   tacacs-server key ZIPSecure
   radius-server host 131.108.110.33
   radius-server key Radius4Me
   snmp-server community Zipnet RO 2
   snmp-server community ZIPprivate RW 2
   snmp-server location 1 Raffles Place, Singapore
   snmp-server contact Allan Leinwand, allan@telegis.net
   !
   line con 0
    password 7 095B59
   line aux 0
   line vty 0 4
    password 7 095B59
    access-class 1 in
   !
   ntp update-calendar
   ntp server 192.216.191.10
   ntp server 129.189.134.11
   !
   end
```

The SingISDN Access Server

The SingISDN on the ZIP network is a Cisco 4500 access server. This access server is set up to handle ISDN dialup clients for IP and can be used as a template for any similar access server on the ZIP network. Each access server needs to have unique network layer addresses because it is impossible to have duplicate network layer addresses on an internetwork. The configuration of this access server features the following:

- ISDN dialup configuration for IP clients
- A local username database for user authentication
- An ISDN rotary group using four ISDN BRI interfaces
- A dialer interface that authenticates PPP sessions using PAP, CHAP, and MS-CHAP
- An access list that permits only specific IP traffic to maintain a current ISDN call

The complete configuration for the SingISDN access server follows:

```
version 12.1
service timestamps debug datetime localtime
service timestamps log datetime localtime
service password-encryption
!
hostname SingISDN
!
aaa new-model
aaa authentication login default group tacacs+ local
aaa authentication ppp default group tacacs+ local
aaa authentication arap default local
aaa authorization exec local group tacacs+ if-authenticated
aaa authorization network local group radius if-authenticated
aaa accounting exec stop-only group tacacs+
aaa accounting network stop-only group tacacs+
enable secret 5 $2$5toY$IJQPTVD4.aEDLwZ8nPrvX.
!
username jim password 7 53633635
username janet password 7 878743465
ip domain-list zipnet.com
ip domain-list zipnet.net
ip domain-name zipnet.com
ip name-server 131.108.110.34
ip name-server 131.108.110.35
ip address-pool local
async-bootp dns-server 131.108.101.34 131.108.101.35
async-bootp nbns-server 131.108.21.70
isdn switch-type basic-dms100
!
clock timezone SST +8
!
interface Loopback0
 ip address 131.108.254.11 255.255.255.255
!
interface Ethernet0
 description Singapore User LAN
 ip address 131.108.1.81 255.255.255.128
 media-type 10BaseT
!
interface BRI0
 no ip address
 encapsulation ppp
 isdn spid1 98050101
 isdn spid2 98060101
 isdn answer1 50101
 isdn answer2 60101
 dialer rotary-group 1
!
interface BRI1
 no ip address
 encapsulation ppp
 isdn spid1 98070101
 isdn spid2 98080101
 isdn answer1 70101
 isdn answer2 80101
 dialer rotary-group 1
!
interface BRI2
 no ip address
 encapsulation ppp
 isdn spid1 91470102
 isdn spid2 91490102
 isdn answer1 70102
```

```
  isdn answer2 90102
  dialer rotary-group 1
!
interface BRI3
 no ip address
 encapsulation ppp
 isdn spid1 91350102
 isdn spid2 91390102
 isdn answer1 50102
 isdn answer2 90102
 dialer rotary-group 1
!
interface Ethernet1
 no ip address
 shutdown
!
interface Dialer1
 description Singapore ISDN Dialup Pool
 ip unnumbered Ethernet0
 encapsulation ppp
 peer default ip address pool isdn-users
 dialer in-band
 dialer idle-timeout 300
 dialer-group 1
 ppp authentication chap ms-chap pap call-in
 ppp multilink
 compress mpcc
!
router eigrp 25000
 network 131.108.0.0
 no auto-summary
!
ip local pool isdn-users 131.108.1.91 131.108.1.106
ip classless
logging trap debugging
logging 131.108.110.33
access-list 1 permit 131.108.0.0 0.0.255.255
access-list 2 permit host 131.108.20.45
access-list 102 permit tcp any any eq telnet
access-list 102 permit tcp any any eq www
access-list 102 permit udp any any eq domain
access-list 102 permit tcp any any eq ftp
tacacs-server host 131.108.110.33
tacacs-server key ZIPSecure
radius-server host 131.108.110.33
radius-server key Radius4Me
snmp-server community Zipnet RO 2
snmp-server community ZIPprivate RW 2
snmp-server host 131.108.20.45 Zipnet snmp frame-relay isdn config
snmp-server location 1 Raffles Place, Singapore
snmp-server contact Allan Leinwand, allan@telegis.net
dialer-list 1 protocol ip list 102
!
line con 0
 password 7 052C092B284B47
line aux 0
password 7 095B59
line vty 0 4
password 7 095B59
 access-class 1 in
!
ntp clock-period 17179886
ntp server 192.216.191.10
ntp server 129.189.134.11
end
```

The Sing2511 Access Server

The Sing2511 on the ZIP network is a Cisco 2511 access server. It is set up to handle analog dialup clients for IP, AppleTalk, and IPX. This configuration can be used as a template for any similar access server on the ZIP network. Each access server must have unique network layer addresses because it is impossible to have duplicate network layer addresses on an internetwork. The configuration of this access server features the following:

- IP, AppleTalk, and IPX access for remote dialup clients
- A backup local username database for user authentication
- A local IP address pool for dialup IP users
- A group-async interface used to configure 16 asynchronous terminal lines
- Terminal line configuration to set up modem-specific parameters and user-session inactivity timeouts

The complete configuration for the Sing2511 access server follows:

```
version 12.1
service timestamps debug datetime localtime
service timestamps log datetime localtime
service password-encryption
!
hostname Sing2511
!
aaa new-model
aaa authentication login default group tacacs+ local
aaa authentication ppp default group tacacs+ local
aaa authentication arap default auth-guest local
aaa authorization exec local group tacacs+ if-authenticated
aaa authorization network local group radius if-authenticated
aaa accounting exec stop-only group tacacs+
aaa accounting network stop-only group tacacs+
enable secret 5 $2$5toY$IJQPTVD4.aEDLwZ8nPrvX.
!
username john password 7 15140403446A
username jane password 7 121B0405
ip domain-list zipnet.com
ip domain-list zipnet.net
ip domain-name zipnet.com
ip name-server 131.108.110.34
ip name-server 131.108.110.35
ip address-pool local
appletalk routing eigrp 25000
appletalk route-redistribution

appletalk virtual-net 3000 Mac-dialup
arap network 2500 Mac-dialup
!
clock timezone SST +8
!
interface Loopback0
 ip address 131.108.254.10 255.255.255.255
 ipx netwrok 2500
!
interface Ethernet0
 description Singapore User LAN
 ip address 131.108.1.80 255.255.255.128
```

```
 appletalk cable-range 4001-4010
 appletalk zone Asia Manufacturing
 ipx network 4010
!
interface Serial0
 no ip address
 shutdown
!
interface Serial1
 no ip address
 shutdown
!
interface Group-Async1
 description dialup pool on Singapore 2511
 ip unnumbered Ethernet0
 encapsulation ppp
 async mode interactive
 appletalk client-mode
 ipx ppp-client Loopback 0
 ipx update interval rip 36000
 ipx update interval sap 36000
 peer default ip address pool modem-users
 ppp authentication pap ms-chap chap call-in
 ppp ipcp dns 131.108.101.34 131.108.101.35
 ppp ipcp wins 131.108.21.70
 compress mpcc
 group-range 1 16
!
router eigrp 25000
 network 131.108.0.0
 no auto-summary
!
ip local pool modem-users 131.108.1.111 131.108.1.126
ip classless
logging trap debugging
logging 131.108.110.33
access-list 1 permit 131.108.0.0 0.0.255.255
access-list 2 permit host 131.108.20.45
!
ipx router eigrp 25000
 network 25000
 network 4010
!
tacacs-server host 131.108.110.33
tacacs-server key ZIPSecure
radius-server host 131.108.110.33
radius-server key Radius4Me
snmp-server community Zipnet RO 2
snmp-server community ZIPprivate RW 2
snmp-server host 131.108.20.45 Zipnet snmp frame-relay config
snmp-server location 1 Raffles Place, Singapore
snmp-server contact Allan Leinwand, allan@telegis.net
!
line con 0
 password 7 052C092B284B47
line 1 16
 session-timeout 30
 autoselect arap
 autoselect during-login
 autoselect ppp
 arap enable
 arap authentication default
 session-disconnect-warning 60
 login authentication default
```

```
 modem Dialin
 modem autoconfigure type usr_courier
 stopbits 1
 rxspeed 115200
 txspeed 115200
 flowcontrol hardware
line aux 0
password 7 095B59
line vty 0 4
password 7 095B59
 access-class 1 in
!
ntp clock-period 17179886
ntp server 192.216.191.10
ntp server 129.189.134.11
end
```

Summary

This chapter has provided the complete IOS configuration commands for routers and access servers on the ZIP network. These configuration commands represent the practical application of concepts discussed throughout this book.

D

I

T

U

Cisco Career Certifications

Cisco CCNA Exam #640-507 Certification Guide

Wendell Odom, CCIE

0-7357-0971-8 • AVAILABLE NOW

Although it's only the first step in Cisco Career Certification, the Cisco Certified Network Associate (CCNA) exam is a difficult test. Your first attempt at becoming Cisco certified requires a lot of study and confidence in your networking knowledge. When you're ready to test your skills, complete your knowledge of the exam topics, and prepare for exam day, you need the preparation tools found in *Cisco CCNA Exam #640-507 Certification Guide* from Cisco Press.

CCDA Exam Certification Guide

Anthony Bruno, CCIE & Jacqueline Kim

0-7357-0074-5 • AVAILABLE NOW

CCDA Exam Certification Guide is a comprehensive study tool for DCN Exam #640-441. Written by a CCIE and a CCDA, and reviewed by Cisco technical experts, *CCDA Exam Certification Guide* will help you understand and master the exam objectives. In this solid review on the design areas of the DCN exam, you'll learn to design a network that meets a customer's requirements for perfomance, security, capacity, and scalability.

Interconnecting Cisco Network Devices

Edited by Steve McQuerry

1-57870-111-2 • AVAILABLE NOW

Based on the Cisco course taught worldwide, *Interconnecting Cisco Network Devices* teaches you how to configure Cisco switches and routers in multi-protocol internetworks. ICND is the primary course recommended by Cisco Systems for CCNA #640-507 preparation. If you are pursuing CCNA certification, this book is an excellent starting point for your study.

Designing Cisco Networks

Edited by Diane Teare

1-57870-105-8 • Available Now

Based on the Cisco Systems instructor-led and self-study course available worldwide, *Designing Cisco Networks* will help you understand how to analyze and solve existing network problems while building a framework that supports the functionality, performance, and scalability required from any given environment. Self-assessment through exercises and chapter-ending tests starts you down the path for attaining your CCDA certification.

Cisco Interactive Mentor

The Cisco Interactive Mentor product line is a series of e-learning solutions designed to provide entry-level networking professionals with the opportunity to gain practical, hands-on experience through self-paced instruction and network lab simulation exercises. This combination of computer-based training with lab exercises offers users a unique learning environment that eliminates the cost overhead necessary with the actual network devices, while offering the same degree of real-world experience. Current releases include:

Router Basics
1-58720-011-2

$149.95

AVAILABLE NOW

LAN Switching
1-58720-021-X

$199.95

AVAILABLE NOW

IP Routing: Distance Vector Protocols
1-58720-012-0

$149.95

AVAILABLE NOW

Access ISDN
1-58720-025-2

$149.95

AVAILABLE NOW

Expert Labs: IP Routing
1-58720-010-4

$149.95

AVAILABLE NOW

Voice Internetworking: Basic Voice over IP
1-58720-023-6

$149.95

AVAILABLE NOW